SECRETS *of a* WELL-BEHAVED DOG

SECRETS *of a*
WELL-BEHAVED
DOG

Understanding Your Dog's Behavior
and Communication for Successful Training

FROM THE EDITORS OF *PETS: PART OF THE FAMILY*

Rodale books may be purchased for business or promotional use or for special sales.
For information, please write to:
Special Markets Department, Rodale Inc., 733 Third Avenue, New York, NY 10017

Printed in the United States of America
Rodale Inc. makes every effort to use acid-free ∞, recycled paper ♲.

Cover design by Joanna Williams
Front cover photograph © Plush Studios/Getty Images
Back cover photographs: (top left) © Chris Amaral/Getty Images; (top right) © Photo Alto;
(center left) © Dimitri Vervitsiotis/Getty Images; (center right) © Photodisc/Getty Images;
(bottom left) © Photodisc/Getty Images
Spine photograph © Photodisc/Getty Images

ISBN-10 1–59486–988–X
ISBN-13 978–1–59486–988–4

2 4 6 8 10 9 7 5 3 1 hardcover

RODALE
LIVE YOUR WHOLE LIFE™

We inspire and enable people to improve their lives and the world around them

For more of our products visit **rodalestore.com** or call 800-848-4735

The Secret Lives of Dogs

AUTHOR

Jana Murphy

RODALE ACTIVE LIVING BOOKS

Editor: Matthew Hoffman
Publisher: Neil Wertheimer
Editorial Director: Michael Ward
Research Manager: Ann Gossy Yermish
Copy Manager: Lisa D. Andruscavage
Copy Editors: Kathryn C. LeSage, Karen Neely
Cover Designer and Design Coordinator: Joanna Reinhart
Associate Studio Manager: Thomas P. Aczel
Book Manufacturing Director: Helen Clogston
Manufacturing Manager: Mark Krahforst

WELDON OWEN PTY LTD

Chairman: John Owen
Publisher: Sheena Coupe
Associate Publisher: Lynn Humphries
Senior Editor: Janine Flew
Senior Designer: Kylie Mulquin
Designer: Jacqueline Richards
Icons: Matt Graif, Chris Wilson/Merilake
Indexer: Barbara Long
Production Manager: Caroline Webber
Production Assistant: Kylie Lawson

Film separation by Colourscan Co. Pte. Ltd., Singapore

CONTENTS

PART ONE

"I'VE ALWAYS DONE IT THIS WAY"

Ancient Instincts and Urges

PART TWO

"I KNOW THINGS THAT YOU DON'T"

The Amazing Senses of Dogs

PART THREE

"I CAN'T BELIEVE THAT YOU LIVE LIKE THIS"

Dealing with Modern Life

PART FOUR

"I Like the Good Things in Life"

The Passion for Food and Fun

PART FIVE

"My Body Makes Me Do It"

When Anatomy Is Destiny

Introduction

Dogs have been part of our families for so long that we often think of them as little (and not entirely well-behaved) humans. Sometimes, we forget that they're an entirely different species. They do things for reasons that have nothing to do with us—reasons that, in some cases, are millions of years old.

Last week, for example, I took Molly, my Labrador retriever, for a walk in the outdoor market near our home. On the sidewalk outside a pizza shop, she stopped to investigate a spot about the size of a pencil point. She gave it a sniff, then flopped on her back and vigorously rolled back and forth. Whatever the spot was, she was rubbing it as deeply into her coat as she possibly could.

Molly was obeying an ancient instinct. Dogs in the wild rolled on things to disguise their natural scents. Molly doesn't have to think about predators or prey, but those old memories still linger. Her rolling was a way of telling the world, "Ain't no one here but us pepperonis."

Dogs do a lot of things like this—things that, from a human point of view, don't make much sense. They bury bones. They walk past their water bowls to drink from the toilet. They chase their tails and steal each other's food. You've probably never been sure why they do the weird and wacky things that they do—until now.

The Secret Lives of Dogs explains the most common and most mysterious types of dog behavior. Take tail chasing. It looks like fun, but it's actually serious business. Dogs used to be hunters. Their eyes and brains are made in such a way that the slightest movement makes them think, "Rabbit!" Before they have a chance to think, "Hey, that's just my tail," their legs are already in motion—and around and around they go.

Dogs smell and hear things of which humans are totally unaware. This explains why many of the "odd" things that they do aren't so strange after all. Nearly every male dog, for example, will lift his leg on fire hydrants and sign poles. Why does he do it? Because he can smell every dog who's been there before, and he knows that future dogs will smell him. He wants them all to know how big and tough he is. Lifting his leg allows him to aim higher than the last guy.

This amazing sense of smell also explains why dogs put their noses in embarrassing places. They don't mean to be rude. They're just taking in loads of information: where you've been, who you've been around, and whether you're happy or sad—all from a quick sniff. A similar thing happens when they stick their heads out car windows, eat unpleasant things in the yard, or cock their heads when we talk. They're using their super-senses to catch up on what's happening around them.

Despite our many differences, dogs and humans get along very well. But occasionally, a dog's natural behavior causes trouble in the family. Destroying furniture. Drooling on the carpets. Biting when playing. Every chapter in *The Secret Lives of Dogs* is packed with practical tips for helping dogs behave better and enjoy life a little more. The "pepper solution" (it has to be red pepper) to dung eating. Why rawhides are better than rubber toys. How changing your posture can eliminate "submissive urination." Even ways to rub dogs' bellies and ears so they groan with pleasure.

Since dogs' breeds play a big role in how they act, we've also included a special feature called "Breed Specific." It explains why Labradors love to play with balls. Why Rottweilers lean on people. Why Akitas chase cats and German shepherds love tug-of-war. And dozens of other breed-specific habits.

To truly appreciate dogs, we have to understand how they think and what they see when they look at the world around them. *The Secret Lives of Dogs* is filled with insights into these wonderful animals. You'll understand them better, and at the same time, you'll discover hundreds of ways to make them happier in today's confusing world.

Matthew Hoffman

Matthew Hoffman
Editor, *Pets: Part of the Family* books

"I've Always Done It This Way"
Ancient Instincts and Urges

Although dogs have been living with people for a long time, some
of their behavior has its origins in their ancestors' days in the wild,
a time when dogs had to be totally self-sufficient in order to survive.

CHAPTER ONE

DISLIKE HAVING THEIR FEET TOUCHED

Memories of Pain

Dogs have very tough paw pads. The pads consist of tissue that's similar to callus, which can be as much as $3/4$-inch thick. It's as though dogs are walking on thick leather soles. They can walk comfortably on surfaces that would leave people wincing and hopping.

The rest of their feet, however, are a lot more sensitive—so much so that they hate having them touched. It seems to be a universal dislike. Regardless of the breed, most dogs will jerk away when you touch their feet, especially on top or between the toes.

This curious sensitivity wouldn't be a problem if it weren't for the fact that dogs peri-

odically need to have their nails trimmed or their toes inspected for stones or burrs. Some dogs will put up with having their feet handled, but others will fight like crazy. It's not uncommon for groomers to charge an extra fee to provide what should be routine claw care.

Don't Mess with My Living

The bottoms of dogs' feet are designed to withstand rugged use, but the tops are not, says John C. Wright, Ph.D., a certified applied animal behaviorist; professor of psychology at Mercer University in Macon, Georgia; and author of *The Dog Who Would Be King*. The tops of the feet are loaded with nerve endings that fire off warnings when they sense pressure that could presage potential injuries, he explains. You can test this for yourself. Touch the bottom of your dog's feet, and he probably won't react. Touch the tops, and he'll pull away or flinch a little. Touch between his toes, and he'll make it clear that he'd really like to be left alone.

"Dogs' feet are essential for them to accomplish almost everything they do," explains

It's easiest to trim dogs' nails when they're on a high, slippery surface. They have to concentrate more on keeping their balance than on struggling with you.

Dr. Wright. "They're used in defense, for hunting, for locomotion, and even for communicating—dogs leave visual markers when they scratch the ground." So dogs get a little nervous when things (or people) that they can't control start touching their feet.

Remembering the Last Time

Dogs have thick, tough claws, and even routine pedicures can be uncomfortable—or worse. "A cut to the quick of the nail is very painful," says Lynn Cox, D.V.M., a veterinarian in Olive Branch, Mississippi. Dogs have good memories of things that have hurt them. The more they've been nicked by nail clippers, the more determined they'll be to keep their feet out of reach.

Bad memories may be compounded by the fact that some dogs only have their feet touched when they're being worked on. Neither nail trims nor first aid are experiences that dogs remember fondly. They come to believe that any foot contact is bad contact, and so they shy away from it.

Now That You Understand...

Lift them up to stop the fear. Dogs who are foot phobic at home sometimes get downright easy-natured when groomers or veterinarians lift their feet. It's not because experts have a magic touch. It's because they put dogs on tables, which are often made of stainless steel. The combination of height and a cold, slippery surface makes dogs think more about stability than about what's happening to their feet. "A high table is a great tool," says Dr. Cox. "I know

A FRIENDLY SHAKE

Shaking hands isn't merely a good social skill. Dogs who learn to shake hands get used to having their feet touched. They get a lot of compliments for their good manners. And they enjoy it so much, you may have trouble getting them to stop.

While your dog is sitting, reach your hand toward him, palm-up, at the usual shaking level. Most dogs will instinctively reach forward, although some won't get the idea unless you pick up the paw and give it a shake. In either case, say "shake" once you're holding the paw. Then praise him a lot. Once he understand that "shake" gets him praise and maybe food, he'll reach out to shake hands at every opportunity.

people who put their dogs on the washing machine or the dryer to trim their nails, and they have no trouble at all."

Have a friend do the work. Another reason that dogs are so cooperative at the vet's is that they're unsure about the whole situation. Dogs are big on routine and hierarchy, both of which get confused when they're away from home. The resulting uncertainty puts them off-guard, which makes it much easier to trim their nails or check their feet, says Dr. Cox. You can achieve the same result by trimming their nails away from home or even by asking (or bribing) a friend to do the work.

Practice young, practice often. Dogs are naturally protective of their feet, but they can learn to accept claw clipping and simple exams when their owners regularly handle their feet, preferably starting when they're young, says Warren Liddell, D.V.M., a veterinarian in Norwich, New York. He recommends touching, rubbing, and holding the feet for a few seconds every day. Gently press your fingers between the toes. Squeeze the pads. Spread the feet and feel around. Get your dog accustomed to the idea

that foot touches aren't a sign of uncomfortable things to come. The more gentle contact he experiences, the more likely he'll be to accept pedicures and exams as he gets older.

FAST FIX Dogs get very nervous when there's uncertainty in their lives, and objects that people take for granted, like nail trimmers, can seem foreign and frightening. A quick solution is to put the clippers somewhere that your dog will see them, like on a low table or a shelf in a bookcase, says Dr. Cox. Don't merely put them out for a few hours on the day that you're going to use them, he adds. Leave them out all the time. This will give your dog a chance to sniff, see, and generally get used to them. He still won't enjoy having his nails trimmed, but at least he'll be less nervous about the shiny, clicky object that you're holding in your hand.

Do one paw a week. Even if it were a medically sound thing to do, doctors would never want to give children an entire lifetime of vaccinations in one visit. It would be overwhelming, to say the least. The same is true of trimming a dog's nails: Doing all four paws at once can be a miserable experience, says Dr. Cox. To reduce discomfort and fear, he recommends clipping just one nail a day. With weekends off, that means you'll do one paw a week. Dogs can tolerate a little discomfort, and doing it slowly will make the process a lot more bearable.

Dogs who are used to having their feet handled from an early age, like this young mixed breed, will be blasé about the experience when they grow up.

CHAPTER TWO

BARKING AT THE MAILMAN

"See—He Went Away"

Looking at Bum, it's hard to imagine a less fearsome dog. At 7 pounds, the tiny Pomeranian looks more like a stuffed toy than a noble protector of hearth and home. But every day at about the same time, Bum undergoes a dramatic transformation. As soon as he hears the mailman's shoes on the walk, he becomes Bum the Terrible, Bum the Protector. He acts as though he'd tear off the mailman's leg if he could only get through the window.

"He's been doing it since he was a little puppy," says Jackie Savard of Tupper Lake, New York. "I don't know why Bum thinks the mailman is such a threat."

Bum probably doesn't have anything personal against the mailman. He's just taking care of his own, says Nicholas Dodman, professor of behavioral pharmacology and director of the Animal Behavior Clinic at Tufts University School of Veterinary Medicine in North Grafton, Massachusetts, and author of *Dogs Behaving Badly*. Every dog

This American bulldog likes keeping an eye on things, and she doesn't miss a chance to give a warning bark. She's protecting her territory, which, from a dog's point of view, is one of the most important things she can do.

has a little watchdog in him. It's something that dogs inherit from their ancestors, who had to defend their territories and limited food supplies from trespassers.

The great thing about mailmen is that they appear to be easy targets. Here's what happens. The first time a dog heard this stranger coming up the walk, he got alarmed.

"He probably backed up a little bit at first, but one brave day, he gave a little bark," says Dodman. His owners came running to see what was causing the commotion. The mailman, of course, dropped off the mail and left. The combination of praise from his owners and the mailman's retreat makes dogs very happy. They just assume that they scared the mailman off. From then on, they feel confident that they can protect their homes from these fearsome visitors, so they keep barking.

"Mailmen, meter readers, United Parcel Service and FedEx couriers, and any other stranger who purposely heads up to the house and then looks as though he's retreating when he gets barked at is going to get the same reception," adds Judith Halliburton, a trainer and behaviorist in Albuquerque, New Mexico, and author of *Raising Rover*.

The Best Time of Day

Nearly all dogs have an instinctive urge to protect their homes, but that's not the only reason they kick up a fuss when the mail arrives. Part of it is merely anticipation. Dogs are attuned to rituals and routines to such an extent that they'd probably be called obsessive-compulsive if they were people. The mail comes every day at more or less the same time. It doesn't matter whether this event is happily anticipated or thoroughly dreaded. Dogs probably begin thinking about it when they get up in the morning, and their excitement grows as the time approaches. By the time the mailman finally arrives, they're keyed up and ready to rumble.

"It can get to be the high point of their days," Halliburton says. Dogs who spend their days alone get particularly excited because they feel as though they've been left in charge. If they don't bark like crazy and warn off intruders, who will? "They figure they're on duty should anyone approach their property."

A sofa under a window provides a great lookout. Dogs who can see what's happening outside tend to bark the most. Moving the sofa may cut down on the noise.

Suspicious Gifts

It's not only mailmen who get dogs worked up. Just as exciting is what mailmen leave behind. Mail that drops through a slot in the door has unfamiliar smells. Dogs are suspicious of new smells, especially when the smells are in their territory. They go to a lot of trouble to put their own scents where they live—by marking around the perimeter of the yard, for example. The idea that someone would come along and put another smell on top of theirs can seem downright offensive.

Some dogs go as far as to shred mail that is dropped through the slot. They don't do it often, of course. Even people who don't mind a little barking get upset when they see the monthly mortgage statement chewed into pieces. These dogs soon find themselves relegated to other rooms.

BREED SPECIFIC

All dogs are territorial, but some breeds have notably strong instincts to protect their homes. Shelties, collies, Labradors, and golden retrievers are among the noisiest barkers. Paradoxically, dogs who were bred specifically for protection, like Dobermans, Rottweilers, and German shepherds, often bark the least. It may be that they have so much confidence that they don't feel the need to bluster.

Now That You Understand...

It's commendable that dogs are sufficiently loyal to want to protect their families. But their barking can drive people nuts. Then there's the issue of bites. Dogs do get out sometimes, and about 3,000 mailmen get bitten every year.

Barking at the mailman isn't always easy to stop. The urge to protect territory goes back hundreds of thousands of years. Dogs can learn to respect the mailman, but it's going to take some time.

Tape a biscuit to the door. Dogs may be protective, but no one ever accused them of being impractical. It's amazing how quickly they'll come around when there's something in it for them. Talk to the mailman and explain the problem, Dodman recommends. Every day after that, tape a dog treat to the door or put the box on the porch. Most mailmen will be more than happy to drop something through the slot. Strangers who bring food are always welcome, and even dogs with strong protective urges will begin to relax within a few weeks.

Rearrange the furniture. Dogs can hear people long before they see them, and that's when barking usually starts. Still, you can keep them calmer by taking away the visual red flags. This may be as simple as moving a chair in front of a window that faces the walk, or pulling the blinds, or keeping your dog in a room where he can't see outside. Your dog may still bark when he hears approaching footsteps, but without the

This golden retriever welcomes the mailman because he gets praised for bringing the mail inside to his owners—proof that rewards are better than scoldings.

actual visual sighting, the barking is less likely to reach a full crescendo.

Say it once, not twice. Trainers always advise people to tell their dogs "no" when they start barking. This is good advice, but only if you do it once. When your dog is barking and you keeping saying "no," it isn't daunting—it's encouraging. Your dog will think you're barking at the mailman too, Halliburton says.

FAST FIX Just as parents are the last ones to know when their teenagers are getting into trouble, people who work all day never realize how much noise their dogs are making until neighbors complain. The corollary, of course, is that it's hard to train dogs when you aren't around to catch them barking. One way to keep them quiet when you're gone is to leave the stereo on all day, with the volume cranked up. Loud music masks outside sounds. Dogs who can't hear the mailman won't have anything at which to bark.

CHAPTER THREE

BURYING BONES

Taking Care of Leftovers

Ancient dogs didn't have people around. No people meant no refrigerators, no artificial preservatives, no ready-to-eat meals, and no safes in which to keep valuables. They survived on whatever they could find or catch. If they managed to get more than they could eat in a sitting, they had to make sure it would be there when they came back to it later.

"They stored spare food by burying it," says Benjamin Hart, D.V.M., Ph.D., professor of physiology and behavior at the University of California School of Veterinary Medicine at Davis and author of *The Perfect Puppy: How to Choose Your Dog by Its Behavior.* "It was a pretty resourceful way of keeping leftovers."

Dirt may be gritty and hard on the teeth, but it's also protective. The temperature in the ground is cooler than it is in the air, so burying food helped it stay fresh longer. Buried food didn't roast in the sun. It didn't immediately get covered with flies and insects, and buzzards couldn't swipe it. All in all, burying food and juicy bones was a very good solution. So good, in fact, that people copied the idea. Until the invention of refrigeration, people stored food in cool underground cellars.

Dogs don't need to bury food anymore because they have more than enough. But when they're faced with an overabundance of rations—and for dogs, having even 1 extra bone in the yard can feel like a tremendous extravagance—they feel that old urge coming on. So they look for a secluded spot, dig a quick hole, and put some goodies away for a rainy day. Not just bones, either. Some dogs bury toys. Others bury other people's toys. More than a few folks have had to trudge into the backyard with a shovel to uncover their 3-year-old's stuffed bear or the remote control for the VCR.

Dogs don't take chances with prized possessions. They'll either bury them for safekeeping or put on their most alert, possessive expressions.

Born to Dig

Not every dog buries bones. In fact, since digging serves no practical purpose anymore, it's gradually disappearing from dogs' behavioral file cabinet. It's possible that in a few thousand years, they'll never bury anything. But in the meantime, a lot of flower beds and gardens get impromptu rototilling as dogs eagerly bury their stuff. Even dogs who have forgotten what dirt feels like will sometimes root up a lawn when they see someone else doing it.

"Dogs mimic other dogs," says Rolan Tripp, D.V.M., a veterinarian in La Mirada, California, who specializes in animal behavior. "If you have a dog who hasn't learned to bury bones or toys and he gets around one who does, he's going to be more likely to do it than a dog who doesn't have any treasure-burying friends."

Dogs imitate people almost as much as they imitate other dogs. They figure that if you're doing something, it must be fun, and they're more than willing to try it themselves. That's why there is generally an increase in digging and burying during the planting months. Dogs spend more time outside when it's warm, and they watch closely as their people bury bulbs in the fall and neat rows of seeds in the spring, says Dr. Tripp. They start thinking that they should be burying things too.

Dogs who are smart enough to dig holes to store their valuables are not always smart enough to realize that some places aren't very

This Australian shepherd loves to dig. He doesn't stop at burying bones—children's toys and the family's footwear may also go underground.

good for digging, at least from a human standpoint. No one cares when a dog buries a bone on the outer acres of a farm. A bone buried in the center of a carefully cultivated plot of Bermuda sod, however, is a problem. And one buried in the corner cushion of the sofa is an expensive disaster. Lots of dogs are perfectly willing to bury things indoors if they don't have a good place outdoors—or if they dislike getting their feet dirty. And lots of owners spend weekends repairing the damage.

Now That You Understand...

Make every bone count. Dogs bury leftovers, not the main meal. That's why a dog with

10 bones may bury 9 of them. A dog with 1 bone, on the other hand, will never let it out of his sight. When you're trying to protect your yard, only let your dog have 1 bone at a time. Throw in a few toys to keep things interesting. Then, once a week, put the bone and the toys away and bring out a new batch, Dr. Tripp suggests. Scarcity and the sense of novelty will make every bone and toy seem too important to put away.

Tie that bone down. One way to keep bones above ground is to thwart one of your dog's most powerful urges—the one that tells him to bury bones in secluded places. Take your dog's favorite bone or toy and drill a hole in one end, says Dr. Tripp. Loop a 4-foot length of chain through the hole and bolt that to a post

in the yard. Dogs who can't walk away with their prizes aren't likely to bury them. And if they do, at least it will be in the spot that you choose. The benefit for your dog, of course, is that he won't have trouble finding it later.

FAST FIX Dogs tend to bury the same bones or toys again and again, and they're invariably the ones they like least, says Dr. Hart. It would seem logical to save them some trouble—and save the yard some damage—by chucking these C-list bones in the trash. This can work if your dog actually sees you throwing the bones away, says Dr. Hart. If he doesn't, the digging will only escalate because your dog will figure that he has misplaced his buried loot and will keep digging until he finds it.

Give him a vault of his own. Rather than trying to stop dogs from burying bones and trashing the yard, sometimes it's easier to encourage them to dig—as long as it's in a spot you can live with. Pick a few square feet in the yard that will serve as an authorized digging zone, Dr. Tripp recommends. Get things rolling by burying a few things yourself while your dog watches. Or take one of his bones, throw a little dirt on top, and encourage him to go at it. As long as the location is sufficiently secluded, most dogs won't have any objection to taking over after that.

Cover his favorite spots. Some dogs will only dig in a few places. If you're lucky, covering the area with chicken wire or canvas weighted down with bricks will make it all seem like too much trouble, and he may quit digging on his own.

BREED SPECIFIC

Dogs with digging in their genes are the ones most likely to bury bones and other treasures. Terriers, such as Irish terriers (left) and dachshunds, are champion diggers because it was once their job to dig deep and flush woodchucks and other rodents from their holes. Dogs from northern lands, such as huskies, also do a lot of digging, because in their native climates they had to dig down to stay warm in winter and cool in summer.

CHAPTER FOUR

CHASING CATS

They're Small and Furry, and They Look like Rabbits

Your dog may not hunt. In fact, he may be hundreds of generations removed from his nearest hunting ancestor. But his body still bears the traits of a hunting machine. Just look at those sharp incisors—they weren't designed for eating dainty bits off a china plate. And consider the eyes. They have thousands more movement receptors than people's eyes do. We see color. Dogs see action.

This kelpie mix knows a good time when he sees it, and he's standing ready for a good chase. The cat recognizes the dog's alert body language and is wisely keeping out of reach.

"Dogs have a chase drive that makes them instinctively go after anything that runs," says Rolan Tripp, D.V.M., a veterinarian in La Mirada, California, who specializes in animal behavior. And cats sure do run. Even when dogs don't have much of anything in mind, the sudden flash of feline movement sends a message to their brains: "Chase." And that's what they do.

Some dogs, of course, wouldn't get up and chase a cat on a dare. Elderly dogs and those with low-key personalities would rather sleep than chase. "Dogs who have been raised with cats since they were pups usually know that cats are just a fact," adds Dr. Tripp. "They're a whole lot less likely to chase than dogs who don't have any feline acquaintances."

Lucky for Cats

While the urge to chase prey thrives in modern dogs, the follow-up urge to kill prey has largely been extinguished. Dogs get excited by cats. They enjoy chasing cats. But once they have them cornered, they forget why they wanted them in the first place.

"Most dogs will corner a cat and then just bark out of frustration because they don't know what to do next," says Dr. Tripp.

Even when dogs have evil intentions, the result is usually the same. Cats are faster and more agile. They can leap tremendous distances and climb sheer surfaces. They usually walk away from chases without a scratch.

Expensive glassware, on the other hand, can take a beating. The usual chase scenario—a scrambling dog in pursuit of a lightning-bolt cat—involves furniture banging, glass breaking, and knee knocking. It's an instinct for pets. For humans, it's a pain in the neck.

Now That You Understand...

Raise a baby gate. Once a chase is under way, it's likely to continue until the cat is out of reach. To expedite the getaway, Dr. Tripp recommends putting a baby gate across the doorway to the kitchen or another cat-only area. Rather than putting it flush to the floor, raise it a few inches. Your cat will be able to zip underneath, leaving the bigger, clunkier dog on the other side.

BREED SPECIFIC

Dogs who have been bred for hunting, guarding, or herding, such as retrievers, Rottweilers, and Border collies, are among the most incorrigible cat chasers. So are high-energy dogs like terriers and Dalmatians. Dogs who are least likely to chase cats (or anything else) include basset hounds, Boston terriers, Great Pyrenees, and Newfoundlands.

Help her over the top. Raised gates only work when the dog is considerably bigger than the cat. When they're both the same size, put up the baby gate and rig a perch on top. This can be as simple as a section of board screwed tightly to the top. Cats are better jumpers than their canine companions, and the perch will allow them to hop up and over, leaving the dogs in their dust.

Interrupt the chase. Even though most dogs don't chase the cats they live with, some find it too much fun to give up. One way to discourage them is to keep leashes on their collars all the time. The minute they lunge, step on the leashes and make a loud noise, suggests Dr. Tripp. Stepping on the leashes arrests their forward momentum and gives them a jolt, and the loud noise makes the whole experience a little uncomfortable. Most dogs will get the hint after awhile that chasing cats has dubious payoffs.

Putting a baby gate or a piece of lattice across a doorway will stop even large dogs, like this Irish wolfhound, from bothering the cats.

Even when they don't lose interest entirely, past experiences of leash jolts will cause them to hesitate for a few seconds—and that's all the time that most cats need to put a safe distance between them and their pursuers.

Like an ex-smoker who takes a puff, however, dogs can get hooked on cat chasing all over again if they get a chance to do it. So you'll have to keep an eye on them all the time.

Cats and dogs get along best when they've been raised together and have been encouraged to develop respect and affection for each other.

The Hustler

All dogs are not created equal. Some are big and some are small. Some are smart and some aren't so brilliant. And some move at a snail's pace while others sprint. Sprinting was the case with Abby. Abby was much less interested in chasing cats than in racing them. And she managed to put one overconfident kitty soundly in his place.

The cat was White Bear. White Bear was fast, even for a cat. He was born with extra toes. When his owner, Carol Vinnacombe of Long Beach, California, asked her veterinarian if her kitten would have any health problems, he solemnly replied that White Bear would be fine, but he'd be very quick on his feet.

White Bear was fully aware of his gift. His favorite game, in fact, was Bait the Dog. "He walks into the room, surveys the dogs, and meows," Carol says. "If that doesn't work, he's not above batting at them with his paws." Carol's two Dalmatians always rose to the challenge, but they never managed to get close before White Bear would dive under the baby gate at the door.

Then Abby joined the family. White Bear wasted no time trying to get a game going with the lanky grey dog. He waved his paw in the air. Abby stood up. White Bear shot off. But when he skidded to the gate, the shocked cat found that Abby was already there and waiting.

It wasn't a fluke. Abby, it turns out, was a greyhound. And not just any greyhound. She was a retired racer who had spent the first 4 years of her life on the track. White Bear's little scam was like a neighborhood hustler challenging a stranger to a one-on-one game of basketball—only to discover that the stranger was Michael Jordan. For the first time in his life, White Bear had been slam-dunked.

Lucky for him, Abby didn't know what she was getting into, either. Once she'd won the race, she just turned and walked away. White Bear still plays his game sometimes, but finally someone besides the Dalmatians knows the agony of defeat.

CHAPTER FIVE

CHEWING SHOES

They Smell Good and Are Easy to Reach

Human feet have about half a million sweat glands, which are always secreting moisture. When feet are tucked into hot, humid shoes, the glands can release ¹/₂ pint of sweat a day. The perspiration, in turn, is loaded with human scents, and that's hard for any dog to resist.

Adult dogs generally understand that just because something smells good doesn't mean they have to chew it. But when they're young, dogs respond to shoes in the same way they respond to anything that gets their attention—by putting them in their mouths, says Kay Cox, Ph.D., an animal-behavior consultant in Gilbert, Arizona.

Added to this natural attraction is that fact that puppies go through a teething phase. Few things make their gums feel better than working over a nice pair of loafers.

It sometimes seems that dogs' interest in shoes is directly related to the cost: The more expensive the shoes, the more likely dogs are to leave them in tatters. But they really don't have a preference, says Gregory Bogard, D.V.M., a veterinarian in Tomball, Texas. They can't tell which shoes come from Saks Fifth Avenue and which come from K-Mart. All they know is that shoes smell exciting and are worth an exploratory chew or two.

"To your dog, that personal smell is the next best thing to you," explains Dr. Cox. In fact, dogs rarely chew up the shoes of people whom they dislike. "If they really hate someone, they might tear their shoes up," she adds. "But most dogs really want to be close to the familiar, pleasant smell of their owners."

Easy to Reach

People always wonder why puppies—and, less often, older dogs—focus on shoes and ignore other human possessions that are also loaded

A smelly tennis shoe left outside to air is too much temptation for this Border collie to resist. She has to explore it—with her teeth as well as her nose.

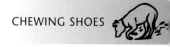

with scents. There are a few reasons for this. Partly, it's the intensity of the smell. A couch cushion will have some human scents, but nowhere near the concentration of a hot, humid pair of pumps.

More important, shoes are singularly convenient. When people leave home for the day, it's normal for dogs to explore a bit. They'll sniff around the living room, the bedrooms, and the closets. Sooner or later, they'll come across a pair of shoes. They're right on the floor, they smell great, and they're just the right size. They may decide that their search is over and commence digging in, says Dr. Bogard.

The Joy of Leather

Some dogs will chew rubber galoshes if that's all they can find. But given the choice, most go for leather shoes. Leather is made from cowhide. Despite all the treatments and tanning and dyes that go into shoe-making, dogs still recognize leather as a substance that's darn close to food.

An added bonus is that leather gets softer and tastier the more dogs chew it, says Dr. Cox. "Once they've started to wear it away, leather massages their gums just like rawhide does. There's a good taste, a good smell, and great mouth appeal, too."

Leather shoes with tassels are especially popular, Dr. Bogard adds. "They're like great-smelling chew toys with tails," he says. "That makes them very hard to resist."

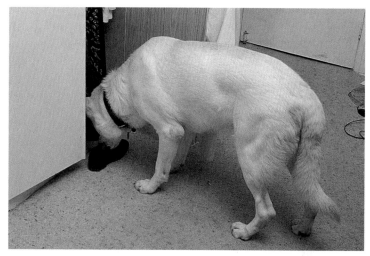

When his folks are away, this German shepherd likes to raid the closets in search of shoes. They smell of his people, and that makes him feel less alone.

Dogs who are into shoes usually aren't very selective, however. Canvas shoes aren't as toothsome as leather, but they're easier to rip into shreds. Dogs enjoy getting that kind of results. Fuzzy slippers are good, too. For one thing, they're warm, which means they cause the feet to exude additional dog-attracting moisture. Plus, all of that faux fur is more than a canine hunter's heart can resist. "I don't think there are many dogs who really think those slippers are alive, but they have a lot of fun pretending they are," says Dr. Bogard.

Now That You Understand...

Put in an insert. Since it's mainly the smell of human feet that makes shoes so tempting, you can make them less so by using shoe inserts. Inserts absorb most of the odors, leaving the shoes themselves relatively scent-free, says Rolan Tripp, D.V.M., a veterinarian in La Mirada, California, who specializes in animal behavior. Of course, you have to remember to remove the inserts when you get home. Otherwise, your shoes will smell as tempting as they always do.

ONLY THE BEST

A decade ago, people going out of town for a few days often left their dogs in boarding kennels, bare-boned establishments that didn't provide much more than a "hot and a cot." But in the last few years, upper-end boarding facilities have begun providing canine guests with everything from organized play sessions to water beds to color TV.

Carol Boerio-Croft, owner of Cozy Inn Pet Resort and Spa in Stahlstown, Pennsylvania, is used to special requests. Some people drop off recipes for gourmet meals. Others bring their dogs' beds and linens. And nearly everyone brings along their dogs' favorite toys.

Some dogs seem a little too pampered, she adds. One regular client always brings along an expensive, almost-new high-heel pump for her dog to chew. "I'm sure pets appreciate the comforts of home," Boerio-Croft says, "but I'd hate to have a dog accustomed to those perks getting too close to my closet."

FAST FIX An easy way to make shoes less appealing is to cover the human scent with a scent that dogs dislike. Dr. Tripp recommends using medicated—and scented—shoe inserts. Or you can spray the insides of the shoes with mint breath spray. Most dogs dislike the smell of mint and will stay away from it. Deodorants containing alum are also a good choice, he says. Use a roll-on deodorant, and put a heavy layer of it on the footpad. If you're using inserts as well, roll it on both sides, he advises.

Teach the difference between shoes and toys. It's rare for dogs to deliberately target shoes or other human possessions. They're just attracted by the scents, and then their natural chewing instincts take over. You have to teach them the difference between shoes and toys, says Dr. Bogard.

Several times a day, bring out a tempting shoe and put it on the floor. Put one of your dog's toys a few feet away. Watch as he heads for the goodies. If he approaches the shoe, tell him "no." When he shifts gears and moves toward the toy, tell him "good boy!" Keep practicing. Periodically move the shoe and the toy farther and farther apart. Most dogs will learn the difference within a few weeks, says Dr. Bogard.

In the early days of training, of course, you'll want to remember to keep your shoes out of reach, Dr. Bogard adds. Young dogs get bored easily and are going to explore. You don't want them to find anything good when you're not around to watch them.

CHAPTER SIX

PAWING BEFORE LYING DOWN
A Comforting Ritual

Everyone has a little bedtime ritual. For children, it's toothbrushing, stories, and lights-out. For their parents, it might be pillow fluffing or putting on satin pajamas. For dogs, it's pawing the ground—or the carpet—before settling in.

"Some dogs' routines are so precise that you can tell even before they start moving what they're getting ready to do," says Emily Weiss, curator of behavior and research at Sedgwick County Zoo in Wichita, Kansas. "You can just see that look in the eye that says, 'Okay, I'm going to turn around four times, paw six times, lie down, sigh, and fall right to sleep.'"

Bowser Was Here

It's only in the last hundred years that dogs have had the opportunity to lie down on fluffy, well-laundered, and comfortable beds. Before that, they had to make their sleeping arrangements in all sorts of rugged, drafty places. They would rearrange the ground a bit in order to create comfortable hollows. It was a bit warmer than sleeping on the surface, and it allowed them to contour the ground to accommodate four legs and a tail, Weiss says.

This kelpie loves her foam bedding—but every time she snuggles down for a rest, she destroys a bit more of it with her paws. It has to be replaced regularly.

A thick pile carpet or a plaid cedar bed doesn't need this sort of treatment, but dogs are creatures of habit. They tend to do the same things they've always done. Every dog develops a slightly different set of bedtime rituals, and for the most part, they'll follow these rituals every time they lie down. "Once they get in the habit of pawing or scratching or circling around before they lie down, they're going to always want to do it," says Vint Virga, D.V.M., a veterinarian at the College of Veterinary Medicine at Cornell University in Ithaca, New York.

Comfort and ritual are only part of the story. Another reason for pawing is that dogs are territorial animals, which means they stake out and claim areas that they consider theirs, says

A freshly dug hole makes a bed that is perfectly tailored for this terrier mix. It is shaped to his body and provides protection from the elements.

Weiss. One way of marking territory is to scratch at the ground. In the wild, dogs who happened by would see the scratch marks and know that the place was occupied. They'd smell the marks, too. Dogs have scent glands in their paws. Pawing at the carpet is one way of depositing their personal scent, she explains.

"I had two males who took turns rumpling up a bath mat," says Betty Fisher, an animal behaviorist and trainer in San Diego and co-author of *So Your Dog's Not Lassie*. "One would go in the bathroom, wad it up, then come back out. Later, the other one would do the same thing." Both dogs wanted to be the last to claim the mat, even though neither of them wanted to sleep on it, she says.

Female dogs may be somewhat more likely than males to paw before lying down, especially if they happen to be pregnant. It's because they have a biological urge to prepare a safe, comfortable nest for their puppies, explains Dr. Virga.

Feels Good to Scratch

From the time they're puppies, dogs will scratch and dig just about anywhere—on the carpet, in the garden, even on linoleum floors. They're not really trying to make a bed in all of these places. They just enjoy scratching. "It feels great on their paws," Weiss says. "If it's hot outside, they'll scratch and get a little cool dirt under their nails. Before long, they're hooked."

This is why some dogs spend an inordinate amount of time pawing the carpet or their beds before lying down. They don't need to make things more comfortable than they already are. They're just enjoying the activity. And since they find it relaxing, it's a natural prelude to taking a nap. "They don't necessarily have a goal in mind," Weiss says. "They do it because it feels good."

Now That You Understand...

It's rare for dogs to do any real damage during their pre-nap pawing. Even though their instincts are telling them to make a comfortable hollow, all they're really doing is following an age-old ritual and going through the motions. But there are exceptions. Some dogs have every intention of making a real bed, and they'll shred cushions and wear away patches of carpet in

BREED SPECIFIC

Many dogs will paw and scratch before lying down, but terriers really get into it. They were bred to dig and burrow after small game, and they paw more than other dogs before settling down to sleep.

order to get it just so, Fisher says. Since you can't stop them from pawing, you'll have to work out ways to accommodate the instinct without sacrificing the house.

Give them a bed of their own. This is by far the simplest solution. Most dogs appreciate having a bed that's theirs and theirs alone. Even when they're reluctant to use it at first, the gradual accretion of personal smells will make it part of their territory, and they'll want to go there when it's time to sleep, Weiss says. Dog beds are made to withstand a lot of abuse, and most have washable covers as well.

Buy a loose-fill bed. As far as comfort is concerned, it doesn't matter all that much what kind of bed you buy. To give the most pawing satisfaction, however, you may want to get a bed that's made from loose fill—from cedar chips, for example—rather than a solid mattress. This gives dogs the opportunity to move the filling around when they paw, which is closer to what they'd experience naturally.

This bullterrier mix loves her beanbag bed. The filling is loose, which means she can paw at it and rearrange it to her own satisfaction.

Put the bed where your dog will use it. No one enjoys spending $50 for a comfortable bed, only to watch their dog give it an indifferent sniff before curling up on a corner of the couch. Since dogs are intensely attuned to territory, you'll need to be accommodating in finding the best place to put the bed, Fisher says. If there's one spot where your dog always settles down to sleep, you'll want to put the bed as close to that spot as possible. And you'll want to keep it in the same area where people spend most of their time, since those are the places that dogs consider home. Dogs like feeling protected when they sleep, and they're more likely to use a bed that's in a corner, she adds.

FAST FIX If your dog has one spot where he always sleeps, you may want to put down a blanket or a soft throw rug. "Putting down throws means I still get to have a nice-looking room, and my dogs have something comfy to sink their paws into," Fisher says. "My dogs are happy, and I don't have to replace the carpets."

CHAPTER SEVEN

DIGGING

A Talent They're Born With

Some dogs have practical reasons for digging. It gets them under the fence. They're convinced that there is something underground worth having. Or they simply want to create a comfy, climate-controlled bed in which they can curl up and go to sleep.

Then there are dogs who couldn't care less about practicality. They dig for one reason and one reason only: It's a heck of a lot of fun. For them, digging is the canine equivalent of sailing on the ocean and enjoying the salty air. They love the smell of freshly turned dirt and the way it feels under their paws. They enjoy the feeling of exhilaration that comes from tossing clouds of dirt behind them. Digging is their sport and their hobby. It requires no special equipment, and they can do it any time and just about anywhere.

Have Skills, Need Job

The reason that dogs are attracted to dirt in the first place comes down to one thing: instinct. Long before L.L. Bean started making cedar-filled beds, dogs dug themselves dens, both for sleeping and for a secure place to raise their pups. They dug to catch burrowing prey and to bury leftovers. Digging was one of the few useful tools they had at their disposal, and they used it often, says Inger Martens, a trainer and behaviorist in Los Angeles and author of *Paws for a Minute*.

Aside from searching around in the garden for treasures or making the occasional great escape, dogs don't have many real uses for digging anymore. That's fine for some dogs and some breeds. Greyhounds and Great Danes, for example, were never much into digging anyway. But others can't leave it alone.

"Terriers were bred to control vermin and snakes, and dachshunds were badger dogs," says

Dogs will sometimes start digging when they see someone else doing it. The smell of all that newly dug earth stimulates ancient instincts, and they can't resist trying it themselves.

James H. Sokolowski, D.V.M., Ph.D., a veterinarian in Vernon, California. "For hundreds of years, breeders picked the dogs that had the most enthusiasm for digging. You can't just turn that off."

Instinct is a powerful force. Add to it generations of specialized breeding, and you have a lot of dogs who will always find a way and a place to dig, even when there's nothing to dig for.

Young and Foolish

Dogs who are destined to dig usually hit their strides between the ages of 3 months and 3 years, says Martens. Some get started after watching another dog do it, or even after watching their owners in the garden. Others don't need any more inspiration than an afternoon of boredom and the desire to try something new. It doesn't take much to get them started. They'll paw at a cricket on the grass, for example, and that leads to more pawing, and pretty soon the entire yard is filled with craters. At that point, they're usually hooked and aren't going to give it up easily, Martens says.

"Dogs need to burn off steam and calories just as people do," Martens adds. "And no matter what else you may think of it, you've got to admit that digging is a great workout."

The Hole Story

Stopping dogs from digging requires counterintelligence and guerilla tactics. You'll never stop them from doing it until you figure out why they're doing it. You can tell a lot from where they're digging and the types of holes they dig.

Dogs dig different sorts of holes for different reasons. This Australian shepherd always digs at the fence line because he wants to get out and explore.

• Holes by the fence mean that dogs are digging to escape—sometimes because something is intriguing them, but mainly because they're bored and looking for action, Martens says. Pets who haven't been neutered, of course, have more compelling reasons to get out.

• Holes by the house are a sign that dogs are lonely and want to get inside where the people are, says Dr. Sokolowski.

• Shallow holes scattered around the yard usually indicate that a dog is trying to get comfortable. They're a type of thermoregulation: Holes are cool in summer and warm in winter, says Dr. Sokolowski. Supplying a wading pool filled with cool water or, in winter, giving

21

dogs a sheltered place with a warm bed will often stop them from digging. These dogs are just trying to get comfortable, and they'd be perfectly content to not have to labor for their comfort.

Now That You Understand...

It's quite easy to recognize dogs who dig just for the thrill of it. They look happy. In addition, dogs who have a specific purpose in mind usually dig when they're alone. Happy diggers, on the other hand, will do it any time. In fact, they may be more likely to dig when people are around, because they want to share their excitement.

It's not impossible to teach dogs to leave the dirt alone, but it's an uphill fight—and the dogs are usually the winners. Compromise is usually a better choice than confrontation.

"We all want our dogs to have nice, complete lives," says Dr. Sokolowski. "If digging is their passion, you can help them find a way to do it that doesn't destroy your property."

1. Pick an acceptable spot. Unless your yard is the size of a postage stamp, there's sure to be a place where you wouldn't mind having a few holes. It can't be too far out of the way, however, because dogs avoid places where they feel isolated, says Dr. Sokolowski. It has to be a place

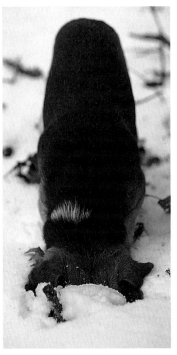

With their sensitive noses, dogs can detect intriguing smells even under snow—and snow is easier to dig than dirt.

where they feel comfortable. Look at the holes your dog has already dug to get clues about her choice of terrain.

2. Bury something good. Dogs aren't going to start digging just because you point to a spot and say, "Dig." You have to make it worth their while. Dig a small hole yourself and bury a bone or one of your dog's favorite toys, advises Dr. Sokolowski. Let her watch while you do it. This will give her the idea, and it won't take long before she notices a familiar, intriguing scent wafting up from the ground. Then she's on her own.

3. Cheer her on. Once she starts tunneling, encourage her. Act excited. Maybe get down on all fours and dig a little yourself. Enthusiasm is contagious. Your excitement will let her know that she's on to something, and she'll keep digging to get more of that good energy.

FAST FIX Your dog may or may not catch on to the fact that you want her to dig in this one place and not somewhere else. If she keeps returning to her favorite holes, you may have to booby-trap them by filling them with rocks and topping them off with a healthy dusting of ground red pepper. Dogs dislike the smell of red pepper, and they certainly don't like digging through rocks, Dr. Sokolowski says.

CHAPTER EIGHT

EATING GRASS

Better Than Antacids

Nearly every dog eats grass sometimes, and some dogs eat it all the time. You would think that veterinarians would have a pretty good idea by now of why they do it. But they don't, mainly because no one has figured out how to ask dogs two important questions: "Do you like the taste?" and "If it tastes so good, why do you throw it up?"

"I swear sometimes that my dog is an Angus," says Marty Becker, D.V.M., a veterinarian in Bonners Ferry, Idaho, and coauthor of *Chicken Soup for the Pet Lover's Soul.* "He lies out in the yard and grazes just like a cow." He doesn't get sick, either, Dr. Becker adds. He just munches happily, then closes his eyes and takes a little nap.

"Dogs explore their worlds with their noses and mouths," Dr. Becker says. "And there's the grass, attractive, sweet-smelling, with an appealing texture; and it's ever-so-accessible on the ground. Why not eat it?"

A Craving for Greens

Dogs are remarkably flexible in their tastes. They'll polish off a bowl of dried dog food, then walk over to see if there's anything good in the trash. If they're still hungry, they'll wander upstairs to see what's in the cat's box. Basically, they'll eat, or at least sample, whatever they find in front of them.

There's a good reason for their liberal tastes. Unlike cats, who evolved solely as hunters, dogs survived by scavenging. When they couldn't catch live prey, which was a lot of the time, they'd eat the ancient equivalent of roadkill. They didn't care too much if had been lying in the sun for a week or was half-buried under old leaves. It was food, and they weren't going to pass it up. When meat wasn't on the table, they'd root around for tender leafy stalks, or roots, or an old polished bone. They simply weren't fussy, and dogs today haven't gotten

These beagles are enjoying a grassy snack. It has a fresh taste they like, and it doubles as medicine when they're feeling ill.

CALL FOR HELP

It's not exactly pleasant when your dog throws up wads of grass on the living room carpet, but he's probably not too sick, either. Once he gets rid of the grass and whatever happens to be irritating his stomach, he'll probably start feeling better soon. Dogs who throw up three or more times in a day, however, need to see a veterinarian, whether or not they've been eating grass, says Sheila McCullough, D.V.M., clinical assistant professor at the University of Illinois College of Veterinary Medicine at Urbana-Champaign.

any fussier. They're predisposed to like just about everything.

In addition, there's some evidence that dogs get cravings for certain foods, says Dottie LaFlamme, D.V.M., Ph.D., a veterinary nutritionist with the Purina company in St. Louis. It's possible that dogs occasionally get a hankering for greens, just as people sometimes go to bed dreaming about mashed potatoes and meat loaf.

It's not as strange as it may sound. Grass was part of their ancestors' regular diets. Dogs are omnivores, which means they eat meat as well as plants. They don't need grassy nutrients any more because most commercial dog foods are nutritionally complete. But dogs aren't nutritionists. They don't know or care that they've already gotten their vitamin or mineral quotients from a bowl of kibble. Their instincts tell them that grass is good, so they eat it. Besides, there's a world of difference between satisfying

the minimal nutritional requirements and having a great meal. And for many dogs, a mouthful of grass clearly tastes great. It's like a salad—they eat some, then want more.

Under the Weather

Even dogs who usually don't eat grass will head straight for the nearest patch when they're feeling sick. They'll gobble a few mouthfuls, retch, and then throw up, or at least try to. Veterinarians still aren't sure if dogs eat grass because their stomachs are upset or if their stomachs get upset after they eat grass. Dr. Becker suspects it's the former, because dogs who are energetic and perky seem to be able to eat grass without getting sick afterward. It seems likely that there's something in grass that does stimulate the urge to vomit.

"The stomach has all kinds of neuro-receptors that respond to what dogs ingest," says Dr. LaFlamme. "They react to acidity, chemical content, and textures. I think the texture of the grass has something like a tickle effect on the stomach, which induces vomiting."

This tummy tickle may explain why healthy dogs can eat grass without getting sick. They take a mouthful, chew it thoroughly and swallow, then reach down for some more. Dogs who are sick, however, appear almost desperate for the grass. They don't chew it carefully or savor the taste. They gobble it. Without the chewing, those prickly little stalks hit their stomachs all at once. This may be what stimulates the urge to throw it all back up—along with whatever was irritating their stomachs in the first place.

"They can't stick their fingers down their throats or ask for syrup of ipecac," Dr. Becker adds. "Eating grass is something that works." And once dogs find something that works, they tend to stick with it.

Now That You Understand...

Keep the grass clean. Unless your dog is in the habit of regurgitating grass on the dining room floor, there's no reason to worry about it, says Dr. Becker. Dogs have been eating grass for thousands or tens of thousands of years, and there's no evidence at all that it's bad for them. That isn't the case, however, when grass has been treated with insecticides, herbicides, or other chemicals. Most products say on the label whether they're dangerous for pets. In any event, you should certainly keep dogs away from grass soon after chemicals have been applied. Most products break down fairly quickly, but they can be quite dangerous if your dog eats them while they're fresh.

Stay away if it's green. You can control what goes on your own lawn, but there's no telling what neighbors put on theirs. Often, the prettiest lawns are the ones that have been most heavily treated with chemicals, says Dr. Becker. Your dog will be better off grazing on lawns that look a little grungier.

Make a broccoli shake. It's just a theory at this point, but some veterinarians believe that dogs eat grass because they're not getting enough fiber in their diets. You may want to buy a higher-fiber food—pet foods for "seniors" generally have the most. These foods can be expensive, however, so you may want to look for

Grass is harmless to dogs, but herbicides and insecticides are not. Try to keep dogs away from grass that you know or suspect has been treated.

other ways to supplement your dog's diet. Most dogs don't care for raw vegetables, but you can run some broccoli or green beans through the blender, adding chicken or beef broth for flavor. Or add a sprinkling of bran to their food.

FAST FIX It's pretty obvious when dogs are feeling sick. When their hangdog, under-the-weather expressions are accompanied by diarrhea or vomiting, an upset stomach is probably the reason. A quick way to soothe an upset stomach is to give dogs a little Pepto-Bismol, says Dr. Becker. Veterinarians recommend giving about half of a tablespoon for every 15 pounds of weight, two or three times a day.

CHAPTER NINE

LICKING FACES

A Show of Love

Dogs use their long tongues for mopping up lunch crumbs, removing mud from their feet, and cleaning their privates. And yet, when they give our faces sloppy licks, there's something endearing about it. Apart from occasional attempts to retrieve bits of glazed doughnut from our chins, dogs lick us because they like us. It isn't a kiss, but it's close.

Almost as soon as they're born, dogs experience the soft warmth of their mothers' tongue, which bathes them with maternal affection, says Gary Landsberg, D.V.M., an animal behaviorist and veterinarian in Toronto, Ontario, Canada. The licking never really stops after that. Mothers take advantage of their puppies' relative immobility during nursing to lick them clean. They also lick their bottoms to jump-start their impulses to relieve themselves.

Puppies do their share of licking too. They lick older dogs' chins and faces to greet them and show respect. And when they're hungry—and puppies are perpetually in search of something to eat—

Dogs lick people's faces to show their respect, though some people aren't as appreciative as others.

licking their mother will sometimes stimulate her to regurgitate a meal, which the puppies regard as an appetizing lunch, says Benjamin Hart, D.V.M., Ph.D., director of the Center for Animal Behavior at the University of California School of Veterinary Medicine at Davis. As dogs get older, they lick each other less often, but they never quit entirely. At the very least, in the absence of hands and hairbrushes, they do each other's hair with their tongues.

A Sign of Respect

Dogs don't lick people because they're hoping for a hot meal. They lick because we're their parents, or at least the head folks in the house. Even when dogs are old, gray, and grizzled, they see themselves in some ways as being our children, and a lick shows how much they respect us, says Dr. Hart.

You can tell a little bit about your dog's personality by how much licking she does, says Dr. Hart. Dogs who are very bold or independent are restrained with their licking because they don't feel as though there is anyone they have to win over. Outgoing, sociable dogs, on the other hand, lick everyone all the time.

Friendly, sociable breeds, like these young golden retrievers, tend to lick people much more than reserved and independent dogs do.

We play a role in all this licking too. It doesn't take dogs very long to learn that laying a wet one on the cheek is a great way to get cooed over and rubbed the right way. So in a way, the instinct to lick is both ancient and immediate; dogs do it naturally, and we encourage them to do it more.

Now That You Understand...

People are never sure how to react to licks. The first emotion is generally "Aw, shucks," closely followed by "Yuck." Imagine where that tongue has been! But it's not as unhygienic as it seems. At worst, says Dr. Landsberg, dog licks are like wiping your face with a slightly dirty washcloth. Not exactly cleansing, but hardly worth worrying about. In fact, there's some evidence that it may be good for you.

In generations past, long before Betadine and antibiotics, people noticed how dogs always licked their own wounds. They suspected that licking may be good for people too. They weren't entirely wrong. Dog saliva does have a mild antibacterial effect, says Dr. Hart, that is certainly good for dogs and doesn't do any harm to people.

As for catching a canine cold, it's not going to happen. Most diseases are only passed within species—from dog to dog or person to person, but not between the two groups. The main exception to this is people with weakened immune systems, who are more susceptible to all sorts of illness, including those passed by overly affectionate dogs.

FAST FIX Dogs have flexible spines, long tongues, and an utter lack of regard for social niceties, which becomes evident when they settle down in public and give their nether regions a long, unctuous licking. It's noisy to listen to and unpleasant to watch, but it's well-intentioned. "People wash, but dogs lick," says Sheila McCullough, D.V.M., clinical assistant professor at the University of Illinois College of Veterinary Medicine at Urbana-Champaign.

Dogs usually don't spend more than a few minutes licking their privates. When they spend longer than that, it's probably because they're uncomfortable. Their bellies and groins have less fur than the rest of their bodies, so those areas are vulnerable to irritation. In addition, dogs often get swollen anal sacs—small sacs inside the anus that contain a fluid used for scent-marking—which make them itchy. A long licking gives relief.

CHAPTER TEN

PROTECTING EMPTY FOOD BOWLS

Memories of Lean Times

If there's one thing that brings out dogs' possessive tendencies, it's food. Among any group of mammals, from lion prides to wolf packs, nothing affects survival as much as getting enough to eat—and eating it before someone else does.

Some dogs have elevated their protective instincts to a speed sport. They hunker over their dishes and inhale the food to ensure that no one else gets a crack at it. All the while, they look around furtively for food thieves. Some get downright aggressive, giving a guttural growl if anyone gets close.

The bowl doesn't have to be full to trigger protective feelings, adds Joanne Howl, D.V.M., a veterinarian in West River, Maryland. "Lots of dogs see their bowls as their possessions," she explains. "They probably imagine that food might appear there at any time. So the bowl isn't just any possession—it's highly prized."

It's not just the bowl they're protecting, but the space around it, Dr. Howl adds. This is due in part to what is called their denning instinct. Dogs in the wild always lived in cozy, enclosed spaces called dens. A den might have been a cave or an abandoned shed. Or it could have been a hollow in the ground, surrounded by trees. Dogs viewed their dens as their castles, and they didn't welcome strangers coming around. So they did whatever they had to do to protect their space.

In addition, dogs like a little peace and quiet when they eat. It's their way of making sure no one gets close enough to steal their food. They may get cranky when

This Labrador is keeping a wary eye on her bowl, just in case anyone tries to make a raid. The fact that it's empty doesn't seem to make a difference.

Friendship never extends to the food bowl. Even dogs who normally get along fine, like these two mixed breeds, will get defensive whenever one approaches the other's bowl.

there's too much activity around their food bowls, even when mealtimes are a long way off. "For a dog, an empty dinner dish is just a meal waiting to happen," says Dr. Howl.

Family Competition

There's nothing like a little sibling rivalry to stir up food-guarding feelings. Dogs who live with other dogs may view each other as competitors for food, treats, toys, and attention, says Robin Kovary, director of the American Dog Trainers Network in New York City and author of *From Good Puppy to Great Dog!* This makes sense because dogs know what other dogs are thinking. They instinctively understand that their food is up for grabs if they don't grab it first.

Competition among dogs has a way of extending to other members of the family. That's when mild protective feelings escalate to baleful glances, growls, or worse. At that point, your dog doesn't view you as a benign and friendly presence. She sees you as a competing appetite.

Hungry, Not Greedy

Some dogs guard their dishes simply because they're not getting enough to eat, Kovary says. Even though about a third of dogs in the United

States are overweight, some dogs still aren't getting all the calories they need, because their owners are overly concerned about keeping them trim. Dogs who are truly ravenous won't be on their best behavior, and they certainly won't let their food bowls out of sight, if they can help it.

Even when a dog's stomach isn't growling, she may protect the bowl if she has gone through lean times. This tends to be an issue for dogs who spent their early months as strays, Kovary says. Like children of the Depression, they remember what it's like to be hungry, and they aren't going to let it happen again.

Since every dog needs a different number of calories, the only way to be sure that your dog is getting enough is to watch her ribs. They should be almost visible, but nicely padded. If they're too prominent—or, conversely, if you can't see them at all—you should make some adjustments to the amount of food that you pour into the bowl.

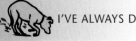
Now That You Understand...

Put the bowl in the middle of a big room. Dogs are most possessive of their bowls when they're put in small, confined places, says Kovary. It's a matter of perception as well as practicality. Dogs who feel crowded get uneasy because they suspect that there is going to be competition for this very valuable resource. And small places are easy to guard. A big, open space, however, would be a chore to protect. Most dogs won't bother.

Move the bowl around. Since it's not only the bowl but also the space around it that dogs protect, Dr. Howl recommends moving the bowl all the time—Monday in the kitchen, Tuesday on the porch, and so on. When dogs eat in different places every day, they attach less importance to the bowl than to the food that's in it.

Make the bowl vanish. No one wants to be washing dog dishes all the time, which is why bowls tend to become permanent fixtures on the floor. Dogs look at them and think, "Mine." You can make the bowl seem incidental and unimportant just by picking it up after every meal, Dr. Howl says.

Toy poodles and other small dogs tend to bond more closely with people than with dogs, whom they see as competitors for affection as well as for food.

Have them work for food. No matter how protective dogs feel inside, they only express it when they're sure they can get away with it. You don't want to make life too easy for them, Kovary says. She recommends making them work before they get fed.

For example, have your dog sit before you put the bowl on the floor. Let her wait there for a minute. Or make her lie down or come when you call or do anything else that you say. This is your dog's "payment" for the meal. Dogs who have to earn their privileges know better than to be grouchy, because they understand from whose hands the food flows.

FAST FIX Probably the quickest way to make your dog less protective is to drop a small treat in the bowl every time she is eating. Make it something special—a morsel of cheese or a piece of hot dog, says Kovary. Your dog will start viewing you more as a waiter than a competitor. In fact, rather than looking suspicious when you approach the bowl, she's going to get downright excited.

CHAPTER ELEVEN

ROLLING IN STINKY THINGS

It's about Bragging Rights

Every morning, Laura Whittaker and her Labrador, Stormy, climb the hill behind her house in Franklin, New York, to feed the horses. Whittaker carries a mug of coffee and a couple of carrots. Stormy runs ahead, happy to see a new day.

It's a peaceful, idyllic time—until Stormy spies a fresh pile of horse dung and decides to take a roll. The invigorated but filthy dog then proceeds to run in circles, coming dangerously close to his disgusted owner as they head back home. Laura goes in the house with her coffee. Stormy stays on the porch.

He's certainly not the only one. Dogs seem driven to roll in filth—the dirtier and smellier, the better. Collectively, they've spent years on the porch because their owners don't want them tracking their odoriferous business inside. The dogs, of course, don't seem to think they stink. If anything, they act happier the dirtier they get, and they're always eager to share their scents with the people they love.

Smells like Home

No one knows for sure why dogs roll in stinky things, but people who study animal behavior have some pretty good hunches.

"My best guess is that dogs like to mark themselves with their territory," says Patricia McConnell, Ph.D., a certified applied animal behaviorist in Black Earth, Wisconsin. "A dog wearing a bit of woodchuck carcass or horse poop on his neck and shoulders is a lot like a guy wearing a big gold chain around his neck. It says something about him and where he lives, something like, 'I'm a dog of means; I own the territory with all this great stuff.'"

It's hard for people to understand how anyone, even a dog, could rate the value of his territory according to its riches of cow pies. This is one of those situations that illustrates how completely different dogs and people are. People appreciate things that are clean and fresh. Dogs like things that are old and smelly.

For this elkhound, happiness is a dead fish on a beach. He's making sure to coat himself with the smell.

Smells that dogs find delectable are often the ones that make people reel. About all you can do is give them a bath and keep them outside until the stench wears off.

There may be a good reason for their off-putting tastes. Dogs have spent eons scrounging for food. It's possible that even the hint of a good meal triggers a sense of elation, says Tony Buffington, D.V.M., Ph.D., professor of clinical nutrition at the Ohio State University College of Veterinary Medicine in Columbus. Out of necessity, they may have developed a unique appreciation for anything that's remotely edible. A week-old carcass certainly qualifies. So does a fish washed up on shore. Even the presence of deer or cow dung suggests that there's a potential meal somewhere in the neighborhood.

Smells Good to Me

Then again, there may be a simpler reason why dogs enjoy coating themselves with horrid things, one that has nothing to do with survival and everything to do with taste. It's possible, explains Dr. McConnell, that they roll in dung,

carcasses, and pond scum because they like the smell. Not just a little, but enough to want to carry it around with them, just as people enjoy dabbing themselves with Chanel No. 5.

"Smell is such a primal sense, it's hard to account for who likes what," says Dr. McConnell. Just as some people enjoy Limburger cheese, dogs may revel in smells that most of us find objectionable. It's hard to criticize their tastes, because they have millions more scent receptors than we do. Our own senses of smell are barely functional compared to theirs. It's possible that they detect pleasing odors of which people are completely unaware.

"I put on gardenia because I like it," says Dr. McConnell. "And when dogs put on dead fish or cow pies, I have no doubt that it smells really good to them. It might even impress their friends."

Now That You Understand...

Dogs have been rolling in dirty things for as long as they've been dogs. It's as much a part of who they are as their barks and wagging tails. They aren't going to quit doing it just because people want them to. Even professional trainers have a hard time making them stop. About all that you can hope to achieve is keeping them away from temptation—and, when that fails, knocking down the odor enough that they're bearable to be around.

Neutralize the smell. Baths are fine for eliminating a little bit of doggy smell, but they won't do a thing for a dog who has rolled on an old catfish. If anything, washing them seems to raise the scent. A better choice may be an odor neutralizer. Available in pet supply stores, these contain ingredients that break down bad odors chemically. Dr. McConnell recommends a spray called Skunk Kleen. "I don't even have to give them a bath anymore," she says. "I spray it on, buff them with a towel, and the stink is gone."

Beat them to it. It's not a glamorous job, but some people have resigned themselves to doing a treasure hunt every few days, looking for things in the yard that their dogs are likely to be attracted to, such as dead mice, deer droppings, and rotten bird eggs. They won't smell good when you pick them up, but at least you won't have to live with the smell for 2 weeks because it's permeated your dog's coat all the way down to the skin.

Give them something better. It isn't easy to convince dogs to ignore their natural urge to roll, but food is always a reliable distraction. "Load your pockets with goodies when you're going for a walk," Dr. McConnell says. "But it's going to take a pretty good bribe."

From a dog's point of view, a smelly mud puddle is great fun to play in—especially when there's a friend to share it with.

PUPPY DOG TALES

The Dog Who Lived for Grunge

Rosie is a Labrador–shepherd mix and, according to her owner, she's the sweetest dog there ever was. Sweet, that is, in terms of her disposition. Rosie's personal aroma, on the other hand, is anything but floral.

"Rosie is a roll-aholic," says Maria Stone, Rosie's owner. "We'll be walking down the sidewalk, and all of sudden she'll be squirming around on her back, trying to get as much of whatever she found onto her hide as she possibly can."

At one time, Rosie lived in rural New Mexico, where she had plenty of opportunities to indulge. "There were pig farms and dairy farms in the neighborhood—more animal crud than she knew what to do with," Maria says. "There were days when Rosie would come in and it was like a whole barnyard had walked through the living room."

Rosie had her rolling apotheosis about the time she reached her 10th birthday. "We were out running, and when I looked over, Rosie wasn't beside me anymore," Maria says. "I ran back, but I wasn't quick enough."

Rosie, she discovered, had found something very old, very smelly, and very dead. And there she was, writhing around, making happy-sounding grunts, and trying to get it all the way down to her pores.

It took 2 weeks, three bottles of dog shampoo, and a couple of gallons of tomato juice to make Rosie reasonably presentable. But after that day, Maria says, she really never smelled sweet again.

CHAPTER TWELVE

LYING ON THEIR BACKS

Good Feelings, Cool Air

Ellen Carpenter was afraid she was going to have to deliver some tragic news to her daughter-in-law, Susan Carpenter of Glocester, Rhode Island. As Ellen stood in the kitchen looking out the window, she noticed that the family's much-loved Samoyed, Buddy, was on the lawn, flat on his back with his legs sticking in the air. The first thought that jumped into her mind was that Buddy had been poisoned. She tapped on the window. Buddy didn't budge. She banged loudly on the glass. There was no response. With tears in her eyes, she walked outside, knelt beside Buddy, and reached out to stroke his stomach.

Buddy rolled his eyes open, licked his chops in gratitude for the belly rub, yawned widely, and went back to sleep.

More than a few people have experienced similar moments of panic. Many animals do go belly-up when they expire. Dogs, however, lie on their backs for the sheer pleasure of it, especially when they're getting ready to take a nap. It's a position that indicates that they're pretty darn happy with life.

"A dog who sleeps on his back is a dog who's really comfortable and who feels very safe," says Cynthia Jacobs, D.V.M., a veterinarian in Clarksville, Arkansas.

It's hard to overestimate the sense of personal security that inspires dogs to assume this position. The belly is their softest, most vulnerable part. Dogs are naturally inclined to keep it protected and out of sight. The only times they lie on their backs are when they're trying to appease another dog (or a person) by showing how helpless they are or when they're feeling so safe and peaceful that they forget all about their instinctive trepidation.

Dogs often lie on their backs as a means of temperature control. The sparse fur on their bellies allows the breeze to reach their skin more easily and cool them off.

This shih tzu mix has it all figured out: a comfortable position on his back, his owner's attention, and the chance of a belly rub, as well.

Feels Good to Me

Once dogs are sufficiently secure to lie on their backs—and in today's pet-loving families, it usually doesn't take very long—they find all kinds of good reasons to do it, says Dr. Jacobs. In hot weather, for example, dogs often lie on their backs as a form of climate control. "They curl up to keep warm and stretch out to cool off," she says. Dogs have less hair and more nerve endings on their bellies than on their backs, so exposing their bellies to the air probably feels very good.

Getting the sun is another reason dogs lie on their backs. Apart from their noses, the belly is the only place that isn't covered with thick fur. Dogs don't think about sunburn, and the sensation of direct sunlight is pleasant. "My dog suns herself by lying on her back and holding a stick in her mouth," says Dr. Jacobs. "You'd think she was in heaven."

Finally, many dogs lie on their backs simply because they know it gets them noticed. When they have reason to believe that a belly rub is on the way, or they hope to invite one, they'll roll over, splay their legs apart, and put their bellies in the most "petable" position. "When your dog rolls over on his back in front of you, he's usually asking for your love and attention," says Jeff Nichol, D.V.M., a veterinarian in Albuquerque, New Mexico. "If he gets a belly rub by doing it, you can bet he's going to be smart enough to do it again soon."

PUPPY DOG TALES

"Bang, You're Dead"

Digger is a 6-year-old terrier mix who has transformed a comfortable body position into performance art. When he was a puppy, he learned to play cops and robbers. The game was simple. Someone would say, "Bang," and Digger would roll over on his back.

It didn't take Digger long to perfect his routine, says Sandy Fitzsimmons of San Jose, California. His stage managers—Sandy's three young girls—were less professional, however. They got so excited by the game that they praised Digger even before the "bang-roll-over" sequence was completed.

As a result, Digger began to jump the gun. Now, rather than waiting for "bang," he keels over as soon as he thinks someone's going to say it. "I have to tell him, 'No, Digger, not yet,'" Sandy says. "He gets all excited and flips over on his back as soon as I point my finger."

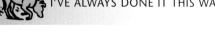
Now That You Understand...

Take the hint. A dog who's lying on his back should look happy and relaxed. If his sides are heaving and his tongue's hanging out, he's probably too hot for comfort and is trying to catch a breeze, says Vint Virga, D.V.M., a veterinarian at the College of Veterinary Medicine at Cornell University in Ithaca, New York. It's not the best form of air-conditioning, however. Most dogs prefer to lie belly-down on a cool surface when they're hot. One way to help them get more comfortable is to hose down a shady area in the yard where they can lie down and cool off. Indoors, encourage your dog to make himself at home in the kitchen, bathroom, or another area that has tile or wood floors, which are much cooler than carpet.

Use sunscreen. Dogs who spend a lot of time lounging on their backs in the sun sometimes get sunburned. Veterinarians recommend applying a sunscreen with an SPF of 15 or higher. It's fine to use human sunscreens as long as they don't contain zinc oxide or PABA, which can be harmful should dogs lick them off.

If your dog is already sunburned, you can apply an over-the-counter anesthetic spray, such as Solarcaine or Lanacane. Anesthetic ointments are helpful, too. It's worth taking care of the irritation because, otherwise, dogs will scratch the area, which may get infected.

Stop the snores. The one problem with dogs who sleep on their backs is that this position can make them prodigious snorers, says Dr. Jacobs. Don't lie awake yourself because your dog looks so cozy that you hate to disturb him. Give him a nudge, she advises. He'll roll over on his side, and that will quiet the snores.

Give him what he wants. Belly rubs are one of the best opportunities people get to bond with pets, says Dr. Nichol. "Dogs don't initiate many of their interactions with their owners," he explains. "Here's one situation where your dog actually gets to ask for what he wants and receive it from you."

Rubbing your dog's belly does more than make him feel great, Dr. Nichol adds. It's also an effective way to remind him of your parental authority. "Because lying on their backs is such a submissive position, every time you give your dog a belly rub, you reinforce your position as the head of the house in the gentlest, most effective way possible."

Dogs instinctively understand that lying on a tiled floor will keep them cooler than settling down on carpet. It's a natural kind of air conditioning.

CHAPTER THIRTEEN

GOBBLING FOOD

Like Money in the Bank

Every day at 9:00 A.M., Willoughby gets his 4 cups of dog food, which he scarfs in 3 minutes flat. Despite his obvious excitement and the exuberance of his feed-me dance, his owner, Jane Rudnitsky of Oneonta, New York, can't tell if he takes any joy in the meal itself. She wonders if he even tastes it.

She has good reason to wonder. Dogs only have about 1,500 taste buds (people have 10,000). They really don't care about having delectable food. They'll happily settle for edible. "They're like my 9-year-old, who inhales meals so he can get back to his computer game," says Marty Becker, D.V.M., a veterinarian in Bonners Ferry, Idaho, and coauthor of *Chicken Soup for the Pet Lover's Soul.* "It's almost a mechanical act for them. The nutrients have to go in, but there's not much passion for the taste."

Most dogs find that leftovers in the trash are every bit as wonderful as fresh food in their bowls. Either way, they usually eat as fast as they possibly can. There's a good reason for this. When your main concern is

Dogs who share a bowl feel compelled to eat as much and as quickly as they can, just to keep others from getting to it first.

getting enough to eat—and in millennia past, dogs could never take this for granted—haste counts more than taste. Modern dogs can dilly-dally over their food indefinitely and not have to worry about it disappearing, but their predecessors weren't so lucky. They knew that food not eaten right away wouldn't still be in the woods waiting for them later.

Saving Up for a Rainy Day

Dogs evolved from wolves, and wolves are prodigious eaters. They're capable of consuming as much as 40 pounds of meat in a sitting, says Rolan Tripp, D.V.M., a veterinarian in La Mirada, California, who specializes in animal

Many dogs will steal as much food as they possibly can, so you may have to feed your dogs separately to ensure that they all get enough to eat.

when they were successful, shared one big meal at the end of the day. But their idea of sharing wasn't the same as ours. Dogs in packs weren't all equal. There were high-ranking dogs, low-ranking dogs, and dogs in between. They ate in order of their ranks in the pack. The leaders ate first and got the choicest bits, while lower-ranking dogs cleaned up the leftovers. It wasn't easy for every dog to get his fill. So they naturally ate as fast and as much as they could, when they could. Dogs have only been living with humans for about 10,000 years, and old evolutionary habits hang on. Dogs today don't have to hunt, and they get more or less the same amounts of food at the same times. But they still have remnants of the urge to fill up fast just in case their food gets taken away. And they eat even faster when there are other dogs in the family. More dogs mean more competition. Whether or not there's a threat to their food, they don't want to take any chances. So they gobble as fast and furiously as they can.

behavior. Ancient dogs and their wolfish ancestors didn't stuff themselves just to be pigs. They were hunters and they had to catch their own meat. They didn't have the luxury of knowing where the next meal was coming from. Maybe Monday would bring a deer, but Tuesday might yield a rabbit or a squirrel or, in many cases, nothing at all. Dogs could easily go for several days without a meal, but only if they were well-fed the rest of the time. They knew enough to fill up when they got the chance.

And speed was important. Dogs used to live in packs, tight-knit groups who depended on teamwork to survive. They hunted together and,

The Price of Gluttony

The passion that dogs put into eating can be a little off-putting to the people who feed them—and who have to watch their terrible manners. There's the drooling and whining. The unseemly snorting as they bury their faces in their food. And, worst of all, the regurgitation that may occur afterward. This, too, is part of nature's plan.

Labrador retrievers like eating so much that most pet-food companies have banned them from the testing rooms. Experts aren't sure why, but Labradors have no discrimination at all and will eat as fast as you put food down—a phenomenon known to veterinarians as Lab lunge.

When wolves stuffed themselves with 40 pounds of meat, their bodies couldn't actually process that much at once. So they would waddle away from the table, throw up a little bit, then eat it to get the nutrients.

Dogs are a lot smaller than wolves, and it doesn't take 40 pounds of meat to turn their stomachs. That's why the kibble you pour in the bowl occasionally gets deposited in the corner a few minutes later. This has nothing to do with physical health or social graces. Their brains and stomachs are telling them that dogs who waste not, want not, and so they follow orders.

Now That You Understand...

Given a chance to raid the food bag, most dogs will instantly revert to their old habits. Even when they don't eat a lot, they do eat fast, and eating fast means that what goes in is going to try to come out. Here are a few ways to protect the floors and keep their stomachs calm.

Give them more time. Dogs learn from experience. If you always pick up the food bowl the minute they're done, they'll figure that they'd better eat faster just in case you pick it up early. Leaving the bowl on the floor for 10 to 15 minutes after it's empty will help them understand that they don't have to rush, says Dr. Becker.

Wet the food. Most dogs like a little gravy with their meals, and moistening dry food with warm water makes it more appealing. More important, it makes it easier to digest, says Dr. Becker. Dogs are less likely to toss up their food when it's not in hard chunks, he explains.

Give them less food, more often. Even though dogs are designed to handle very large meals, it's better for their digestion to eat smaller amounts, more often, says Dr. Tripp. Veterinarians often recommend feeding dogs at least twice a day. Some say it's better to feed them three, four, or even five times a day. The total amount of food will be the same, but the leisurely pace will help ensure that it stays where it's supposed to.

FAST FIX Putting a large object in the middle of your dog's food bowl will force him to coax out each bite. This means he'll have to eat more slowly, says Dr. Becker. It doesn't matter what you put in the bowl, as long as it's not appetizing and it's big enough that it won't get swallowed accidentally. A large butternut squash works well. For small dogs, a tennis ball is fine as long as they don't show more interest in the ball than in their food.

PART TWO

"I Know Things That You Don't"
The Amazing Senses of Dogs

Dogs see the world in ways that we can hardly imagine. Their senses of smell and hearing are vastly better than ours, while their vision leaves something to be desired. When they act in ways that seem unusual to us, they're often responding to something of which only they are aware.

CHAPTER FOURTEEN

BARKING AT BUTTERFLIES

They're Very Tempting Targets

Debra Doyle lives in Walls, Mississippi, and her dog, a Chow Chow named Bear, is perfectly suited for rural life. Bear likes looking out the window and watching the world go by. He gets especially excited when butterflies pass. There's something about their slow, fluttery, unpredictable movements that make him stand up and bark … and bark.

Bear's hardly the only dog who gets excited by butterflies. "Dogs are hardwired hunters, so they want to chase after anything that passes by," says Katherine Houpt, V.M.D., Ph.D., a diplomate of the American College of Veterinary Behaviorists and a professor in the College of Veterinary Medicine at Cornell University in Ithaca, New York.

Dogs who are truly hunting, however, don't bark much because that would alert their prey, she adds. In Bear's case, the "prey" is on one side of the glass, and he's on the other. There's something out there he wants to chase, but he can't get at it. He barks out of frustration. Even if the window weren't there, he'd still bark because the odds of catching a butterfly aren't very good. If he really thought he had a chance for success, he'd be very quiet, Dr. Houpt explains.

One reason dogs get so excited—and frustrated—by butterflies is that butterflies seem as though they'd be easy to catch. They're big, they flutter close to the ground, and they don't move very fast. So dogs keep trying, and nearly every time the butterflies stay just out of reach. It drives dogs crazy because no matter how often they fail, the urge to chase is extremely strong, says Mark Plonsky, Ph.D., a dog trainer and professor

Dogs look out windows for the same reason people do—to see if anything interesting is happening. A passing butterfly can bring on a barking frenzy.

POOCH PUZZLER

Why do dogs eat flies?

Dogs dislike insects. They don't like the sensation of prickly insect feet crawling on them, and the buzzing of flies probably irritates them as much as it does us. Combine this antipathy with their natural hunting instincts, and it's easy to see why they often go snapping at flies, then swallow them when they succeed in catching them.

"When you watch dogs going after flies, you'll see that they stalk them like prey, and they seem to get real joy out of catching one," says Kay Cox, Ph.D., an animal-behavior consultant in Gilbert, Arizona. They're probably indifferent to the taste, she adds. "You don't see dogs chewing and savoring their flies," she says. "Instead, what you see is the 'Aha!' satisfaction of having caught them."

of psychology at the University of Wisconsin at Stevens Point.

"That pull is almost magnetic," he says. When a dog can't keep up with the creature that's taunting him, he has to do something. That may mean barking. Or running in circles. Some dogs will open their mouths and let loose with a whole series of yawns—the canine equivalent of taking a big breath and counting to 10.

Something to Talk About

Apart from giving voice to their hunting instincts, dogs bark at butterflies as a way of being social. These are usually the same dogs who bark when they hear or see something out of the ordinary. They know that something is happening, and they want to share the news.

"Some dogs are just naturally more inclined to be verbal than others," says Kay Cox, Ph.D., an animal-behavior consultant in Gilbert, Arizona. "It can be any dog, but beagles, terriers, and poodles are the ones who seem to do it the most. They want to tell you about everything."

It's not necessarily the butterflies themselves that get these dogs so excited, Dr. Cox adds. It goes back to their breeding. They were bred to bark as a way of communicating with hunters. "They were supposed to bark to scare up quarry, to tell the hunter when they had it in the tree, and so on. But they don't have any work-related use for that communicative ability anymore, so they find an outlet for it on their own," she says.

Even dogs whose ancestors never hunted will often bark at butterflies as a way of guarding their territory. It's hard to imagine that any dog would think of a butterfly as posing much of a threat, but they react that way to pretty much anything that comes into their space. The butterflies unknowingly contribute to the habit because, sooner or later, they fly away. "When a dog barks and barks at something, and it goes away, he invariably thinks he did it," says Dr. Houpt. A dog

Anything that moves is going to attract a dog's attention, and a large, bobbing balloon is the perfect target for a leap and a snap.

who has conquered one butterfly will feel very happy. He'll want to repeat the satisfying experience—with bigger and louder barks—every chance he gets.

Now That You Understand...

Keep your voice low. No one enjoys listening to round after round of senseless barking. After a while, nearly everyone responds with a loud bark—"Quiet!"—of their own, which only makes their dogs bark more.

"When your dog barks and you yell, he really thinks you're barking with him," says Dr. Cox. "And so he'll bark even louder."

Since dogs use their barks as a way of communicating with others in the family, it's often enough to let them know you've gotten the message. Keeping your voice low and quiet, acknowledge what your dog has seen. Tell

him "butterfly," advises Dr. Cox, and follow that with a low-key "quiet." Just as quietly, lead him somewhere where he can't see outside. He'll know you've heard what he has to say, and that will be enough for him, she explains.

FAST FIX Since dogs who are in the house can't hear butterflies outside, you can stop the barking just by closing the blinds, says Dr. Cox. You can also use the blinds as part of a training exercise. After you tell your dog "quiet," shut the blinds. He'll get quiet right away. After a few seconds, open the blinds again. With a little practice, he'll learn that barking less lets him have what he loves—the view out the window—while noisy barking always gets the blinds closed, she says.

Bribe him for quiet. When your dog barks at butterflies and keeps barking until you notice him, try ignoring him the next time. Let him bark as long as he likes. In the meantime, go get a dog treat and go about your business. As soon as your dog stops barking on his own, give him the treat and tell him "good quiet," says Dr. Cox. Some dogs will start barking less after just a few rewards, and nearly all dogs will get quieter within a few weeks of practice.

Dogs will spend hours stalking and snapping at flies, but they hardly ever manage to catch one.

CHAPTER FIFTEEN

EATING DUNG

Following the Crowd

Mother dogs do whatever they have to do to take care of their young. One of their duties is to lick the pups' genitals and bottoms in order to jump-start their ability to urinate and have bowel movements. Another motherly duty is to keep the nest clean. So after revving up their puppies' insides, they eat what comes out.

Dogs have only a fraction of the tastebuds that humans do, so this unpleasant duty doesn't faze them. And from their point of view, it has to be done. Apart from the need for basic housekeeping, eating the puppies' stools once kept dog families alive. Dung has a powerful scent, and it would have advertised the presence of puppies to every hungry predator within sniffing distance, explains Jo Ann Eurell, D.V.M., a veterinarian and animal-behavior specialist at the University of Illinois College of Veterinary Medicine at Urbana-Champaign.

Dogs aren't the only animals who eat the stools of their young. Horses, cats, and many other mammals do it too. But there's a difference. Most animals take care of their young, then never eat dung again. Dogs, on the other hand, sometimes get a taste for it. They keep going after it every chance they get.

He Did It First

Dogs have always lived in groups. First, they lived with other dogs. Now, they live with people. As with all highly social animals, including humans, they're very impressionable. They learn how to play by watching other dogs play. They

Mother dogs often eat the stools of their puppies to keep the nest clean and to remove any odors that may lead predators to the litter.

Puppies often imitate what older dogs do. There are times when that includes imitating their least desirable behavior—eating dung.

learn proper etiquette by following the examples of their elders. And they often eat dung for no other reason than they saw another dog doing it, says Dr. Eurell.

One reason that this habit is so common is that every dog watched his mother do it. Most puppies sample dung at some time or other. But most of them seem to give it up.

Doesn't Taste Bad

Children will often do crazy things because they saw their friends do them first. But once is usually enough. They won't jump out of a tree or put their fingers in a candle flame after the first painful experience. Dogs, however, will return to dung again and again.

Most experts have had to conclude that there's more at work than simple imitation. If dogs hated the taste of dung, they wouldn't keep eating it. But they do. So there has to be something about it that they like.

This isn't all that surprising. Dogs have always been scavengers, Dr. Eurell explains. They'll eat roadkill as readily as their suppers. Old trash, pond muck, and dead sparrows on the lawn are no less appetizing. Dogs start getting hungry whenever they sniff something with a pungent smell, and dung certainly does smell.

Not all dung tastes the same, of course. Dogs seem to have different preferences. Some are attracted to the stools of deer, cows, or horses. Others will eat the stools of other dogs. And a great many dogs are attracted to cat droppings, possibly because cat foods are very high in protein and the dogs are going after undigested nutrients.

Look at Me

Dogs, no less than children, crave attention. And they do whatever it takes to get it, including things they know you hate. This probably explains why some dogs only eat dung when their owners are around to watch, says Dr. Eurell. It's

probably the equivalent of a 6-year-old saying a dirty word and then watching for his parents' reaction. "Look at me," the dog is saying.

Boredom has something to do with it too. Dogs entertain themselves by putting things in their mouths. When not much is happening, they often nose around the yard, picking up sticks and putting them down, even mouthing rocks on occasion. Since they aren't offended by the smell or taste of dung, it's just another thing for them to pick up, play with, and explore.

Now That You Understand...

Dogs occasionally eat so much dung that they get sick to their stomachs. For the most part, however, it's not likely to make them sick—although they may get worms from eating the stools of an infected animal. "Their digestive tracts are very forgiving," says Robin Downing, D.V.M., a veterinarian in Windsor, Colorado.

The people who live with dogs, however, are less forgiving. For one thing, it's an ugly sight that no one wants to watch. There's also the fact that dogs who eat dung have heart-stopping bad breath. "It takes some serious devotion to get past that," says Dr. Downing.

FAST FIX Veterinarians sometimes recommend adding garlic, canned pumpkin, or Accent meat tenderizer to a dung-eating dog's food. Assuming that it's his own dung that he's attracted do, these ingredients may give it a taste he dislikes—although it's hard to imagine that anything could make it taste worse than it already does. This isn't a perfect solution, but it does work for some dogs, says Dr. Eurell. A product called For-bid, available in pet supply stores, does the same thing and may help, she adds.

Add some seasoning. People won't eat food with too much salt, and dogs won't eat dung that has been sprinkled with ground red pepper. Taking a few minutes each day to season the stuff your dog usually eats—in the litter box, for example—will make it less appetizing. Even if your dog does take a bite, he'll wonder what the heck he's gotten into.

This isn't something that you can do halfway, however. If you do it for just a day or two, your dog will be resourceful enough to sniff out something that hasn't been treated. The idea is to treat the dung long enough that he assumes it's always going to taste like that. And once he gives it up for a while, he may forget all about it, says Dr. Eurell.

Switch to a concentrated food. Average dog foods are designed for the average dog. They have an abundance of nutrients, but some dogs simply need more than these foods provide. They may turn to dung as a way of supplementing their diets. It's worth switching to a premium dog food, says Dr. Downing. These foods provide highly concentrated nutrition in a form that's easy for dogs to digest. If their bodies' needs are being met, they may be less likely to look for extras, she explains.

Feeding your dog two or three times a day may help, too. Dogs who eat only once a day get hungry between meals. Feeding them more often will keep their stomachs satisfied, and they'll be less likely to forage on their own, says Dr. Downing.

CHAPTER SIXTEEN

ATTRACTED TO VERTICAL OBJECTS

It's Where the Big Dogs Go

When people and dogs go for walks, it's almost as though they're on completely different trips. "I see all the same things I saw the day before—the same trees, the same mailboxes, the same fire hydrants," says Mark Plonsky, Ph.D., a dog trainer and professor of psychology at the University of Wisconsin at Stevens Point. His dog, however, is "seeing" with his nose. The scents he encounters are changing all the time.

A tree by the sidewalk, for example, contains hundreds of scents humans don't know exist. But dogs recognize them as clearly as we see the branches and the leaves. They're especially attuned to the smells of other dogs. A quick sniff tells them who's been there before them, how big and dominant they were, whether they were male or female, even if they were in good health. "That tree might as well be a signed guest book," says Dr. Plonsky.

The reason vertical objects such as telephone poles and fire hydrants have so much appeal is that they provide a canvas for dogs to project their social aspirations. In their world, size makes a difference. Bigger dogs can "claim" more territory than smaller ones. "The thinking seems to be, 'The higher I urinate, the bigger other dogs will think I am,'" say Emily Weiss, curator of behavior and research at the Sedgwick County Zoo in Wichita, Kansas. Some dogs go so far as to choose the highest tree on a hill, and then try to mark the highest spot on that tree.

Some dogs are so determined to get their marks up high that they get downright athletic. Some raise their legs over their heads in order to

An essential part of this golden retriever's routine is checking out who's been visiting his district. It makes his daily patrol around his territory more interesting.

If sniffing starts at the front gate and continues at every fence post until you arrive home, it makes for a very long walk. Dogs who are leash-trained are easier to manage—and to keep moving.

achieve more upward trajectory, Weiss says. Others back up to trees with their hind ends in the air. Some even stand on their front legs in order to get extra height.

Their efforts don't go unnoticed by other dogs. "Even dogs who don't leave a mark of their own usually want to stop and investigate who's been around," Weiss says. Bragging aside, it's a good way of staying on top of the neighborhood news.

Looking for Love

For dogs who have been neutered, hydrants and other vertical objects are mainly an opportunity to share some gossip—their mating instinct isn't very strong. Dogs who are intact, however, have a very practical reason for aiming high. Big dogs

tend to be the most dominant, and dominant dogs are more attractive to the opposite sex. For males, hitting a high spot on a tree is an opportunity to announce their availability as well as their status, Weiss says. For females, sniffing the different levels gives them a variety of mates to choose from.

The messages contained in a droplet of urine—and a dog's ability to detect them—are hard for humans to imagine. Dogs have nearly 20 square inches of scent-detecting membrane. Humans only have $1/2$ square inch. In addition, dogs have a small mass of nerve endings in the roof of the mouth called the Jacobson's organ. It responds only to odors linked to food and sex. When a dog sniffs urine markings on a telephone pole, the Jacobson's organ fires off a signal to the hypothalamus, the part of the brain that is responsible for controlling sex drive and appetite.

Now That You Understand...

This fascination with all things upright wouldn't be an issue if dogs took themselves for walks. But there's usually a human at the other end of the leash. A walk around the block can take an impressively long time as dogs do their sniff-and-mark routines. While dogs do need an opportunity to get their bearings and catch up on the latest gossip—and to leave some of their own—there's no reason it should take all day.

Dogs who are leash-trained know that they're not supposed to stop until their owners give them the go-ahead. If your dog hasn't had basic obedience, you're going to have to teach him to heel. And the only way he'll learn that is by watching you all the time to see when you want him to stay close or when it's okay to take a break. "When he's keeping his eyes on you, he won't be wandering off exploring new smells," Dr. Plonsky adds.

He has developed an unusual technique for teaching dogs to watch him. "I spit food at them," he explains. During the early stages of training, Dr. Plonsky puts tiny pieces of cooked hot dog in his mouth, one at a time. Periodically, he'll pop one out so the dogs can get it. "Once they've done it a few times, they learn not to take their eyes off my face," he says.

Keeping a dog focused on you is one way of stopping him from investigating every tree he passes. This Border collie is intent on the ball in his owner's hand.

The Smell of Boy

Most dogs spend their free time sniffing fire hydrants and tree trunks. But some use their talented schnozzles for a higher purpose, as a bloodhound named Mac proved one day when a neighborhood child wandered away from home. No one had a clue where he was, and his parents were afraid that he might have gotten lost in the nearby forest.

The police, after a preliminary (and unsuccessful) search, called Mac's owner, Captain Paula Wyatt of the Hopewell Sheriff's Department in Virginia. Mac is trained in search-and-rescue, but even so, the situation didn't look good, Paula remembers. The boy had been gone for more than 12 hours—more than enough time for his scent to have faded. Worse, the police, neighbors, and other dogs had already been searching for hours, covering the boy's scent with their own.

Paula asked for something belonging to the boy. Someone gave her a pillowcase. She held it out, and Mac sniffed it thoroughly. Then Paula snapped on his harness, and they started the search. Everyone stood back and watched as the excited bloodhound went to work. He aimed right for the woods. He crisscrossed his own tracks, followed a stream, stuck his nose in the water now and then, and took detour after detour. It seemed like he was going in circles—but then, that's how a lot of children get around. Mac knew what he was doing.

In the end, after searching for almost 2 hours, Mac ran right up to the boy, who was sitting on a log in the nearby woods. He greeted the boy by licking him from head to toe.

CHAPTER SEVENTEEN

COCKING THEIR HEADS

A Way of Capturing Sound

It wasn't by accident that advertising for RCA once featured a dog cocking his head in front of a speaker horn. There's something about this position that most people find utterly adorable. Dogs know it, too—which is why they do it, even when they aren't trying to hear anything in particular.

"We give them a positive response, and they remember that," says Emily Weiss, curator of behavior and research at Sedgwick County Zoo in Wichita, Kansas.

The Better to Hear You

Dogs don't start off cocking their heads to get human approval, of course. They do it for a very practical reason. Tilting the head to the side puts one of the ears up and forward. By turning an ear in the direction of fuzzy or inaudible sounds, dogs are able to hear a little more clearly, explains Rolan Tripp, D.V.M., a veterinarian in La Mirada, California, who specializes in animal behavior.

We often forget how confusing human speech is for dogs. Even though dogs understand some of what we're saying, most of our conversation is just a blur of sound to them. Usually, they just ignore it. They can tell from our body language and eye movements when we're saying things that concern them. Once something attracts their interest, they'll often perk up their ears and tilt their heads slightly in order to figure out what's going on, Weiss says.

Dogs rarely cock their heads when sounds are coming from the sides, since their ears are already in prime hearing position. They mainly do it when people are in front of them, since the sound waves aren't traveling directly toward the ears, explains Weiss.

You'll see this more in puppies than older dogs, adds Dr. Tripp. It's not that puppies have more trouble hearing. They just haven't been around us long enough to figure out what's important and what isn't. So they respond to almost any sound with a little head-cock, especially when we're looking at them at the same time. They know something interesting is happening, and they don't want to miss a thing.

Human speech is confusing for dogs. They often cock their heads to make sense out of the babble of noise. The movement allows them to capture every bit of sound.

51

Natural Limitations

The way a dog's ears are designed may play some role in how much he cocks his head. Pricked-up ears may be slightly more efficient than other ear shapes, since sound waves are able to go right in. Floppy ears present a problem. The sound waves have to pass through a big, heavy earflap before reaching the eardrum. This probably doesn't make a big difference, but dogs with heavy, hanging ears may have to work a little harder in order to hear what's being said, says Dr. Tripp.

"The inside of a dog's ear is shaped like a cup," Weiss adds. This design allows the ears to scoop in sound waves—but only when the opening is unencumbered.

When dogs are trying to pinpoint the source of a sound, they'll cock their heads to bring things into clearer focus.

When dogs cock their heads, gravity pulls one of the earflaps away from the auditory canal. Essentially, this opens the "cup" and allows more sound to flow in, says Dr. Tripp. This may be particularly important for Lhasa apsos, Maltese, and Pekingese, who tend to have a lot of hair in their ears. "If you put a little cotton in your ear, loosely covered it with a hat, and tried to hear, you'd have pretty much the same effect," he says.

Head cocking also helps dogs see a little better. Unlike people, who generally see things more clearly the closer they are, dogs don't see well at all when things are less than a few feet way, says Christopher J. Murphy, D.V.M., Ph.D., professor of ophthalmology at the School of Veterinary Medicine at the University of Wisconsin at Madison. When you're right next to your dog and he's cocking his head, he may be trying to bring you into focus, he explains.

Now That You Understand...

Dogs hear a lot better than people do, partly because their ears are incredibly mobile. They have 15 different muscles that can move the ears in all directions. This helps them detect and understand sounds no matter where they're coming from. Head cocking is just another tool they use to hear clearly. Dogs shouldn't be doing it all the time, however. When they are, they may need some extra help to hear.

Speak in a higher voice. One way dogs decide what's worth listening to and what isn't

CALL FOR HELP

Even though it's normal for dogs to cock their heads in order to hear (and see) better, they shouldn't be doing it too often. A dog whose head seems to be in perpetual tilt mode probably has an ear problem that isn't going to get better on its own, says Rolan Tripp, D.V.M., a veterinarian in La Mirada, California, who specializes in animal behavior.

A damaged eardrum or an inner-ear infection can make it hard for dogs to hear, he explains. In some cases, ear problems can throw off a dog's internal sense of balance, which will also cause him to tilt his head. "Any time a dog carries his head tilted for more than a few minutes, he needs to visit his veterinarian," says Dr. Tripp.

Dogs with ear infections often shake their heads as well as tilt them, Dr. Tripp adds. Use a flashlight to light the inside of your dog's ear. If you see redness or a discharge, or if you smell an unpleasant odor, he probably has an infection and is going to need antibiotics to knock it out.

Stand where he can see you. Even though a substantial portion of a dog's brain is devoted to sound, a dog always uses his other senses to augment what he's hearing. Standing in front of your dog will allow him to watch your face, eyes, posture, and body movements while you talk, explains Dr. McConnell. Even if your dog isn't hearing clearly, he'll be able to gather a lot of information from your body language about what you're trying to tell him.

Trim the ears. Dogs with unusually hairy ears may hear a little better if you remove some of the fluff, says Dr. Tripp. You can use blunt-ended scissors to trim some hair from the outer part of the earflaps, but groomers usually prefer plucking. Dogs don't enjoy having their ears plucked and will often put up a fight, so you may want to pay a groomer to do it for you.

Dogs who tilt or shake their heads constantly may have an ear infection. Use a flashlight to check for redness or discharge. If the ear looks irritated, you need to see a vet.

is by the sound frequency. High-pitched sounds get their attention, probably because they resemble the sounds made by traditional prey such as rabbits and chipmunks. Pitching your voice upward will get your dog's attention and let him know that he needs to listen carefully to what you're about to say, explains Patricia McConnell, Ph.D., a certified applied animal behaviorist in Black Earth, Wisconsin.

CHAPTER EIGHTEEN

HANGING THEIR HEADS OUT CAR WINDOWS

They Smell Things We Don't

People need to get over the idea that all things intelligent belong exclusively to humans. Our dogs undoubtedly consider us to be handicapped, nearly disabled, by our astonishingly poor sense of smell. Experts estimate that dogs can catch a whiff of something that's one million times less concentrated than what humans can detect. With so much sniff power, it's hardly surprising that they stick their heads out car windows. They could care less about the scenery. What they're after are smells.

"If you're driving through town at 30 miles an hour and your dog has his nose out the window, he knows where the bakery is, where the butcher shop is, which street leads to the local McDonald's, and maybe even what the mayor had for breakfast," says Myrna Milani, D.V.M., a veterinarian in Claremont, New Hampshire, and author of *DogSmart*.

More Speed, Better Smells

Dogs assume a characteristic expression when they put their faces into the wind: Their upper lips curl, their noses wrinkle, their eyes partly close, and their ears fold back. It looks as though they're experiencing a moment of ecstasy—which they probably are—but mainly they're concentrating. "It's as though they're closing down all the rest of their senses to focus on this one," says Dr. Milani.

There's a world of fascinating scents outside the car. This mixed-breed dog loves to hang her head out the window and sample every one of them.

All dogs, from huge Great Danes to tiny terriers, have extraordinarily acute senses of smell. Their scenting ability is enhanced when they are moving quickly, which is one reason that they take advantage of open car windows.

Smells are so important to dogs that they have two separate systems for detecting them. One is the nose system. It consists of a huge amount of tissue called olfactory epithelium, which is loaded with scent receptors. This area takes up about $1/2$ square inch in humans, but up to 20 square inches in some dog breeds. As air moves over the tissue, odor molecules settle in millions of scent receptors. The more air flow there is, the more scents dogs detect.

"Dogs' sense of smell is enhanced when they're moving quickly," adds Vint Virga, D.V.M., a veterinarian at the College of Veterinary Medicine at Cornell University in Ithaca, New York. In the evolutionary scheme of things, this probably made them better hunters because they could load up on scents while chasing prey.

Dogs have a second smelling system that's headquartered in their mouths. Near the upper incisors is a tiny duct that leads to a specialized gland called Jacobson's organ. It's designed to capture and interpret the most primitive types of smells. Dogs depend on it to identify other dogs, choose a mate, and smell prey. When dogs scrunch up their faces in the wind, it looks like they're catching flies, but what they're really doing is catching scents, says Dr. Milani.

The Road Hound

Riding a motorcycle requires proper balance and a low center of gravity, neither of which dogs have in abundance. This is regrettable because riding in the open air is their favorite way to sniff the breeze. Jon and Vicki Marsh of Frankfort, Indiana, found a way to overcome nature's limitations and allow their Rottweiler mix, Indy, to experience life on the road. He rides in a sidecar attached to their Honda Gold Wing, with his nose pushed forward and goggles securely covering his eyes.

Indy started riding motorcycles when he was 6 months old, and it has become his favorite pastime. In some ways, he's a better passenger than people are, Jon adds. Indy doesn't shift around too much, which helps the motorcycle stay balanced.

Riding a motorcycle isn't without risks, of course. The main problem is other drivers who can't believe what they're seeing, Jon says. They slow down at first, then speed up and get as close as they can to make sure their eyes aren't playing tricks on them—that what they're seeing really is a robust Rottweiler riding a little to the right of center, with his ears blown back and a very happy look on his face.

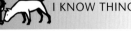

BREED SPECIFIC

Dogs don't see very well, so they're usually indifferent to passing scenery. Dogs called sighthounds, however, depend on their eyes more than on their noses. For Afghans, salukis, and greyhounds, riding in a car provides a visual as well as an emotional thrill.

These dogs are attracted to things that run—and when they're in a speeding car, everything outside looks like it's running. Wide-open windows aren't recommended for sighthounds because when they see something "running," they tend to do what nature intended—dive after it and commence the chase.

Now That You Understand...

Veterinarians are always telling people not to let their dogs put their heads out the windows because a ladybug doing 65 miles an hour can do serious damage. But people do it anyway because their dogs love it and it's hard to resist. Rather than having to make a choice between safety and canine satisfaction, here are a few compromises you may want to try.

Strain the air. Now you can do for cars what you've always done with windows at home—put up screens. Products called window vent guards are designed to fit into any car window. You can put them in and take them out in seconds, and they fold small enough to fit in the glove box, says Dr. Milani. The screens don't interfere with scent-laden air. Your dog will still catch a good breeze, but without the risk of catching debris in the face. The guards are available from pet supply stores and catalogs.

Give an inch. Open windows wouldn't be so dangerous if dogs were satisfied to sit in the backseat and breathe deeply. But from their point of view, nothing beats climbing halfway outside—and every year, a few dogs lean too far and actually fall out, says Dr. Milani. She recommends opening the window far enough so that your dog can put out his nose, but not so far that he'll stick out his whole head. He'll still get the sensory rush, but without the risk.

Lock him in place. Seat belts are a good idea even if your dog doesn't see open windows as an invitation to freedom. Pet supply manufacturers have developed a variety of safety harnesses that are designed to lock into existing seat belts. Buckling dogs in their seats keeps them from roaming, protects them in the event of an accident, and puts them in a prime position to catch the wind without having to poke their heads out the windows.

A window vent guard lets dogs catch scents while keeping debris out of their eyes and noses.

56

CHAPTER NINETEEN

AFRAID OF THUNDER

A World Turned Upside Down

At any given moment, about 2,000 thunderstorms are raging around the world, with lightning hitting the ground 100 times a second. What this means is that there are more than 2,000 reasons for dogs to dive under the bed, howl at the sky, and claw, chew, or bark their way through the house, looking for comfort from the storm.

"The thing about thunder is that we're not just talking about noise," says Myrna Milani, D.V.M., a veterinarian in Claremont, New Hampshire, and author of *DogSmart*. "There's a whole big scary event that comes along with it."

Dogs' senses are much sharper than ours. They hear, smell, and sense things with a clarity that we can hardly imagine. Because they hear higher and lower frequencies than we do, the sound of thunder is more intense. Their hearing is sensitive, so the volume is much higher. Then there are the changes in atmospheric pressure that accompany storms, and the gusting winds that bring sudden changes in airborne scents.

"With all that, plus lightning, thunder, and rain, a storm is nothing less than a full assault on the senses," says Dr. Milani. "Thunder is one thing most dogs pin their fears on, but it's not the only one. It's just the most obvious and the most disruptive."

In addition, dogs aren't able to understand what's causing all the commotion. You can't tell them that storms are a normal meteorological phenomenon. All they know is that the world has suddenly changed, and it's not a change for the better.

When thunderstorms are raging, a dog's natural instinct is to take cover in an enclosed place, such as under the bed, where he'll feel safer.

A Shocking Night

PUPPY DOG TALES

Linda and Reese Gardiner's dogs aren't afraid of thunder, but they are afraid of fire, and for good reason. One summer night in their home in Davie, Florida, the Gardiners were sleeping soundly in their beds. Both of them are deaf, so the thunder booming outside didn't disturb them. Their two poodles, Peanut and Pepper, were paying very close attention, however.

Peanut and Pepper haven't had formal training as service dogs, but both of them alert the Gardiners to sounds that the people wouldn't otherwise hear. When the phone rings, for example, one or both dogs will let them know. They do the same thing when someone comes to the door at night. Storms don't bother them, but they do listen carefully to what's out there. On this particular night, their vigilance paid off because a falling power line hit the house and ignited the air conditioner.

Both dogs immediately bounded onto the bed and nudged the Gardiners to wake them up. Then they ran to the window, back to the bed, and to the window again, trying to draw the couple's attention. Linda finally got out of bed, looked out the window, and saw the sparks. She quickly shut off the air conditioner, and the sparks died out.

The danger past, Peanut and Pepper both curled up and went to sleep, happy that they'd done a good night's work.

Good Intentions, Bad Results

No one knows why some dogs are terrified of thunder while others are oblivious. The fears tend to be worse in big dogs, which has led some experts to speculate that they may be able to hear low-frequency rumblings that smaller dogs miss. In addition, breeds who work closely with people, such as Labrador retrievers, suffer most, probably because these dogs feel that it's their job to protect their people, and storms leave them feeling helpless because they can't bark or bite away the danger. "Here's something that they see as a threat and can't do a thing about," says Dr. Milani. "It makes them feel totally out of control."

The way that people react to their dogs' nervousness has a lot to do with how well the dogs cope with storms, adds Betty Fisher, an animal behaviorist and trainer in San Diego and coauthor of *So Your Dog's Not Lassie.* Dogs who are frightened look to their people for reassurance. When the people seem upset—not because of the storm, but because their dogs are obviously terrified—the dogs think something like, "Wow, they're scared too! I guess this really is a problem."

"The best way to handle storms is to pay as little attention to your dog as possible until it's over," Fisher says. "Let him stay near you, but don't baby him. When dogs hear worried tones in our voices—especially the tone that says, 'It's okay, mommy's here'—they become convinced that there's really something to be afraid of."

A similar thing occurs when people try to coax dogs out of their hiding places. All the dogs want is a place to feel safe. They can't understand why people are sticking their heads under the bed and trying to bribe or pull them out. They've never seen people acting that way before, and it freaks them out.

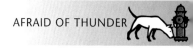

A sleeping bag creates a cozy, den-like space in which dogs can burrow down and ride out the storm in comfort.

Now That You Understand...

Hold them like Mom did. Mother dogs control and reassure their pups by holding them behind their ears or on the bridges of their noses. You can give dogs the same feelings of re-assurance by buckling them into special collars such as the Gentle Leader or the Halti. Unlike traditional collars, which go around the neck, these are like harnesses that slip over the nose and behind the ears. They're perfect for dogs who are trembling because of thunder. "It's like behavioral acupressure," says Dr. Milani. "They give your dog the same kind of feeling that a 3-year-old child has when mom or dad is standing behind him and holding him by the shoulder."

Putting dogs on leashes during storms helps too, Fisher adds. Leashes are symbols of parental authority, and dogs will relax when they know that someone else is in charge of things.

Tranquilize them with a sleeping bag. Dogs naturally gravitate to small, enclosed places, which is why they often lie down in the midst of shoes, clothes, or other things on the floor—it's their way of creating a little den. The urge to hide is especially strong when they're frightened. Dr. Milani recommends unzipping a sleeping bag and putting it where your dog usually spends her time. She'll appreciate the comfort, and the thick folds will allow her to burrow in and create a little enclosed space.

Give an herbal sedative. Some of the same natural tranquilizers that work for people also work for dogs. Supplements with ingredients such as melatonin and chamomile, available in pet supply stores and catalogs, can make it much easier for dogs to relax during storms, says Elizabeth Brown, D.V.M., a veterinarian in Sarasota, Florida.

Try a soothing touch. A technique called Tellington Touch, which isn't quite acupressure and is not quite massage, has been shown to help dogs relax. One stroke that seems to ease storm anxiety is the ear touch. Hold the ear between your thumb and forefinger and give gentle strokes, moving from the base to the tip.

CHAPTER TWENTY

LOSING TOYS BETWEEN THEIR PAWS

Too Close to See

If dogs wore glasses, they'd all have bifocals that were thin at the top and as thick as Coke bottles on the bottom. They can see fairly well at a distance, but reading *The New York Times* is beyond them. Most dogs can't focus at all on objects closer than $1\frac{1}{2}$ feet away. That's why a seemingly smart, highly sensitive dog can lose a rubber cheeseburger that's lying directly under his nose.

The reason for this canine farsightedness lies in their paws: Dogs don't have opposable thumbs the way people do. "They don't need to be able to closely examine things at arm's length," says Christopher J. Murphy, D.V.M., Ph.D., professor of ophthalmology at the School of Veterinary Medicine at the University of Wisconsin at Madison. "As they've evolved, they've needed to be able to catch sight of prey at a distance and keep it in view while they try to run it down." Objects that are just a paw's length away aren't likely to get up and run away, and dogs don't need to see them clearly.

Even if dogs had 20/20 vision, they might not bother looking at things close-up. A large portion of a dog's brain is devoted to processing smells. They depend on smell far more than their other senses, including sight. A dog who is frantically searching for a toy that he knows was right there a minute ago isn't using his eyes very much. All of that head turning and body positioning is an attempt to pull in scent molecules from all directions. It's his sense of smell, not his eyes, that will lead him to the prize. Finding things by smell probably isn't as fast as seeing them clearly, but in the long run, it's just as accurate.

Dog who tend to lose their toys may have less trouble when the toys are large, like this German shepherd's ball. It's also blue, a color that dogs easily see.

A Unique Blind Spot

Blurry vision isn't the only reason dogs lose things that are right in front of them. Unlike people, they have a small (or not so small, depending on the breed) anatomical disadvantage: a very big nose. It's rather like a blind spot in the car—they just can't see around it. The bigger the nose, the bigger the blind spot, says Dr. Murphy.

Once again, this wasn't a disadvantage in the evolutionary scheme of things. Dogs who hunted needed to know what was happening off to the sides and far in front of them. Their eyes are set far apart, which allows them to see an area that encompasses 240 degrees. (Humans, by contrast, can see about 180 degrees.) A tennis ball may disappear when it's right under a dog's nose, but he'll spot it in an instant when it's off to the side.

Dogs see moving things even better, adds Mark Plonsky, Ph.D., a dog trainer and professor of psychology at the University of Wisconsin at Stevens Point. Their eyes are exquisitely sensitive to motion, whether from a rabbit rustling the bushes or a tennis ball rolling across the lawn. Things that are motionless, however, might as well not even be there. Dogs just can't see them as easily.

Now That You Understand...

Since dogs will never have great eyesight—as they get older their vision may get even worse—they can use a little help finding things that, to people, appear to be in plain sight. Rather than

These racing greyhounds can see moving objects extremely well. Once an object stops moving, however, they're much less likely to spot it.

waiting for their noses to kick in, you can make their toys a little more visible.

Pick colors they can see. Dogs don't see colors anywhere near as well as people do. They're essentially color-blind when it comes to distinguishing reds and greens. This can be a problem when, say, they're looking for a green tennis ball on a green lawn. Dr. Plonsky recommends buying toys that are yellow or blue. Dogs can see these colors, and the toys will stand out more clearly against the background.

FAST FIX Dogs who are perpetually losing their toys will have a lot more fun if you simply buy them bigger toys. They're easier to see and keep track of. Your dog will spend less time searching and more time playing, says Dr. Plonsky.

These miniature schnauzers love their hedgehog toy. It's yellow, so it's easy to see. And a small bell inside the toy helps them keep track of it when it's in motion.

Buy toys that make noise. Dogs hear a lot better than people do. In fact, they depend on their sense of hearing almost as much as their sense of smell, says Ralph Hamor, D.V.M., a veterinarian and specialist in ophthalmology at the University of Illinois College of Veterinary Medicine at Urbana. For older dogs especially, balls with little bells inside can be a big help. Even if your dog has trouble seeing the ball, the ringing will lead him to it every time.

Balls with bells don't make noise unless they're moving, of course. So you may want to get a few sets of toys: noisemakers for times when you'll be playing with your dog and larger, brightly colored toys that he'll be able to find when he's playing by himself.

Play in the dark. The eyes contain structures called rods and cones. Rods are responsible for detecting light, and cones for detecting color. As you might expect, people have lots of cones. Dogs have mostly rods. This is why they hardly notice colors but can see better in the dark than we can. So don't stay inside after supper. Take your dog outside and throw his toy for a while. That rubber cheeseburger may be invisible to you after dark, but your dog will find it right away.

Mark toys with scents. The smellier things are, the easier it is for dogs to find them, says Dr. Plonsky. This is especially true when the scents are meaty. Rubbing your dog's ball with a piece of hot dog or wiping it with chicken broth will make it hard to miss. "I can hide my dog's toys in places where there's no way he can see them. But as long as the toys smell, it's as though there's a big neon sign over them," he says. "Dogs' sense of smell is so powerful, it's almost as though they 'see' things with their noses."

BREED SPECIFIC

Labradors and other retrievers usually have very good eyesight. They needed extra sharp vision in order to see and retrieve downed birds. German shepherds and Rottweilers, on the other hand, have a genetic tendency to be short-sighted.

CHAPTER TWENTY-ONE

SNIFFING PRIVATE PLACES

Getting to Know You

People have lots of ways of greeting each other: nods, kisses, handshakes, waves, and high fives, to name just a few. Dogs keep it simple. They sniff each other's bottoms.

Dogs do a lot of things differently from people, and for the most part people are tolerant of these differences, figuring to each species, its own. Not so with rude sniffing. It's obnoxious when dogs do it to people, and it's not much better to stand around while they take their time doing it to each other.

It's not a mystery why dogs sniff each others' privates. Every dog carries ID in his back pocket, so to speak. On each side of the rectum is an anal sac, which contains a strong-smelling fluid. This fluid is the equivalent of a dog's thumbprint, says Char Bebiak, an animal behaviorist and head trainer at the Purina Pet Care Center in Gray Summit, Missouri. With a quick sniff, dogs can tell more about each other than

we could determine by rifling through one another's wallets. "Dogs can tell the sex, age, health, reproductive status, diet, and mood from those smells," says Bebiak. "They get all the information they need to decide whether they want to associate with that dog and what kind of relationship they ought to have."

When dogs meet people, they use the same tried-and-true method that works so well with their peers. It may be uncomfortable and embarrassing for us, but dogs know what they're doing. "Private places offer dogs a lot of information because the scents are more intense than those from other parts of the body," says Robin Kovary, director of the American Dog Trainers Network in New York City. Dogs can pick up as much information about health, hormones, and tension levels from sniffing people as from sniffing other dogs. Research has shown, in fact, that dogs sniff with such accuracy that they may be able to detect some types of cancer or the onset of seizures before people have a clue about the problem.

When dogs meet other dogs, they always give each other a thorough sniffing. Unless they're taught more polite alternatives, they'll take the same approach when they meet people.

Human Interference

A dog who greets people by shoving her nose into their bottoms needs to be taught to stand back and use another, more polite kind of greeting. But you don't want to interrupt dogs when they're doing their usual meet-and-greet with each other. People who tug their dogs away from each other before they've finished their traditional introductions are inadvertently creating social tension, Kovary explains.

The sniffing ritual is designed in part to help dogs establish who has the more forceful personality and deserves extra respect. This is an essential component of all their introductions as well as of the interactions that follow. Interrupting this step by tugging dogs away from each other leaves them uncertain about their respective roles. They may solve this uncertainty by getting physical. So instead of watching a leisurely sniff, you may find yourself in the middle of a fight.

Tugging on the leash in the midst of a dog-to-dog introduction creates another kind of tension as well. Dogs read body language very quickly. When you pull your dog away from another dog, the leash will pull her head upward. This is the position that dogs assume when they're being threatening. So you could inadvertently start a fight by pulling your dog into a position that says, in effect, "And so's your mother."

"Sniffing is the main way dogs sum one another up, and you don't want to make it hard for them to assess a new situation and a new dog," Kovary says.

Now That You Understand...

A nose thrust may be acceptable among dogs, but it's not so pleasant for the two-legged visitors in their lives. Every dog can learn to greet people in more acceptable ways. The secret, Kovary says, is to teach them an alternative to that ancient, secret handshake they know so well.

Start with a shake. The standard greeting among people is the handshake, and dogs can learn it too. Have your dog sit, then stick out your hand, putting it slightly below her nose. Most dogs will instinctively raise a paw to meet it. If your dog doesn't get it and won't raise a paw, pick up her paw for her and give it a shake. Then say, "Good shake!" and

Dogs need time to sniff each other. You don't want to pull them apart, because it can create social friction that can lead to fights.

This clever mixed breed has learned to give a high-five when he meets new people. It's more polite than sniffing their bottoms.

give her something to eat. Keep practicing, and have other people do it too. As long as there's the potential for food, dogs will remember this trick and try it every chance they get.

BREED SPECIFIC

All dogs rely on smells to understand the world and the people they're meeting, but they don't all put their noses in people's crotches. Large dogs are much more likely to do it, for the simple reason that their noses are at the perfect height to reach peoples' privates. Smaller breeds sniff what they can reach. The lowest smell center on the human body is the feet, and that's invariably what they go for.

Take her everywhere. Dogs spend most of their time at home, and when they do get out they're so excited and hungry for information that they can hardly keep their noses to themselves. Take them out in public more often so they meet a lot of new people. Eventually, they'll start getting blasé about the whole thing, in part because they'll have collected so much information in the past that they won't feel the burning need to collect more, says Bebiak. This will make it easier for them to remember to sit and shake rather than lunge and sniff.

FAST FIX Dogs despise the smell of minty breath spray, and you can take advantage of this to discourage them from sniffing people. When you're going to be in a situation in which your dog will be meeting new people, arm yourself beforehand with a canister of breath spray. When she moves in for the inevitable sniff, quickly spritz some of the spray toward her mouth. Aim downward so that the irritating spray doesn't hit her eyes. The unpleasant smell and taste, combined with the *psst* sound, is a very strong discouragement, Kovary says.

This type of "aversion therapy" works because dogs link the unpleasant experience with the behavior that caused it, and the memory will stay with them. For the most part, however, dogs learn fastest when they're praised for doing things right, rather than scolded for doing them wrong, Kovary adds. So reward your dog well when she sits and shakes. You should even reward her when she does nothing at all. As long as she's not sniffing, she's being a good dog and deserves a special treat.

PART THREE

"I Can't Believe That You Live like This"

Dealing with Modern Life

The world that we take for granted is a strange place for dogs. They've been living with humans for only a few thousand years, so they continue to do things the way that they always have, making small adjustments along the way.

CHAPTER TWENTY-TWO

HUMPING LEGS

It's All about Power

No one would mind if their dogs only humped other dogs at the appropriate mating times. It's how they reproduce, and if their level of discretion leaves something to be desired, well, dogs will be dogs. But some dogs aren't very selective about the objects of their affections. They'll try to hump arms, legs, teddy bears, sometimes even cats.

This type of indiscriminate humping isn't about mating. Even a dog who is frenzied by hormones knows the difference between a receptive partner and someone's leg. It's not even about pleasure, although that may play a role. Dogs mainly hump because they're trying to assert themselves. The longer they get away with it, the more powerful they feel, says Bernadine Cruz, D.V.M., a veterinarian in Laguna Hills, California.

Coming of Age

Humping usually starts during a dog's adolescence—between 6 months old and 2 years old, depending on the breed. This is the time when reproductive hormones

Dogs are always trying to prove that they're tougher than the next guy. Some do it by humping. Others do it by putting their feet on another dog's back, as this 6-week-old bulldog puppy is doing.

are starting to reach adult levels, and some dogs go a little bit crazy. "They reach sexual maturity before they reach emotional maturity," says Dr. Cruz. "They just don't know what to do with themselves."

Humping is not strictly a male behavior, Dr. Cruz adds, although males are the worst offenders. Unlike females, whose hormones ebb and flow with their reproductive cycles, males maintain fairly steady hormone levels all the time. The hormones themselves don't cause humping, but they make dogs more likely to do it. That's why neutering or spaying is the best way to reduce or eliminate this unpleasant behavior.

Young Rebellion

There's another reason that males are more likely than females to latch on to human legs, one that has nothing to do with reproductive urges. Males are just more competitive. They're always trying to prove—to people as well as to other dogs—how big and tough and independent they are. Humping is just one way in which they push the boundaries and assert their dominance within a family, says Dr. Cruz.

Watch a litter of puppies at play, and you'll see that they spend quite a bit of time climbing on top of each other. The more assertive dogs may take advantage of their position and throw in a little humping. It's their way of saying that they are, quite literally, top dogs. "They hump to show their dominance more than for any other reason," says Dr. Cruz. "My Pomeranian humps my Lab because she's much more concerned with rank than he is."

Once dogs are out of the litter and living with people, the same instinct remains. Human legs don't have special appeal, but they're accessible and easy to wrap paws around. "In the wild, dogs never mount dogs who are higher in rank than they are," Dr. Cruz explains. The only time that a dog tries this with people is when there's some confusion in his mind about who's in charge and who isn't.

It's not that dogs make conscious decisions to assert their authority. They hump as naturally as they bark or steal food off the table—it's just something they do. Even those who understand that they're not supposed to do it may forget themselves—when visitors come to the house, for example, or when people are on the floor

CALL FOR HELP

Dogs who hump people's legs almost always develop the habit when they're young. A dog who has never humped before but is suddenly doing it a lot should get a checkup because he could have a urinary tract infection. Humping may help ease the discomfort, says Bernadine Cruz. D.V.M., a veterinarian in Laguna Hills, California.

Humping is almost always a behavioral problem, Dr. Cruz adds. Dogs who hump legs and get away with it may experiment with other, more aggressive types of behavior. You should get some help, either from your veterinarian or from a professional behaviorist or trainer, if your dog doesn't give it up on his own.

playing with them. "If your dog wants to lord it over his stuffed toys or other dogs, you may not care," says Dr. Cruz. "But it's never okay for him to do it to a person."

Now That You Understand...

Give a motherly warning. You don't want to leave any doubt in your dog's mind that humping legs is a nasty habit. Discipline dogs the same way that their mothers would—by grabbing the scruffs of their necks, giving a quick shake, and shoving them away, Dr. Cruz recommends. "Don't try to lift your dog by his neck; but pull up that scruff, shake him quickly, and tell him no," she says.

Brandy Oliver, a dog-behavior consultant in Seffner, Florida, gives an even more specific command: She tells her dog, "No hump." "Now that I've had to use that command in some awkward situations, I wish that I'd come up with something else, like 'Play nice,' or 'Don't mess around,'" she adds.

Don't let him lean. Humping is generally the last link in a chain of physical liberties. Maybe your dog is always pushing against or leaning on your legs. Or he may insist on licking your face or climbing onto your lap. Physical pushiness is a sign that dogs are feeling free to do pretty much whatever they want. Once they get away with some aggressive physical contact, it's natural for them to push the boundaries further. You may want to encourage your dog to keep his distance, by pushing him away with your knee when he leans, for example, or by walking away when he's getting in your face, says Dr. Cruz. Once he understands that you only get physical when it's your idea, he'll be less likely to take liberties in other ways.

Let some air out of his ego. Dogs need to understand that no matter how exalted they feel around other dogs, they're always second banana in their dealings with people. Rather than dealing with the humping directly, it may be more effective to deal with the underlying attitude. Make dogs work

Dogs who are physically pushy—always climbing into people's laps or leaning against them—may take it one step further and start humping.

for everything they like, Dr. Cruz advises. Have your dog sit before you give him food. Have him lie down before you give him a toy. Have him do something—anything—before you do anything for him. When you reinforce your position of authority, your dog will be less inclined to be disrespectful.

FAST FIX It's rare for dogs to just walk up to someone and start humping. It usually happens when there's been a lot of excitement or physical contact—because someone is wrestling with them, for example. Keep games less physical while you're training your dog to keep his hips to himself, Dr. Cruz recommends. Physical contact is fine, but rough-and-tumble games may make it hard for him to remember what's he's not supposed to do.

CHAPTER TWENTY-THREE

DRINKING FROM THE TOILET

Cool, Fresh, and Tasty

Wine connoisseurs don't drink a fine Bordeaux from plastic cups. Draft lovers know that beer tastes lousy from cans. So it shouldn't come as much of a shock that some dogs like water best when it's served in a nice porcelain dish.

"To people, a dog who drinks from the toilet is just gross," says Ilana Reisner, D.V.M., Ph.D., a diplomate of the American College of Veteri-

nary Behaviorists and a visiting fellow at Cornell University School of Veterinary Medicine in Ithaca, New York. "But to a dog, the toilet is a constantly freshened source of good water."

Before dogs had people laying out their food and water every day, they had to provide their own refreshments, Dr. Reisner explains. They developed a knack for choosing the cleanest, freshest water from the sources they had available. Those who didn't were sure to get parasites or other water-borne diseases. With no veterinarians or medications in sight, these dogs passed away. Those who learned the ropes, on the other hand, lived to reproduce, and their puppies instinctively knew what they should and shouldn't drink.

While their judgment certainly isn't perfect, dogs have good reasons for choosing the toilet bowl over their water dishes. Consider how people like their water: cool, freshly poured, and out of a clean glass. The toilet is probably in the coolest room in the house. The water in the toilet gets changed more often than the water in their bowls. And porcelain make a nice goblet that doesn't alter the taste of water like metal or plastic bowls may.

The toilet is just the right height for this American bulldog, who comes into the bathroom several times a day to get a drink. The water is cooler than in her bowl, and she seems to like the taste.

Feels like Home

People tend to be squeamish about bathrooms. We worry about germs. We scour and scrub to eliminate every last scent. We shut and lock the doors and demand total privacy. We do everything we can, in short, to keep our bathrooms separate from the rest of our lives.

Dogs, on the other hand, aren't squeamish at all. Consider their usual habits. These are animals who will eagerly sniff, roll on, and devour month-old roadkill. Who view cat boxes as convenient sources of takeout. Who greet each other (and people) by sniffing backsides. From their point of view, the bathroom is just an extension of their naturally earthy tastes. They don't think about off-putting odors when they drink from the toilet, says Reisner. If anything, they probably like the smell.

Cleaner Than You Think

There's no question that toilets are germy environments. Even an immaculate, freshly scrubbed bowl contains thousands, if not millions, of bacteria. But dogs don't care. After all, they didn't evolve in the dining room at the Plaza Hotel. For most of their evolutionary history, they lived in pretty rough surroundings. As a result, their immune systems are remarkably sturdy. Toilets may not be clean by our standards, but for dogs they're almost as hygienic as Perrier.

"A dog who drinks from a stagnant puddle, a lake, or a pond is exposed to more potentially hazardous germs than one who drinks from a toilet," says Dr. Reisner, who says she's never

CALL FOR HELP

Whether dogs drink from their appointed bowls in the kitchen or make detours to the commode, they always need to drink a lot of water—up to 5 to 7 percent of their weight every day. A 100-pound dog, for example, should have at least 5 pints (a pint equals 1 pound) of water a day, says Lynn Cox, D.V.M., a veterinarian in Olive Branch, Mississippi.

Dogs don't always drink as much as they should, however. Or, more commonly, they drink more than they should. Dogs who are suddenly drinking more than usual could have diabetes, kidney disease, or other physical problems, says Dr. Cox. This is why many veterinarians recommend keeping the toilet lid closed—not because the water is harmful, but because it makes it hard to tell when a dog's need for fluids has spiked upward.

Regardless of where your dog gets his refreshment, you should call your veterinarian if he's spending extra time at the water bowl, especially in cool weather or when he hasn't been particularly active, Dr. Cox advises.

heard of a dog getting sick from sipping potty water. This doesn't mean that dogs can't get sick from drinking toilet water, Dr. Reisner adds. A toilet that's stopped up or hasn't been cleaned since the Eisenhower administration will contain enough germs to trigger a day or two of diarrhea or vomiting. More worrisome than germs are chemicals. In our perpetual battle to keep bathrooms clean, we pour all sorts of chemicals into toilet bowls and tanks. Some of these products taste perfectly fine to dogs, but can make them ill if they drink enough.

Now That You Understand...

Even though toilets are sanitary enough for quenching canine thirst, most people prefer to keep the lids closed. Mainly, it's about etiquette. No one wants to listen to their dog noisily lap-

Some dogs become quite adept at opening closed toilet lids. The only way to stop them may be to weigh down the lid with something heavy, such as a large book.

ping up a toilet-water cocktail. And no one wants to clean up the trail of spittle and water that invariably follows.

Invest in a new water bowl. Some dogs drink out of the toilet because they like the taste. Others do it because they dislike the water in their regular dishes. It's not the water itself that's usually the problem, but what the water is served in. Plastic dishes, for example, absorb odors and may give water an off taste, says Dr. Reisner. Switching to a metal or ceramic dish—and washing it regularly—can make your dog's usual water supply a little more palatable—and make him less interested in finding alternatives, she says.

Put the bowl somewhere else. Dogs definitely like their water cool. Water that sits in a sunny kitchen may be 10°F warmer than water that's kept in a cool, tiled bathroom. If you don't have a different place to keep the bowl, put in a few ice cubes every time you change the water, says Lynn Cox, D.V.M., a veterinarian in Olive Branch, Mississippi. Dogs will appreciate the extra coolness as well as the crunchy ice.

FAST FIX The men in the family will undoubtedly need reminders, but the easiest way to keep dogs out of the toilet is to lower the lid. Unless, that is, you happen to live with a very smart and determined dog who learns to uncap the toilet on his own. If that happens—and some dogs like toilet water so much that wedging their noses under the lid is hardly an insurmountable obstacle—you'll either have to keep the bathroom door closed or secure the toilet lid by putting something heavy on top.

CHAPTER TWENTY-FOUR

DESTROYING FURNITURE

It's a Teenage Thing

It's remarkable what people will put up with. Carol Lea Benjamin, a dog trainer in New York City, remembers an overzealous husky who dug all the way through a couch. When his owners bought another couch, he tore that one up, too. Rather than buying couch number three, they called Benjamin, author of *Dog Training in 10 Minutes*.

"That was probably the most destructive dog I've ever seen," she says. "Two couches is pretty impressive. I told them that I'd be a lot cheaper than replacing more furniture."

Luckily, few dogs who set their sights on furniture run up that kind of tab. Most don't even need professional counseling. But they do need to learn that furniture is made for people to use, not for dogs to shred. And that can take some work and patience.

Something to Do When There's Nothing to Do

Nearly every dog was originally bred to do some kind of work. Working dogs were busy all the time. Dogs today, however, spend most of their time lounging inside while their owners are at work. They don't get as much exercise as they used to, and they get bored.

"The biggest reason that they start chewing, scratching, and ruining things in the house is because they don't get enough exercise," Benjamin says. Furniture is always accessible; it comes in an appealing variety of tastes and textures; and it's covered with great smells. Dogs with energy to burn and time on their paws may find it hard to resist.

"Dogs chew a lot of things just because they are there," adds Brandy Oliver, a dog-behavior consultant in Seffner, Florida. "Maybe your dog is leaning against the table leg. She gives it a lick. It doesn't taste bad, so she decides to take a chomp. Before you know it, it's a pile of splinters."

When high-energy dogs like this young American bulldog don't have enough to do, they get bored—and bored dogs often become destructive.

74

Mainly a Phase

Adult dogs occasionally tear up furniture, but for the most part this is a problem with younger dogs. When they're teething, for example, they'll chew on just about everything. Puppies aren't big enough to do a lot of damage. Dogs who are in adolescence—anywhere from 6 months old to 2 years old, depending on the breed—are the ones who tear things up the most, Benjamin says.

Adolescent dogs are a lot like human teenagers. They're somewhat wild. They seethe with energy. They haven't had a lot of training, and their hormones are driving them nuts. "People look at their dogs and all their problems around this time and ask themselves, 'What have we gotten into?'" Benjamin says.

Dogs do outgrow this destructive stage, but they can do a lot of damage in the meantime. Trainers often recommend applying a dog repellent such as Grannick's Bitter Apple to areas that dogs are abusing. It may help, but dogs who are truly driven to chew and destroy may not even notice that it's there.

Now That You Understand...

Keep an eye out for crumbs. In the age of television and Monday-night football, the couch has become the modern dinner table. Food invariably spills, and the alluring scents are the closest things to engraved invitations that dogs get. Once they start licking, chewing and digging are sure to follow, Benjamin says. Keeping a napkin on your lap and cleaning up crumbs before the odors get into the furniture will help prevent problems later.

Puppies need to chew to relieve the pain of teething. Once they get their teeth into furniture, they'll often keep at it and give it a thorough working-over.

Give her a toy box. Dogs sometimes get confused about what is and isn't appropriate to chew. Oliver recommends filling a small box with dog toys—rawhides, squeaky toys, tennis balls, whatever your dog enjoys. Put it right next to the furniture that she's been working over. "Every time she heads for the furniture, tell her, 'No chew,' then tell her 'Look in the toy box,'" she says. Most dogs will quickly learn what the words mean, especially if you get them started by occasionally salting the box with a couple of dog biscuits.

Keep her active. Dogs need a lot more exercise than most of them usually get. "If you can give your dog 10 minutes of exercise before you leave the house each morning, she'll burn off some of the energy that can make her destructive during the day," Benjamin says. Just as important, exercise provides bonding time that dogs need to feel secure—and secure dogs are the ones who are least likely to be destructive. "It would be great if we could all take our dogs to the beach for 3 hours on the weekend, but what they need more is to know that they're remembered," she says.

FAST FIX There's something about wood that dogs find hard to resist, and a table leg can be a lot more toothsome than an old rubber ball. Oliver recommends giving dogs sticks to chew. They're somewhat like bones—tough enough to provide tooth resistance, but soft enough to show results—and that makes dogs happy.

"When our dogs were puppies, we had hunks of sticks all over the house, but they never chewed the furniture," Oliver says. "If I had to choose, I'd clean up bits of stick again—they're much easier to replace."

An Indoor Excavation

Chewing and digging are nice, but smelling is even better. Getting to good smells, however, may require chewing and digging. Skye, a 2-year-old Chinook, proved to be a capable excavator when she was put in a room that contained the family's prized heirloom sofa.

It didn't take Skye long to realize that the sofa was a veritable mine of intriguing scents. She was determined to get to the bottom of things—literally, as it turned out. "She worked her way through the top fabric, right where our cat used to sleep," says Patti Cancellier of Rockville, Maryland, Skye's owner. "She went through the foam, down through the original fabric, all the way down to the old horsehair stuffing."

Within an hour, Skye had dug a hole that was $1^1/_2$ feet in diameter. Patti was appalled not only because of the destruction but also because her husband was home at the time of the excavation and didn't notice what was going on. But despite her irritation, she couldn't blame Skye. The sofa contained almost 100 years of scent history, and the little dog just had to explore.

Patti took pictures of Skye posing in front of the couch, just as a reminder of how much trouble puppies can be. Now that Skye has outgrown her chewing phase, Patti says, she's going to take a chance and have the sofa re-covered again.

This mixed-breed dog happily chews on his ball for hours. Like most dogs, he's less likely to chew furniture when he has an acceptable alternative.

The problem with sticks, of course, is the splinters. These aren't a problem for most dogs, but some dogs will actually swallow them. Watch your dog for a while. If she's content to just gnaw, she'll probably be okay. If she actually swallows the bits, you'll have to find something else for her to chew. Even a small splinter can cut her tongue or gums. Splinters can also damage her digestive tract.

CHAPTER TWENTY-FIVE

AFRAID OF CLIMBING STAIRS

Memories of Crash Landings

Nicki, a miniature dachshund, was sitting on the deck one afternoon when a black cat wandered through her yard. Her instinct was to chase, and in her excitement she forgot to be cautious on the steps. She paid for it by taking a painful tumble.

She wasn't seriously hurt, but mentally she was a changed dog, says her owner, Lois Ives of Norwich, New York. Nicki refused to set foot on stairs after that, and nothing Lois tried would convince her to ascend or descend on her own.

"Most dogs learn to handle stairs with reasonable grace and ease," says Benjamin Hart, D.V.M., Ph.D., professor of physiology and behavior at the University of California School of Veterinary Medicine at Davis and author of *The Perfect Puppy: How to Choose Your Dog by Its Behavior*. But some dogs never get the hang of it, or, like Nicki, they have a bad experience and never again feel comfortable climbing.

A Long Way Down

Dogs instinctively know that it's not a good idea to get too close to the edge of a cliff—and from their point of view, stairs can look an awful lot like a cliff when they're standing at the top, says Dr. Hart.

Most dogs encounter their first staircases when they're puppies. They're just as nervous as children encountering their first escalators. But after their initial apprehension, they're willing to take a chance. Gingerly at first, and with increasing confidence, they make their way up and down. It doesn't take them long to figure out that stairs aren't very hard to navigate.

Older dogs, on the other hand, can get very set in their ways. If they first discover stairs later in life, they're going to be reluctant to give them a try, no matter how much their owners cajole them. All they hear is the voice of Mother Nature, telling them they're standing on the brink and should forget about it. So they stay securely at the bottom or the top, refusing to venture onto that dangerous middle ground.

"It's harder for an adult dog who hasn't tackled steps before than it is for a puppy,"

CALL FOR HELP

Some dogs are truly afraid of climbing stairs, but others avoid them because they've developed arthritis or hip problems and climbing hurts, says Warren Liddell, D.V.M., a veterinarian in Norwich, New York. Arthritis mainly occurs in older dogs, and it can be treated with medications or, less often, with surgery. It's worth taking your dog in for a checkup if he has recently begun avoiding stairs, even if he otherwise seems healthy.

says Warren Liddell, D.V.M., a veterinarian in Norwich. The cut-off point seems to be about 6 months of age. Dogs younger than 6 months old are open to new things. Dogs older than that are conservative and not at all eager to take chances.

"Remember What Happened Last Time?"

Dogs learn from experience just as people do. And Nicki, a graduate of the school of hard knocks, took her lesson seriously.

"A dog who has fallen down a flight of stairs, even as a puppy, may remember it for the rest of her life and be nervous around stairs because of it," says Dr. Hart.

With the exception of dogs with physical problems such as arthritis, falling down a flight of stairs is unlikely to cause serious injuries. But that doesn't make them any more likely to re-member the experience fondly, says Dr. Liddell. Dogs who are unusually timid or nervous may be reluctant to ever put themselves in danger again. That's when owners find themselves in the position of having to choose between car-rying their dogs up and down stairs or giving in to the situation and allowing their dogs to stay on the ground floor all the time.

A Bid for Attention

Regardless of why dogs are frightened by stairs, the usual human response is to beg and plead with them to make the climb. This involves a lot of petting and reassurance. Dogs put two and two together very quickly. If making a stink

about ascending or descending brings the family running, any attention-loving dog is going to do it every chance she gets, says Judith Halliburton, a trainer and behaviorist in Albuquerque, New Mexico, and author of *Raising Rover*. This type of attention-driven behavior can be very hard to change. Dogs love the attention, but it invari-ably makes things worse.

"When we beg, plead, push, pull, or carry dogs up or down the stairs, they just get more apprehensive," says Halliburton. Even when the fears don't escalate, the theatrics do. Either way, the stairs become a psychological barrier that's difficult to overcome. At this point, you'll have to be more creative at getting them up and down on their own.

BREED SPECIFIC

Any dog can be afraid of stairs, but there's only one breed that's truly born to climb. The Norwegian lundehund was bred to hunt for birds called puffins that live in rocky cliffs. Over generations of breeding, lundehunds became increasingly adept at climbing. They even developed extra toes to give them better traction on the cliffs.

Lundehunds are rare today, in part because they were so successful. When puffins were declared an endangered species in the early 1900s, people stopped breeding lundehunds. Today, there are only about 2,000 lundehunds in the world. But they still have six or seven toes instead of the usual five, and they can outclimb any other breed.

Most dogs like food a lot more than they fear stairs. A trail of food ending with a delectable piece of hamburger will help most dogs overcome their nervousness.

the jackpot—and a dog who conquers stairs once will usually be willing to do it again.

Start with a single step. Sometimes fear is stronger than appetite. Dogs who won't climb stairs even to get a bite of bacon need more help. "When dogs face the staircase, they may see something insurmountable," Halliburton says. "They need to be taught to look at just one step and eventually go from there."

1. Just get their paws on the first step. It doesn't matter how you do it—with food, gushing encouragement, or anything else. Once they've made it that far, praise them like crazy, then walk away and do something else for awhile, Halliburton says. One challenge is enough for the day.

2. Then go up one level. It may take time and patience, but nearly every dog will be willing to mount that first step. After that, the rest is easy. Once a day or so, encourage your dog to take the next step. Make a big deal of it when she does. Then, as before, walk away and leave her to stay on the step or climb down, as she prefers. From a dog's point of view, climbing 2 steps isn't all that different from climbing 10. Helping her focus on the small picture—a single step instead of the whole staircase—will encourage her to take the chance.

Now That You Understand...

Put the best food out of reach. Dogs will do anything to satisfy their stomachs, which is why food bribes are very effective at getting them up and down stairs. The idea isn't to make the food easy to get, however. Put a so-so treat on the first or second step, a better treat a step or two higher, and something really great higher still, says Dr. Hart. Then stand back while your dog ponders what's really important to her. Sooner or later, her nose is going to lead her to

CHAPTER TWENTY-SIX

HOWLING AT SIRENS

A Vaguely Familiar Sound

New Guinea singing dogs are famous for their ability to harmonize. These rare, wild dogs live on the isolated island from which they take their name. Unlike most dogs, who have been deliberately bred to have features such as wide-set eyes and docile dispositions, the singing dogs have evolved without interference from human beings. And they've spent about 6,000 years perfecting their singing skills.

"One dog leads, and the rest join in with an intricate chorus that runs up and down the scale," says Janice Koler-Matznick, an animal behaviorist in Central Point, Oregon, who studies the singing dogs. "It's like hearing a lead singer with a doo-wop group behind him."

The rare New Guinea singing dogs have a call that carries for miles. It allows them to keep in touch across the valleys of their mountainous homeland.

Nobody has to teach singing dogs to howl. They're born knowing how to. In fact, Koler-Matznick has seen a dog who was raised away from the pack sing perfectly in tune the day he met his peers.

To some extent, nearly every dog shares this rare breed's love of music. All that dogs need is someone—or something—to get them started.

Modern Sounds, Ancient Instincts

Anyone who lives in a suburban neighborhood has discovered that the wail of sirens is invariably followed by the wail of dogs. For a long time, experts believed that dogs howled at sirens because the high-pitched noise hurt their ears. But then people noticed that the dogs didn't seem to be in pain. If anything, they seemed pretty happy when they howled. And the louder one dog howled, the harder others would try to keep up.

It seems likely that dogs don't object to sirens at all. Rather, these neighborhood canine choruses are more like sing-alongs. Dogs who howl at sirens are reaching back into their genetic pasts. "The sound frequencies that dogs hear in the sirens probably are similar to the group-chorus howls made by wolves, coyotes, and other wild dogs," says Melissa Shyan, Ph.D., a certified applied animal behaviorist and associate professor of psychology at Butler Univer-

That's *Amore*

Any dog can howl, but Regal the beagle can truly sing. The distinction isn't always obvious when Regal is just sort of humming along, but his talent emerges when he launches into his full-throated version of "That's *Amore*." He brings more to his song than just volume. He can sort of carry a tune, too—at least you can tell that he's trying.

Regal's owner, Rachelle Divitto of Cleveland, didn't recognize his talent right away. For a long time, in fact, she thought he was complaining about her taste in music. But it was obvious that Regal was happy, not pained, when he howled. So like any good mother, she encouraged him to express himself.

Regal didn't howl at just any music, she adds. Most tunes left him thoroughly indifferent. But his favorites gradually emerged, and "That's *Amore*" was right on top. Whenever it came on, Regal would sit back, arch his neck, and start howling. Rachelle was impressed enough by his talent that she entered him in a singing contest called Search for America's Best Singing Pet.

This is why, one day in 1997, Regal found himself at the South Street Seaport in New York City, singing "That's *Amore*" for a crowd that included New York mayor Rudolph Giuliani. Regal won the contest, along with a private session in a recording studio and a featured spot in an advertisement for the contest's sponsor.

Regal's victory never seemed to go to his head. As far as Rachelle can tell, he's still singing his heart out just for the joy of hearing his own voice. But now he has an award to prove his talent, and that's worth something.

sity in Indianapolis. "Dogs are distantly related to these wild canines, and the sound of the siren triggers a deep-down instinct to respond."

The whole business is somewhat puzzling. When you listen to a police siren and then listen to dogs howling, it's hard to imagine that dogs actually confuse the two sounds. Most probably don't. All it takes is one dog getting duped into howling. Once he gets started, his neighbors have something real to respond to. So they join in. "It's a social event," says Dr. Shyan.

It's easy to understand why people were convinced that dogs were suffering headaches every time a fire engine went by. To human ears, it sure sounded as though they were in terrible pain.

No Practical Purpose

Howling made sense thousands and thousands of years ago. A howl can be heard a lot farther away than a bark can. Dogs who lived in groups and engaged in coordinated hunts needed to communicate with each other even when they out of each other's sight. Howling was a way of sharing important information like where they were, whether it was time to start a hunt, and when strangers were entering their territory.

Howling makes almost no sense today, however. In fact, dogs probably aren't even sure why they do it, says Dr. Shyan. But on some level, howling must be important, because dogs keep doing it. Judging from the enthusiasm with which they sing out, apparently it makes them feel good and allows them to declare their kinship with their buddies in the neighborhood.

BREED SPECIFIC

Basset hounds and beagles are among the most prolific howlers because they've been bred to chase prey and bark them into trees until the human hunters arrive.

Now That You Understand...

Give them something else to listen to. Dogs clearly enjoying howling more than people enjoy listening to them, and they aren't going to give it up willingly. But if you interrupt their songs, they may forget what they were doing. Crank up music on the stereo, Dr. Shyan recommends. This will interfere with the siren sounds that your dog hears and will give him less to respond to.

FAST FIX Apart from masking the sounds of sirens, a sudden blast of loud music is distracting. Dogs will stop howling to think about this new sound. That's the time to shift their attention to something else. Roll a ball across the carpet or flip them something to eat. The urge to howl usually passes after a minute or two, so a quick distraction is pretty effective at restoring quiet, Koler-Matznick says.

Teach them voice control. No one enjoys midnight howl-athons, but a lot of folks get a kick out of their dogs' natural musical talents. Most dogs will learn to sing after getting a few lessons.

1. Go into another room—or, if you're practicing outside, go a few yards away—and give a long, wailing howl of your own. Make sure your dog can't see you, Dr. Shyan says. If he can, he won't see the need to communicate by howling—he'll just come running over.

2. Make yourself sound wolfish by starting with a long howl, followed by several short yips—dogs' way of saying, "C'mon and sing with me now." Then be quiet for a few seconds to give your dog time to respond. If he doesn't, try a few more howls.

It may take a little time for your dog to figure out what the heck you're doing. But if he's a natural howler, he'll catch on quickly and will start singing along. "I have to hold my ears once I get my dogs started," Dr. Shyan says. "But they love to howl with me."

Although howling serves little practical purpose these days, many dogs still love to throw their heads back and give voice to the wild dog within.

CHAPTER TWENTY-SEVEN

SAYING HELLO BY JUMPING UP

Closing the Vertical Gap

At 6 weeks, a Great Dane standing on her hind legs is about a foot tall. Six months later, she's closer to 6 feet. That's a lot of dog to have jumping on you when you come through the door. Even if you live with a cocker spaniel or a Pekingese, jumping up is a lousy greeting. It ruins stockings. It gets muddy paw prints on your pants. And it bothers the heck out of people who don't want to get that intimate with your dog.

Here's the paradoxical thing. Yes, some people really dislike it when dogs, their own or someone else's, jump on them. But dogs, on the other hand, do it all the time because they think they're being polite. This is one of those cases in which human and canine expectations diverge, leaving bad feelings on the human side and disappointment on the dogs'.

A Problem of Reach

The next time you take your dog to the park, watch how she greets and is greeted by other dogs. They start by sniffing each other's mouths, then move around to sniff the back ends. All of this is considered proper and polite behavior among dogs, and they assume it's the way they should greet people as well, says Kimberly Barry, Ph.D., a certified applied animal behaviorist in Austin, Texas.

Here's the hitch. Dogs don't have any trouble sniffing our bottoms—they'd do it all the time, given a chance. But the first part of the greeting, the mouth sniff, isn't possible because we're so much taller than they are. Except for very short people with very tall dogs, the only way this is going to happen is if dogs get up on their hind

Part of the canine greeting ritual is to sniff and lick faces. Because people are so much bigger than they are, dogs try to bridge the gap by jumping up.

83

This Norwich terrier will do almost anything to get close to his owner's face. Jumping up won't get him high enough, so he's using his paws to get more reach.

legs or, in the case of small dogs, fly off the ground. They don't actually get a good sniff while they're airborne, of course, but their instincts tell them that this is a reasonable way to solve the problem.

Some dogs are more reserved than others in their greetings. Chows, Akitas, and Rottweilers, for example, are more standoffish than other breeds and rarely jump up to say hi to strangers. Terriers and golden and Labrador retrievers, on the other hand, will jump on just about anyone. And nearly all dogs will lovingly assault their owners if they think they can get away with it, says Sarah Wilson, a trainer in Gardiner, New York, and coauthor of *Paws to Consider.*

People have something to do with this as well. Dogs first learn their manners when they're puppies. Puppies are drop-dead cute when they put their little paws in the air, and most people make quite a fuss over them. So they keep doing it as they get older. What's cute in a puppy isn't very cute in an 80-pound German shepherd.

Oh, Does This Bother You?

With their thick fur and hard heads, dogs are a little like linebackers suited up for a game. They can slam into each other all day without feeling much of anything, because physically they're not very sensitive, says Wilson. They engage in a lot of full-body contact. "Often, they'll plow into other dogs the same way they plow into people."

Various breeds differ quite a bit in the amount and types of physical contact that they indulge in, Wilson adds. Toy breeds tend to jump up on their little legs and then hang on until someone picks them up. Greyhounds are more aware of their own physical space and usually keep a little distance. Retrievers, on the other hand, love contact. "They will slam into people, lick their faces, and be totally unaware that they've knocked you over and broken your glasses," says Wilson.

Now That You Understand...

Turn greetings into meetings. Dogs do their run-and-jump routines because they're so eager for attention that they can hardly stand it. So give them some attention. Turn the usual homecoming into a quick training workout, Wilson recommends. For a few weeks, every time you walk in the door and your dog jumps up, snap on a leash and practice some obedience drills. That is not what your dog had in mind when she came running over. It takes the edge off her excitement. "I practice 'sits' and 'downs' with them until they're absolutely sick of me," Wilson says. "They start to think, 'Gee, I guess I really don't need this much attention,' and they start to back off on their own."

Turn your head to the side. Everyone has had the disheartening experience of rushing to meet someone only to be met in return with profound indifference. It's enough to make you think twice about showing that much enthusiasm next time. Dogs react the same way, says Dr. Barry, who recommends giving your dog no attention when you walk in the door. Ignore the jumping. Ignore the pleading eyes. Sit down and read a newspaper. Give her a chance to settle down. At that point, invite her over and lavish her with all the attention you want. This teaches a valuable lesson: "I get ignored when I'm hyper, and I get my ears stroked when I'm calm. Hmm."

Pull them sideways. Leashes aren't only for going for walks. You can use them to teach dogs all sorts of things, including the benefits of staying grounded. Once again, this trick involves a little training. Once or twice a day, put a leash on your dog. You can either hold the end or let the leash drag on the floor. Then wait until someone comes to the door at an arranged time. The minute your dog launches her usual jump, grab the leash and pull it sideways. "The idea isn't to haul your dog off to the side, but to give enough of a pull to make her stop and think about what she's doing," Wilson says.

Dogs who jump up need to be kept on a leash whenever people are coming over. A quick tug on the leash will pull them off-balance and let them know that they're doing the wrong thing.

The sideways pull is critical, she adds. Dogs don't like being pulled off-balance. Your dog won't stop jumping immediately, but if you do this every time she jumps, she'll start to investigate other, calmer ways of greeting people.

FAST FIX Nothing gets a dog's attention more effectively than food, and dogs who are eating aren't going to waste time jumping up, says Brian Kilcommons, a behaviorist and trainer in Gardiner, New York, and coauthor of *Paws to Consider*. "Hold a treat at your dog's eye level when you walk in," he suggests. "Toss it off to the side as you head past her, and she'll learn to look for the treat instead of jumping up."

CHAPTER TWENTY-EIGHT

SAYING HELLO BY PEEING

Pure Emotion, Total Respect

People greet each other by making eye contact, shaking hands, and asking about the weather. More formal greetings—at Buckingham Palace, for example—might involve a curtsy or bow. For the most part, anything between "Hey!" and "Ma'am" is considered polite.

Dogs have greetings for different situations too. An informal introduction begins with a face sniff, followed by a sweeping sniff down the length of the body, and concluding with a sniff around the rear. When they're greeting someone they really want to please or someone who really intimidates them, they give the ultimate courtesy: They pee.

It's hard to imagine urine as a form of flattery, but among dogs it symbolizes tremendous respect, says Kimberly Barry, Ph.D., a certified applied animal behaviorist in Austin, Texas.

Dogs view every individual as being a little more or a little less important than the rest. To keep questions of rank crystal clear, dogs use body language to show respect to superiors and power to subordinates. They have many ways of expressing respect. Avoiding eye contact is one. Crouching down is another. When the message still isn't getting across, peeing on the floor clears up any ambiguity. It can be loosely translated as "You're the boss."

Together at Last

Splashes of urine aren't only a status signal. Dogs will sometimes urinate accidentally when they're so excited that they can hardly hold still. This usually occurs in young dogs, although adults sometimes do it too, says Sandy Myers, a behavior consultant at Narnia Pet Behavior and Training in Plainfield, Illinois. Part of the reason is bladder control—younger dogs don't have much. It doesn't help that the most exciting time of day—when their owners walk in the door—coincides with the time when their bladders are fullest. "It's a tough combination," Myers says.

When dogs want to show respect and submission, they go belly-up. They may even pee a little to reinforce the message.

Submissive peeing mostly occurs in dogs who lack confidence. You can boost the self-esteem of small dogs by making them feel taller. For example, put them on a table and run through a few obedience commands while they're up there.

It's easy to tell the difference between excitement and submissive urination, Dr. Barry adds. "Dogs who crouch down very low or roll on their backs are peeing to show that they're submissive," she says. "Dogs who greet you by jumping and wiggling around are peeing because they're overexcited."

My Apologies

The same dogs who urinate when they're excited also tend to do it when they get into trouble, says Myers. And they do it for nearly the same reason. While some dogs are tough as nails, most aren't. When the people they love raise their voices, they'll do everything in their power to make the people happy again. They can't write notes or send flowers, so they pee. It's the equivalent of saying, "Sorry, sorry, sorry."

Dogs do this with other dogs too, and for good reason. The bigger, madder, more intimidating dog immediately recognizes the humility in the gesture. She'll usually walk away, satisfied that she has made her point.

Now That You Understand...

Make them feel taller. Every dog has a little bit of a Napoleon complex. No matter how big or small a dog is, she wishes she were bigger. Dogs who are insecure are especially conscious of height. These are the ones who are most likely to splash the floor in the foyer.

You can't make your dog any taller, but you can make her feel taller—and this can work wonders for her self-esteem. Teach your dog to climb up on a picnic table or some other elevated surface outside, Myers recommends. Let her get comfortable, then practice a few "sits" or "downs." Better yet, bring someone—a person or another dog—over to meet her. "It's amazing how much a little height can do for a dog's self-assurance," Myers says.

Get low and reach up. Dogs read our body language in ways we can hardly imagine. Take a welcoming rub on top of the head. For people, this is a natural show of love. For dogs, however, it's a sign of domination, especially when it's accompanied by direct eye contact. Dogs who are nervous about confrontations will get even more nervous, and nervous dogs are the ones who tend to pee when their owners come home. Dr. Barry recommends abandoning the head rub and replacing it with a rub under the chin. This is how dogs greet older or more dominant dogs, and they view it as a very gentle salutation.

Come home quietly. People are just as happy to see their dogs at the end of the day as their dogs are to see them. But this isn't the best time for energetic greetings, Dr. Barry says. Coming home quietly and not making a fuss will go a long way toward keeping things drier.

Go out as soon as you come in. Rather than having your homecomings in the hall, Myers recommends opening the door, then immediately stepping back outside, letting your dog follow. The extra physical space will make your arrival a little less overwhelming, and your dog will also have a chance to relieve herself before she gets worked up.

Help her learn self-control. Unless your dog is still a puppy, it's unlikely that she's going to learn to control her bladder any better. But she can learn to control her emotions generally. The less excited she gets, the less likely she'll be to make a mess, Myers says. By far the best way to teach dogs to control their exuberance is to teach them basic obedience. For one thing, dogs who have learned to listen for instructions are generally calmer than those dogs without any training, she explains. Just as important, when your dog does start getting worked up, you can just tell her "sit" or "lie down." This is the canine equivalent of chill-out time. "They need you to set the tone by giving them something to do when they get excited," Myers explains.

FAST FIX Probably the easiest way to help dogs overcome their damp greetings is to ignore them when you come home, says Dr. Barry. This may sound coldhearted, but your dog really doesn't need you to fuss over her at that particular moment. In fact, showing total nonchalance will help her understand that homecomings aren't such a big deal after all.

This Hungarian vizsla is learning basic obedience lessons to help her control her emotions, which will also help her control her bladder.

For this to be effective, however, you can't give even a halfhearted greeting. Sail right past your dog when you walk in, Dr. Barry recommends. Act as though you don't see her. Sit down and read the paper. Do some dishes. Do not give your dog any energy at all. This will give her time to get used to your presence. Her excitement will taper off, and that's when you can spend some time together.

This "I-don't-see-you" technique is particularly effective if you accompany it by tossing a treat on the floor away from you as you walk in, says Brian Kilcommons, a behaviorist and trainer in Gardiner, New York, and coauthor of *Paws to Consider.* The lack of reciprocal excitement on your part, and that the fact that something very interesting just hit the floor, will give your dog something else to think about. By the time she remembers you, the edge will be off her excitement, he explains.

CHAPTER TWENTY-NINE

RAIDING THE TRASH

It's Mighty Tasty

For dogs who have figured it out, trash cans are like the corner coffee shop, the neighborhood diner, and an all-you-can-eat buffet rolled into one. There's only one difference, which has nothing to do with the quality of the food: Trash cans are completely self-service. Dogs get hungry, they take what they like.

Of all the mystifying things that dogs do, this is the easiest to explain, although it's among the hardest for people to swallow. "Dogs will do just about anything for food, and the trash can does not have the same negative associations for them that it has for people," says Tony Buffington, D.V.M., Ph.D., professor of clinical nutrition at the Ohio State University College of Veterinary Medicine in Columbus.

Dogs have good memories. A dog who has scored one good meal from a trash can is going to keep coming back. Some dogs play trash cans almost like slot machines. It doesn't matter how often they lose. They keep coming back, hoping against hope for another big win. Sooner or later, they get one. Trainers refer to this type of now-you-win, now-you-lose scenario as intermittent reinforcement. It's almost better than winning all the time, because scarcity makes the heart grow fonder. For dogs, there's no stronger kind of encouragement than occasional victories, says Sarah Wilson, a trainer in Gardiner, New York, and coauthor of *Paws to Consider.*

Putting the trash can away in a cupboard isn't enough to deter tenacious scroungers. This Australian shepherd knows how to nose open the door to get to the good stuff inside.

Smells like Supper

Dogs have a far better sense of smell than people do, so you'd think they'd be even more disgusted by trash smells than we are. But there's no accounting for taste. "The fact that dogs have a more acute sense of smell doesn't mean that the same smells that send us running do the same for them," says Dr. Buffington. Quite the opposite. The smellier things are, the more dogs seem to like them.

The list of canine comestibles includes rotten meat, moldy bread, spoiled sour cream, and all the other things that make trash, well, trash. As long as it's potentially edible, dogs are going to be attracted to it, says Dr. Buffington. "I can't think of any natural smell that dogs really dislike," he adds. "They like it all."

The reason that dogs like practically everything comes from their evolutionary history. For eons, they were hunters and scavengers. To survive, they ate just about every terrible thing that you can think of. If it didn't make them sick—and in many cases, even if it did—they figured that it was better to eat now and ask questions later.

Survival isn't a factor anymore, but they continue to scavenge, and trash makes good pickings. The things they find there, however, may not be edible at all. "I once treated a dog who ate a can of sardines, can and all," says Donn W. Griffith, D.V.M., a veterinarian in Dublin, Ohio. It's not uncommon for dogs to get blocked intestines from things they eat, he explains. They also get liver problems or, when they tackle unusually hard items, broken teeth. "There's a whole host of physical problems that may be caused by eating garbage."

Dogs today certainly don't need the calories, but the instinct to get extra is thousands of years old. A lid is no protection.

Now That You Understand...

It's difficult to keep dogs out of the trash because the rewards they find there are powerfully motivating—so much so that dogs have learned to raise tightly closed lids and even open pantry doors when trying to get at them. Since they aren't going to give it up voluntarily, you may have to try more creative solutions to keep your trash stashed.

Make the trash less rewarding. Just as good tastes attract dogs to trash, bad tastes may

BREED SPECIFIC

The dogs who get into trash the most are the ones who are tall enough to reach it, like golden retrievers and Rottweilers. Smaller dogs, such as Chihuahuas (right), are equally tempted but don't have the same opportunities.

keep them away. Try booby-trapping the trash with stuff that will assault their taste buds, recommends Julia Jones, a service-dog instructor for Canine Companions for Independence in Santa Rosa, California. For this to work, however, you have to use bait that smells good enough for them to approach but tastes bad enough to keep them away once they've sampled it. Here are some suggestions.

• Cut a hot dog into pieces and coat the pieces with hot-pepper sauce.

• Put a few slices of bread on top of the trash and give them a liberal dousing with vinegar.

• Dust the top of the trash with baking powder. It contains a compound called alum that is harmless but tastes terrible to dogs. Sprinkle it on when you go to bed at night. If your dog drops by for a midnight snack, the taste will send him packing.

Rig an alarm. Dogs understand that they aren't supposed to root through the trash, which is why they generally go after it during the day when people are at work or at night after we've gone to bed. Since you can't watch your dog all the time, you may want to set up an alarm. There are several ways to do this. One is to hang a chain of bells from the side of the trash container. The sudden jangle will do more than startle your dog. If you're lucky, he will think that the trash had something to do with that awful noise, and he'll decide to stay away after that.

Another type of alarm is a mousetrap-like device called a Snappy Trainer. Available in pet supply stores, it's designed to give a loud snap when it's jiggled. If you put it on top of the trash, when your dog comes around it will go off like a gunshot and scare the heck out of him, says Judith Halliburton, a trainer and behaviorist in Albuquerque, New Mexico, and author of *Raising Rover.*

Turn the bin around. Kitchens aren't always designed in such a way that you can put trash containers out of reach. What you can do, if the bin has a hinged lid, is turn it around so that the side that opens faces the wall. You'll still be able to get at it, but it will be harder for your dog to get into position to nose the lid open.

Lock the lid. Department stores sell locks that are designed to prevent toddlers from opening trash cans. What works for children works equally well for dogs, says Jones.

Give him an extra meal. Dogs aren't necessarily starving when they raid the trash, but they're much more likely to go after free food when their bellies are a little empty. Dr. Griffith recommends feeding dogs two or more times a day. Since dogs tend to go after the trash at night, feeding them before you go to bed may be enough to keep them out of the trash.

CHAPTER THIRTY

RUNNING AROUND AFTER BATHS

Better Than a Blow-Dry

Tazzie is a 2-year-old red Border collie who loves the beach but hates getting wet. "She's very happy to stand in water up to her ankles," says Dawn Curie Thomas, D.V.M., Tazzie's owner and a veterinarian in Santa Barbara, California. "Any wetter than that is too wet for her."

When it's time for a bath, Tazzie pulls out all the stops to avoid the inevitable. "I pull out the towels, and she just disappears," says Dr. Thomas, who is also the author of *The 100 Most Common Questions That Pet Owners Ask the Vet.*

"You wouldn't think that the house had a dog at all." Once she's been found, Tazzie turns into 50 pounds of dead weight, hoping that her owner will give up and go away. When the bath is finally over, Tazzie runs around like a mad dog, desperately trying to get dirty again.

School's Out

Even dogs who enjoy baths will usually emerge from the water with a burst of super canine speed. They shake like crazy, then lunge for something dry—carpets or couches when they're inside or patches of dirt when they're out—to rub and squirm against. Sometimes, they're dirty again before all their fur is dry.

"When you bathe dogs, you have them totally controlled," says Bernadine Cruz, D.V.M., a veterinarian in Laguna Hills, California. "When they finally get out of the water, they're like kids who have been turned loose on the playground after being cooped up all day."

Dogs don't like being forced to do things. Once baths are over, they celebrate by shaking and running around.

Most dogs don't get bathed very often, so it's a big event in their lives. Love it or hate it, they emerge from the water totally stimulated. They just have to have a little running frenzy to release some of that energy, says Dr. Cruz.

What's That Awful Smell?

The whole concept of baths is lost on dogs. They're perfectly happy when their skin and fur are well-coated with their natural scents and oils, along with whatever they've been rolling in lately. "The last thing they want is frou-frou perfume on them and water in their ears," says Dr. Thomas.

Dogs who tear around madly after baths are probably trying to make themselves smell more like dogs again, which is why they often roll their wet, newly clean selves in the dirtiest stuff that they can find. "They may be trying to get rid of the 'stink' of the shampoo," says Dr. Cruz.

If your dog gets truly manic, you may find that it's easier to take him to a groomer for his baths. A basic wash and dry usually costs about $20 for small dogs and $40 for larger dogs. Groomers have deep tubs, professional-quality combs and brushes, and a lot of experience keeping dogs under control. Your dog will be cleaner than you've ever seen him. Of course, he's still going to roll in the first puddle that he finds when he gets home.

Now That You Understand…

Give a dry bath. One way to keep dogs clean without the house-drenching frenzy is to give them waterless baths. Pet supply stores sell

Why do dogs shake when they're wet?

Humans are the only animals who reach for towels when they're wet. Birds and nonhuman mammals, dogs included, get rid of excess water by giving themselves a good shake. They have to do it because the sensation of water on their fur (or feathers) is akin to having a tickle in the throat. It's irritating. Giving a vigorous shake is like have a good cough. It makes them feel better right away, says Benjamin Hart, D.V.M., Ph.D., professor of physiology and behavior at the University of California School of Veterinary Medicine at Davis and author of *The Perfect Puppy: How to Choose Your Dog by Its Behavior.*

Dogs do the most shaking when fur high on their bodies gets wet, Dr. Hart adds. In fact, researchers have found that the shake itself begins high up on the body, then works down to the toes, with the tail shaking last. A dog with wet ankles won't do anything more than lick off the moisture, while a dog who's soaked up to his ears will shake it all off.

All that shaking isn't so good for your walls, but it's very good for dogs. It removes a lot of water quickly, and it helps prevent health problems such as ear infections and skin irritations. So even though their mothers aren't telling them, "Get out of those wet clothes before you get sick," dogs instinctively listen to Mother Nature and do the next best thing.

a mousselike product that you rub into the coat then brush out. It cleans and softens the fur without leaving an oily residue, and it doesn't

Dry shampoos will clean dogs' coats without giving them a chance to shake everywhere. The shampoos are massaged in, a sensation that dogs prefer to being bathed.

some of the postbath hijinks by making baths less exciting and more business-like, says Jan Stewart, a dog groomer in Granada Hills, California.

• Before chasing after your dog and dragging him to the tub, set out every-thing that you need for his bath—the shampoo, conditioner, brushes, and towels, Stewart says. This way, you won't have to go looking for last-minute sup-plies, and your dog won't have time to have second thoughts about getting scrubbed. Moving quickly is essential.

require any water. Since it's more like giving a massage than a bath, dogs aren't as inclined to run around and get dirty immediately after-ward, says Dr. Thomas.

FAST FIX An easy way to keep dogs clean is to dust their coats with a mixture of cornstarch and baby powder, then brush it through their coats. The powder soaks up skin oils and helps eliminate the usual "doggy" smell. Your dog will still run around afterward, but without a water-filled coat, he'll pick up less grit and grime than he would after a conventional bath.

Get organized and move quickly. Since dogs don't get a lot of baths, they always get worked up when you try to lift them into the tub or soak them with a hose. You can eliminate

• Wear your dirtiest jeans and an old T-shirt, or put on a swimming suit. You're going to get wet, whether you like it or not. You may as well be prepared for it.

• As soon as the bath is over, snap a leash onto your dog's collar and get him outside. There's no way to stop dogs from shaking and running around, but you can take them to a location where the mess won't be a problem.

• Keep them in the bathroom after the bath is done. The postbath burst of energy only lasts a few minutes and simmers down quickly. As long as you have an easy-wipe bathroom without fancy carpets or expensive woodwork, it's easiest to wash your dog, give him a quick towel off, then leave the bathroom and shut the door. He'll still zip around, but the mess will be confined and he won't have a chance to get dirty before his coat is dry.

CHAPTER THIRTY-ONE

PREFER HUMAN BEDS TO DOG BEDS

Status, Comfort, and Room to Roll

If dogs had the opportunity to sleep-test beds, you can imagine what the winners would be. Over there are the dog beds: lumpy, bumpy, and tucked out of the way somewhere. Over here are the human beds: big, soft, high off the drafty floor, and occupied by people. From a dog's point of view, they're the best real estate in the house.

"People's beds are great places for dogs to be," says Brandy Oliver, a dog-behavior consultant in Seffner, Florida. "They smell great, and they're a place dogs can go when they want some company."

Nearer to You

Dogs aren't solitary animals the way cats are. They have spent most of their evolutionary history living with families of dogs. When night fell, they all curled up next to each other, says Benjamin Hart, D.V.M., Ph.D., professor of physiology and behavior at the University of California School of Veterinary Medicine at Davis and author of *The Perfect Puppy: How to Choose Your Dog by Its Behavior*. Sleeping close together kept them warm. It made them happy and secure. Now that they live with people, they want to continue this time-honored and comforting ritual, he explains.

More important than comfort is closeness. Dogs get lonely when they sleep by themselves in a laundry room or basement. "It's the company that makes the bed the place to be," says Dr. Hart. "Some people want their dogs on the bed and encourage them to jump up. The praise dogs get for coming aboard is probably all the motivation they need to do it every night."

Left to their own devices, in fact, quite a few dogs would choose to sleep near the bed,

Human beds have lots of attractions for dogs. They're big, soft, and high off the ground—but best of all, that's where the company is.

but not in it. That king-size mattress offers the ultimate in comfort, but there's a lot of activity up there. People roll around. They shove with their legs. They hog all the covers. "A lot of dogs start out on the bed at the beginning of the night and wind up on the floor," says Dr. Hart. They may come up for the closeness, but they'll climb back down for more serious sleeping.

Height Makes Might

There's another reason dogs gravitate to the bed, one that has nothing to do with comfort or closeness. Imagine a small executive who sits in a very large chair. That's how dogs perceive the bed. In their world, height is power. A shy, retiring dog, for example, will be very careful about raising his head so that it's higher than a more-assertive dog's. An assertive dog, on the other hand, will stretch his whole body upward in order to appear taller than he is. Sleeping on the bed automatically adds a few feet to a dog's stature, and that can be quite a perk, says Sarah Wilson, a trainer in Gardiner, New York, and coauthor of *Paws to Consider*.

There's nothing wrong with indulging a dog's quest for upward mobility. You have to be careful, however, that he doesn't take advantage of what he perceives as his privileged status. He may start lording it over other pets—growling when the cat dares to climb up, for example. Some dogs go even further. "Since I'm as tall as the people," their thinking seems to go, "I'm allowed to grumble when they push into my spot."

"For people, the bed is just a place to sleep, but for dogs, it's one of the ways they figure out what their social status is in the household," Wilson explains. A dog who feels that he has

---

SWEET DREAMS

Dogs have gotten pretty spoiled lately. Rather than sleeping on cold ground the way they used to, they curl up on beds that are as cozy—and nearly as pricey—as anything humans buy.

Water beds. Dogs with arthritis or other joint problems will appreciate a heated, puncture-proof water bed, which comes with a removable, washable cover.

Cedar-filled beds. Sweet-smelling cedar is a natural flea and tick repellent. But cedar beds can be lumpy, and most dogs prefer a mixture of cedar and a softer filling.

Sleeping-bag beds. For dogs who like getting under the covers, sleeping-bag beds are just the ticket. They look just like sleeping bags, only they have flexible rings at the openings to keep them open. They're sized just right for small dogs.

Folded-blanket bed. An old-fashioned bed is one of the least expensive—and also one of the best. Take an old blanket, fold it a few times, and put it where your dog likes to sleep. Since blankets are filled with human scents, they provide the ultimate in doggy comfort.

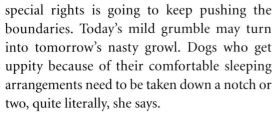

special rights is going to keep pushing the boundaries. Today's mild grumble may turn into tomorrow's nasty growl. Dogs who get uppity because of their comfortable sleeping arrangements need to be taken down a notch or two, quite literally, she says.

A dog who's accustomed to sleeping in the bed isn't going to give it up voluntarily, she adds. Even if you don't let him up before you go to sleep, he's going to try to sneak up once you're asleep. The easiest way to keep him out of your bed is to make his own bed a very comfortable place to be.

Now That You Understand...

Put his bed next to your bed. "Though dogs can adapt well to sleeping by themselves, they like to be in the same room with their families at night," says Dr. Hart. He recommends putting the dog's bed next to yours. He'll be able to smell you. He'll hear you breathing. And he'll know he's important enough to share the same general space, if not the bed itself.

Make his bed bigger. "You can't expect a German shepherd or a Rottweiler to be able to stretch out on a 3-foot round bed and be comfortable," Oliver says. Even though dogs sleep curled up most of the night, they need additional room to spread out when they feel like it. The bed should be as long as your dog is when he's stretched full length. For bigger dogs, you may need to put two pillow-type beds side by side.

Spend some time in his bed. Dogs climb into bed with people because it makes them feel important. You can make their beds feel just as

Dogs are less likely to hog people's beds when they feel that their own beds are special. A visit from his owner—as well as a pet and a few treats—is enough to convince this Labrador mix that his own bed is the place to be.

special by visiting them yourself. "Sit on the floor and pet your dog while he's in his bed," Oliver suggests. Occasionally stashing a biscuit in his bed is a good incentive, too, she adds.

FAST FIX It's not really the contact with your body that dogs crave at bedtime, but all of the other sensory stimulations that come with the territory, smells especially. Oliver recommends taking one of your old blankets and putting it on your dog's bed. It's loaded with your personal scents, and that will probably be enough to keep him happy.

CHAPTER THIRTY-TWO

UNRAVELING TOILET PAPER

Always Good for a Laugh

If ever there's a time when dogs look like mischievous toddlers, it's when they're sitting on the bathroom floor surrounded by ribbons of toilet paper. The expression on their faces says, "Oh, did I do that?" Once they see you laughing, they'll happily tear into it again.

"They may start pulling at the toilet paper because they're bored or curious, but once they get going, it's just plain fun," says Janine McInnis, D.V.M., a veterinary behavior specialist in Dallas.

Toilet paper is fun because it engages all of a dog's senses, says Emily Weiss, curator of behavior and research at Sedgwick County Zoo in Wichita, Kansas. "Toilet paper is soft and light, and it flips and flutters," she points out. "The roll makes a great noise when dogs turn it. And best of all, the pile just keeps getting bigger and bigger. For dogs who are really captivated by visual stimuli, the ever-growing white thing they're making is a huge reward for pulling on the roll."

The Paper Chase

Dogs can entertain themselves for quite a while with a roll of toilet paper, but what makes it really fun is the reactions of their owners. Nearly everyone laughs when they see their dogs' antics for the first time, and their dogs remember that. "Even if you respond with a shriek, that high-pitched shout sounds a lot like a puppy's yelp," says Weiss. "It translates to 'Let's go play!'"

Unraveling the roll is just part of the game. The other part is running through the house

This Rhodesian ridgeback puppy likes nothing better than to run up and down the stairs until they're festooned with toilet paper.

with the paper flapping. That's the part a lot of dogs really enjoy, says John C. Wright, Ph.D., a certified applied animal behaviorist; professor of psychology at Mercer University in Macon, Georgia; and author of *The Dog Who Would Be King*. Toilet paper rolls aren't very firmly anchored. Dogs get a lot of satisfaction from working them free from their holders and showing everyone in the family what they've done, he says.

Not everyone appreciates replacing a roll of paper, only to see it in shreds a few hours later. But you should consider yourself lucky when you have a puppy who limits himself to this shred-and-chase game—it means he's not destroying something else, Dr. McInnis says. "It's a whole lot easier to clean up toilet paper than to replace carpet or hang new curtains or bring in a new couch. Usually, closing the bathroom door does the trick."

Now That You Understand...

Toilet paper isn't expensive, and it doesn't make too much of a mess. Most people don't mind when their dogs shred a few rolls. Of course, no one enjoys reaching for the roll only to discover that the dog, once again, has taken it away—or left behind a soggy, tattered mess that's only good for the trash.

Make it clatter. Most dogs outgrow this unraveling phase, but some keep doing it because it's so much fun. Discipline may not

BREED SPECIFIC

Australian shepherds, Border collies, Australian cattle dogs (left), and other herding dogs have been bred to control things with their mouths. They tend to grab anything that moves and flutters, and the loose end of a toilet paper roll is just about perfect.

help, because it only takes a few seconds for dogs to turn a roll of toilet paper into streamers—meaning, it's hard to catch them in the act. One way to discourage them is to set a booby trap, says Weiss. Put an empty can or two on top of the roll. Put a few marbles inside the cans. When your dog gives the paper a pull, the cans will tumble, making a noisy clatter. After a few frights, most dogs will be convinced that grabbing the roll isn't as much fun as it used to be, she says.

FAST FIX People don't always realize that toilet paper unrolls two ways. When you hang it with the loose end on the outside, it's easy for dogs to unravel it by giving a pull. A quick solution is to reverse the roll so that it hangs with the loose end facing the wall. It will still spin when your dog paws it, but it won't unwind. This takes a lot of the fun out of the game, Dr. Wright explains.

Another solution is to switch from a horizontal holder to one that holds the paper upright. The loose end won't hang down, and most dogs won't bother giving it a spin.

PART FOUR

"I Like the Good Things in Life"

The Passion for Food and Fun

Having fun and stealing the limelight are what dogs live for. Their playfulness is what makes them so great to have around. When you understand what they enjoy the most, you'll discover ways to make each day even better.

CHAPTER THIRTY-THREE

LIKE HAVING THEIR EARS RUBBED

It's a Chemical High

Duncan is a stickler for routines, especially routines that feel good. A 10-year-old bearded collie in York, Maine, Duncan has a none-too-subtle way of getting what he wants. Every morning at the same time, he gets up from his favorite place on the floor and sits on Karen Norteman's feet, which is about the last thing she needs as she's getting ready for her long commute to her job with a Boston computer company. But she has learned

that Duncan isn't about to get up from his foot-squishing position and let her put on her socks and shoes until he gets what he's after. Since Duncan weighs about 47 pounds, she can hardly ignore him.

"When Duncan gets his ears rubbed, he moans and groans and sings like a musical instrument," Norteman says. "He likes to have his back rubbed too, but that doesn't give him anywhere near the ecstasy he gets around the ears."

Nearly all dogs loving having their ears rubbed. You wouldn't think this would be such a common phenomenon. After all, there are hundreds of breeds, and all of their ears are different. Papillons' look like wings, German shepherds' are sharp peaks, and basset hounds have big, hanging floppies. But they all love a little ear work just the same.

"It's pretty much universal," says Allen Schoen, D.V.M., director of the Center for the Advance-

This Great Dane's expression shows that he's a sucker for an ear massage. The ears are filled with nerves, and dogs like having them touched.

ment of Veterinary Alternative Therapies in Sherman, Connecticut, and author of *Love, Miracles, and Animal Healing*. "Dogs crave affection and touch from their owners, so a rub on the ears meets a basic need for communication."

Pure Nerves

Ears are one of a handful of nerve centers on a dog's body that are extra-sensitive to touch. The only other places that are nearly as sensitive are their bellies and the nooks between their toes, says Christine Makowski, D.V.M., a veterinarian in Landenberg, Pennsylvania.

When you rub a dog's ears, the pleasure she feels is intense. And the good feelings don't stop on the surface. Their ears contain nerve branches that extend to the internal organs, says Dr. Schoen. When you rub them, your dog doesn't just feel good on the top of her head. The pleasure comes from inside her body too.

Because the ears are such a hotbed of nerves, they're the primary target of people who practice acupuncture and acupressure. Putting pressure on the ears sends nerve impulses right through the body. "There's essentially an entire map of the body on the ear," Dr. Makowski explains. In fact, many acupuncturists only work on ears, because they can treat the whole body that way.

Chemical Bliss

It's not uncommon for dogs to get so relaxed and blissful when they're getting their ears rubbed that they slip into happy sleep. It's not only because they're feeling comfortable.

CALL FOR HELP

Unlike humans, who have fairly straight ear canals, dogs' ear canals make a few sharp bends. This means they are at high risk for getting ear infections. Dogs who have always loved having their ears rubbed but are suddenly wincing and pulling away probably have an infection and need to be checked out.

Rubbing the ears sends nerve impulses to the hypothalamus and pituitary glands, says Dr. Schoen. These glands secrete endorphins, pain-killing, feel-good hormones that make dogs feel relaxed, even euphoric. When you rub your dog's ears, she's essentially getting high on her own hormones.

So is the person doing the petting. Researchers at the University of Pennsylvania in Philadelphia, the University of California, Los Angeles, and elsewhere have found that people get a lot of the same benefits that their dogs do. Rubbing dogs' ears triggers a flood of human endorphins. This in turn helps people relax and even lowers blood pressure.

Not for Everyone

Just as people don't want strangers coming up and rubbing their backs, dogs are particular about who rubs their ears. It's not a matter of snobbery. It's just that dogs have their own ways of relating to each other. One thing of which they're very much aware is height. Dogs with strong personalities will deliberately put their paws or heads on top of other dogs' heads. They couldn't care less about the ears. They're just showing that they're big enough and tough enough to do it—it's a power move. Should another dog attempt the same thing with them, it's a declaration of war.

Dogs don't expect people to act the same way dogs do, but they instinctively get uncomfortable when people they don't know loom over them or reach down to rub their ears. It's a show of familiarity that they don't like. Once they know you and like you, of course, all this changes. They know that you have the right to rub their ears, and so they sit back and enjoy it.

Dogs with more laid-back personalities, on the other hand, are accustomed to having other dogs do the head-over-head thing. In fact, they'll invite it by tucking their heads, crouching down, and rubbing the tops of their heads under a more dominant dog's chin. It's their way of showing respect. Even if they've never seen another dog, they understand that people play the same dominant role and that their ears are fair game. This is true of family members, of course, but also of people they've never met before. Power isn't an issue, so they'll take all the attention that they can get.

Most dogs fall somewhere in the middle and are neither dominant or submissive. They'll accept ear rubs from people with whom they feel comfortable, but they may be a little nervous about strangers with outstretched hands.

Now That You Understand...

It's pretty hard to rub dogs' ears in ways they dislike. To launch them straight to cloud nine, however, you need to hit as many of the nerves as you can.

Starting at the base of the ear, hold the flap between your thumb and forefinger, Dr. Makowski suggests. Very gently pull the ear straight out from your dog's head, letting your fingers slide as you go. If you do that about four times, moving your fingers each time so they slide over a different section of the ear, you'll hit just about every hot spot, and your dog will be very, very happy.

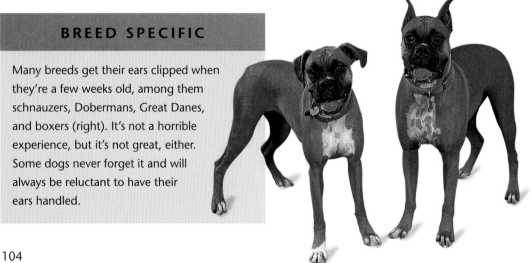

BREED SPECIFIC

Many breeds get their ears clipped when they're a few weeks old, among them schnauzers, Dobermans, Great Danes, and boxers (right). It's not a horrible experience, but it's not great, either. Some dogs never forget it and will always be reluctant to have their ears handled.

CHAPTER THIRTY-FOUR

LOVE HAVING THEIR BELLIES RUBBED

The Best Kind of Affection

When it's a belly rub she's after, Hazel knows exactly how to get it. In fact, the 7-year-old basset hound in Zebulon, North Carolina, has a routine that she follows night after night. She eats dinner. She asks for, and gets, three Meaty Bone treats. She takes a sip of water from her bowl. Then she hops her 48-pound self up on the couch, puts her head on a pillow, and rolls on her back—and scans the room for volunteers.

This terrier mix's idea of bliss is to sit on her owner's lap and to have her belly and chest stroked.

She doesn't have to wait long. Everyone in the family makes an *aw* sound and lines up to rub Hazel's lightly furred belly. Hazel, of course, eats it up.

Hazel isn't the only dog who does the belly-up routine. If there's such a thing as a universal pleasure center among dogs, it's the belly. The skin on their bellies is thinner than skin elsewhere, and there's not a lot of fur. As a result, the belly is exquisitely sensitive to touch, says Robin Downing, D.V.M., a veterinarian in Windsor, Colorado.

"One of the reasons we think of dogs as our best friends is that they have some remarkable similarities to us," adds Jeff Nichol, D.V.M., a veterinarian in Albuquerque, New Mexico. "They enjoy physical affection just like we do." A dog who's getting his belly rubbed enjoys the attention. He likes the nice sensations. And he likes knowing that he can attract people like a magnet just by rolling over and putting his feet in the air.

Ultimate Trust

Dogs use body language to convey very specific messages. Rolling on their backs and exposing their bellies is a sure sign of submission. It's a way of telling other dogs, "I'm at your mercy; do

105

Going belly-up is a sign of submission. It's how dogs express their trust and affection. It also feels good, as this Staffordshire bull terrier can attest.

what you will." A dog who's being threatened and wants to avoid a fight will expose his belly to signal his noncombatant status. Conversely, a dog who's at peace and relaxed will go belly up just because he feels safe to do so. "That position is the ultimate in vulnerability," says Dr. Downing.

People only reveal their softer sides to those they love and trust. It's the same with dogs. It takes a lot of trust for them to expose their bellies in front of people, and that's one of the reasons that belly rubs are such blissful experiences.

"When your dog looks at you, lies down, and flops over for a belly rub, that says something about the relationship you have with him," says Dr. Nichol. "It tells you that your dog knows that you are in charge, that he loves and trusts you, and that he's happy with that arrangement."

The unique thing about this behavior is that it presents one of the few opportunities that dogs have to set the agenda. "It's usually the people who decide when to spend time with their dogs," says Dr. Downing. "We choose when we'll go for a walk, when we'll take a ride in the car, when we'll sit on the deck and throw tennis balls. But here's an opportunity for dogs to say, 'I'd like to spend some time with you now.'" They know that their people will be more than happy to comply.

Selective Love

Some dogs are promiscuous with their affection. They'll roll over for anyone at just about any time. This is especially true of Labrador retrievers, who are known for their people-pleasing personalities. It's not uncommon, in fact, for Labradors to walk around a room, pause in front of each person they come to, and flop onto their backs.

Other dogs are much more cautious about revealing themselves. It's not a matter of love or affection, just one of temperament. "There are dogs who love you but who just don't want to be that vulnerable," says Dr. Downing. Her own dog, a 5-year-old pug mix, is a case in point. Despite his diminutive size, he's an assertive, dominant dog. He wouldn't dream of having his

Why do dogs kick their legs when you rub their bellies?

One minute, you're casually rubbing your dog's belly and he's lapping it up. Then, all of a sudden, your hand is caught in a windmill of whirling back legs and claws, driving you away. What makes a pleasurable belly rub turn into a leg kick?

Most of the time, it's because you've hit a tickle spot, says Jeff Nichol, D.V.M., a veterinarian in Albuquerque, New Mexico. The areas between and below the ribs are loaded with nerve endings, and when you hit several of these nerve endings at the same time, it tickles and makes dogs uncomfortable.

A reflex action may be involved as well. Just as your doctor can make your leg kick by rapping your kneecap, it's possible to make dogs kick by inadvertently hitting one of their many reflex points.

Dogs aren't uniformly ticklish. The same pressure and place that sends one dog's leg into overdrive may elicit nothing more than a happy sigh from another. You'll just have to rub different places and see what happens.

belly rubbed. "As much as he loves me, he's just not that kind of dog," says Dr. Downing.

Akitas are known for being independent and somewhat reserved. They're less likely than most dogs to ask for or even tolerate a belly rub. The same is true of huskies, Alaskan malamutes, and other breeds with strong, assertive personalities.

Now That You Understand...

Rubbing your dog's belly is about as foolproof as anything can be. "Once a dog rolls on his back, the message is pretty much, 'Touch me anywhere; I'm yours.' You can't do much wrong," says Dr. Nichol. Still, every dog likes having his belly rubbed in a slightly different way. Here are some of the pleasure points.

Rub where he can't scratch. Nearly all dogs love having their chests rubbed. This is partly because the chest and chin are areas that puppies lick when they want to show respect, and dogs instinctively respond to the gesture with affection. It's also a place that they can't scratch very easily. Rubbing the chest shows love and respect, and maybe relieves an itch or two at the same time.

Work on the bare belly. Because there's very little fur on the belly around the belly button, this is probably the most sensitive place to rub. Most dogs love it, says Dr. Downing.

Play with pressure. "Some dogs like to be rubbed vigorously, as though you were toweling them after a bath, and some prefer little strokes or circles," Dr. Downing says.

Most dogs are suckers for a belly rub, but dominant and reserved breeds such as Akitas (left) may not appreciate the intimacy.

107

CHAPTER THIRTY-FIVE

Sitting on People's Feet

Better Than a Security Blanket

Dan Hickox's dog, Homer, is only truly happy when sleeping in one place—on Dan's feet. Homer stakes them out for midmorning daydreaming, afternoon naps, and nighttime snoozes. He doesn't care where the feet are. He sits on them when they're on the floor, on the couch, under the kitchen table, or on the bed—anywhere he can catch them staying still long enough for him to settle down.

There's no getting around the fact that dogs love feet and everything associated with them. They adore shoes and socks, and most of all, they love the smelly tootsies themselves. "Your feet are the part of you that your dog knows best," says Sarah Wilson, a trainer in Gardiner, New York, and coauthor of *Paws to Consider.* "They're right there on the floor with her; they're full of the smell of you; and lots of times, they're the only part of you that dogs are allowed to sit on."

One reason that dogs like feet so much is the same reason that most people steer clear of them. For such a small body part, feet pack a whole lot of scent. Each foot has about 125,000 sweat glands. That's enough to keep plenty of smells percolating, especially when the feet are encased in socks

Large dogs, such as this chocolate Labrador, are too big to comfortably sit on laps the way small dogs can. Sitting on feet is the next best thing.

and shoes. Dogs draw a huge portion of their knowledge of the world from their sense of smell. And feet sure do smell.

Close to You

Rich aromas aren't the only things about feet that dogs find attractive. They also depend on them as sort of a human tether. "There are some dogs who worry that their owners will get up and leave without them noticing," says Nicholas Dodman, professor of behavioral pharmacology

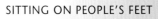

and director of the Animal Behavior Clinic at Tufts University School of Veterinary Medicine in North Grafton, Massachusetts, and author of *Dogs Behaving Badly*. "They don't want their people to get very far away, so they sit on them."

Large dogs are more likely than small breeds to choose a podiatric perch. Small dogs can scramble into laps when they want to keep track of their people. Big dogs are too bulky for that kind of cuddling. Sitting on feet gives them similar feelings of closeness and reassurance.

Of course, there are plenty of dogs who simply want to be near the people they like. They're not all that desperate for attention or reassurance—they just like the closeness. "You don't cuddle up with your husband on the couch because you don't want him to sneak away without you noticing," says Wilson. "You just like the physical contact."

Now That You Understand...

Some dogs crave foot contact more than others, and there's not much you can do about it. Keep your leather shoes in the closet and be grateful that your dog wants to be close to you. Dogs who are truly anxious about being abandoned, however, need some extra reassurance.

Schedule cuddle time. Dogs who know they can depend on getting attention at certain times of the day or in certain places are less likely to demand it the rest of the time. Set aside 5 to 10 minutes each day when your dog can sit on your feet, lick your face, and generally revel in physical contact, Wilson recommends. She'll come to depend on these regular meetings and look forward to them—and she'll be less

Feet are smelly and easily accessible—two factors that make them irresistibly attractive to dogs.

desperate the rest of the time because she'll know something good is coming.

Protect your space—but just a little. Dogs who are insecure are constantly crowding their people, and they can get frantic when the people are out of sight. The only way they'll feel more confident is if they're gradually weaned from clingy contact, says Rolan Tripp, D.V.M., a veterinarian in La Mirada, California, who specializes in animal behavior.

Once or twice a day for a few weeks, attach a leash to your dog's collar and tie it to something a few feet away from where you're sitting. You want her to be close enough that you're in sight, but too far away to make physical contact. She'll whine at first, but eventually she'll give up and lie down. As soon as she's been still for a minute, toss her a cookie and tell her how great she is. Most dogs catch on very quickly that a little separation can make the stomach fonder. Once they've figured that out, your feet will get a break, Dr. Tripp explains.

CHAPTER THIRTY-SIX

BITING WHEN PLAYING

So Excited They Can't Stand It

Boys ages 5 to 9 are bitten by dogs more than any other group of people—5 times more, to be exact. The reason that these poor kids seem to be bite magnets is that they're boisterous, aggressive, and seething with energy. In other words, they act a lot like young dogs, and young dogs bite each other when they play.

"Animals play much rougher than people do," says Betty Fisher, an animal behaviorist and trainer in San Diego and coauthor of *So Your Dog's Not Lassie*. This isn't a problem when they're playing among themselves. They have thick fur that protects them from each other's teeth. People, with their soft skin and hairless bodies, are much more vulnerable. Adult dogs understand this, but puppies don't. "When they get really caught up in a game, they can get carried away and forget who they're playing with," she says.

Dogs from 6 months to 2 years old do the most biting. Like human teens, they have more energy and strength than judgment. Plus, they're constantly testing boundaries, Fisher adds. Even when they know they're not supposed to bite, they'll try just to see what happens.

Dogs usually bite when everyone is running around and getting worked up, says John C. Wright, Ph.D., a certified applied animal behaviorist; professor of psychology at Mercer University in Macon, Georgia; and author of *The Dog Who Would Be King*. The faster and more furious the game, the more stimulated dogs get. At that point, they're prepared to match playful aggression with more aggression. And once they're caught up in the camaraderie and competition, they may forget all their good manners and do rude things, including jumping on people, knocking over lamps, and biting.

Their Mothers Didn't Raise Them Right

Some lessons need to be taught at home. For dogs, one of the most important lessons they'll

Even gentle dogs sometimes bite when they get overexcited, such as when they find someone to play with and chase.

ever learn is that biting is bad manners. Mom dogs and other puppies in the litter have a very effective way of discouraging bites. They bite back, giving a little extra oomph for emphasis. It doesn't take dogs long to learn that biting invariably invites stronger bites in return. By the time they're 8 weeks old, most pups have learned that biting their elders and playmates is a bad idea, even when they're playing. And most of them carry this knowledge into their human families.

However, if a puppy is taken away from his siblings and his mother too early—especially before 6 weeks of age—he won't have learned the proper etiquette about biting, says Dr. Wright. At this point, it's up to his human "littermates" to teach the lessons that the poor pup didn't get earlier.

It's not always easy to do, mainly because of instinct: Puppies have an instinct to bite, and people have an instinct to swat the of-fending muzzle. This teaches dogs two things, says Dr. Wright. "They find that they can stop someone from swatting them by biting their hands and holding them. Second, they may decide that any hands coming toward them are fair game for biting."

You Just Don't Understand Me

To their credit, most dogs give hints before they haul off and bite someone, says Dr. Wright. During play, they'll get progressively mouthier up until the point when they actually clamp down. More often, bites occur when dogs are sick of playing. They'll show their reticence by pointedly looking away from whoever is trying to engage them. Or they'll turn their backs or lie down and try to ignore what's going on. Anyone who ignores these hints is likely to get nailed.

Dogs also bite when they don't like the way someone is playing, Dr. Wright adds. For example, people have an inclination to pull dogs' ears or to roll them over and pin them down when they're wrestling. Some dogs will put up with this all day, but others won't stand for it. "Dogs are smart enough to figure out that biting is a quick and easy way to stop games that aren't fun," says Dr. Wright. "And once they find a strategy that works, they stick with it."

Now That You Understand...

Talk like Mom. Since dogs tend to bite when they're acting childish, you can often stop them by acting motherish, which means giving a low, authoritative *grrr*. Dogs hear this sound a lot when they're puppies, especially when

POOCH PUZZLER

Why do dogs lick after biting?

For proof that dogs have tender hearts, watch what happens when they accidentally bite someone: They'll quickly give the area a gentle lick. "When you cringe or act surprised, your dog will lick you to appease you," says John C. Wright, Ph.D., a certified applied animal behaviorist; professor of psychology at Mercer University in Macon, Georgia; and author of *The Dog Who Would Be King*. "It's not necessarily that he feels bad because he bit you, but because he sees you're upset."

When dogs start biting too hard, one way to stop them is to blow on their noses. This young Rhodesian ridgeback doesn't like the sensation and is starting to back off.

they're nursing and their teeth start coming in. They take Mom's threats seriously, and memories of her warnings stay with them. Growls get their attention and make them think twice about what they're doing.

Turn your back. "If you want to show your dog that you don't like the way he plays, stop moving, extricate whatever part of you he has in his mouth, and turn your back on him," says Fisher. This sends a very clear signal that you aren't happy and won't play unless your dog learns to keep his teeth to himself.

Use an extension. Rather than letting dogs mouth your hands, it's better to use toys, towels, or ropes as intermediaries. Anything that puts distance between your hands and their mouths will work better than hand-to-hand—or hand-to-mouth—games, says Dr. Wright.

Play at your level. Dogs love it when people get down on all fours and wrestle, head butt, and generally roughhouse with them. Physical games are fun, but some dogs have a

natural tendency to be dominant. Seeing a person on all fours makes them think they're dealing with a doglike equal, one whom it's perfectly acceptable to bite, Fisher says.

Dogs have a natural respect for height, however. Keeping your head and shoulders higher than your dog's will help him understand that you're the one he needs to respect, not the one he's allowed to bite, she explains.

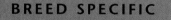 **FAST FIX** A quick way to extricate toys—or hands—from overeager jaws is to blow on dogs' noses. They find this quick blast of air very distracting and will relax their jaws. "If you and I were playing a game and I suddenly blew on your nose, you'd stop whatever you were doing and ask me what the heck I was doing," Fisher says. "It's the same with dogs."

BREED SPECIFIC

Border collies, shelties, and other herding dogs have a hard time controlling their mouths when they're playing. This is mainly because they've been bred to herd livestock, and biting is one of the tools they use.

CHAPTER THIRTY-SEVEN

CHASING BALLS

It Just Comes Naturally

Pet supply stores sell an enormous variety of toys—rubber tug-toys, pull ropes, and squeaky cubes, to name just a few. These high-end gizmos may catch people's eyes, but they often leave dogs yawning. As any child who has turned a stick into a spaceship can attest, the best toys are usually the simplest. And nothing is simpler than a ball.

"I have to watch my dog when we go to the pet supply store," says Carol Lea Benjamin, a dog trainer and author of *Dog Training in 10 Minutes.* "He'll pick up a ball and carry it right out of the store in his mouth."

Balls are so attractive, in fact, that larceny is common. Dogs in parks have been known to stake out the tennis courts, waiting for an errant ball to fly over. Little League games have been interrupted by dogs running into the outfield to grab slow grounders. And more than a few children have gone to bed crying because family dogs have shredded—or at least slobbered on—their favorite balls.

Born to Chase

Wild dogs—and their ancestors, the wolves—weren't stealthy, silent hunters the way cats are. They had to chase their suppers. The fastest, most-eager runners were the ones who got the most to eat, and they lived long enough to have plenty of puppies. Multiply this by a few thousand generations, and the result is an entire species with an instinct to run and chase.

Dogs certainly don't confuse a baseball in the yard with a running rabbit. But the love of chasing has been deeply bred into them. What

Dogs no longer need to hunt, but they still love to chase. Balls provide all sorts of fun—they can be chased as well as caught on the fly and rolled along the ground with the nose.

POOCH PUZZLER

Why do dogs prefer tennis balls?

Even dogs who are blasé about balls generally will get a happy gleam in their eyes when they're given a tennis ball. There's something about these colorful, fuzzy globes that dogs find strangely intoxicating.

This is partly because of the size. Tennis balls are small enough for most dogs to hold comfortably, and large enough so they don't slip down their throats, explains Carol Lea Benjamin, a dog trainer in New York City and author of *Dog Training in 10 Minutes*.

More important, tennis balls have a soft, spongy surface, which is perfect for picking up and retaining scents. "They get a very personal scent from the dog's mouth as well," she says. "They can smell that it's their ball."

Best of all, tennis balls have a springy texture that dogs adore. When they chew, the balls squish down, then pop right back. "That bit of compression is a great workout for their jaws," Benjamin adds. "Some dogs feel lost when they don't have a tennis ball to chew."

Plus, dogs have the opportunity to carry balls back to their owners, and this makes them feel as though they're fulfilling their life's mission, says Dr. Houpt. It's precisely what their parents, grandparents, and great-grandparents did, and they're carrying on the tradition.

"One of the things that makes dogs great pets is that they're so adaptable," Benjamin adds. "They're born with a drive to chase prey. When they chase balls, they're translating that drive into a game instead."

Now That You Understand...

Play with bright balls. Dogs don't see colors very well, so it doesn't matter very much what colors the balls are that your dog plays with, as long as they're not green or red, colors which are hard for them to see. Also, they should be brightly colored rather than muted. Most of a dog's vision comes from structures in the eyes called rod receptors. Rods are only sensitive to black and white. Brightly colored balls stand out more against the background and are easier for dogs to see.

Throw balls across their line of sight. How many times have you tossed a ball right at your dog, only to watch him lose sight of it? There's a reason for this. Dogs' eyes are set farther apart than ours. They can easily see movement off to the sides, but they have a lot of trouble seeing things that are right in front of them. They'll have more fun with balls when you toss them across their line of sight rather than right at them.

Set aside some throwing time. Some dogs are born chewers and will work over a ball as

they once did for business, they now do for fun, explains Katherine Houpt, V.M.D., Ph.D., a diplomate of the American College of Veterinary Behaviorists and a professor in the College of Veterinary Medicine at Cornell University in Ithaca, New York.

Chasing is just one reason dogs love balls. Catching is the other. Many dogs have been bred to hold things in their mouths. A ball isn't as exciting as a downed duck, but the sensation of holding something is probably very satisfying.

You can encourage reluctant dogs to come to you by using two tennis balls. Entice your dog with one ball, then throw it. Then use the second ball to encourage him to come to you again.

enthusiastically as they'll splinter a stick. Most dogs, however, won't even notice a ball that's just sitting there. If you want your dog to get the most fun out of his ball, you have to set aside some time for throwing it. "I play tennis with my dogs a couple times a week," says Inger Martens, a trainer and behaviorist in Los Angeles and author of *Paws for a Minute.* "I hit the balls, they chase them, bring them back, and line them up for me to hit them again."

Practice the two-ball technique. Since dogs often go bananas for balls, you can use them as motivators when you're doing basic training, Dr. Houpt says. Training with balls is actually better than training with food. Balls have no calories. They make it easy for dogs to get a lot of exercise. And they help dogs get used to watching your every move, which is essential when you're teaching obedience, she explains.

BREED SPECIFIC

Dogs who were bred for hunting and retrieving, like terriers and golden and Labrador retrievers, are the ones most likely to get excited about balls. Dogs bred for protection, such as Akitas, tend to be indifferent.

Balls are especially useful for teaching the "come" command, Benjamin says. This command is tricky because dogs who are playing and having a good time aren't always paying attention to the person at the other end of the yard. When you're holding a ball, however, you can be sure you'll have your dog's undivided attention, she explains.

She recommends using two balls. Hold one of the balls in your hand so that your dog can see it. When his eyes are riveted on you, tell him "come." Wait until he comes and sits in front of you. Then throw the ball. Maybe he'll bring it right back, and maybe he won't. It doesn't matter too much because you'll be holding a second ball. He'll want that one just as much as he did the first one. Tell him "come" again, have him sit, and then swap balls for another throw. Dogs love this game because they get a chance to run, retrieve, and play with you. After a while, they'll come running whenever they hear the word come, whether you're holding a ball or not.

CHAPTER THIRTY-EIGHT

CHASING THEIR TAILS

Might Be a Rabbit

Even though she has mellowed a lot since she was a puppy, there are two things that get Hopie, a 6-year-old dachshund, totally riled up. The first is when her owner, Cindy Poole of Roxbury, New York, gets the leash out in the morning. The second is when the school bus pulls up outside and crowds of yelling, giggling children pile out.

Hopie has to deal with her excitement somehow, and a few barks just aren't enough. So she chases her tail.

"Lots of dogs chase their tails when they've got energy and excitement that they don't know how to handle," says Alice Moon-Fanelli, Ph.D., clinical assistant professor in animal behavior at Tufts University School of Veterinary Medicine in North Grafton, Massachusetts. For some dogs, the big event is going outside after being cooped up all day. Getting out of the tub is always exciting. And the sight of a leash is a sure-fire call to action. "For some dogs, chasing their tails is something to do when they really don't know what to do," says Dr. Moon-Fanelli.

Why Turn to the Tail?

Dogs have all sorts of ways of showing excitement. They roll over and over on their backs. They jump up on their hind legs. They run around in circles and bark. These are all normal outlets for energy and excitement, and dogs do them all of the time. Tail chasing is less common. Researchers are not sure why dogs do it, but they suspect it may have something to do with their hunting pasts.

This bullterrier mix chases her tail from time to time just for the fun of it. For some dogs, however, tail chasing can become an emotional compulsion.

Dogs originally got their meals by hunting, usually small prey such as rabbits. Their brains and eyes are wired in such a way that they're intensely aware of quick movements. It's possible, says Dr. Moon-Fanelli, that some dogs catch a glimpse of their tails, get excited, and, without thinking about it, try to catch the pesky things. They rarely succeed, of course. So they keep trying.

"We don't have any reason to believe that dogs really think their tails are prey to be captured," says Dr. Moon-Fanelli. "But that basic instinct may be what gets them started."

All for Show

Even if dogs initially see their tails as bushy little squirrels, it shouldn't take them long to realize their mistake. Yet some dogs keep chasing—not just once or twice, but all the time. They may simply think it's fun, especially when the people they live with think it's fun too.

"Tail chasing is pretty cute when dogs first do it, and a lot of people make a big fuss over it," says Kathy Gaughan, D.V.M., assistant professor at Kansas State Veterinary Medicine Teaching Hospital in Manhattan. Dogs enjoy an appreciative audience. When they discover that something gets them a lot of attention, they'll keep doing it.

But this has a downside. Like actors who are always "on," some dogs get such a thrill from performing that they keep doing it even when the curtain is down. Tail chasing is hard work, and they run themselves ragged until they collapse in a panting heap on the floor. Then they get up and do it again.

CALL FOR HELP

Dogs who compulsively chase their tails have always been thought to have personality disorders. In some cases, however, the behavior may be triggered by seizures. Dogs who chase their tails even when they appear to be miserable or totally unaware of their surroundings may have a neurological problem and should be seen by a veterinarian.

Coping with Confusion

Dogs who chase their tails aren't necessarily as happy as they appear, Dr. Gaughan says. When they don't know how to deal with a situation, such as meeting a strange dog, chasing their tails acts as a distraction. It buys them time while they think about what they're going to do next.

This sounds like a silly way to cope with confusion, but people do similar things, says Dr. Gaughan. It's called displacement behavior. Suppose you're having an internal debate about whether to complain about the service in a restaurant or just to keep the peace and keep eating. While you're making up your mind, you may rap your fingers on the table or fiddle with the napkin. The physical activity is a stalling tactic, and it helps dispel some energy at the same time. Dogs who chase their tails may be doing something similar, Dr. Gaughan says.

Any stressful situation can lead to tail chasing, adds Char Bebiak, an animal behaviorist and head trainer at the Purina Pet Care Center in Gray Summit, Missouri. "Dogs aren't able to say, 'Hey, take a break; it's stressful,'" she says. "Instead, they turn to a behavior they know, as a way of calming themselves."

Dogs who chase their tails all the time may have a compulsive personality disorder, Dr. Moon-Fanelli adds. One clue is whether they do other odd things as well. For example, dogs who chase their tails also may chase shadows or the moving sunlight on the carpet. Or they'll groom themselves constantly. Compulsive behaviors can be quite serious, and often need medical treatment, she explains.

Chasing the Pain

Dogs do a lot of things that are utterly mystifying to people, but sometimes the underlying reason is the simplest one imaginable. Some dogs chase their tails because they hurt, and they want to give them a lick and bite for relief.

"Sometimes, a dog gets her tail caught in a door, stepped on, or injured in a fight, and no one even knows it's wounded until they call their vet because they're worried about the tail

chasing," says Dr. Gaughan. Once the problem is taken care of, the tail chasing will stop as well.

Now That You Understand...

It's good entertainment to watch dogs chase their tails, but you don't want to encourage it. There's no way to predict which dogs will do it for fun and which will become truly obsessed.

"It can be like turning something on and then not being able to turn it off," Dr. Moon-Fanelli says.

It's best for your dog if you totally ignore her when she starts chasing her tail. Don't tease dogs with laser light toys, either, Dr. Gaughan adds. These toys can lead to the same type of compulsive activity that tails can. In fact, some dogs have been known to go nearly crazy chasing sunbeams or even moving shadows.

Even dogs without tails find these appendages fascinating. If they can't chase their own, they'll go after someone else's.

118

CHAPTER THIRTY-NINE

CHEWING STICKS

It Keeps the Jaws in Shape

One look at a dog's mouth tells you that it was designed for serious business. Those intimidating teeth suggest this was a creature whose ancestors had to rip, tear, and crunch to get themselves fed. Holding those teeth are strong jaws, capable of biting with several times more strength than human jaws.

Shredding a stick isn't quite the same as tearing supper apart, but it's good practice: One reason dogs chew sticks is that it helps them keep their jaws strong, says Char Bebiak, an animal behaviorist and head trainer at the Purina Pet Care Center in Gray Summit, Missouri. At one time, they got nutrition from every part of their prey, including the tough skin and bones, Bebiak says. Dogs in the wild probably chewed on sticks just as much as modern dogs do, as a way of staying in shape for the next meal.

"Sticks let dogs really work their jaws. And even though they may not need to hunt anymore, the urge to keep their mouths strong hasn't diminished all that much," Bebiak says. That's why dogs today, whose food isn't much harder than a rice cracker, continue to chew sticks, sometimes covering the yard with piles of wood chips. It gives them chewing satisfaction that they might not get anywhere else.

Chewing sticks serves several purposes: It passes the time, helps clean teeth and give jaws a workout, and gives dogs the satisfaction of destroying something.

Even dogs who aren't thinking about chewing will often do it once they have sticks in their mouths, adds Jeff Nichol, D.V.M., a veterinarian in Albuquerque, New Mexico. Dogs put all kinds of things in their mouths—not just sticks, but stones, old shoes, and leaves. It's their way of exploring new things. "Once something is in their mouths, regardless of why they picked it up in the first place, lots of dogs just start chewing," he says.

Once they've chomped down, sticks provide instant gratification, he adds. They have a firm texture and a little bit of crunch, which dogs enjoy. Plus, they're relatively easy to shred, and dogs enjoy seeing that they're making progress.

Looks Right, Tastes Good

From the time they're puppies, most dogs are attracted to sticks more than most objects they come across. This is partly because wood is easy to chew, but it's also because of the shape—sticks look more or less like bones. Bones are what dogs would be eating if we didn't pour their food into ceramic dishes. They like the meaty flavors of bones, and the marrow inside is an excellent source of nutrients, Bebiak says.

Sticks don't taste at all like bones, of course, and dogs do know the difference. But sticks have their own appeal. They have a musky, earthy taste that seems to appeal to dogs. And of course, they can find them just about anywhere. "The logic seems to be, 'If I had a bone, I'd chew that. But since I don't, this will do,'" says Dr. Nichol.

Now That You Understand...

Veterinarians worry about stick chewing because dogs will occasionally swallow what they chew. A mouthful of splinters isn't likely to cause problems, but swallowing a large hunk of stick may. While some dogs do get overeager and gulp sticks as soon as they're small enough to swallow, most just chew and spit, so to speak, says Cynthia Jacobs, D.V.M., a veterinarian in Clarksville, Arkansas. Still, you'll want to be safe. Here are a few things to watch for.

Clear the yard of fruit branches. Dogs aren't very selective about the types of sticks they chew. This can be a problem if you have apple, pear, or other fruit trees. The wood has a rich, aromatic taste that dogs like, but it also contains small amounts of toxins that can upset dogs' stomachs, says Dr. Jacobs.

Other types of wood can also make dogs sick—in some cases, seriously so, says Dr. Jacobs. Branches from azaleas and trees such as black walnut, black cherry, red oak, black locust, yew, and red maple contain substantial amounts of poison. Dogs who chew enough of the wood can get very ill, she says. If you're not sure what type of wood your dog is chewing, keep it out of reach until you can make sure it's not one of the hazardous varieties.

Limit the size. If your dog is going to chew sticks, make sure they're too big to fit all the way in his mouth, Dr. Jacobs says. Smaller sticks have a way of getting stuck, and more than a few

Puppies need to chew to relieve the pain of teething. If they can't find sticks, they'll make do with a substitute such as a broom.

Small sticks may get swallowed or stuck inside dogs' mouths. The safest sticks to let them have are big ones, but remember to replace them before they're chewed into splinters.

dogs have found themselves with their jaws locked open because a stick got wedged inside. Big sticks have a way of turning into lots of little sticks, however. Once piles of debris begin accumulating, you'll want to clean them up before your dog has a chance to take them back into his mouth.

Make sure he's not a swallower. Most dogs just chomp and shred their sticks, leaving the wreckage on the ground around them. They don't actually ingest much, says Dr. Nichol. Some dogs, however, swallow what they chew. Besides the risk of choking or intestinal blockages, dogs who actually eat sticks sometimes use them in place of regular food. "Sticks don't begin to meet your dog's nutrition requirements," he says. "If he's making a habit of eating them, you should steer him toward a chew toy that he can play with but won't be likely to swallow."

BREED SPECIFIC

Rottweilers, Dobermans, and other "protection" dogs are among the most enthusiastic stick-chewers because they've been bred to work with their mouths. In addition, all of the retriever breeds are known for chewing.

FAST FIX If your dog is determined to chew and swallow sticks, you're going to have to keep him away from them and give him something safer. The problem with rubber toys is that a lot of dogs don't like them very much. A good alternative may be sterilized bones. Available in pet supply stores, sterilized bones are hard enough to last a long time, but they still have a little bit of give. And they don't break down into splinters or tiny bits, says Dr. Nichol.

The choicest sterilized bone, however, isn't going to taste anything like sticks—or bones, for that matter. That discourages a lot of dogs from giving them a try. You can overcome this by basting the bones. Soak them for 10 to 15 minutes in beef or chicken broth. The meaty flavor won't last long, but it will get your dog's interest. Once he starts chewing, there's a good chance that his instincts will kick in and keep him going. Once he's chewed the bone for a while, it will take on his personal scent, and that will make it even more attractive.

CHAPTER FORTY

Eating the Cat's Food

Stolen Food Is the Best, Especially When It Smells

For a couple of old fogies, Cocoa and Tar get along pretty well. Cocoa, a 10-year-old dachshund, and Tar, a 20-year-old black cat, peaceably share a house and a yard almost all the time. Conflicts only arise at mealtimes. Cocoa tries every trick in the book to score some of Tar's food. It doesn't matter whether there's food in her bowl or not; she always tries to get the cat's. She has tried being sneaky, bold, and begging, but neither Tar nor her owner, Renee Martin of Olive Branch, Mississippi, will let her get away with it.

Still, Renee can't help but be impressed with Cocoa's persistence. "If there's any way Cocoa can get that cat's food, she's going to try," she says. "She doesn't seem to care that she never wins. She keeps at it anyway."

Mmm, Sure Smells

At pet food companies, nutrition scientists and veterinarians put a lot of energy into making dog and cat food healthy. Taste is important, too, but more for cats than for dogs. Dogs have some pretty nondiscriminating ancestors, who were just as likely to eat something they found dead on the side of a ravine as something they hunted down themselves. They cared a lot more about filling their bellies than about how food tasted.

Cats are different. They're very particular about what they eat. In fact, some cats will literally stop eating if they can't have foods they like, says Joanne Howl, D.V.M., a veterinarian in West

Some dogs see cats as competitors for food and their owners' affection. Stealing their dinner makes dogs feel that they have the upper hand.

River, Maryland, and coauthor of *Your Cat's Life*. To create appealing meals, manufacturers use the best quality fish, meat, and other ingredients. More important, they make sure that cat food is really smelly, because cats won't eat it unless the odor announces itself loud and clear.

Dogs are attracted to cat food for the same reason they're attracted to week-old carrion. They like anything that smells. And cat food sure does smell. Given a choice between their nutritious but relatively bland food and that stinky bowl of cat food, they'll go for the cat food every time.

Even if cat food didn't taste and smell so great, dogs would probably go for it because they like variety, says Robin Kovary, director of the American Dog Trainers Network in New York City. "Dogs will put just about anything new, from cigarette butts to a Danish, in their mouths to check them out," she says. "Cat food is novel and it's yummy. That makes it pretty irresistible."

Friendly Competition

As if the tempting taste and aroma of cat food weren't enough of an attraction, dogs have another, more emotional reason for eating it. They're greedy for the good things in life—affection, attention, the best spot on the couch, and food. They view cats as rivals for all of these good things. If they can sink their teeth into their rivals' food, that's kind of like shopping with someone else's money.

"Dogs get jealous of cats," says Dr. Howl. "Eating the cats' food is a subtle way for a dog to get one over on them."

Actually, all stolen food tastes best, and a dog will happily raid another dog's bowl, even if the food is exactly the same as his own. "Dogs who want to show that they've got some authority in the house will eat the other dog's food first to make the point," Kovary says.

A Little Too Rich

Dog food is about 20 percent protein. Cats, who are carnivorous, need more protein—their foods are at least 30 percent protein. A dog who eats too much cat food is going to get diarrhea and an upset stomach. If he keeps eating it, he's going to get fat. His snacks from the cat bowl won't do his owners any good either, since cat food usually costs two or three times more than dog food.

The opposite scenario, that of a cat filching dog food, would be much more serious. Dog foods contain an amino acid called arginine, which cats can't digest. In fact, dog food can be life-threatening for cats. Since they very rarely eat it, however, this isn't likely to be an issue, says Dr. Howl.

Now That You Understand...

Dogs are predictable about committing the same indiscretions again and again. Once they develop a taste for cat food, they'll go to great lengths to keep getting it. Obviously, putting the cat's food in a bowl on the floor isn't going to stop them. Since cats are more agile than dogs and more adept at getting into places that dogs can't, it's easy enough to find places where the food will be safe from canine crooks.

Install a food protector. One way to keep the cat's food safe is to install a chain lock on a cabinet or utility room door. Depending on its length, such a lock will allow the door to open just enough to admit a cat, but not enough to let a dog get to the goodies inside. If you happen to have a very small dog, of course, this isn't going to work very well.

If your dog is truly committed to eating the cat's food, you may need to put the food behind a closed door—in a closet, for example—and install a cat door, Dr. Howl says. An easier solution may be to put a baby gate across the door-

way to the kitchen or utility room. Install it so it's a few inches above the floor. The food will be protected and your cat won't have any trouble getting in and out. If you happen to have a dachshund or another short breed, put the gate close to the floor and attach a small ledge on top. This will let your cat hop up and over.

Put the food high. Cats are the Michael Jordans of the animal world. They can jump astonishing distances without running starts. Dogs, on the other hand, couldn't do a slam dunk if they tried. Putting the cat's food on a high shelf or bookcase won't inconvenience the cat at all—most cats, in fact, prefer eating up high—and your dog won't be able to get at it.

FAST FIX Cats are intrigued by small, enclosed places. You can take advantage of this to create a safe food stash. Turn a wooden box upside down—packing crates work well because they're sufficiently heavy that dogs can't easily tip them over—and cut out a cat-size hole. Your cat will be in and out of the box all day, playing as well as eating, and your dog won't be able to squeeze his muzzle through, says Dr. Howl.

One way to foil cat-food thieves is to put the cat's dish up on a high place. The cat will feel safer, and the dish will be harder for the dog to reach.

CHAPTER FORTY-ONE

PREFER RAWHIDES TO RUBBER TOYS

Chewing and Swallowing Beat Just Chewing

The difference between chewing on rubber and chewing on rawhide is like the difference between chewing bubblegum and eating candy. Gum is great, but candy—well, who wants gum?

This concept explains why expensive rubber toys tend to lie forgotten under cushions on the couch, while rawhide chews are eagerly grabbed the instant they hit the floor. Rawhide chews are made from cow or water buffalo skin. They taste salty and a little meaty, and they have a nice texture—just what dogs like. And because rawhides absorb flavors, manufacturers can add an extra something that rubber-toy makers can't: Tasty bastes such as chicken, beef, and peanut butter. Dogs eat them up.

Rubber, of course, comes from plants, and there aren't many dogs who will pick a plant-and-chemical-based product over one that's nice and meaty.

Food versus Fun

It's not really fair to compare rawhides to rubber toys. Even though they're both designed for chewing, rawhides are a type of food, and rubber toys are, well, toys. They're meant to be played with and chewed, not swallowed. It's not impossible for dogs to eat rubber, but most don't. What they will do is throw rubber toys in the air, chew them for awhile, then toss them around some more.

"Rubber chew toys have a lot of mouth appeal," says Joanne Howl, D.V.M., a veterinarian in West River, Maryland. "The companies that make them do some really clever things with the textures, shapes, and firmness to make them fun for dogs to carry around."

One thing that dogs like about rubber toys is the squeezy factor. The more they bite down,

A rawhide bone will keep this American bulldog occupied for hours. It also cleans her teeth and gives her jaws a good workout.

the more the rubber bounces back up. This gives jaws quite a workout, which dogs enjoy. But most dogs don't settle down to gnaw on rubber toys they way they do with rawhide. They play with them, and they want people to play with them. Rubber toys are great for throwing. They hold up better than tennis balls. They stay relatively clean in the backyard, and they're a perfectly acceptable pacifier for dogs who like having something in their mouths all the time.

People like rubber toys too. For one thing, they're nearly indestructible, although dogs who try hard enough can sometimes reduce them to little rubber bits in a few hours. It's cheaper to buy one or two rubber toys than bag after bag of rawhides. And unlike rawhides, which have calories, protein, and fat, rubber toys won't make dogs fat—no matter how much they indulge.

Now That You Understand...

Get the right size. "If you give your 120-pound dog an itty-bitty rawhide bone for a treat, he's going to swallow it in about 2 minutes," says Dr. Howl. Rawhide is safe as long as dogs chew it up before swallowing, but large pieces may get stuck in their intestines, she explains. This usually won't cause medical problems, but it can lead to diarrhea.

Rawhide packages usually specify what size dogs the treats are for. This is only a starting point, says Dr. Howl. Watch your dog to see how long it takes him to finish a chew. It should take 2 days or more. Anything that he finishes quicker than that is probably too small, and he's going to have tummy trouble.

Rubber toys are better than rawhides for outdoor use because they're resilient, less likely to harbor germs, and easy to wash.

Beware of bastes. Dogs love flavored rawhides, but some of the flavors may not love them back. Dogs who are sensitive to the ingredients in different bastes may get diarrhea or other digestive complaints, says Dr. Howl. Try giving your dog unflavored rawhides to see if things improve.

Restore the flavor. Some dogs will only chew basted rawhides. The flavors don't last forever, however. Once the baste is gone, dogs will often abandon the chews and ask for new ones. Rawhides are expensive, so it's worth restoring used chews to their former flavorful selves.

Mark Beckloff, co-owner of Three Dog Bakery treat shops, based in Kansas City, Missouri, has developed a number of bastes, such as low-sodium tomato sauce thinned with a little water and spiced up with cheese, or beef broth thickened with a little flour and water, or simply beaten eggs. Dip the rawhides in the baste, then bake them in a 250°F oven until the baste dries.

Dogs love all three flavors, which usually will have to be reapplied every few days.

Keep rawhide inside. Rawhides that have been chewed and slobbered on for a few days become magnets for bacteria. In fact, the diarrhea that dogs sometimes get after chewing rawhides is probably caused by germs that had a chance to multiply. Bacteria in the house are less likely to be a problem, so that's where your dog should do his chewing.

Rubber toys are perfect for outside chewing, adds Char Bebiak, an animal behaviorist and head trainer at the Purina Pet Care Center in Gray Summit, Missouri. Rubber is impermeable, so bacteria are unlikely to multiply. Plus, you can easily wash the toys whenever they get too grungy.

Make rubber better. For dogs who don't like or can't tolerate rawhide but still want to chew, you'll need to get rubber toys that have taste appeal. Toys such as Kong, available in pet supply stores, are designed to be stuffed with food, such as peanut butter or cheese. Rubber toys that smell and taste like a peanut butter sandwich are in a whole different league from plain rubber. Even when the food is gone, dogs will continue to gnaw, chew, and paw them to get to the flavors inside.

A Difference in Tastes

The reason that beef, chicken, and peanut butter rawhides are such big sellers is that people are convinced their dogs will like them. The dogs, however, wish that someone would ask their opinion for a change. It's not that dogs don't like beef and chicken. They do. But what they really, really like, and what their owners never seem to buy, is something a little more pungent: garlic.

The Pet Factory, a rawhide manufacturer based in Mundelein, Illinois, has tested untold numbers of taste combinations. The testers, of course, are dogs. The one chew that dogs love best is called the Field Chew, which has been basted with garlic, liver, and brewer's yeast. This is far from the company's top seller, however, because people are convinced their dogs want something beefy. In addition, the ingredients, from a human point of view, are a little off-putting.

"We don't call it the 'Garlic, Liver, and Brewer's Yeast Bone' for a reason," says Doug Van Treeck, general manager of the Pet Factory. "No matter how great it tastes to dogs, it just doesn't appeal to people."

This may explain why one of the company's rawhide products has been flavored with vanilla. Vanilla is a ho-hum flavor for dogs, but people love the smell, so that's what they take home.

CHAPTER FORTY-TWO

PLAYING TUG-OF-WAR

The Thrill of Competition, the Joy of Chewing

Dogs start pulling almost from the time they're born. Their first instinct is to latch on to their mothers and pull—it gets the milk flowing. Then they pull on their littermates' tails. They pull on their blankets. They pull on everything they can get their mouths around, and they keep pulling throughout their lives. "You'd have a hard time finding a dog who'll walk away from a game of tug," says Kennon A. Lattal, Ph.D., a certified applied animal behaviorist in the department of psychology at West Virginia University in Morgantown. "The mouth is the only grasping tool they have available, and tugging is almost what they're designed for."

Winning the contest isn't just about getting possession of the Frisbee. It's a chance for one dog to prove his superiority over the other.

It's Good to Win

Dogs are just as competitive as people—maybe more. The games they love best nearly always have clear winners and losers. Losers come away from games knowing that they're a rung down on the social ladder. Winners come away with bragging rights.

Tugging is a wonderful game because there's no ambiguity at the end. One dog tugs and gains the prize. The other goes home empty-handed.

"If you have a dog who's very submissive, letting him win at tug-of-war can give him the confidence boost that he needs," says writer Steve Dale of Chicago, whose syndicated column "My Pet World" appears in papers nationwide.

Dogs who are unusually assertive, on the other hand, tend to win a lot at all games. They love tug-of-war because it's another opportunity to show how strong and talented they are. For this reason alone, it's a good idea not to let them beat you too often when you're playing tug-of-war, says Dr. Lattal. It will only feed their already overstuffed egos.

A Controversial Game

For every dog who loves tug-of-war, there's a trainer who's not so sure. Because it's such a competitive game, it can bring out a dog's worst instincts as he pits himself against his owner.

A dog who goes head-to-head with people may start thinking that their relationship is always a level playing field, and that's not an attitude that you want a dog to have.

Dogs with unusually dominant personalities or those who have shown signs of aggression probably shouldn't play tug-of-war at all, says Dr. Lattal. For most dogs, however, it's a healthy kind of competition. It gives them a chance to get physical and stretch their bodies. And it's an acceptable outlet for some of those canine urges that often get expressed in other, less acceptable ways.

"They can mouth all they want, slobber if they want, and pull as hard as they like, and it's all fine," says Dale. In fact, tug-of-war is about the only way that dogs can indulge two of their passions—chewing and interacting with people—at the same time.

Now That You Understand...

Choose your tug toy. Dogs who truly adore tug-of-war will start viewing everything as a potential toy. To avoid spending the rest of your life prying socks from your dog's jaws, pick one or two tug toys—a length of rope works well, as do the 2-handled rubber pullers sold in pet supply stores—and never use anything else, says Dr. Lattal.

Stack the odds. It's hard to play tug-of-war with strong dogs because, pound for pound, they're a lot stronger than we are. To keep the game from ending too quickly, use a tug rope that has a loop for gripping at your end and is tapered at the dog's end. This reduces the amount of pressure he can put into his grip,

Dogs love playing tug, but it's important to keep the game under control and to ensure that you win more often than they do.

giving you a distinct advantage. This may sound unfair, but your dog won't know the difference. More important, it ensures that you'll win most of the time, which will help your dog accept the fact that you're the leader after all.

Stop when you hear sound effects. Tug-of-war is always competitive, and it's normal for dogs to make little *grrr*'s when they're giving it their all. But growling has a way of turning into snarling, and snarling can lead to biting, says Dr. Lattal. Bites that occur during tug-of-war are usually accidental, but that hardly matters. They signal a level of aggression that's going to cause all kinds of problems—not just during the game itself, but in other ways.

Growling means it's time to stop the game, says Dr. Lattal. Put down the tug toy. Go into the kitchen to get a treat. Then make your dog sit before you hand it over. What you're telling him is that, regardless of the game, you're the one he has to listen to, and proper behavior and discipline are still expected.

CHAPTER FORTY-THREE

GETTING WET

It's Cool, Refreshing, and Filthy

There are dogs who like water and dogs who won't have anything to do with it. Then there's Dancer. A 3-year-old Land-seer Newfoundland, Dancer loves water so much and swims so well that she could be a lifeguard. In fact, Newfoundlands are so adept in the water that breeders have developed a swimming test that human swimmers would struggle to complete. For Dancer to pass the test, she had to dive into a river and retrieve a life jacket and a cushion, in that order, that were floating 50 feet from shore. Then she had to swim 75 feet out to a rowboat with two occupants yelling for help, pass them a line, tow the boat to shore, and beach it. Finally, she had to "save" her own handler, Joyce Echon of Aliquippa, Pennsylvania, when she went into the water.

Labradors were bred to work in water. Like this puppy, they'll usually take every chance to swim or splash in whatever water they can find.

"Dancer has been swimming since she was 10 weeks old," Echon says. "She took to the water like a duck."

People have been breeding water dogs for a long time. These are the dogs who enjoy the water most. "Golden, Labrador, and Chesapeake Bay retrievers; Newfoundlands; and poodles all have strong histories with water," says Sandy Myers, a behavior consultant at Narnia Pet Behavior and Training in Plainfield, Illinois. "Their ancestors were bred because they showed enthusiasm for wading in without hesitation. After all, no hunter wants a retriever who doesn't want to get his feet wet in a swamp."

More Than Genetics

Much as people try to predict dogs' personalities according to their breeds, every dog is an individual. There are plenty of Labradors who hate getting wet and plenty of dry-dock dogs who will splash right in. "I've seen a West Highland terrier who'll dive into anything and swim underwater with his eyes wide open, and there are Labs who don't even want to take a bath," says Char Bebiak, an animal behaviorist and head trainer at the Purina Pet Care Center in Gray Summit, Missouri.

Since hunting isn't as popular as it used to be, many breeders don't worry if their dogs take to the water or not. The love of water has

become less of an innate characteristic than it used to be. Still, dogs keep getting wet. "They like water for a lot of the same reasons people do," says Vint Virga, D.V.M., a veterinarian at the College of Veterinary Medicine at Cornell University in Ithaca, New York. "It's cool and refreshing and fun to play with."

Deep in Muck

Even though dogs and people both like water, they differ in their choices of swimming holes. Give dogs a choice between a sparkling-clean swimming pool and a deep, murky, mucky puddle, and most will take the muck every time. No one is sure why they do it, but it's probably because way back in their evolutionary pasts, it made sense to cover their personal smells with something else.

"Just like hunters wear camouflage or special scents to conceal themselves from their prey, dogs may have an urge to put on the smells of their environment to make them blend in," Dr. Virga says. A dog who reeked of dirty water was essentially telling both prey and predators, "Ain't nothing here but a bunch of slime."

This may explain why dogs will fight like crazy when you give them baths, then rush to the nearest puddle as soon as you let them out.

Now That You Understand...

Dry those ears. Dogs who spend a lot of time in the water have a high risk of getting ear infections. Those with big, floppy ears, such as beagles and Labradors, have the highest risk because their ears trap moisture. Taking a minute

A big expanse of dirty water just adds to the fun of a game of chase for these three salukis.

to swab the insides of your dog's wet ears with the corner of a towel will reduce the risk of infections, Dr. Virga says.

Rinse their feet. Just as wet ears are prone to infections, wet feet can also be a problem, especially when dogs have been wading in dirty, bacteria-filled water, says Lynn Cox, D.V.M., a veterinarian in Olive Branch, Mississippi. He recommends rinsing your dog's feet with clean water after she has been wading. Or you can wipe the pads and between the toes with baby wipes.

Take your own water. Dogs who wallow in pond water usually drink a lot of it too. Their digestive tracts are much tougher than ours, and they're unlikely to get seriously ill. But even a mild infection can cause diarrhea, so it's worth giving them water from home. The more fresh water your dog drinks—adding $1/2$ cup of beef broth to a gallon of water will make it much more interesting—the less likely she'll be to imbibe a few quarts of pond water.

PART FIVE

"My Body Makes Me Do It"

When Anatomy Is Destiny

Living with dogs means encountering a wide-ranging spectrum of four-pawed faux pas. They don't mean to be rude. It's just that their bodies make them do things that humans wouldn't dream of doing.

CHAPTER FORTY-FOUR

AVOIDING HARDWOOD FLOORS
The Risk of Rollovers

It all started when Brendan Murphy of Olive Branch, Mississippi, dropped a grape. Francine, the family's yellow Labrador, scrambled to be the first one to get to it. She lost her footing on the hardwood floor and kicked it away instead. Determined, she lunged again. She slid straight into a wine rack, sending a red Bordeaux crashing to the floor. The startled, wine-spattered dog finally grabbed the grape, made her way through the rubble, and retreated to the relative safety of the carpet (white, unfortunately) in the next room to eat her prize.

Brendan, who's 6, thought it was pretty funny. "Francine didn't mean it," he said. "She just needs some practice on slippery floors."

Francine bounded right back onto the slippery wooden floor an hour later, but lots of dogs aren't so brave. After taking one hard fall, they may remain nervous about these treacherous surfaces for years afterward.

Clumsy by Nature

Anyone who's taken a turn on skates knows what it feels like for dogs to venture onto a hardwood floor. "It's how walking on ice is for people," says Benjamin Hart, D.V.M., Ph.D., professor of physiology and behavior at the University of California School of Veterinary Medicine at Davis and author of *The Perfect Puppy: How to Choose Your Dog by Its Behavior.* "Dogs have a hard time getting their footing, so they slip and slide. They know that if they fall, it's going to hurt."

Part of the problem is that dogs can't spread their front legs in order to get traction. When

Covering wooden floors with rugs or mats will help prevent dogs from slipping. The mats should have rubber backings for a better grip.

they try, especially when they do it quickly, it tends to hurt. After doing the splits a few times, they learn to avoid hardwood floors when they can. When they can't, they pick their way carefully across.

In addition, dogs don't have the kind of balance that people—or cats—take for granted. Their paw pads tend to be dry and callused, which reduces the amount of traction they can generate. And unlike cats, who have the ability to retract their claws, a dog's nails are always out, which reduces traction power even more, says Merry Crimi, D.V.M., a veterinarian in Milwaukie, Oregon.

Dogs who have grown up around hardwood floors know how to balance and have less of a problem, Dr. Hart adds. But those who are encountering them for the first time can have a hard time adjusting.

The Bigger They Are, The Harder They Fall

It's usually big dogs who have the most trouble with wood floors, says Jeff Nichol, D.V.M., a veterinarian in Albuquerque, New Mexico. Partly, this is because they have long legs and heavy bodies. When they fall, they fall hard. They also have a high center of gravity that works against them on slick surfaces.

"It's hard for them to stop falling once they lose their footing," Dr. Nichol says. "When a big, heavy dog lets one leg slip out from under him, it's going to go straight out, and there's not a lot he can do to stop it."

Another reason big dogs struggle with wood floors is that many of them have hip dysplasia,

CALL FOR HELP

Dogs who are most nervous about hardwood floors tend to be those who have other aches and pains and are wisely concerned about hurting themselves more. German shepherds, Labradors, and golden retrievers have a high risk of developing arthritis. Even if they don't fall, just slipping on a floor can cause a sudden jolt of pain, says Jeff Nichol, D.V.M., a veterinarian in Albuquerque, New Mexico.

If your dog is unusually gingerly about stepping on slick floors, or he's starting to have trouble getting up or getting around, he may have joint problems that need looking into. Veterinarians have begun doing hip-replacement and other types of joint surgery, but most dogs will improve with anti-inflammatory medications, Dr. Nichol explains. There are a number of new drugs that can reduce the pain and swelling of damaged joints without causing the side effects of some of the older drugs.

says Dr. Nichol. This is a hereditary condition in which one or both hip joints aren't as stable as they should be. Dogs with hip dysplasia may be a little clumsy, and the pain of slipping or falling is one they're likely to remember.

"Dogs who fall a few times are going to get anxious around the floors that trip them up," says Dr. Nichol. "They often get this head-down, hunkered-down, 'Oh, no, I've got to cross over this again' body language that tells you how much they hate it."

Now That You Understand...

Flip on a night-light. Dogs see a little better in the dark than people, but they're nothing like cats. Things that go bump in the night are often dogs trying to find the water bowl. The danger zones tend to be where carpets suddenly give way to wood floors. The unexpected transition from solid to slick can send them flying, says Dr. Crimi. She recommends using night-lights in areas where dogs have to walk across hardwood or polished linoleum floors. They're less likely to fall when they can see that the surface is changing, she explains.

Keep the nails short. Dogs with long toenails are at a disadvantage the minute they step on hardwood floors. The nails themselves are hard and skittery, and when they get long, dogs spread their toes slightly as they walk. This reduces stability and balance, says Dr. Nichol.

Most dogs need their nails trimmed every month or so. Older dogs need trims more often because they don't get as much exercise, which means the nails don't wear down as quickly as they grow.

Dogs dislike having their nails trimmed, so it's always a struggle to keep them short. You'll want to be conservative when doing the cutting. If you look carefully, you'll see a pink line, called the quick, extending from the base of the nail toward the tip. (For dogs with dark-colored nails, holding a flashlight to the nail will reveal the quick.) The quick is loaded with nerve endings and blood vessels. As long as you cut below the quick so that you don't cut into it, most dogs will learn to put up with occasional trims, says Dr. Nichol.

Make a path. Dogs who are perpetually slipping and sliding will be much happier if you make a path across hardwood floors, using rubber-backed mats or carpet runners. Don't depend on unbacked carpets or throw rugs because they slide around too much, advises Dr. Nichol.

Play on the carpets. It's fun to roll balls across hardwood floors and watch dogs go skating after them. Some dogs like this, too, but it's not a safe way to play, says Dr. Nichol. Slipping puts a lot of pressure on muscles, joints, and ligaments. And dogs who take a hard fall can damage their joints. Any game that requires running, twisting, or turning should be done on a carpeted area or outside, he advises.

A carpeted floor provides the best indoor playing surface for dogs. They can get traction and are less likely to slip and get hurt.

CHAPTER FORTY-FIVE

DOGGY BREATH

Bad Hygiene, Worse Appetites

Ebbie is a therapy dog who accompanies her owner, Cynthia Whittaker of East Meredith, New York, when she delivers Meals on Wheels to elderly neighbors. A 2-year-old yellow Lab, Ebbie has adoring eyes and a constantly wagging tail. Everyone looks forward to her visits.

Except for one thing: Ebbie's breath is rotten enough to curl hair, and her well-meaning kisses are often received with grimaces of disgust. Whittaker tried brushing Ebbie's teeth, but it didn't help at all.

Ebbie is hardly the only dog with horrific halitosis, which is why "doggy breath" has become a cliché for any odor that's unpleasantly pungent. Part of this is due to hygiene. We all know what our breath smells like when we don't brush our teeth for a day, and dogs never brush theirs. In addition, dogs put their mouths in all sorts of places. They chew moldy tennis balls and lick their bottoms. They eat trash—and the older and smellier it is, the more they like it.

"If your dog helps himself to the cat box, then comes over and gives you a big wet kiss, you're going to smell it," says Robin Downing, D.V.M., a veterinarian in Windsor, Colorado. "That type of bad breath, mercifully, will go away on its own."

Bad Teeth, Bad Smells

For many dogs, however, the bad breath never goes away. Veterinarians estimate that nearly 90 percent of dogs have periodontal disease. This is a condition in which a bacteria-laden film called plaque hardens on the teeth, causing gum infections that often result in a rotten kind of smell, says Dr. Downing.

It's a fairly recent problem, she adds. Dogs who lived in the wild didn't live very long, usually 5 or 6 years. They weren't around long enough to get tooth decay. Dogs today live 12 or more years. The window of opportunity for

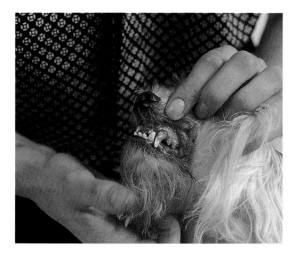

Gum disease, which sets in when food particles rot and harden on the teeth, is suspect number one when dogs develop persistent bad breath.

137

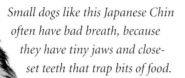

Small dogs like this Japanese Chin often have bad breath, because they have tiny jaws and close-set teeth that trap bits of food.

dental problems to set in—with the resulting smelly breath—is much bigger than it used to be.

Diets have also changed. Dogs get their food delivered in a dish. It's convenient, tasty, and easy to chew. So easy, in fact, that their teeth don't get much of a workout. As plaque accumulates, dogs' breath begins to stink. Contrast this to wild dogs. They were hunters. For their suppers, they tore apart chunks of meat and spent hours working over bones. Every meal provided tooth scrapings that a dental hygienist could only envy.

Finally, humans have bred dogs with small jaws and close-set teeth. Food particles easily get trapped, and infection in one place easily spreads to another. Tooth decay has become a real problem, and so has smelly breath.

I Can't Believe I Ate the Whole Thing

Dental problems are one cause of doggy breath, but they're not the only one. Dogs have table manners that, with all charity, can only be called gross. They stuff themselves silly, then release windy burps. They tip over trash cans and devour the contents. They eat discarded junk that they find on the sidewalk. It's not the healthiest diet, and their stomachs pay the price.

"You can tell how dogs are doing on the inside by how they smell on the outside," says Dr. Downing. "Bad breath that comes and goes is probably the result of temporary stomach upset or dietary indiscretions." Other internal problems can also cause bad breath. Dogs with kidney disease, for example, often have breath with a sour, metallic smell.

Now That You Understand...

Scour their teeth with rawhide. "Thick, knotted rawhide bones are terrific for dogs' teeth," says Dr. Downing. As the rawhide gets softer from being chewed, it works like a sponge to clean the teeth.

Dogs just adore trash and will pick it up from anywhere. Naturally, their breath isn't particularly sweet after a smelly snack from the gutter.

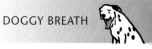

Encouraging dogs to drink after they've eaten will help wash away food particles that attract bacteria and cause bad breath.

What's good for the teeth isn't necessarily good for the stomach, Dr. Downing adds. Big dogs tend to swallow big chunks of rawhide, which can give them diarrhea when they eat too much of it.

Switch to a tooth-cleaning diet. A recently developed dry dog food called Hill's Prescription Diet t/d (the "t/d" stands for tartar diet) doesn't shatter like conventional kibble when dogs bite down. It stays partly intact. This means that each piece of food momentarily wraps around a tooth and scours the surface, Dr. Downing explains. It won't remove plaque that has already formed, but it will prevent new deposits from accumulating.

Buy clean-breath toys. Dogs who are chewers enjoy tearing into rope toys, which act like dental floss and clean between their teeth. In addition, pet supply stores sell chew toys with grooves and ridges. "If you put a little dog toothpaste in the grooves, your dog will brush his own teeth while he's chewing," says Dr. Downing.

Brush their teeth now and then. The best way to improve dogs' breath is to brush their teeth a few times a week. You can use a doggy toothbrush, but many people find that it's easier to rub the outer surfaces of the teeth with a small piece of gauze wrapped around a finger. (The inner surfaces are pretty much self-cleaning because they're constantly bathed with saliva.) Friction alone will remove much of the plaque, but you'll get better results using a toothpaste made for dogs. These come in appetizing (for dogs if not for people) flavors like malt and meat, Dr. Downing says.

Mix fresh vegetables into their food. It's too bad that dogs don't like parsley, because it contains compounds that act as natural breath fresheners. Fresh vegetables, however, are almost as good. Uncooked baby carrots and green beans clean the teeth—if your dog will eat them.

FAST FIX Dogs who drink water after eating are less likely to have bad breath, because water rinses away food particles that bacteria feed on. Dogs prefer fresh water, so changing it often is the best way to encourage them to drink, says Dr. Downing.

Veterinarians sometimes recommend flushing the teeth and gums with a Water Pik. An alternative is to let them drink directly from the hose, which many dogs enjoy doing.

CHAPTER FORTY-SIX

DROOLING WHEN THE FOOD BAG RATTLES

Too Excited to Swallow

Nearly 100 years ago, Ivan Pavlov and his dogs became famous worldwide for their demonstrations of what came to be called the conditioned response. Pavlov would ring a bell, then feed the dogs. After a while, the dogs started drooling the minute they heard the dinner bell, whether dinner was forthcoming or not.

Ever since then, everyone's assumed that food—or the mere idea of food—will make dogs salivate. It does, but so do many other things. In fact, dogs will drool almost anytime they get excited, says Jeff Nichol, D.V.M., a veterinarian in Albuquerque, New Mexico.

"If you've watched a 2-year-old at a Disney movie, you may have seen the same principle in action," says Dr. Nichol. "They get so wrapped up in the excitement of what they're watching, they just forget to swallow."

Research has shown that the salivary glands kick into overdrive when dogs (and people) start thinking about or actually smelling food. It's the body's way of starting the digestive process. But all sorts of thing can trigger a similar

Dogs often drool when they get excited. The sight of dinner being prepared is more than enough to start this mixed breed salivating. Other dogs may drool at the sight of sticks or the prospect of a walk.

response. The anticipation of a walk or going for a ride will turn many dogs into veritable faucets.

"I had an Airedale once who stood in rapt fascination over a turtle for about 45 minutes," Dr. Nichol remembers. "And for 45 minutes, he drooled a steady stream on the floor. He just completely forgot everything else except what he was watching."

We often joke about people who can't walk and chew gum at the same time. That's actually a pretty good comparison of what happens with excited dogs. They can't concentrate and swallow at the same time.

Some breeds, such as Newfoundlands, drool more than others because they have loose lips that catch saliva and frequently overflow.

Great Danes. These dogs have been bred to have pendulous lips. This has created little pockets inside the mouth that act as drool basins, explains John Simon, D.V.M., a veterinarian in Royal Oak, Michigan, and author of *What Your Dog Is Trying to Tell You*. It's not that they drool more than other breeds. It's just that the lip pockets frequently fill up and overflow.

Now That You Understand...

Withhold the leftovers. A dog who drools at the rattle of kibble is going to drool even more at the prospect of steak scraps or other fatty leftovers from the human table. It's not merely great-tasting food that causes heavier salivation—rich foods can upset a dog's stomach. A simpler diet won't stop drooling, but it may reduce the deluge somewhat.

Dress him in style. Tying a bandanna around your dog's neck is an easy way to blot the moisture and keep the fur on the chest dry. Fold the bandanna in half, corner to corner, and tie it around your dog's neck so that the triangle hangs over the chest. Bandannas look stylish and will go a long way toward keeping the fur—and your pants legs and the furniture—a little drier.

Provide a place setting. Since dogs do their heaviest drooling when they're eating (or waiting to eat), you may want to buy a package of paper place mats and put them under your dog's bowl. You'll have fewer puddles to clean up when he's done.

Designed to Drool

Hot weather and simple physiology also explain why dogs get moist around the mouth. They respond to heat—as well as to stress—by panting. Their humid exhalations create a lot of moisture. Since they pant with their tongues out, all of that moisture runs downhill instead of backward toward the throat. Forget swallowing. They may lick their chops to mop up the moisture, but for the most part, they just drip, says Dr. Nichol.

Even dogs who don't drool very much in the kitchen may do it in the car. One of the first signs of car sickness—or anything else that upsets the stomach—is heavy drooling.

Drooling tends to be exaggerated in basset hounds, bulldogs, Saint Bernards, mastiffs, and

CHAPTER FORTY-SEVEN

LICKING THEIR FEET

Nearly Everything Makes Them Itchy

Imagine going through life without being able to scratch certain parts of your body. People are lucky in this regard. We have long arms and fingers that can reach just about anywhere. It isn't so easy for dogs. Despite their flexible spines and mobile hind legs, there are spots that they can't reach very well, such as the tops of their noses, the bases of their tails, and especially the bottoms of their feet.

Dogs' paw pads are loaded with nerve endings and are unusually sensitive, says Jeff Nichol, D.V.M., a veterinarian in Albuquerque, New Mexico. "When dogs get itchy, the feet are the place most likely to be affected." Since they can't use one paw to scratch the other, they use their tongues and teeth, and the biting and slurping can go on for hours.

There are several reasons that the feet are so prone to itching. For one thing, dogs don't wear shoes, which means their feet come into contact with all sorts of irritating, itchy things. In addition, they get allergies just as often as people do.

Dogs can be allergic to many things, and it's mostly their feet that feel the effects. Even walking or lying on newly mown grass can be enough to make them itchy, and they'll bite and lick their feet to get relief.

The main symptom of canine allergies is itchy feet. What they're allergic to doesn't matter all that much, Dr. Nichol adds. Food, pollen, dust, and fleas are all potential allergens that seem to affect the feet worst of all. Some dogs get itchy feet just from walking across a newly mown lawn.

Pause for Pedicures

Unlike cats, who happily spend hours grooming themselves each day, dogs are singularly grungy. They don't worry much about dirt. In fact, they seem to go out of their way to get dirty. Despite this general indifference to hygiene, they take very good care of their feet. At least a few times

a day, they inspect their feet closely, then lick and bite away things that happens to be stuck, like pebbles, burrs, or splinters, says Craig N. Carter, D.V.M., Ph.D., head of epidemiology at Texas Veterinary Medical Diagnostic Laboratories at Texas A & M University in College Station.

Normal foot grooming shouldn't take more than a few minutes, Dr. Carter adds. Dogs who lick or bite their feet all the time aren't simply being clean. There's something wrong, and they're trying to get relief.

Despite their passion for keeping their feet clean, dogs don't like it when anyone else touches them, says Dr. Carter. This may be because the feet are somewhat ticklish. It's not uncomfortable when they lick their own feet, but they don't want anyone else to do it. Even when they're among other dogs, the feet are off-limits. It may be that they have an instinctive aversion to having their feet handled.

"A dog's feet are everything to him," Dr. Carter adds. "Dogs depend on them to survive, so it's no wonder that they're protective about letting anyone touch them."

Now That You Understand...

Soak them in oatmeal water. The colloidal oatmeal sold in pharmacies is very helpful for reducing itching, says Dr. Nichol. Put a few inches of cool water in the tub or a basin, mix in a handful of the oatmeal, and let your dog stand in the solution for a few minutes. Even if you don't add oatmeal, cool water shrinks blood vessels in the feet, which will help reduce itching.

Protect the skin with fatty acids. Some dogs get itchy feet because they aren't getting

---

CALL FOR HELP

Allergies themselves are usually mild, but the way in which dogs react to them can be a real problem. Some dogs lick and bite their feet for hours, day after day. The constant moisture and friction can result in deep, hard-to-heal sores called lick granulomas. The sores are painful and often get infected, and they rarely respond to home treatments. Any sore on the paws that doesn't start getting better within a few days needs to be treated by a veterinarian.

---

enough fatty acids in their diets. Fatty acid supplements, available in pet supply stores and from veterinarians, can be very effective. They don't work quickly, however, so it may be a month or two before you notice any improvement.

Ask your vet about food allergies. People who are allergic to the proteins in certain foods will usually get hives or upset stomachs. Dogs with food allergies are more likely to get itchy feet. The only way to tell if your dog is allergic to something that he's eating is to put him on a totally different diet—one that contains none of the ingredients in his usual food. You can buy hypoallergenic foods from veterinarians and in pet supply stores. If food allergies are the problem, the itching should clear up in 8 to 10 weeks. At that point, ask your veterinarian to recommend a food that's less likely to cause itching later on.

Use antihistamines. Allergies can be difficult to identify, and some veterinarians don't

Petroleum jelly applied to dogs' paw pads once or twice a day will create a barrier against itch-inducing allergens.

Get rid of fleas. Flea bites themselves aren't very itchy, but some dogs have allergic reactions to flea saliva. The easiest way to get rid of fleas is usually with either an oral drug such as Program or a topical liquid called Advantage. Both of these products will control fleas much more effectively than sprays or powders, says Dottie LaFlamme, D.V.M., Ph.D., a veterinary nutritionist with the Purina company in St. Louis.

Don't bother with bad tastes. A traditional (and ineffective) remedy for foot licking is to coat the paw pads with a bad-tasting ointment such as Grannick's Bitter Apple. While this and other repellents may keep dogs away from your shoes or the furniture, they won't help with foot licking, because the itching is usually too intense—dogs aren't going to let a little bad taste get in the way.

bother. Instead, they advise treating the symptoms with antihistamines. Diphenhydramine (Benadryl) can be very helpful, says Dr. Nichol. He recommends giving 1 to 2 milligrams for every 8 pounds of weight.

FAST FIX Coating your dog's foot pads with petroleum jelly once or twice a day will help trap moisture and keep them from cracking and itching, says Dr. Carter. Unlike most hand creams and lotions, petroleum jelly also creates a strong physical barrier that will help keep molds and pollens off the pads.

BREED SPECIFIC

Despite their tough appearances, Dobermans and German shepherds (right) are real pussycats when it comes to sore feet. They're no more likely than other breeds to have foot problems, but they do tend to be more sensitive to pain and will complain more.

CHAPTER FORTY-EIGHT

Smelly Gas

It Depends on the Menu

All mammals produce intestinal gas, and dogs are no exception. Compared to cows, which produce upward of 60 quarts of gas a day, dogs are relatively modest in their output. What they lack in quantity, however, they make up for in pungency—their gas is unusually smelly. Even a small dog can clear a large room, and bigger dogs, especially those who are real food-hounds, can be downright unpleasant to be around.

"Part of the reason we notice dogs' gas so much is that dogs haven't been taught to hold it in," says Dottie LaFlamme, D.V.M., Ph.D., a veterinary nutritionist with the Ralston Purina Company in St. Louis. "They don't go out of the room to pass it."

Protein In, Smells Out

The intestinal tract is filled with bacteria that help process foods and aid in digestion. As part of their natural metabolism, the bacteria release clouds of sulfurous gases, which gives intestinal gas its unpleasant smell. The more protein there is in the diet, the stronger the smell.

Cows and other herbivores produce a lot of gas, but there isn't enough meat-based protein in their diets to create large amounts of sulfur gases. Dogs, on the other hand, eat a lot of protein—quite a bit more than most people, says Dr. LaFlamme. They don't necessarily have a lot of gas, but when they do, it's powerful stuff.

It's not only protein that contributes to high-octane gas—it's also the type of protein. Many commercial dog foods get their protein from animal by-products—feathers, for example, or ground-up bone. These ingredients are harder for dogs to digest than protein that comes from "whole" foods, such as chicken meat or eggs, says Dawn Curie Thomas, D.V.M., a veterinarian in Santa Barbara, California,

Dogs love human foods, but their bodies often can't cope with them. The result is often more gas than usual—and it will be smellier than usual, too.

and author of *The 100 Most Common Questions That Pet Owners Ask the Vet.* The harder the body has to work to process protein, the more flatulent a dog is going to be, she explains.

Food Allergies and Sensitivities

A surprising number of dogs are sensitive to ingredients in their food. For example, milk is a common ingredient in dog food, but many dogs have a condition that makes it difficult for them to digest it. This condition, called lactose intolerance, can make dogs extremely gassy, says Dr. LaFlamme.

Food allergies are another problem. Dogs who are allergic to ingredients such as soy or wheat aren't able to digest their food efficiently and tend to be gassy. They often get diarrhea as well.

One way to tell if your dog is sensitive to something in his diet is to write down every single thing he's had to eat within the 24 hours preceding the gassy episodes. Sometimes something as simple as switching to a different brand of treats will make intestinal gas a little less unpleasant. Your veterinarian may recommend putting your dog on a diet called an elimination diet. He'll be given a hypoallergenic food containing ingredients he's never had before. If the gas goes away, you'll know that something in his food was causing it.

Now That You Understand...

Switch to a premium food. Sometimes just switching from a low-cost dog food to a premium brand such as Innova will reduce gas, says Susan Wynn, D.V.M., a veterinarian in

Switching to a premium food that contains high-quality ingredients will usually help decrease dogs' flatulence.

Marietta, Georgia. Read labels before you make the change. What you're looking for is a food that lists whole ingredients such as chicken, beef, lamb, and egg at the top of the ingredient list. If you see the word by-products among the first few ingredients, you'll know the food is going to be more difficult to digest.

Experiment with flavors. Every dog reacts differently to different foods. If you notice the gas is increasing when your dog eats a beef-and-potato-based food, switch to one with lamb or rice, or even one containing venison or rabbit and potato.

Ask your veterinarian about lower-protein foods. Since it's mainly protein that makes a dog's gas so smelly, you may want to switch to a lower-protein food, especially if your dog has been eating a high-performance chow. Some foods supply more protein than dogs need. You can cut back without compromising good nutrition. Protein is a key ingredient in

Fewer rawhides can mean less gas. Dogs who swallow bits of rawhides, rather than just chewing them, often get gas from the excess protein. In addition, the large amount of air that they swallow while chewing them can also cause flatulence.

every diet, however, so talk to your veterinarian before making the change, says Dr. Thomas.

If you do decide to change foods, do it gradually. Dogs who are suddenly switched from one food to another tend to get diarrhea, says Dr. Thomas. You can make the transition more comfortable—and less gassy—by adding a little bit of the new food to your dog's usual diet for a few days. Each day, gradually increase the amount of the new food while cutting back on the original. You'll know in a month if switching foods is going to help, she says.

Take human foods off the menu. Dogs will eat just about anything, but their bodies aren't designed to handle most of the foods people eat. "Table scraps are often the culprit," says Dr. LaFlamme. "If you're slipping your dog

bologna or cheese or ice cream, that may be what's causing the problem."

Get rid of the rawhides. Dogs love these tough, chewy little treats, but rawhides don't always love them back. They're very high in protein, and dogs who eat a lot of them tend to get gassy—not just because of the protein, but because they swallow buckets of air while chewing them, says Dr. LaFlamme. Give your dog some other treats for a few weeks and see if the air improves, she suggests. Or give him larger, tightly tied rawhide bones, which take longer to eat.

Give digestion a hand. You can buy a gas-reducing product called CurTail in pet supply stores. It's a digestive enzyme that helps break down foods in the intestine, leaving less fodder for gas-producing bacteria, says Dr. Thomas.

Feed your dog more often. Dogs who eat their food all at once tend to have more gas than those who eat smaller amounts more often, says Dr. Thomas. She recommends feeding dogs two, three, or even four times a day. Your dog will still be eating his usual amount, but spreading out the serving times will help the intestines work more efficiently, she explains.

BREED SPECIFIC

Many German shepherds have a hereditary condition in which they don't produce enough digestive enzymes. This doesn't necessarily affect their overall nutrition, but it can result in foul-smelling gas. Other gassy breeds include boxers and bulldogs. These dogs have short, flat faces and short respiratory tracts. They gasp quite a bit and tend to swallow air when they eat, which can result in extra gas.

CHAPTER FORTY-NINE

LIFTING THEIR LEGS WHEN THEY PEE

Hitting Heights for Bragging Rights

At the San Diego Zoo, there's a sign near the rhinoceros enclosure that reads, "Stay back at least 20 feet and beware when I turn my back to you." The reason for the warning is that rhinos like to mark their territory with urine—and when you consider that the average male rhino weighs 4,500 pounds and is the second-largest land animal, you can imagine what happens when they do.

It's a funny thing about animals and their territory: They often make it a point to announce what belongs to them, and they exaggerate how much space they themselves actually occupy. Bears, for example, make scratches on

trees—not down low, but as high up as they can reach. Wild cats back up to rocks and trees and urinate upward. Dogs lift their legs and do the same thing.

"They're leaving their scent where other dogs will smell it, and they put it as high up as they can, so that it will appear that a big, macho dog has been there," says James H. Sokolowski, D.V.M., Ph.D., a veterinarian in Vernon, California. The best way for them to gain that extra height is to lift a leg, tilt their bodies slightly to the side, and aim for the highest spot.

Urine is loaded with pheromones, chemical scents that tell a lot about dogs—their sex, their social status, even what they eat. "It's amazing how much information dogs are able to gather from a scent," says Dr. Sokolowski. Every dog's urine has a different smell, so these scent markings are very personal signatures. They allow dogs to tell the world about themselves, and other dogs are very interested in learning more.

This dog is lifting his leg way above his hip so that he can make his mark as high as possible up the tree. Other dogs who find the scent will think he's bigger than he really is.

Dogs often investigate when another dog is lifting his leg. It's the canine equivalent of getting the news as soon as it's printed.

Aiming High, Aiming Low

Marking territory via leg lifting is mainly a guy thing, especially among dogs with big macho personalities, says Liz Palika, a trainer in Oceanside, California, and author of *Love on a Leash*. It doesn't matter how big they really are, she adds. They want to seem big. "I've seen a little beagle arch his back like a contortionist to get his urine up high," she says. "But I also know a 150-pound Newfoundland who never lifts his leg at all."

All of this leg lifting isn't as random as it appears. Dogs who share territory—in today's world, common territory may be the perimeter of a yard, a fire hydrant on a city street, or the trees in a public park—have developed an etiquette for who pees where. A boisterous, take-charge dog will always aim high. The quiet, more submissive dog who follows him is going to add his scent to the message board, but he doesn't want to appear arrogant or challenging. So he aims a little lower.

"If you take an intact male to the park, he might want to mark as many as 20 bushes and 15 light poles," Palika adds. "A neutered male would be more likely to hit only two or three places."

Female dogs also leave chemical scents when they urinate. Since they aren't as concerned as males with marking territory or making social displays, they usually squat rather than lift their legs. Some females, of course, have personalities that are every bit as outgoing and assertive as any male's, and these dogs sometimes lift their legs, Dr. Sokolowski says. So do females who have had medical problems that were treated with male hormones.

Not As Easy As It Looks

Just as it's a challenge for a person to stand on one foot, a dog has to learn to comfortably stand on three. It takes time for dogs to develop a good sense of balance, and puppies often struggle in the beginning. Dr. Sokolowski's dog, a Pekingese named Ming Tu, is a case in point. On his first attempt, he wound up flat on his back, spraying in the air.

"There are a lot of clumsy young males who fall while they're learning to pee with their legs up, but with practice they eventually learn to keep their balance," says Palika.

Dogs start working on their form when they're about 9 months old, and they keep practicing and perfecting it until they get it right. By the time they've reached a year and a half, the age of sexual maturity in most dogs, they're comfortable with the concept and are starting to think about refinements—such as marking higher in order to impress all the other dogs who will come after them.

Now That You Understand...

The urge to lift and water wouldn't be a problem if dogs only did it once or twice in the course of a walk. But dogs who are concerned about power and social status have an intense need to spread the word. This makes for some very slow walks—and worse. "Some dogs even mark inside people's homes," Palika says.

Since standing on three legs requires more concentration and balance than standing on four, you can take advantage of dogs' momentary distraction to teach them that they're not supposed to stop at every vertical object that they see. "When your dog lifts his leg, give the leash a tug," Palika says. "Tug just hard enough so that he has to put his leg down to catch his balance. When he does, give a command such as 'Don't pee.'" As long as you do this consistently, your dog will learn that he's only going to get a couple of chances to empty his bladder. He'll be more likely to do it all at once, rather than saving it up and releasing it a little at a time.

It doesn't take children very long to learn that there are appropriate times and places to urinate, and dogs can learn it too. The lesson "go potty" is among the easiest of all to teach, says Palika.

1. "Go outside with your dog when you know he has to go to the bathroom," Palika says. "The best time to practice is first thing in the morning, when you know he'll have to go."

2. As soon as your dog starts getting into position, tell him, "Go potty." He was going to do it anyway, so this step is easy.

3. As soon as he's done, give him a treat. Act as though it was all your idea and he's a great dog for listening and doing what he's told.

If you start this lesson when your dog is a puppy and you practice it every time he goes outside, he'll learn to control himself until you say that it's okay for him to go.

A slight tug sideways with the leash will pull dogs off balance and tell them that they don't have to sniff—or mark—every smell they come across.

CHAPTER FIFTY

TAIL WAGGING

Sending Messages, Revealing Moods

When you want to know what dogs are thinking, all you have to do is look at their tails. Tails are almost always in motion, and every motion means something different. "You can tell when a dog is feeling happy, aggressive, submissive, or worried just by looking at the wag of the tail," says Liz Palika, a trainer in Oceanside, California, and author of *Love on a Leash*. "Their tails always reflect their emotions."

The wag that we're most familiar with is the happy wag. Some dogs are so happy, in fact, that wagging their tails just isn't enough. They wag their entire back ends. "I love to see dogs with their rumps shaking," says Cynthia Jacobs, D.V.M., a veterinarian in Clarksville, Arkansas. "You know as soon as you see them that they are happy dogs and that they can't wait to meet you."

For all of this mobility and self-expression, tails aren't very sensitive, Dr. Jacobs adds. This is why dogs with big tails can walk through the house thumping furniture and knocking lamps off tabletops without noticing the destruction going on behind them. They don't even feel it.

Talking to You

Nature didn't give dogs expressive tails for the benefit of humans. They're really designed for long-distance communication with other dogs. Tails generally fly high above dogs' backs, allowing them to use them like flags to send messages from far away. They don't depend on this feature very much today, but it mattered a lot when dogs lived with other dogs. They could gauge the intentions and moods of strangers before they came within biting range.

Thousands of years of human interference have made tails less effective than they used to be. Greyhounds, for instance, have been bred so

The status of each dog is reflected in his tail. The big black dog signals dominance by holding his tail the highest. The other dogs are lower-ranking, so they hold their tails lower.

that their tails are perpetually held low or tucked between their legs. To other dogs, they look like they're always scared. Alaskan malamutes, on the other hand, have been bred to have their tails up all the time. They sometimes get into fights because they mistakenly convey the message that they're trying to be dominant.

Then there's the issue of docking. Airedales, cocker spaniels, and some other breeds have their tails docked, or cut short, when they're a few days old. This may look good in the show ring, but it leaves these dogs with a stubby appendage to do the job that their whole tails were meant to do. Dogs manage to adjust, but they probably lose a little bit of subtlety in their communications, says Dr. Jacobs. They appear to make it up in other ways—for example, by using their eyes or ears to convey messages that otherwise might be shown with the flick of a tail.

While all dogs use their tails in similar ways, there are some differences among breeds. Some hunting dogs, for example, have been bred to wag their tails constantly while going after prey. They only quit wagging when they've found what they're looking for. Herding dogs, on the other hand, have been bred to

A Tail of Recovery

When April got hit by a car, the prognosis was terrible. Her tail and both of her back legs were broken, and her veterinarian didn't think she'd walk again. "And she'll never wag her tail," he told Larry Anderson, April's owner and a Web site designer and computer programmer in Saint Cloud, Florida.

Against all odds, April proved him wrong. A month after the accident, she was able to stand. A month after that, she was walking. Soon after that, her tail started to wag—not as vigorously as before, but enough to show that she was coming back.

It's not much of a tail anymore, Larry admits. It's bulbous in the middle and a little on the crooked side. But it works, and it makes Larry happy every time he sees it. "When I come home, April moves it as fast as she ever did," he says.

American cocker spaniels usually have their tails docked, or cut short, in order to meet the standards of the American Kennel Club.

not move their tails very much, because vigorous wags could excite the animals that they're trying to herd.

Now That You Understand...

Experts in canine communication have identified many tail themes and variations. Here are the ones you'll see most often.

High and slowly swishing. Veterinarians hear it all the time: "I can't believe he bit me—his tail was wagging." People don't understand that wags aren't all the same and that there's a big difference between a happy wag and what experts call a swish. Dogs who raise their tails and slowly swish them back and forth aren't happy. "This usually happens when a dog is thinking dominant thoughts and is ready to back them up," Palika says.

Tail swishes are part of a whole communication package that includes puffing up the neck and moving the ears forward. Each of these things makes dogs look bigger and more ferocious. It warns other dogs or people to stay away.

Low and barely wagging. Just as dogs raise their tails when they're blustering, they lower them when they're intimidated. It's a sign of appeasement, a way of saying "Please don't hurt me—look how small and helpless I am."

Wagging madly. This is the wag that people like to see. Depending on the breed, the tail may be upright or pointing backward like a ruler. In

A thrashing tail could alarm these sheep, which is why herding dogs like this kelpie have been bred to keep their tails still while they're working.

either case, it will be beating the air wildly. This always signals a happy, enthusiastic dog.

TAXES AND TAILS

Until fairly recently, all dogs had long, expressive tails. Then, a few centuries ago, humans decided to make a few changes—not for the sake of the dogs, but, as often happens, to collect a little money.

The practice of docking, or cutting tails short, started in England. Dogs back then were divided into two groups—those who worked for a living, and those who were kept only for their owners' pleasure, explains Liz Palika, a trainer in Oceanside, California, and author of *Love on a Leash*. People who owned luxury dogs were required to pay a tax. Working dogs were tax-free. To collect taxes efficiently, officials needed to distinguish the workers from the loungers. So they came up with the idea of docking the working dogs' tails.

As the years went by and people got used to seeing certain breeds with truncated tails, this became a breed standard, an agreed-upon look that sets one breed apart from the rest. Many of the same breeds who get their tails docked today had working ancestors in the old country. Paradoxically, what began as a mark of common working dogs is now a sign of the canine elite—dogs who are deemed worthy to represent their breeds at the Westminster Kennel Club Dog Show and other prestigious dog shows.

CHAPTER FIFTY-ONE

THROWING UP
The Price of Opportunity

Dogs throw up so often and for so many reasons that veterinarians rarely bother trying to figure out what caused a particular episode. Essentially, they blame it on fate. "We call it GOK disease," says Robin Downing, D.V.M., a veterinarian in Windsor, Colorado. "It stands for God Only Knows."

Maybe it's because they get so much practice, but dogs don't seem to mind throwing up. Unless they're seriously ill with something, they aren't likely to lose much energy or even miss a meal. "Dogs have a much higher tolerance for physical discomfort than people," says Karen Campbell, D.V.M., a professor of small-animal medicine at the University of Illinois College of Veterinary Medicine at Urbana-Champaign. "Throwing up doesn't bother them nearly as much as us."

Feed the Mouth, Bill the Stomach

In order to understand dogs' facility for throwing up, it helps to understand how they view food in general. Their ancestors were hunters—but unlike most animals who hunt, they weren't very good at it. Dogs learned quickly that if they wanted to survive, they had to eat everything—fresh game, carrion, bones, even dirt and grass. And because their meals were sporadic, they got in the habit of really packing it in whenever they had the chance.

After eons of evolution, dogs have become totally nondiscriminating about food. They like everything. But not everything likes them back. "Dogs usually get upset stomachs because they've eaten spoiled food, too much food, or

Dogs will eat anything that smells—and anything that's sufficiently pungent has the potential to make them sick.

food that's too rich," says Dr. Campbell. They also tend to get sick when they eat rough things like bones or grass, which irritate the stomach.

Vomiting isn't good for carpets and wood floors, and it certainly isn't pleasant to witness or clean up. But it's fundamentally a healthy thing for dogs to do, says Tony Buffington, D.V.M., Ph.D., professor of clinical nutrition at the Ohio State University College of Veterinary Medicine in Columbus. "Dogs have much shorter intestinal tracts than people do, so they can clear the whole thing faster," he says. "Considering all the questionable things dogs eat, being able to get them out fast has a lot of survival value."

Can't Stomach Being Alone

We all know the feeling of stomach butterflies, which tend to swarm when we're nervous. Dogs get them too. There's a physical reason for this. Anxiety causes the stomach to produce more acid. The irritation, if it's strong enough, can stimulate stomach contractions that result in throwing up.

Probably the main source of stress for dogs is the one that's hardest to avoid: spending time alone. Nature never intended dogs to live apart from their canine—or, more recently, their human—families. Many dogs get anxious when they're alone, which can give them a queasy feeling. This is why people sometimes come home and find evidence that their dogs have been violently ill, even though the dogs seem to be perfectly healthy.

Small dogs tend to throw up more than bigger ones, Dr. Campbell adds. The reason is

> **POOCH ?? PUZZLER**
>
> ### Why do dogs always throw up on the carpets?
>
> Put a dog in a large room with a vast expanse of easily cleaned tile. Should he need to throw up, he'll invariably wander off the tile and onto a carpet to lose his lunch. The more expensive the carpet, it seems, the better the odds that he'll hit it.
>
> It's not entirely a coincidence. "Dogs have a strong instinct not to soil the spaces where they sleep, eat, and drink," says Myrna Milani, D.V.M., a veterinarian in Claremont, New Hampshire, and author of *DogSmart*. They're not really aiming for carpet, she adds. What they're doing is going as far as possible from their usual living area. And if that area happens to include an expensive Oriental rug, well, that doesn't bother them at all.

simple: They have little stomachs. Even a little bit of overindulgence can push them to the heaving point. The opposite happens too. Small stomachs may not hold enough food to last all day. The resulting hunger spasms can trigger bouts of vomiting, she explains.

Now That You Understand...

Give their bellies a break. Dogs with flu or other stomach viruses may keep getting sick as long as there's food in their stomachs, says Dr. Downing. She recommends putting them on a fast for a day. Going without food for 24 hours gives their stomachs a chance to recover, and they'll start feeling better fairly quickly.

Cook some rice and hamburger. A strange thing about dogs is that even when they've been throwing up, they'll often gobble their food just the same—then get sick some more. Dr. Downing recommends putting them on a rice-and-hamburger diet for a day or two. This combination is easy to digest and will help prevent a relapse, she explains.

Give them extra fluids. You don't want dogs to drink a lot of water when they've been throwing up, because that can stimulate more heaving. But it's important to replace the fluids that vomiting has removed from their bodies. Once the worst of the sickness is over, replace

CALL FOR HELP

Dogs throw up all the time, and usually it doesn't mean very much. You can get a good idea of how serious it's likely to be just by watching how they feel afterward. "If your dog throws up and doesn't look back, don't worry about it," says Robin Downing, D.V.M., a veterinarian in Windsor, Colorado. Dogs who are acting mopey, however, or who have vomited five or more times in 24 hours, need to see a veterinarian. Serious vomiting can be caused by poisoning, ulcers, or other internal problems. You should get help right away.

your dog's usual water with Pedialyte, recommends Lynn Cox, D.V.M., a veterinarian in Olive Branch, Mississippi. Available in drugstores, this solution contains essential minerals called electrolytes. It will help prevent dehydration and keep dogs healthy. Pedialyte comes in several flavors. Most dogs prefer the orange, says Dr. Cox.

Dogs love human food, but it's frequently too rich for them to digest, which is why they may throw up afterwards.

FAST FIX Some of the same over-the-counter medicines that people use also help pets who have been throwing up. When your dog has been sick, try giving him one chewable Pepto-Bismol tablet for every 25 pounds of weight. "They usually like the tablets better than liquids," says Dr. Cox.

If you don't have tablets, it's fine to give liquid Pepto-Bismol, Dr. Campbell adds. The usual dose is half of a tablespoon for every 15 pounds of dog, two or three times a day.

CHAPTER FIFTY-TWO

YAWNING AT THE VET'S

Instant Calm

There's a lot of yawning going on out there, and only some of it's at bedtime. Marathon runners yawn before races. Musicians yawn backstage before concerts. Brides yawn before weddings. And dogs yawn when they're waiting in the veterinarian's office.

Fatigue has little to do with all of these mouth-open, tongue-curling yawns. Research has shown that yawning causes instantaneous changes in the body, in dogs as well as in people. Heart rate goes up. Bloodflow to the brain increases. The lungs fill to capacity, taking in oxygen and whisking away carbon dioxide. All of these changes help dogs dispel anxiety, gather their wits, and focus on the tasks at hand, explains Ronald Baenninger, Ph.D., professor of psychology at Temple University in Philadelphia and a leading authority on yawning.

Few things in a dog's life are as exciting—and as nerve-racking—as waiting to see the veterinarian, adds Joanne Howl, D.V.M., a veterinarian in West River, Maryland. Even before they walk in the door, they're barraged with smells from unfamiliar (and sick) animals, strange people, and medications, antiseptics, and cleaners. Dogs can probably smell other dogs' fear as well as the nervousness of their owners, she says. It's not a reassuring environment, and it makes most dogs feel rather apprehensive. To calm themselves, they yawn— and keep yawning. "It helps them center themselves when they're really excited or agitated," Dr. Howl says.

Getting Pumped

Yawning helps dogs cope with all kinds of stress, not just stress that's caused by strange or frightening things, says Dr. Baenninger. Dogs who are

Even a routine visit to the veterinarian is a stressful experience. Yawning helps a dog to feel calmer and more focused.

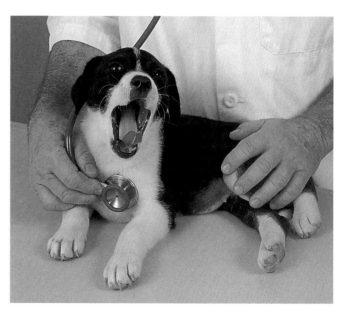

The water is making this Dalmatian nervous. Yawning releases tension from his body and floods his tissues with energizing oxygen.

anticipating something good will often yawn a few times to get their minds and bodies prepared. It gives them a surge of energy and helps control their eager agitation. "When I grab a leash, my dogs wake up fast, stretch, and give a big yawn. Then they're ready to go," he says.

Yawning was especially helpful back in the days when dogs had to catch their own suppers. Ancient dogs, just like dogs today, spent a lot of their time sleeping. It wouldn't do for them to be groggy after waking up, especially when a likely meal happened to wander by. They had to make the transition from dead-sleep to full alertness almost instantly, and yawning helped them do it.

All meat-eating animals use yawning as a kind of wake-up pill, Dr. Baenninger explains. Slower-moving, plant-eating animals—cows, for example—don't yawn very much. "They don't really have to get their energy up for much of anything," he says.

Mom Needs a Break

Puppies start learning about yawns within a few days of being born. Apart from doing their own yawning, they learn to watch their mothers' yawns. A yawn from Mom is a sign that it's time for the pups to settle down. Mother dogs

probably don't use yawns as a deliberate form of communication, but when they're feeling comfortable and relaxed, their puppies naturally relax as well.

As adults, dogs will yawn to calm themselves in many situations. In training classes, for example, yawning can reach epidemic proportions. "You see it a lot in dogs who are really eager to please but don't know how," says Dr. Howl. Dogs who start getting frustrated will often yawn as a way of taking a mental break, she explains.

They do the same thing in veterinarian's offices. Some dogs will yawn nearly nonstop, especially when they're in the waiting room and aren't sure what's going to happen. Once an examination is underway, a yawn or two is a good sign, says Dr. Howl. "Sometimes I'll see a really tense dog on the table, and I'll start talking to her and petting her to settle her down," she says. "When she gives that big yawn, I know she's starting to come around."

Now That You Understand...

Yawn back. For dogs as well as people, the memory of Mom gives a lot of comfort. You can rekindle this soothing memory as a way of calming dogs when they're feeling anxious. The next time you're at the vet's, and your dog is looking nervous, give a big yawn of your own. Many dogs will respond the same way people do when someone yawns—by yawning back, says Dr. Baenninger.

It's best to start doing this when dogs are still young and are naturally attuned to watching for yawns, says Dr. Howl. If you start early, you can use this trick throughout their lives to keep them calm at the veterinarian's and in other stressful situations.

Take a break. A sleepy yawn now and then doesn't mean very much, but dogs who are giving one yawn after another are anxious about something. Yawning back isn't going to calm them down. What they really need is a break from the situation, says Dr. Howl. Rather than staying in the veterinarian's waiting room, for example, find out how much time there is until your appointment. If there's time, take your dog outside. A quick walk or even a big breath of fresh air will stimulate some of the same physical responses as yawning, she explains. Your dog will feel calmer and will be less upset when you come back inside.

People who train dogs always watch for yawns because they invariably mean their dogs

How Kelsey Learned the Ropes

Kristen LaCroix of Aurora, Illinois, didn't plan to teach Kelsey, her 8-year-old beagle mix, to yawn on command—although she might have if she'd thought of it. As with all puppies, Kelsey was particularly adorable when she curled her little pink tongue and gave a big yawn. "Every time she yawned, she made a cute little sighing noise," Kristen says. "I would always look at her and say in a really stupid voice, 'Bi-i-ig yawn!'"

The message wasn't lost on Kelsey, who realized that yawning seemed to make her owner very happy. One night she had the opportunity to prove how alert she really was. Kristen and her husband, Pete, had guests over for dinner. Pete was telling them about Kristen's fascination with Kelsey's yawns. To demonstrate, he said, "Bi-i-ig yawn," imitating Kristen's voice. Kelsey, right on cue, ran to the table and gave a big, arching yawn.

After that, of course, Kristin couldn't resist telling Kelsey to yawn, and Kelsey is always happy to oblige.

have reached the end of their attention spans. They start yawning when they simply can't take in any more information. Pushing them at this point will increase their frustration and trigger even more yawning. Yawning means that it's time to do something else for a while, says Dr. Howl. Throw a ball. Run around for a few minutes. Give them a cookie. Even a short break will help them dispel nervous energy and shake the cobwebs from their brains.

Credits and Acknowledgments

(t=top, b=bottom, l=left, r=right, c=center, F=front, C=cover, B=back)
All photographs are copyright to the sources listed below.

PHOTOGRAPH CREDITS

Ad-Libitum: Stuart Bowey, i, viib, ixc, 2b, 3c, 4b, 5b, 6t, 7b, 9t, 10b, 11b, 12b, 14b, 15t, 16b, 17t, 18t, 19b, 20b, 25t, 26b, 28b, 29t, 30b, 32t, 34b, 35t, 36b, 38t, 39b, 41b, 42b, 44b, 46t, 48b, 49t, 50b, 51b, 52b, 53b, 55t, 56b, 57b, 63b, 65t, 67b, 70b, 71b, 73c, 74b, 76b, 84t, 85b, 87t, 88t, 89b, 91t, 92b, 94t, 95b, 97t, 98b, 99t, 101b, 102b, 105b, 106t, 107b, 108b, 110b, 112t, 115t, 116b, 121t, 122b, 124b, 125b, 126t, 127b, 129t, 134b, 136b, 137b, 138b, 138t, 139t, 140b, 141t, 142b, 144b, 144t, 146t, 147t, 150b, 152b, BCbl

Auscape International: Francais/Cogis, 133c, 156b; Gehlhar/Cogis, 13t; Hermeline/Cogis, 60b; Lanceau/Cogis, 23b, BClc

Australian Picture Library: 43b, 158t; Carnemolla, 153t

Bill Bachman and Associates: Bill Bachman, 22t, 59t

Norvia Behling: ivt, xb, 21t, 33b, 37b, 45b, 100, 104b, 113b, 128b, 148b, 157b, BCtl

Walter Chandoha: 149t

Bruce Coleman Limited: Adriano Bacchella, 131t; Erwin and Peggy Bower, 80b; Jane Burton, 8b, 82c, 120b; Jorg and Petra Wegner, 119b, BCtr

Kent and Donna Dannen: 109t

Matt Gavin-Wear: 86b, 75t

Robert Harding Picture Library: 83b

The Image Bank: Frank Whitney, 27t

Ron Kimball Photography: Ron Kimball, xii, 132

NHPA: 31b

The Photo Library: 61t

PinchMe Design: Jacqueline Richards, 54b, 151b

Dale C. Spartas: 40, 66, 145b, 154b

Renee Stockdale: 64b

Stock Photos: ii

Tony Stone Images: John Brown, FC

Judith E. Strom: viiit, 62t, 68b, 118b, 130b, BCrc

The publisher would like to thank the following people for their assistance in the preparation of this book:
Peta Gorman; Sally Gorman; Tracey Jackson; Aliza Pinczewski; The Royal Society for the Prevention of Cruelty to Animals, Yagoona, N.S.W., Australia; Danielle Wilkes

Special thanks to the following people who kindly allowed their dogs to be photographed:
Steve Allen and "Ren"; Len Antcliff and "Bozie"; Aruna Basmayake and "Nikki" and "Maggie"; Tara Beath and "Jax"; Corinne and Don Braye and "Minne"; Sue and Michelle Burk and "Jacko"; Pam Cohn and "Jesse"; Lynn Cole and "Abel" and "Suzie"; Lindy Coote and "Boo"; Adrian Cox and "Polly"; Donna and Tom Devitt and "Kinka"; Frances Farac and "Madison"; Annette Fitzgerald and "Bundy"; Bev Flowers and "Jack"; Kevan and Verena Gardner and "Floyd"; Gwynneth Grant and "Max"; Roger Goldsinch and "Buzz"; Kerri Hancock and "Marley"; Lindy Haynes and "Babar"; Richard Hennassey and "Beau"; Philip Jacobs and "Casper," "Rogue," and "Tinker"; Emilia Kahrimanis and "Lulabel"; Sherrie Martin and "Max" and "Sam"; Paul McGreevy and "Wally"; Andrew McIntyre and "Abby" and "Daisy"; Louise Moore and "KC" and "Zammy"; Judith Neilson and "Pepa"; Karl Pitt and "Bengie"; Simmone Pogorzelski and Shaun Lawrence and "Jackson"; Jacqueline Richards and Nick Wiles and "Skipper"; Jennifer Saunders and "Barney" and "Kitty"; Ann and Richard Stevens and "Cassie"; Alex Syriatowicz and "Socrates" and "Cassiel"; Cassandra and Jason Toogood and "Saba"; Amanda Trickey and "Rusty"; Sarah-Jane Vaux and "Dessa"; Russ Weakley and Anna Gregg and "Max," "Bob," and "Harry"; Annabella Zanetti and "Frank"

Index

Boldface page references indicate photographs. Underscored references indicate boxed text.

Dogspeak

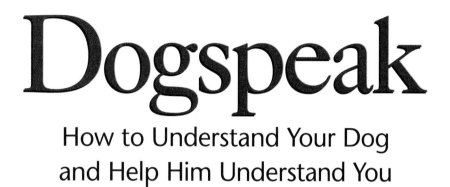

Dogspeak

How to Understand Your Dog and Help Him Understand You

From the Editors of
Pets
part of the family™

Edited by Matthew Hoffman

Consultant: Paul McGreevy, B.V.Sc., Ph.D.,
veterinarian and lecturer in animal behavior at
the University of Sydney, Australia

Rodale Press, Inc.
Emmaus, Pennsylvania

Pets: Part of the Family public television series
is generously underwritten by PETsMART,
PETsMART.com, and Fresh Step cat litter.

Notice

This book is intended as a reference volume only, not as a medical manual. The information given here is designed to help you make informed decisions about your pet's behavior. It is not intended as a substitute for any treatment that may have been recommended by your veterinarian. If you suspect that your pet has a serious behavior problem, we urge you to seek competent help.

Printed in the United States of America on acid-free ∞, recycled paper ♻

Library of Congress Cataloging-in-Publication Data

Dogspeak : how to understand your dog and help him understand you /
   edited by Matthew Hoffman.
        p.   cm. — (Dog care companions)
   Includes index.
   ISBN 1–57954–049–X hardcover
   1. Dogs—behavior.   2. Human-animal communication.   I. Hoffman,
Matthew.   II. Series.
   SF433.D654   1999
   636.7'088'7—dc21   98–52352

     ISBN 1–57954–182–8 paperback

Distributed to the book trade by St. Martin's Press

4 6 8 10 9 7 5 3   hardcover
           10   paperback

OUR PURPOSE

To explore, celebrate, and stand in awe
before the special relationship between us
and the animals who share our lives.

Pets
part of the family

Dogspeak

CONTRIBUTING WRITERS

Susan Easterly, Elaine Waldorf Gewirtz, Bette LaGow,
Susan McCullough, Arden Moore, Liz Palika, Audrey Pavia

RODALE BOOKS

Editor: Matthew Hoffman
Publisher: Neil Wertheimer
Editorial Director: Michael Ward
Research Manager: Ann Gossy Yermish
Copy Manager: Lisa D. Andruscavage
Cover Designer and Design Coordinator: Joanna Reinhart
Associate Studio Manager: Thomas P. Aczel
Book Manufacturing Director: Helen Clogston
Manufacturing Manager: Mark Krahforst

WELDON OWEN PTY LTD

Chairman: John Owen
Publisher: Sheena Coupe
Associate Publisher: Lynn Humphries
Senior Editor: Janine Flew
Project Editor: Kathy Metcalfe
Copy Editor: Lynn Cole, Laura J. Wallace
Senior Designer: Kylie Mulquin
Designer: Jocelyne Best
Picture Researcher: Jenny Mills
Illustrator: Chris Wilson/Merilake
Icons: Matt Graif, Chris Wilson/Merilake
Indexer: Garry Cousins
Production Manager: Caroline Webber
Production Assistant: Kylie Lawson

Film separation by Colourscan Co. Pte. Ltd., Singapore

CONTENTS

PART FOUR

FAILURE TO COMMUNICATE

PART FIVE

PUTTING IT TO WORK

Introduction

Webster's hasn't come out with *The First International Dogtionary,* and that's a shame. Dogs and people have been living together for thousands of years, but despite that, our communication skills are still pretty rocky. We say "Come!" and our dogs hear "Smell the tree over there!" They politely sniff us by way of introduction, and we get offended at their rudeness. We ask them to sleep on the bed, only to watch them take over the couch. Sometimes it seems as though we're speaking different languages.

Which we are. No matter how intelligent and alert they may be, dogs have ways of hearing, seeing, and thinking about the world that are totally different than ours, and this invariably leads to confusion.

I once met a beautiful Irish setter in a park in New York City. He was tossing a tennis ball in the air with his mouth, scrambling after it, and tossing it again. When he saw me he ran over, dropped the ball on the grass, and stared up at me eagerly, his tail whipping the air behind him. I bent over to pick up the ball—and froze when

I heard an ominous *grrr*. Had this friendly Dr. Jekyll turned into Mr. Hyde? I looked at the dog and he looked back, his tail beating a little more. I reached for the ball again. *Grrr*.

A soggy tennis ball wasn't worth getting nailed for, so I walked away. "That's one confused pooch," I muttered.

When I got home I told the story to an animal behaviorist friend of mine, who immediately set me straight. The dog wasn't confused at all, he explained. I was. The dog's "happy" signals all meant the opposite of what I thought. The staring, the wagging tail, and the alert expression were actually challenges. In a playful sort of way, the dog was daring me to pick up the ball. By misunderstanding "dogspeak," I essentially committed a canine faux pas.

The editors at *Pets: Part of the Family* decided to unravel this confusion once and for all. After all, one of the hardest parts of living with dogs is that they can't tell us in words what they're feeling or when they're happy or sad. They can't explain why they're chewing shoes, having accidents in the house, or are terrified of thunder. They can't explain why one training technique is working and another isn't. It's up to us to work out what they're trying to say—and to make sure that they understand us, as well.

We talked to dozens of the country's top behaviorists, trainers, and veterinarians, and asked them to explain the complex world of canine communication and to show us how to communicate a little better, whether we're working out the rules of a ball-toss game or having a heartfelt chat about our dogs' lavatory habits.

Dogspeak is their answer. It's a complete "dogtionary" to help you communicate more effectively and affectionately with the dogs in your life. Much to our surprise, we discovered that barking is just one way—and a minor one, at that—in which dogs communicate. To really understand dogs, you have to *look* at what they're saying. Whether the position of their ears indicates that they're happy or sad. The difference between a friendly tail-wag and a warning tail-swish. When eye contact means "I love you" and when it means "Keep away." Even dogs' facial expressions tell a lot about what they're feeling. *Dogspeak* includes more than 170 photos and illustrations so you can see exactly what to look for.

Communication goes both ways, of course, so this book is packed with tips showing how to help your dog understand you. When to raise your voice higher and when to pitch it low. "Strong" words dogs respond to. The best and worst names for dogs (dogs named Mo sometimes get confused because it sounds like "no"). Hand movements they respond to and those that make them nervous. And much more.

Every page of *Dogspeak* provides fascinating glimpses into dogs' inner lives: How they see. What they really hear. Why smell is so important. You'll also learn some amazing ways to use this information to communicate a little more clearly. And that's what good relationships are all about.

Matthew Hoffman

Matthew Hoffman
Editor, *Pets: Part of the Family* books

PART ONE

WHAT'S YOUR DOG SAYING?

Dogs have plenty to say, but they don't say it the same way we do.
Dogs talk to humans and other dogs through body language and facial
expressions, and by barking, whining, growling, and howling.
They also depend on their senses of smell and hearing,
which are far more sensitive than ours.

CHAPTER ONE

TALK TO YOUR DOG

Dogs are an important and well-loved part of the family. You'll be sharing
your life with your dog for a long time, so improving your relationship
through better communication will have long-term benefits for both of you.

Dogs have an uncanny ability to understand what people are feeling. They don't hold grudges. They love us despite our flaws, and they're there for us day after day. Our relationships with dogs can outlast jobs, friendships, and even marriages. So it's hardly surprising that most people talk to their dogs. They really are our best friends.

"Dogs are full-fledged members of families," says Marty Becker, D.V.M., a veterinarian in Bonner's Ferry, Idaho, and co-author of *Chicken Soup for the Pet Lover's Soul.* "Although we don't speak a lick of Labrador, direct communication is going on between us and our dogs all the time. Dogs sense our moods and allow us to be completely ourselves."

It's not only the human members of the family who appreciate the close ties. In addition to the obvious perks—free food, comfortable places to sleep, and regular belly-rubs—dogs get tremendous emotional fulfillment from their relationships with us. They're naturally social and see people as part of their pack—the canine equivalent of a happy home. "Lying around and listening to us talk is part of what being in this human pack is all about," says Mary Merchant, a therapy dog evaluator for St. John's Ambulance Corps in Powassan, Ontario, Canada.

When they lived in the wild, dogs roamed in close-knit groups called packs. For this golden retriever, his human family has become his pack.

Breaking the Barriers

Even though our relationships with dogs have some "human" qualities, such as mutual respect and affection, there's an inevitable distance between us. We belong to different species, after all, and we see the world and communicate in entirely different ways. Sometimes dogs are

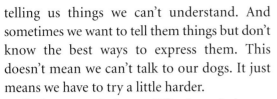

telling us things we can't understand. And sometimes we want to tell them things but don't know the best ways to express them. This doesn't mean we can't talk to our dogs. It just means we have to try a little harder.

"When people have difficulty relating to dogs, it's usually because they assume that dogs are just like them," says Jeff Nichol, D.V.M., a veterinarian and a newspaper columnist in Albuquerque, New Mexico.

But dogs aren't like people, which is why words and gestures that have such resonance with us mean nothing at all to them—or, in some cases, mean precisely the opposite of what we're trying to say.

Hugging is a good example. Among people, a full-body hug is a wonderful sign of affection. But dogs don't feel that way. The nearest they come to hugging is when one dog, in an attempt to dominate, pins another dog's shoulders with her paws. So dogs may perceive hugs—from humans or other dogs—as signs of competition rather than affection.

While dogs are more likely to misconstrue gestures than words, they don't have a lot of words to choose from. That's why spoken communication can be the hardest barrier to breach.

Not that this stops anyone from trying. People talk to their dogs all the time—about their day at work, whether a new pillow is comfortable, or if it's time to take a walk. Dogs have impeccable manners and always look interested, even though most of the words are probably just a blur of noise. But the words don't matter all that much because, except for their names and a few commands that they understand, dogs mainly respond to intonations and body lan-

guage. But dogs do understand some words and phrases, as long as they're simple, spoken plainly, and used consistently.

"A long string of words—like 'Sit, sit, sit, I said, sit'—has no meaning," Merchant says. "It just goes over your dog's head."

Perhaps the best way to communicate more clearly is to spend more time paying attention—not just to your dog's barks, but also to her gestures and body language.

"It takes a lot of practice to be a good listener because we often have preconceived notions of what our dogs are saying," says Laurel Davis,

POOCH PUZZLER

Why don't dogs watch television?

You would think that *The Incredible Journey* or *Lassie* reruns would get any dog's attention, but most dogs don't show a lot of interest in television, regardless of what's on. This is partly because their eyesight isn't very sharp. They're more likely to respond to television sounds, such as barking or phones ringing, than to television images, which probably appear pretty blurry to them.

In the future, however, dogs may spend a lot more time in front of the tube. Big-screen televisions and the development of digital signals have made televised images incredibly lifelike. "With these TVs the pixels are extremely dense, giving an image and sound like never before," says John C. Wright, Ph.D., a certified applied animal behaviorist and professor of psychology at Mercer University in Macon, Georgia. "Your dog may perceive the dog on TV as being real."

Are some dogs multilingual?

German, Italian, Swahili—whatever the language, most dogs can understand it, if only because they comprehend the body cues and tone of voice that go with the words.

Some languages, however, are more effective than others for getting a dog's attention. The hard-edged, gruff sound of German has more of a "commanding" ring to it than the lyrical, lighter tones of French, for example. A dog who's given a command in German may not have a clue what the word means, but it'll sound important enough to warrant a check of the speaker's body language to see what's expected.

Misty, a Border collie mix, was multilingual. She could react to commands given in Latin, French, Spanish, and English, says Joanne Howl, D.V.M., a veterinarian in private practice in West River, Maryland. Dr. Howl would look at Misty, lift her index finger and thumb, say "Bang, you're dead," or "Tu es morte" and Misty would fall over, stick her legs in the air, and dramatically "die" on cue.

Dogs also seem to be multilingual when it comes to reading the body language of different breeds.

"When dogs approach another dog with their tails pointed straight up, it's viewed as a threat," says John C. Wright, Ph.D., a certified animal behaviorist and professor of psychology at Mercer University in Macon, Georgia. "But a German shepherd somehow knows that a beagle always walks with his tail up. The German shepherd can discriminate the difference in meaning."

D.V.M., a veterinarian in private practice in Asheville, North Carolina. "If you take the time to listen, you can learn a lot from your dog."

Seeing the World Their Way

Dogs are perfectly at home in the human family, but conflicts are nearly inevitable because dogs and people live by different rules and can see similar situations in entirely different ways. For example, you get excited when the mail arrives, but your dog hears an intruder; she looks lazy when she won't move away from the door, but she's probably issuing a challenge; you buy her an expensive dog bed, but she keeps climbing into the armchair—not, it turns out, because it's softer, but because it's higher, and that makes her feel more powerful.

Talking with dogs involves much more than giving commands. It requires understanding why they do the things they do. The most important thing to remember is that dogs originally lived in cohesive, highly structured societies called packs. Nearly everything your dog does, from rolling over on her back to grumbling when you tell her to get off the couch, is motivated by her desire to establish her place in the family "pack."

That's not to say that every dog wants to be the boss; in fact, most prefer not to be. But they derive tremendous comfort from knowing what their status is in the family, says John Loomis, owner of Alibi Obedience and Agility Training School in Jacksonville, Arkansas. That's why one of the main rules in human relationships—the rule that everyone is created equal—never works with dogs.

"It's not what you say but how you say it that counts," explains Janice DeMello, a trainer in Somis, California. When you're telling your dog to get off the furniture, don't make it sound like a request. Requests work with people but rarely with dogs. When giving commands, make them sound like commands—firm and authoritative. Your dog will understand that you mean business, and, more important, she'll be reminded that her status in the family is lower than yours. Rather than resenting this, she'll be able to relax because she'll know exactly where she stands.

Talking with dogs isn't just about telling them to do things. It's about understanding what they're feeling at any particular time. Dogs aren't very verbal, but their body language, facial expressions, and movements provide tremendous insights into what they're thinking and feeling. "You can learn a lot about your dog just by watching her," says Amy Ammen, director of Amiable Dog Training in

Communicating effectively with dogs isn't just about giving clear verbal messages, you also need to understand their motivations for doing things.

Milwaukee and author of *Training in No Time.* When you watch dogs closely, you'll learn to recognize more than the obvious emotions like happiness or sadness. You'll know when they're feeling restless or bored, when they want attention, and even what they're about to do next.

Dogs are as complex as people, and they often give conflicting signals. The tail may be saying "Play with me!" while the eyes are saying "I'm feeling pretty tense right now." This is why you can't follow the same rules when dealing with all dogs. But once you're familiar with your dog's usual habits and expressions, you'll know exactly what she's feeling—and, most of the time, what she's trying to tell you. You'll develop a strong sense of empathy, and that's what friendship is all about.

BREED SPECIFIC

German shepherds are among the most popular service dogs because they're very skilled at understanding what people want them to do. This has less to do with native intelligence than with their instinctive urge to please their owners. More than most breeds, German shepherds are attuned to the people they spend time with, which makes it easy for them to learn spoken commands, hand signals, facial expressions, and body language.

How Dogs Talk with Dogs

Dogs are expert communicators, using not only their voices, but also body language, facial expressions, and scent. Other dogs get the messages far more quickly than we do, but if you watch closely, you'll soon learn what they are saying to each other.

Dogs don't waste much time getting acquainted. Within seconds of meeting, they've worked out one another's sex, age, and status, and come to a tacit understanding as to which dog has the higher status. At that point they'll either begin to play or go their separate ways. Or, if there is some dispute about who is top dog, they may settle the argument with a brief, but rarely serious, tussle.

It seems amazing that dogs can collect so much information so quickly, but it's really not surprising. Like people, dogs rely on more than just their voices to communicate. They use everything from body language and scent to facial expressions to say their piece.

What Dogs Have to Say

Dogs have plenty to say, and much of it harkens back to their past. Because they're pack animals, they spend time sorting out their status—who fits where in the social structure, and who gives the orders. They also talk about establishing and defending their territory and possessions, such as food, toys, or even (in their view) humans.

"Although their emotions don't linger like ours, dogs also feel fear, excitement, happiness, stress, uncertainty, and confusion," says Chris Kemper, a dog trainer in Dallas, Texas. And, unlike people, dogs have no reason to camouflage their emotions. Simply watching how they act and react when they're together will give you a good idea of what they're trying to say.

Both these dogs are communicating many things with their body language. The keeshond (left) is interested in his new friend, but is maintaining dominance by standing stiff and tall. The Welsh springer spaniel's pose is friendly, but definitely submissive.

Learning to Communicate

During the first seven or eight weeks of life, puppies learn the basics of communication from the best teacher of all—their mother. For instance, when she wants to start weaning them (about the time those sharp little puppy teeth come in), she'll curl her lip at them. This warns them to back off, says Wendy Volhard, a trainer in Phoenix, New York. "If they persist, she'll growl a little. If she still hasn't gotten through, she'll really growl, which lets them know she means business," she says.

Conversely, the mother lets them know what's acceptable by ignoring or casually accepting their actions. "If one pup is grabbing another's ears just in play, not to hurt him, his mother lets him know, by ignoring his behavior, that what he's doing is fine," says Marge Gibbs, a trainer in Lincolnshire, Illinois, and a columnist for *The American Kennel Club Gazette*.

Puppies quickly learn to talk to each other, too. Because they play by biting, an important message is, "Hey, that hurts." When one puppy bites a littermate too hard, the victim squeals, letting the biter know he went too far. Puppies soon learn to "inhibit" their bites, which ensures they'll all get along. "You can yelp like a puppy to stop them from biting you," says Volhard. "It's far more effective than any verbal command because you're speaking their language."

Talking with Body Language

Throughout a dog's life, body language will remain his most important way of talking to other dogs. He'll use his eyes, tail, ears, and general

POOCH **?? ?** PUZZLER

Why do dogs form barking chains?

If you live in a neighborhood with more than one dog, you will have heard the infamous "barking chain," the canine equivalent of a musical round. One dog starts the din, and soon others in nearby yards join in.

Sometimes they're all barking at the same thing, such as when a bicyclist passes each house. But at other times, it's anybody's guess what got that first dog started.

"With group activities, sometimes it's a matter of trying to look—or in this case, sound—bigger than you are," says Mark Feinstein, Ph.D., an animal behaviorist and dean of cognitive sciences at Hampshire College in Amherst, Massachusetts. "You see this with clustering behavior in cattle, and perhaps the barking chain is a similar thing."

Some dogs, however, are less likely to join in. Large working breeds, such as Kuvaszok or Maremma sheepdogs, would be among the first to bow out of the barking chain because they've been bred to live among their charges, and making too much noise would upset the herds. But scent hounds such as bassets and bloodhounds are very vocal, as are terriers, whose traditional role was to bark to let their owners know they'd found game or vermin.

stance to let them know what's on his mind. When two dogs meet, the first thing they do is establish their rank. A dog who wants to say, "I'm confident, I'm fearless, and what are you going to do about it?" does so by putting his head, tail, ears, and hackles up and by making eye contact. If another dog of lesser rank wants

These Rhodesian ridgebacks are having a great time play-fighting. The lower-ranking dog is submitting by rolling over with his belly up.

to reply, "Not a thing, boss," he'll lower his tail and ears and possibly crouch or lick his lips.

When a dog wants to invite another dog to play, there's no mistaking his message. "He's happy, panting, grinning, and his tail is wagging so hard that his whole rear end is wiggling," says Gibbs. He may drop into a play-bow, then back up and pretend to run—anything to entice his friend to a quick game of tag or roughhousing.

On the other hand, if they've been playing hard and one dog decides he's had enough, he'll start ignoring the other dog. If that doesn't work, he might raise a lip, growl, or even snap to get the other dog to back off.

Dogs don't stay angry very long, and one of the dogs will usually try to bring things to a friendly level again. He'll do this by using many of the same gestures he used as a puppy when he wanted some care and consideration. "He will lick the other dog's mouth, roll over, and expose

his belly," says Kemper. Or he might use other appeasing gestures, such as flattening his ears, lowering his body and squinting. It's his way of saying, "Treat me nicely, please."

The Role of Play-Fighting

As well as being fun, play-fighting is one way dogs sort out the pecking order. It's also a great way for a lower-ranking dog to challenge, even briefly, another dog whose position he'd never seriously consider usurping. "Often two dogs will stage a mock fight—no blood, just lots of snarls and tussling," says Kemper. "You'll see one laying his head over the shoulders of the other, showing his dominance. In the end, the lower-ranking dog will usually roll over onto his back, which is his way of saying 'uncle.'"

Going belly up is a classic sign of submission from puppyhood, when a pup learned he'd be safe if he rolled over and let the other guy win. A dog won't hurt another who has given in.

Most play-fighting, even at its most genial, has its roots in dominance displays. And some breeds take things a bit more seriously than others, says Gibbs. "Labradors love to play rough, but put some of the herding or Nordic breeds such as malamutes or huskies into the mix and it may become a fight."

Communicating with Scent

For dogs, there's a whole realm of scent-based communication that humans can't even begin to imagine. Dogs can detect and identify

A Body Language Primer

A dog like this vizsla (below) can tell a lot about another dog just by looking at him and noting what the different parts of his body are doing.

Eyes
- Direct eye contact means a dog is feeling bold and confident
- Casual eye contact means he's contented
- An averted gaze means deference
- Dilated pupils indicate fear

Ears
- Relaxed ears mean that a dog is calm
- Erect ears show that a dog is alert and attentive
- Ears that are up and forward mean a dog is challenging or being assertive
- Ears that are laid back indicate that a dog is worried or scared

Body movements
- Pawing is an appeasing gesture
- Licking another dog's face is an invitation to play or a sign of deference
- Play-bowing (front legs extended, rump up, tail wagging) is an invitation to play and a sign of happiness
- Draping the head over another dog's shoulders is a sign of boldness
- Freezing in place means a dog is frightened
- Rubbing or leaning against another dog is a companionable gesture

Mouth and lips
- Panting means that a dog is feeling playful or excited, or maybe he's just hot
- A dog with the mouth and lips closed is uncertain or appeasing
  - Licking the lips is a sign a dog is worried or is being appeasing
  - A relaxed mouth means a dog is calm
  - Lips pulled back are a challenging or warning sign

Hackles (the hair on the shoulders and hips)
- Raised hackles indicate arousal, either because a dog is frightened or is challenging another dog
- Smooth hackles show a dog is calm

Tail
- A relaxed tail means a dog is calm and at ease
- Tail held straight out, wagging rhythmically and slowly, means that a dog is cautious or on guard
- Tail down indicates worry or uncertainty
- Tail held up and wagging fast indicates excitement
- An erect tail is a sign of alertnesss
- A tail between the legs is a sign of fear

smells that humans don't even know exist because dogs' olfactory glands are literally a million times more sensitive to some smells than ours are.

Though we may turn up our noses at the most typical dog greeting—the nose-to-rear-end method—it works well for them. The anal sacs just under a dog's tail contain glandular secretions that vary in composition from dog to dog. Dogs can tell with one sniff more than we'd ever get from a phone call: The other dog's age, sex, rank, health, and whether he or she has been altered.

Dogs pick up and deliver scent messages everywhere they go. One of the main ways they communicate with other dogs is with urine marking. The smell of regular urine differs from the urine that's used for marking. By leaving their mark in various places, dogs let other dogs know that they're claiming possession of this territory. Male dogs are much more inclined to this behavior than female dogs. They're telling any potential intruder, "Enter at your own risk." Even if your dog would actually welcome the company, this behavior is ingrained.

Sniffers can determine the "attitude" of the dog that previously marked. "I once saw a very dominant male dog mark a tree," Kemper says. "Later, a more submissive dog smelled the spot and immediately backed up—he seemed to have a submissive reaction to the urine itself."

Some stud dogs in the show ring have been known to mark their handlers' legs, says Mary Merchant, a collie breeder and therapy dog evaluator for St. John's Ambulance Corps in Powassan, Ontario, Canada. That's because, when faced with so much competition, they feel

Scent-marking is one of the main ways dogs like this Labrador communicate, which is why even a short walk can be interrupted with a dozen toilet breaks.

driven to stake their claim to what is rightfully theirs—in this case, their owners.

On a walk, you'll likely see your dog sniff and urinate at the same places. "He probably smells another dog, thinks, 'Oh, no, that's my tree, not yours,' then re-marks the tree," explains Kemper.

Urine is not the only thing that leaves interesting messages for other dogs to find. Just try pulling a dog away from a pile of another dog's stools. This encounter is just about as good as meeting the other dog in person, since when they do meet, it's the rear end that initially gets the most attention.

When your dog makes a deposit while on a walk, or even in your yard, he may immediately scratch and kick at the ground, perhaps even tossing the stools around. Experts think this is yet another way a dog marks his territory, by spreading his scent as far as possible.

Talking with Voice

Humans are verbal creatures, so it's natural for us to expect that barking is the main way that dogs communicate with each other. To a dog, though, barking is far less important than other forms of communication, such as body language or scent marking.

Still, barks, whines, howls, and growls have a place in the dog dictionary. How your dog "talks" depends on his mood and what he wants. To tell what your dog is really saying, you need to look at a sound in context.

Barking

Barking is the dog equivalent of human conversation. It's a great way to get the attention of a human or another dog. It also announces a dog's territory, and helps relieve stress. Different barks mean different things:

- A series of high-pitched barks means your dog's worried or lonesome and wants attention.
- A single bark in his regular voice means he's curious and alert and is making contact.
- Quick, repetitive, high-pitched barks mean your dog's feeling playful, or has spotted something he wants to chase.
- A low, repetitive bark—the sort your dog makes when a stranger approaches—means he's feeling defensive or protective.

Growling

Growling is an unmistakable warning sign. Dogs use it to tell other dogs or humans to back off. They also growl when they're frightened.

- When your dog combines a growl with a dominance posture, he's feeling aggressive.
- When he combines a growl with a submissive posture, he's feeling fearful or defensive.
- A growl during play isn't aggressive.

Howling

Howling is a dog's equivalent of using the phone—it's how he gets in touch with other dogs, even when they're miles away.

- A sing-song howl is used to contact other dogs, and means your dog is curious or happy.
- Plaintive, mournful howls signal distress.

Whining or Whimpering

Whining and whimpering hark back to puppyhood, when these sounds got him attention.

- When your dog is excited or lonesome, he'll whine or whimper to get your attention. These can sound like yawns.
- When he's stressed, fearful, or worried, he'll give repetitive, squeaky whines that may be punctuated with shrill yaps.

BREED SPECIFIC

Some dogs unwittingly challenge others because their ears and tails are naturally in an "aggressive" position. Breeds with pricked ears and tails over their backs, like Akitas, basenjis, and Alaskan malamutes, may get extra attention from dominant dogs because they look ready to fight, even when aggression isn't on their minds. Pups who've recently had their ears cropped, such as Great Danes, Doberman pinschers, and boxers, can also unintentionally set off warning bells in other dogs.

CHAPTER THREE

How Dogs Talk with People

When dogs want to talk with people, they do more than just bark.
They use an eloquent range of body language to say what
they're thinking and tell you what they want.

A dog looks longingly at his leash and paces back and forth in front of the door. The message is obvious: "Hey, I want to go outside." Another dog stands stiffly, his ears up and his tail sweeping slowly back and forth. His body language and his low, throaty growl are saying, "I don't like this situation and you'd better watch out."

Yet another does a full-body dance, barks, and wets the floor whenever his owner comes home. His message is, "You're number one in my book, and I'm peeing just to show that I know you're in charge."

Then there's Sir Loin, a people-pleasing black Labrador who lives with Marty and Teresa Becker in Bonner's Ferry, Idaho. Sir Loin adores having his belly rubbed, and his usual con is to step in front of the Beckers, collapse in an exaggerated fall, and roll onto his back, with his belly exposed and his tail wagging at turbo speed.

"If we're rushing and don't have time to rub his belly, he hangs his head and pouts," says Dr. Becker, a veterinarian and co-author of *Chicken Soup for the Pet Lover's Soul*. "His message is very clear: We've disappointed him."

Each of these dogs is delivering a different message, but they have one thing in common: a rich vocabulary that consists of body language,

Some messages are as obvious as this terrier mix's "Let me in" plea. Others are harder to interpret.

eye contact, behavior, barks, and a variety of other vocal sounds.

Dogs can't master the spoken word, but they don't really need to because they're already experts at getting their owners' attention. Why bother with words when a playful bark, a wagging tail, a cocked head, a lifted paw, or a soulful look in the eyes can deliver such unmistakable messages?

Signals You Should Know

There are slight differences among different breeds, and even among individual dogs, but all dogs communicate in more or less similar ways. People can usually tell what their dogs are feeling by glancing at the ways they're standing or moving, or just by looking at their eyes. But some of their signals aren't that obvious. Here are some of the main ways in which dogs communicate with people—and, in some cases, with other dogs as well.

Barking. There are many reasons dogs bark. It can mean they're having fun or are feeling frightened or lonely. It can mean they want attention or that they hear a strange noise that they think their owners should know about. The tone of barking changes with the dog's motivation, says David S. Spiegel, V.M.D., a veterinarian in private practice in Wilmington, Delaware, who specializes in behavior problems. "A panicked or anxious dog barks in a tone and pattern that we recognize as distress. This is meant to draw us near to help him."

While most dogs bark to say something, others do it just for fun, or out of habit, or because they're bored. This kind of barking can go on all day, and your dog will soon become the neighborhood nuisance.

Chewing. Chewing is natural and dogs get a lot of fun and satisfaction from doing it. Except for puppies who haven't yet learned household rules, dogs quickly learn what is and isn't appropriate for them to chew. So it's rarely a mistake when an adult dog rips up a pair of loafers or chews up a magazine, says Suzanne B. Johnson, Ph.D., an animal behaviorist in private practice in Washington, D.C. Chewing usually means they're anxious or bored. It can also mean they have too much energy and aren't getting enough exercise to dispel it.

Leaning. Dogs are enormously tactile and they don't respect "personal space" quite as much as people do. It's very common for dogs to get close to people and lean against their legs. Our usual reaction is to reach down to scratch their heads—which may not be the response they were after at all.

Dogs who merely lean, as opposed to a catlike rubbing back and forth, may be attempting to expand their personal space by taking over yours. It's sometimes the canine equivalent of leaning forward aggressively and saying "I'm tough and I can do as I like."

Conversely, some dogs lean as a way of expressing affection and establishing possession, much as people put their arms around each other when walking down the street. "My dog, Kira, will lean against me to prevent me from going somewhere else," says Joanne Howl, D.V.M., a veterinarian in private practice in West River, Maryland.

And sometimes, of course, a lean just means your dog is a little itchy and is rubbing against your legs to scratch a hard-to-reach spot.

This boxer is leaning against his owner's legs to show affection and "possession" of him.

13

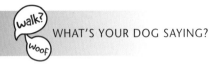

This young Labrador licks his owner's face in a gesture of deference and affection.

Leg humping. Nearly all dogs at some time in their lives show a little too much interest in people's legs. It's an unpleasant habit that's not only confined to male dogs. Most dogs either outgrow it or give it up once they've been neutered. Some dogs, however, do it all the time. It's not about sex, it's about power. Dogs who hump people's legs are saying "I'm higher on the totem pole than you," explains Jeff Nichol, D.V.M, a veterinarian and newspaper columnist in Albuquerque, New Mexico.

Licking. At one time, most experts believed that dogs licked people's faces for the same reason they licked their mothers'—as a way of getting something to eat. Today, a dog lick is generally considered more of a tribute than an attempt to solicit food. A dog who licks your face is reaffirming his subordinate status and saying that he loves and respects you. "He's telling you that you're the most wonderful thing that ever walked this Earth," says Dr. Nichol.

Limping. It's not unheard of for dogs to sprain their legs, but it occurs a lot less often than their theatrical limps might suggest. Many dogs employ this classic "pay attention to me" signal, and even experts can get fooled. One rainy evening in New York City, Robert Eckstein, D.V.M., Ph.D., a specialist in animal behavior at the department of biology at Warren Wilson College in Asheville, North Carolina, fell victim to the acting ability of a pooch pretender.

"I spotted this stray dog walking on three legs as though his fourth leg were injured beyond use. Once inside my apartment, the dog ran at full speed on all four legs and jumped on the bed. Mission accomplished."

Mouthing hands. Dogs who wrap their muzzles around your hand without using their teeth are giving a friendly greeting. This is common in Labradors and other retrieving dogs who have been bred to gently carry game back to their owners, says Laurel Davis, D.V.M., a veterinarian in private practice in Asheville, North Carolina. Muzzle-wraps aren't always gentle, however. When dogs are playing, one will often use his mouth to shut another's muzzle. Dogs who use their teeth, even in a controlled way, on people are getting way too aggressive, and this type of behavior is often followed by other forms of aggression.

Nose-nudging. Dogs love to push people with their noses. Most of the time it just means they want affection, says Dr. Nichol. "Or he considers the chair that you're in to be his favorite place and he wants you to move out of the way so he can take possession," he adds.

Smiling. Chesapeake Bay retrievers are known for curling their upper lips whenever they feel happy. Alaskan malamutes and Samoyeds are also well-known for their smiling expressions. Most dogs, however, don't smile in the same way that people do. If anything, they tend to assume a grinlike expression when they're feeling threatened and aggressive and want people to see their teeth.

Tongue-flicking. Dogs who repeatedly flick their tongues up to lick their noses are invariably uneasy, says Judy Iby, a registered veterinary technician in Milford, Ohio, and author of *The New Owner's Guide to Cocker Spaniels.* They often do this when they're assessing a new situation or debating whether or not to approach a stranger, she says. It's also common for them to flick their tongues when they're concentrating extra hard, such as during an obedience session.

Yawning. People usually yawn when they're tired or bored, but among dogs, yawning is often a signal that they're feeling stressed. A good yawn briefly lowers their blood pressure and helps them stay calm, says Dr.

Howl. She once treated a frightened collie mix, who crouched and shivered on the floor. After Dr. Howl stroked her head and body for a few minutes and spoke some soothing words, the dog let out a huge yawn and stood up.

"After three or four more good yawns, she had calmed down and become my best buddy," says Dr. Howl. "It was fascinating to watch the anxiety pour out of her body."

Lost in Translation

People and dogs speak different languages, so it's not uncommon to misinterpret the messages being passed back and forth. Sometimes we don't understand what our dogs are telling us. More often, they attempt to tell us things, but we don't even recognize that what we're seeing or hearing is a message.

Suppose your dog has started digging holes in the backyard and nothing you do will make him stop. This is more than a behavior problem: It's probably your dog's way of saying that he's a little bored with the daily routine and lack of mental stimulation, and he's trying to shake things up. Knowing the motivation for your dog's behavior is the key to changing it—or, when it's good behavior, encouraging more of it.

When dogs feel a little stressed, they'll often yawn to calm themselves down.

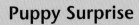

Puppy Surprise

It was late November and a winter storm was coming in—not the best time to deliver a litter of puppies. But dogs can't ignore the call of Nature any more than people can, so that's precisely when a Great Pyrenees named Seminole disappeared from Beverly Coate's farm in Stigler, Oklahoma.

For three days, Beverly looked for Seminole and her new pups. Temperatures were dropping, the wind was picking up strength, and rain was turning to freezing sleet. "I kept thinking about her and telling her in my mind to come and get me," Beverly says. Maybe it was a coincidence, but her positive thinking paid off. At 8:00 P.M., a weather-worn but insistent Seminole showed up in the barn—without her pups.

Seminole ran right to Beverly. She barked and pawed and did everything she could think of to get her attention. "She seemed very agitated with me for taking too long to find the flashlight," Beverly says. "Even though she looked hungry and thirsty, she refused food or water. She just wanted to go."

The two headed into the nearby woods. Sometimes Seminole walked at Beverly's heels, and sometimes she gave her a tug as though providing directions. About a quarter-mile away, Seminole led Beverly to a cedar thicket—and to her litter of nine beautiful pups.

Because dogs are companion animals, it's natural for them to prefer being with their owners than off by themselves. Many of the signals dogs give, from tail-wags to chewing on table legs, are really bids for attention. A dog who grabs his owner's wallet and starts running around the house isn't trying to get change for a twenty. He does it because he knows his owner is going to chase him. When that happens, he'll have succeeded in getting someone to play, and that's what he was after all along.

Every dog acts up (and acts out) occasionally, and it doesn't mean that terrible psychological forces are at work. The messages that dogs try to send are often quite simple: "I'm lonely," or "I'm jealous," or "I'm bored." They don't misbehave because they're trying to get even or cause problems. And they don't misbehave deliberately to tell you what's bothering them. "These acts are not usually deliberate communications with their owners," says Dr. Howl. "They are expressions of what's going on in the dog's mind."

When translating dogspeak, it's helpful to consider your dog's breed, says Steve Aiken, an animal behaviorist in Wichita, Kansas. You can't ignore a dog's inherent tendencies because they're sure to come out one way or another.

"Because terriers were bred to dig out and kill underground rodents, it's natural that they will want to go excavating in your backyard," Aiken says.

You don't have to like that instinct—any more than you have to appreciate a Labrador's instinct to chew—but you can work with it, Aiken says. Some people provide their dogs with authorized digging areas, places where they can excavate to their heart's content. and nearly everyone gives their dogs nice things to chew. By understanding what dogs need, Aiken says, you can give them what they need before they have to ask.

CHAPTER FOUR

CAN YOUR DOG READ YOUR MIND?

Some dogs seem to have extraordinary powers. They can find their way
home over great distances and can even predict earthquakes.
Some people are convinced that dogs can read minds, as well.

They rouse themselves from naps and wander to the door minutes before their owners pull into the driveway—long before they could have heard the sound of an engine or the tires on the road. Dogs who usually love car trips will run away when it's time to go for their annual shots. Some dogs can sense when their owners are going to have a seizure, and others can detect early-stage skin cancer—in some cases, with 99 percent accuracy. To the human mind, these and other forms of "mind-reading" are nothing less than astonishing, but for dogs, they're all in a day's work.

"I've been a pet lover all my life and a veterinarian for more than 20 years, but I still can't explain how lost dogs find their way back home or act as healers when we're sick or in need," says Marty Becker, D.V.M., a veterinarian in Bonner's Ferry, Idaho, and co-author of *Chicken Soup for the Pet Lover's Soul*. "I don't know if they read our minds or our hearts, but they constantly amaze me by what they pick up."

Mind Over Car

People have been speculating about dogs' extrasensory powers for centuries. Most experts have dismissed stories about canine prescience as being coincidence, at best, or even outright fraud. But one scientist isn't so sure. Rupert Sheldrake, Ph.D., former director of studies in biochemistry and cell biology at Cambridge

No one's sure how they do it, but but some dogs can find their way home from hundreds of miles away.

University, England, and author of *Seven Experiments That Could Change the World*, describes an experiment conducted by an Australian television crew. Having heard that a mixed-breed dog named JT could accurately predict the return of his owner to her home in Manchester, England, they decided to check it out. They designed an experiment in which JT and his owner were recorded simultaneously, with the images being projected on a split-screen television. The test showed convincingly that whenever JT's far-away owner headed for her car to go home, JT would move to the French doors of his home and settle down to greet her. The return trips were entirely random, yet JT got his timing right 85 percent of the time.

"I've collected a database of more than 2,000 pet stories, and there seems to be no clear dominance by breed or intelligence levels," explains Dr. Sheldrake. "The key behind telepathic pet phenomena seems to be the degree of bonding between the pet and his owner."

In the Realm of the Senses

No one can say for sure whether dogs can predict the future or read their owners' minds. But experts agree that dogs and many other animals have senses that go beyond what we can easily imagine, which may explain their uncanny ability to travel great distances without benefit of a compass or map. Homing pigeons use both the configurations of the stars and the Earth's magnetic fields to find their way home. Flocks of monarch butterflies spend their winters in Mexico, then fly back to the Rocky Mountains in Colorado. And there are many verified stories

POOCH PUZZLER

Can dogs predict earthquakes?

Scientists aren't sure how they do it, but some dogs are able to predict earthquakes long before the first tremor shakes the ground. Along with high-tech scientific instruments, dogs (and other animals) are considered an essential part of national earthquake warning systems in Japan and China. Experts have found that hours or even days before earthquakes, dogs begin pacing and acting restless. They bark at nothing and, in some cases, run away from the area.

In 1975, officials in the Chinese city of Haicheng were sufficiently alarmed by unusual animal behavior that they ordered 90,000 residents to evacuate the city. Hours later, a massive earthquake struck. It measured 7.3 on the Richter scale and destroyed 90 percent of the city's buildings. Without the early canine warning, the human tragedy would have been much more severe.

Researchers around the world, including members of the United States Geological Society, have studied how dogs seem to know about earthquakes. They speculate that dogs may detect high-frequency noises deep inside the Earth—noises that are too high for humans to hear. It's also possible that dogs sense electrostatic charges in the atmosphere or vibrations in the Earth. "Dogs have much more acute senses of hearing and smell than we do," says Robert Eckstein, D.V.M., Ph.D., an animal behaviorist in the department of biology at Warren Wilson College in Asheville, North Carolina. "They sense aspects of the real world that we aren't aware of."

of dogs finding their way home after moving to new cities hundreds of miles away.

Even though JT's story suggests that dogs are able to communicate over great distances with their owners, researchers suspect that the explanation has less to do with telepathy than with their incredible senses.

Seizure dogs are a good example. Increasingly used as an "early-warning system" by people who have epilepsy, these dogs have the amazing capacity to warn their owners of oncoming seizures as much as an hour before they occur. This advance notice allows their owners to take precautions, such as sitting down or moving away from stairs, so that they don't injure themselves when the seizure strikes.

The ability to detect seizures sounds as though it could only happen in a high-tech laboratory—or in a late-night science fiction movie. But there's a perfectly plausible explanation, says Roger Reep, associate professor at the University of Florida College of Veterinary Medicine in Gainesville. It's possible, he explains, that dogs are able to predict seizures because their highly developed sense of smell allows them to detect chemical changes in the brain that precede attacks.

In fact, many stories of canine "telepathy" are probably due to dogs' superior senses as well as their superlative observational skills, says Robert Eckstein, D.V.M., Ph.D., an animal behaviorist in the department of biology at Warren Wilson College in Asheville, North Carolina. "Since dogs mainly communicate nonverbally, it's very likely that they read our bodies, not our minds," Dr. Eckstein says. This may explain why your dog suddenly jumps up and looks at you expectantly just when you're thinking of taking him for walk or filling his food bowl. People are always giving off unconscious signals. Your dog probably reads the various movements of your body—the way you glance at the cupboard door or shift your weight, or even changes in your breathing. Some body language is so subtle that another person would never notice it. But dogs notice because at one time their survival depended on their powers of observation. When they lived in tight-knit groups called packs, each dog needed to know how the other dogs were feeling or what they were about to do. Dogs learned that being observant gave them an advantage in the struggle to survive, and they still haven't lost touch with their ancient heritage.

Mental Connections

While most scientists doubt that dogs can read minds, some vets believe that dogs do it every day—and that it's possible for humans to read their pets' minds, too. Laurel Davis, D.V.M., a veterinarian in private practice in Asheville, North Carolina, incorporates in her practice both mainstream veterinary medicine and occasional forays into telepathy. She believes that people have a natural ability to communicate telepathically, an ability that's often strongest in children and tends to become rusty in adults.

Even people who have never given a thought to telepathy have the ability to communicate with their pets, says Dr. Davis. She tells the story of a woman who had just attended an animal communication seminar. After it was over, she saw a man and a big dog sitting in a parked car.

MIND TO MIND

Communicating across the species isn't just the stuff of science fiction. When you're ready to try a little telepathy yourself, here's what professional animal communicators advise.

• Set aside a few minutes when you can give your dog your full attention, preferably in a quiet area where you won't be disturbed. Prepare a few questions or messages you want to communicate.

• Take a few deep, relaxing breaths to focus your energy and clear your mind of distractions.

• Say your dog's name in your mind. At the same time, form a detailed mental picture of what he looks like. The image you form should be as detailed and complete as possible.

• Mentally ask your dog a question or give the message you want him to receive. It's important to focus on the words—not by saying them out loud, but by allowing them to form in your mind.

• Relax totally and be prepared for whatever message you receive. In some cases you may hear actual words. More often, you're likely to receive a mental picture or feeling. You may receive a strong feeling that your dog is happy and content. Or you may get a mental image of what he's doing when you're gone or why he's been acting in an unusual way lately. Whatever message you receive, you need to acknowledge it mentally so that your dog knows you received it.

Don't be surprised if you don't receive any mental images at all, adds Laurel Davis, D.V.M., a veterinarian in private practice in Asheville, North Carolina. Most people aren't accustomed to using their minds to communicate with their dogs, and it takes time and practice to learn how to "listen" closely. But it's worth trying. "By talking with dogs on a telepathic level, I've found them to be wiser than you'll ever know," says Dr. Davis. "They are very spiritual."

She decided to try some of the things she had learned at the workshop. She stood still in the parking lot and for 10 minutes spoke mentally with the dog. Then she walked over to the car to say "Hi." The dog greeted her warmly, to the amazement of the owner, who said that his dog had a history of extreme aggressiveness and had never before let anyone near the car.

Patty Summers of Evington, Virginia, is a professional animal communicator. She believes that thought exchange between people and their pets isn't based on the physical senses but on true telepathic communication.

"Because telepathic communication is beyond verbal and isn't physical, it can be done from a distance," she says. "Animals often tune in to their people. They want to know where they are and what they're doing. When someone's coming home, he's probably thinking of heading home. His animal picks up on that thought."

Dr. Davis says she has used her mind to "talk" with dogs who were miles away. She begins these conversations with an ice-breaker, such as asking about their likes and dislikes. (She often finds they really love a particular ball or hate dry dog food.) Once she has established a rapport, she asks them specific questions to help resolve specific problems.

"When I communicate this way with animals, I have to be careful not to let preconceived notions of what I think they're saying or doing enter into the picture," she says. "It takes a lot of practice to be a good listener to dogs."

Mental telepathy takes practice, says Dr. Davis. Even if you aren't able to pick up signals from your dog right away, you can be pretty sure that your dog will hear you—not the actual words, perhaps, but the warmth and positive feelings you're putting out.

Psychic Sasha

Damon Miller couldn't figure out how she did it. On mornings when he planned to stay home from work, Sasha, his white German shepherd, almost went berserk with pleasure. On regular work mornings, she was quiet and almost seemed dejected. The amazing thing was that Sasha seemed to know his plans even before he got dressed in the morning.

Damon and his wife, Kathie, wondered if something was tipping her off. Damon, a dentist in Merlin, Oregon, didn't have a fixed schedule. Sometimes he took Wednesdays off. Occasionally he worked weekends. He rarely announced beforehand when he was going to stay home. But Sasha always knew. She seemed to be reading his mind.

Or maybe she was reading his socks. Damon and Kathie finally realized that Sasha started getting excited—or dejected—as soon as Damon took his socks from the bureau drawer. Brown socks, which he always wore to work, meant he was leaving the house. White socks meant it was going to be a fun, let's-play kind of day. "When Sasha spotted white socks being removed from the drawer, she would jump up and down and act excited," says Kathie. "Damon would pat Sasha's head to confirm that this was 'white socks day,' and they'd head out to his wood shop in the garage and spend the day together."

Was Sasha reading their minds or reading the clues? The Millers still don't know for sure. "We just know that she hated being left at home," Kathie says.

CHAPTER FIVE

THE NOSE KNOWS

One of the main ways that dogs communicate is with their sense of smell.
They sniff other dogs to learn about their age, sex, and status. They can even tell
a lot about a person's mood by the way he smells.

There's a powerful instrument that can detect tobacco wrapped in 27 layers of polythene or locate termites that are silently demolishing the foundations of a house. This instrument isn't a technological marvel created by humans, and you don't need an advanced degree to use it. It's the canine nose.

Among humans, the most important senses are sight and hearing. Among dogs, the sense of smell is paramount. A dog's sense of smell is up to a million times more sensitive than a human's.

Dogs can detect scents we don't even know exist, and they can identify the faintest of smells, even when they're heavily masked by other scents—such as the odor of trace amounts of heroin that have been hidden in pungent aniseed. A dog's sense of smell is often more powerful than the best scientific instruments, which is why dogs have been used to detect not only drugs but also gas leaks and explosives, and to find people lost in the wilderness or buried in avalanches.

Dogs can smell things humans can't because they have more nasal membrane than we do. We

The canine sense of smell is more sensitive than any machine, which is why Customs officers use dogs to search airline passengers' luggage for narcotics.

have about 65 square inches of nasal membrane, while dogs have about 900 square inches—an area that's greater than that of a dog's whole body, says Bruce Fogle, D.V.M., Ph.D., a veterinarian and author of *The Dog's Mind*. The nasal membrane is packed with olfactory receptors, specialized cells responsible for detecting scents.

A German shepherd typically has about 220 million olfactory receptors, while a human has about 5 million, says Mark Plonsky, Ph.D., a psychologist and dog trainer at the University of Wisconsin in Madison. It's believed that the bigger the dog and the longer his muzzle, the keener his sense of smell. German shepherds, for example, aren't just better at sniffing out scents than humans are, they're better at it than some other breeds. A fox terrier, for instance, has 150 million olfactory receptors, and a dachshund has about 125 million.

Dogs have an additional advantage. Their noses are always wet, as anyone knows who has woken up to the sensation of a cold, wet nose. It's believed that this sheen of moisture acts almost like Velcro, trapping scent molecules as they waft by. Along with the sticky mucus in the nasal passages, this allows dogs to collect and store large numbers of passing molecules.

Scents don't just drift conveniently into their noses. A dog's nostrils act like little antennas. Dogs wiggle them to collect scents and figure out where they're coming from.

When your dog raises his head and sniffs, he's breaking his normal breathing pattern to gather some new information. The air currents are abuzz with news, and he can hardly wait to tap into them and find out what's going on. "He has to actively sniff to pull the scent into the olfactory

Detective Down Under

Rex, a wire fox terrier, lived happily in a suburb of Sydney, Australia, for most of his eight years. But when his owners, Rae and Ted Humphries, started spending more time away from home, they decided it would be best for Rex if he went to live with friends more than 20 miles away. "I didn't like the idea of his being lonely all day without us, and I thought he'd be better off where he'd have more company," Rae says.

Rex, however, had different ideas. He ran away from his new home the day after he arrived. His new owners searched the neighborhood for days, but Rex was nowhere to be found. They had to accept that he wasn't coming back.

Three months later, Rae heard a scratching at the back door one evening. She opened the door and there was Rex. "He was thin and his coat was caked with dirt," she says. "But despite his sorry state, he was so happy to see me."

She couldn't imagine how Rex managed to find his way across railroad tracks, traffic-filled highways, and open land to find his family after all those months. "You hear about dogs having a wonderful sense of smell, and I can only imagine that Rex put his to good use to find us," she says. "After that escapade, we knew he had to stay with us."

Dogs like this pharaoh hound sniff the air to collect scent molecules and locate where smells are coming from.

23

sensors, and when he doesn't, he's effectively turning his nose—or his sense of smell—off," says D. Caroline Coile, Ph.D., a neuroscientist in Ochlocknee, Georgia.

What all this means is that dogs have the ability to take in and identify scents that humans don't even know exist.

The scent molecules gleaned with each sniff are ultimately distilled and transported to various parts of the brain, much of which is devoted to remembering and interpreting them. Dogs have the ability to tap into this scent storage bank throughout their lives.

"Odors have a powerful influence on both the behavior and the physiology of the dog," says Dr. Fogle. "Smell memories last for life and affect almost all canine behavior." Scents tell them where they are, who a dog or person is, and even what state of mind that other creature happens to be in.

of information by reading the scent messages that other dogs have left.

The urine of female dogs in heat, for example, contains different pheromones—scent molecules—than that of dogs who are out of season. The males, of course, are eager for this information.

It's not only urine that contains scent signals, says Ian Dunbar, Ph.D., a veterinarian and author of *Dog Behavior*. The anal glands, stools, and saliva also contain olfactory information that dogs are keen to get hold of.

Even though dogs introduce themselves by sniffing each other's faces, it's the back ends that get the most attention. A quick sniff reveals a lot: how old a dog is, which sex, neutered or intact, relative or stranger. Scents also reveal a dog's confidence and social status, and what his mood happens to be at the moment. Dogs synthesize all of this information and figure

How Dogs Communicate with Scent

A dog who raises his leg on a tree isn't being indelicate. He's essentially pinning a notice on the community bulletin board. The scents in urine are as unique as the fingerprints among humans. Dogs who sniff trees, electric poles, and fire hydrants are gleaning tremendous amounts

By putting his nose to work this Border collie is learning the age, sex, and status of other dogs that have been visiting his neighborhood.

These Picardy shepherds are indulging in the usual sniff routine, which enables them to collect a lot of personal information.

out very quickly what their relationship with another dog is likely to be.

Although dogs do the sniffing routine longer with dogs they don't know, even house mates will sniff each other frequently. Behaviorists aren't sure why dogs continue to sniff even when they know each other intimately. It may simply be the dog equivalent of saying "How are you today?" and catching up on the gossip.

A dog's fascination with smells doesn't stop with sniffing. Even dogs that have lived indoors all their lives appear to have an instinct that tells them to get dirty and roll in smelly things at the first opportunity. "It's camouflage," says Torry Weiser, a dog trainer in San Francisco. "What they're doing is using the scent of another creature to disguise themselves from something they're preying on and to get closer to it." Dogs don't have to think about prey and predators very much anymore, but the urge lives on.

"They seem to be having a great time doing it," Weiser adds. "It's not perfume to us, but it certainly is to them."

What Human Scents Tell Dogs

Your dog knows your scent and has it filed in his memory, along with the smells of all the other people he's been introduced to. Some people your dog will remember with affection, others with fear and loathing—and his "scent memory" will be triggered every time he meets them.

The one smell dogs value most is the smell of their owners. "It's a familiar smell that conveys comfort and safety," says Weiser. That's why experts recommend leaving an article of worn clothing with your dog when you have to leave for any length of time. The piece of clothing has your smell on it, and it gives comfort to him.

And like it or not, your dog can tell a lot about your mood just by your smell. A person's body odor is believed to change depending on his or her mood, and dogs are thought to be able to pick up on this.

Research has also shown that "happy tears" contain different chemicals than "angry tears," and some experts believe dogs can tell the difference—and know right away whether to nuzzle your hand or give you a wide berth until you've calmed down.

Perfume, deodorant, cigarette smoke, and other odors that linger on skin and clothing all combine to make up a person's individual smell. Changing that composite smell "picture" in some way—using a new perfume or none at all, for instance—can confuse a dog and dull his

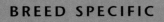
BREED SPECIFIC

Dogs bred to hunt, track, or retrieve, such as bloodhounds, beagles, Norwegian elkhounds (right), and Labrador retrievers, appear to have the best sense of smell. But any dog's sense of smell can be improved with the proper training.

Norwegian elkhounds have an astonishing sense of smell and can detect game up to three miles away.

ability to recognize someone as quickly as he normally would.

Dogs don't care if you're sweaty or have something pungent on your hands, but there are odors that do turn them off. Among these are citrus smells, such as lemon, lime, and orange, and spicy smells like red pepper. They particularly dislike the smell of citronella, which is why it's often used in spray form to keep dogs away from certain areas.

There are odors that turn dogs on, too, and often they're ones that turn us off. The trash smells like a smorgasbord to our dogs, but if we smell it at all, it's the opposite of delectable.

Sometimes, because of illness or accident, a dog's sense of smell can become impaired. "Dogs with a loss of smell seem to do just fine," says Dr. Coile. They'll tend to rely more heavily on their other senses to give them the essential information they need, she explains. They may start to eat less, though. The smell of their food is important to them, even more than the taste. That's why veterinarians often advise warming food when dogs lose their appetites. Warming food boosts the aroma, which may get them eating again.

NOSES AT WORK

Working dogs use their sense of smell to hold down serious jobs. Among the canine professions that call for a good nose are drug sniffing, explosive detection, and rescue work. Specially trained scent dogs can also locate people trapped in avalanches and under rubble.

In California, a group of beagles is employed by the U. S. Department of Agriculture at airports and postal facilities to detect fruits, plants, and meats that are being illegally transported into the state.

Research has shown that dogs' noses contain infrared receptors that are sensitive to temperature. Combined with their sharp sense of smell, these receptors help dogs to detect humans buried deep in snow.

Dogs can also be trained to track people who have gotten lost in wilderness areas. And they can detect shed human skin cells in places where people have recently been.

CHAPTER SIX

BEYOND HUMAN HEARING

Dogs have astonishingly good hearing, and they pay more attention
to sounds than people do. You can take advantage of their
superior hearing to help them learn more quickly.

Can you hear the squeak of a mouse inside a wall, the ultrasonic beep of a dying smoke alarm battery, or the faint sound of a thunderstorm long before it arrives? Not a chance—but for dogs, these and other faint or high-pitched sounds are as loud and clear as the ringing of a bell.

Their superior hearing dates from when they lived in the wild, and the ability to hear the slightest of sounds could mean the difference between getting a meal and going hungry.

Though the need to listen for a meal is long gone, dogs still rely on their hearing to make better sense of the world around them.

Experts have discovered that dogs can hear sounds from four times farther away than people can. That means that what a person can hear from a hundred yards, a dog can hear from a quarter-mile. Dogs are also able to detect very high frequencies that humans are oblivious to.

Dogs may not be able to see with crystal clarity, but they more than make up for that with their exquisitely sensitive hearing. It lets them know that you're coming home long before you pull into the driveway, and they can tell when you're upset no matter how hard you try to keep your voice steady.

A very effective way to work with dogs, whether you're trying to get their attention or helping them learn new commands, is to take advantage of their hearing. Not only do they hear things we can't, they hear things differently. You can use these differences to help dogs learn more quickly, feel more secure, and understand what you're saying.

This Labrador always knows when his owner is coming home because he can distinguish the sound of her car from any other.

Why Dogs Hear So Well

Before dogs became domesticated, hearing was an essential sense for survival. Their sharp hearing alerted them to danger, let them communicate with other dogs far away, and enabled them to detect even the smallest and most cautious prey. The changes in the brain that occurred over thousands of years still guide dogs today. Experts have found, for example, that while the human brain is largely devoted to such things as learning and memory, much of a dog's brain is devoted to sound, says Katherine A. Houpt, V.M.D., Ph.D., a veterinary behaviorist and professor of physiology at Cornell University in Ithaca, New York.

One of the reasons dogs hear so much better than people do is that their ears are bigger. They're also cup-shaped, which enables them to trap all the available sound waves and funnel them into the eardrum. Another advantage is that their ears are as mobile as antennas. Dogs have 15 different muscles that move the ears up, down, and sideways. And they can move one ear at a time—a talent that eludes most people—which lets them detect and pinpoint sounds coming from any direction.

With all of this anatomical sophistication, dogs can do some amazing things—like hearing when a cat's nosing around their food, even when they're sound asleep three rooms away. They can tell, using hearing alone, whether the

SIREN SONG

The high-pitched wail of a siren can launch even quiet dogs into howling harmonies. Dogs can hear sounds at very high frequencies, and experts once suspected that the wail of sirens hurt their ears, just as fingernails against a chalkboard drive some people crazy.

The problem with this theory is that dogs never seem uncomfortable or unhappy when they're howling at sirens. Quite the opposite, in fact: Many dogs seem to relish it. "There's absolutely no evidence that these sounds hurt their ears," says John C. Wright,

Ph.D., a certified applied animal behaviorist, professor of psychology at Mercer University in Macon, Georgia, and author of *The Dog Who Would Be King.*

The most likely explanation, he says, is that dogs evolved from wolves, and wolves howl to greet their pack-mates and to communicate across distances. Dogs are a long way from wolves, but some of the old instincts remain. It's unlikely that they confuse sirens with the greeting of another dog, but they still respond the way they're supposed to—by howling back.

POOCH PUZZLER

Can dogs spell?

Some dogs get so excited when they hear words such as "walk" or "cookie" that their owners develop a kind of code to prevent themselves from going bananas. Rather than saying "walk," for example, they'll spell it out and say "w-a-l-k."

But it usually doesn't take dogs long to learn that w-a-l-k means it's time to run about and bark until someone finally picks up the leash.

Even though dogs can't spell, they're perfectly capable of learning complex sound patterns and linking these sounds with what they mean, says Torry Weiser, a dog trainer in San Francisco. "If you spell a word such as 'walk' each time you get ready to take your dog out, eventually, he'll figure out what it means," Weiser explains.

food that slipped from the cutting board was an uninteresting brussels sprout or a tempting piece of meat. Even when they're running around in the backyard, they'll know you're home the instant your key hits the lock.

Dogs' superior hearing makes their world a very interesting place—and also one that's vastly different from a human's world.

"It's hard to imagine what a dog's world must be like," says D. Caroline Coile, Ph.D., a neuroscientist with a special interest in canine sensory systems in Ochlocknee, Georgia. "What we do know is that they certainly have a much richer auditory life than we do."

Despite their excellent hearing, dogs aren't overwhelmed by the variety or volume of the sounds they hear any more than people are overwhelmed by the range of the things they see. Anything dogs aren't interested in or don't need to know, their brains filter out. That's why they can sleep through a noisy conversation in the next room but will wake up the instant someone says their name. Similarly, when someone fills the laundry tub to wash a sweater, some dogs hide because they think it's bathtime—but they'll ignore the sound of the kitchen sink being filled for doing the dishes. They only tune in to the things that might affect them, says Dr. Houpt.

Some of the things that attract a dog's attention are the same things people wish they could hear but can't—like the sound of someone slipping over a back fence into the yard. This is one situation in which a dog's superior hearing is a real favor to the family. But just like car alarms, sometimes a dog's hearing can be a little too sensitive. Dogs will occasionally erupt in a sudden burst of barking because they hear something that the people in the family can't see or hear, and couldn't care less about.

Being able to hear high frequencies has surprising

This Labrador can hear the sounds of small animals under the snow, so he does what comes naturally—he investigates by digging.

benefits for some dogs. The cry of a bat, for example, is way too high for most creatures, including cattle, to hear. That may explain why cattle in South America often get attacked by vampire bats, but dogs seldom do. It seems that dogs can hear the bats' cries and so can avoid becoming the source of their next meal, says Bruce Fogle, D.V.M., Ph.D., author of *The Dog's Mind*.

It seems that all dogs, no matter what their size or breed, have roughly equal hearing abilities, says Rickye Heffner, Ph.D., professor of psychology at the University of Toledo in Ohio. Small dogs don't hear higher frequencies better than large dogs do, and large dogs are no better at picking up low noises than smalls dog are.

Ear type doesn't have much effect on hearing, either. Floppy-eared dogs and prick-eared dogs have fared about the same in tests,

Gretchen on Guard

No one knows the benefits of canine hearing better than Jessica Maurer of Portland, Maine. If it weren't for the keen ears of Gretchen, her 11-year-old Samoyed, Jessica and a few of her friends might not be here to tell the tale.

Jessica, her roommate, and two neighbors had just sat down at an outdoor table in Jessica's backyard. They were about to eat when Gretchen suddenly stood up and began to growl. Jessica looked over and saw that Gretchen was staring up at the 80-foot sycamore tree that loomed over the table.

That's when they heard a loud popping sound. Realizing the tree was about to fall, they scrambled to get out of the way. Jessica's roommate didn't move quickly enough, and her legs were injured. But everyone else got away in time—thanks to an alert dog with very remarkable hearing.

PUPPY DOG TALES

A dog's ear size and shape don't affect how well he hears. Floppy-eared dogs like the Cavalier King Charles spaniel (right) hear just as well as prick-eared ones like the Belgian shepherd (left).

says Dr. Heffner. Surprisingly, dogs with floppy ears can hear almost as well with their ears in the normal, droopy position as when they're taped up to expose the ear canal.

One thing that is breed-related is the likelihood of a dog being born deaf. This is caused by a genetic disorder that is associated with white and blue merle coat colors. "It can crop up anywhere, but it crops up a lot in Dalmatians," says Dr. Heffner. Other breeds commonly affected include Australian cattle dogs, Australian shepherds, Boston terriers, English setters, and Old English sheepdogs.

But dogs who are deaf learn to compensate in other ways. "Dogs spend 80 to 90 percent of their time communicating without a sound," says Suzanne Clothier, a trainer and co-owner

of Flying Dog Press in St. Johnsville, New York. They pay close attention to body language, faces, and eyes to help them understand each other and people. Dogs who are deaf learn to "read" people very well.

A Sound Approach

Since dogs are attuned to and excited by high-pitched sounds—probably because these were the sounds made by their traditional prey—the best way to get their attention is by pitching your voice upward, says Clothier. Speaking in a high voice is perfect during training or when you're calling your dog, she explains. It's also an effective way of letting your dog know when he has pleased you.

Dogs also respond to lower tones, presumably because these sounds resemble the growls or grumbles they hear almost from birth—first from their mother when she wanted to reprimand them, and later from dogs who growled to send the message "Leave me alone" or "Don't touch that, it's mine."

Unlike high tones, which tend to make dogs happy and excited and less likely to obey instruction, low tones make them slightly nervous because they associate these sounds with "top dogs." You can use this to your advantage when dogs aren't doing what you want by speaking in a deeper, growl-like voice. They'll understand that you really mean business and so will be more likely to obey you.

You can also get results by playing with the volume of your voice. Shouting will get a dog's attention, but may be counterproductive because it can also scare or intimidate him. Lower volumes will often work better than a shout. For example, whispers can be very effective once a dog is paying attention. Dogs are intrigued by whispers just as humans are, and they'll do the canine equivalent of leaning closer to hear exactly what you're saying.

POOCH PUZZLER

Do dogs like music?

Many dogs seem to react with pleasure when their owners turn up the stereo. They may lie down peacefully at their owners' feet while mellow New Age or classical music is playing, or prick their ears up at the sound of more strident pop music. Experts suspect it's not the kind of music that gets their attention as much as our reaction to it.

"Our dogs are experts at reading body language," says Steve Aiken, an animal behaviorist in Wichita, Kansas. "When we listen to music we enjoy, our bodies show it. We may sway, dance, or hum, but generally any music that improves our mood will result in body language that our dogs like to see. Our bodies say we're happy, so our dogs are happy."

It *is* possible for dogs to develop musical preferences, Aiken says—but there's a very strong likelihood that they'll form a taste for the same sorts of music that their owners prefer to listen to.

When we listen to music that pleases us, dogs may learn to make a positive association toward that style.

"It's not that they're hanging out to hear the latest Pavarotti recording," Aiken says. "But it's obvious that we enjoy listening to him, and that makes them happy, too."

PART TWO

THE BARK SIDE

Dogs depend mainly on scent and body language to communicate, but they do use their voices—both to talk to each other and to us. You can tell a lot about what dogs are thinking by the way they bark. And since barking is their native language, you can communicate more clearly by occasionally barking back.

CHAPTER SEVEN

THE LANGUAGE OF BARKING

Dogs have different barks to convey different messages. They use some barks to speak with other dogs. Other kinds of barks are meant to get their owners' attention or to show that they are happy and excited. Still other barks indicate that they're nervous or anxious.

A few thousand years ago, barking made a lot more sense than it does today. Even though wild dogs lived together in packs, they often went their separate ways during the day to hunt for food or look for mates. Barking enabled them to communicate across great distances. It served both as a long-distance phone call and a community bulletin board—a way of talking to one dog or the entire pack. And unlike scent and body language, which are dogs' preferred ways of communicating, barking didn't leave a physical trail for predators to follow. So even though wild dogs—and their ancestors, the wolves—didn't bark a lot, it came in handy on occasion.

From an evolutionary point of view, barking isn't a very useful trait any more. For one thing, most dogs live in apartments or houses, so they don't need to communicate across great distances. And since dogs live mainly with humans and not other dogs, barking isn't a great way to communicate. It's like going to Rome and only speaking English: People know you're saying something, but haven't the slightest idea what.

Here's the curious thing. Even though barking is less useful today than it used to be, modern dogs do it a lot more than their ancestors did—not because it's a great way to

When living in the wild, dogs barked to communicate across great distances. These Munsterlanders have all their friends close to home, but the tradition continues.

communicate, but because they're not very mature. Like children, they often bark merely to hear themselves speak.

Perpetual Adolescence

As any parent can attest, adolescence is a noisy time. That's equally true among dogs, who can be real chatterboxes when they're growing up,

BARKS AND VARIATIONS

The basenji (left), a breed that originated in Africa, is a medium-size, handsome dog with a distinctive, tightly curled tail. An unusual shape of the larynx, or voice box, is thought to be responsible for the fact that basenjis don't bark. "But they make every other noise under the sun," says Mary Merchant, a therapy dog evaluator for St. John's Ambulance Corps in Powassan, Ontario, Canada. Their most common noise is halfway between a chortle and a yodel.

Despite their rather odd vocalizations, basenjis are quiet more often than most dogs, probably because they once hunted in packs, and being noisy isn't helpful when you're trying to sneak up on your supper.

Another unusual vocalist is one of the world's most elusive wild dogs, the New Guinea singing dog (right). Found in the mountainous interior of Papua New Guinea, these small, red-and-white dogs have a strange bark that sounds like a rooster's crow. The sound travels tremendous distances and helps the isolated packs stay in touch, says Mark Feinstein,

Ph.D., an animal behaviorist and dean of cognitive sciences at Hampshire College in Amherst, Massachusetts. Even singing dogs that never have any physical contact talk to one another over the valleys.

The dogs are naturally solitary and have been called the night dog or black dog—not because of their coloring, but because they're seldom seen, only heard. There's a small colony of singing dogs at Amherst College. The best way to get them to "sing," says Dr. Feinstein, is to walk out of their sight. They'll start vocalizing right away. "They're trying to make contact," he says.

says Mark Feinstein, Ph.D., an animal behaviorist and dean of cognitive sciences at Hampshire College in Amherst, Massachusetts. In the wild, dogs quickly move through adolescence as they mature and begin taking care of themselves. But in today's world, dogs are always dependent on their owners. In a sense, they never grow up entirely. They continue barking

A Bark Saves a Life

PUPPY DOG TALES

A dog who won't stop barking can be a real nuisance. But Nan Duff, a nurse in Ben Avon, Pennsylvania, owes her life to one dog's determined yaps.

Early one summer morning, Nan's chocolate Labrador, Duncan, began barking—and barking. He barked so loud and so long that Nan's neighbor, Lisa Grillo, wondered what was up. "This barking was very different from the way he usually barked," Lisa recalls. "It was high-pitched, like a yelp."

Lisa phoned Nan to ask what was going on. When she didn't answer, Lisa called the police. Then she went outside and saw Duncan, still barking, in the bedroom window of Nan's home across the street.

The police arrived and broke a window to get into the house. They were greeted by Duncan, who raced upstairs to Nan's bedroom. The officers found Nan unconscious in bed, with Duncan at her side. She was taken to the hospital, where doctors learned that her blood sugar was frighteningly low. Nan, a diabetic, had lapsed into a life-threatening coma.

Nan recovered and was amazed when she learned how Duncan had called for help in the only way he could. For his lifesaving effort, Duncan received the Pennsylvania Veterinary Medical Association's Human–Animal Bond Award, which rewards animals whose heroic deeds best exemplify the close bonds between people and their pets.

It's not a coincidence that dogs started barking a lot more when they were domesticated. Their new owners realized that barking could be a useful trait. It warned them when strangers were approaching, it alerted them to the presence of game, and it let strangers know that this was a dog to be reckoned with. Barking was so useful, in fact, that people deliberately bred those dogs who barked the most, and the "vocal" genes were passed on through the generations.

For most people, of course, barking is more of a nuisance than anything else—but dogs keep doing it. That's partly because we often inadvertently encourage barking. For example, people who are walking their dogs will often touch the top of their dogs' heads and admonish them when they make a noise—cues that dogs often take to mean they're doing a great job and should keep it up. A similar thing occurs when sleep-deprived owners stick their heads out the window and yell at a dog to pipe down. Barking dogs are often seeking a reply—any reply—and if it happens to be a human who answers, that'll do fine.

Interpreting Barks

Dogs bark for all sorts of reasons. Apart from greeting other dogs, they bark to ask for attention or to show that they're happy and excited.

because their domestication has them stuck in adolescence, says Dr. Feinstein.

"It's young dogs that are almost always the barkiest," adds Deborah Jones, Ph.D., a dog trainer in Akron, Ohio. They rarely stop barking completely, but when they're older and more experienced, they tend to bark less. "Once they get better at reading and sending the more subtle body language clues, they quiet down," says Dr. Jones.

Barking helps them blow off steam and relieves stress as well as boredom. Dogs have a number of different barks, which convey entirely different messages. By listening to the pace, pitch, and overall tones, you can get a pretty good idea of what your dog's trying to say.

Strong and Steady

Dogs often respond to strangers approaching or things they hear outside with a series of single barks, or with a quick, repetitive *wooo-wooo-wooo-wooo-wooo*. This type of barking is a warning. It's not meant to tell the intruder to go away, but to let the owners know that something is amiss. "He doesn't want to handle this potential threat all by himself, so he calls for reinforcements," says Dr. Jones.

You can't tell from listening to this type of bark whether the intruder is a human or

When a dog barks at strangers from inside the car, his bark will be strong and steady because he's warning you of possible danger.

Even though dogs no longer need to hunt for food, they still have a strong instinct to chase small animals—or at least to bark at them.

another dog. But your dog's body language will provide additional cues, says Dr. Jones. If a strange dog approaches, for example, your dog will probably do a lot of running forward, then stepping back. "But if the other dog is an old pal, look for play-bows, tail wagging, and happy, upright ears."

Dogs give similar greetings when people they recognize come to visit. Even though the bark is low-pitched and regular, it almost sounds happy—a message that will be reinforced by happy panting and tail wags.

Fast and Furious

Dogs don't have the best vision in the world, and from a distance, a running rabbit probably doesn't appear all that different from a person zipping by on in-line skates. So they respond the way they would to anything that's moving quickly, with a high-pitched, fast bark that says,

A cocker spaniel holds the world record for persistent barking—an amazing 907 barks in 10 minutes.

BREED SPECIFIC

Nearly all dogs bark occasionally, but some breeds have a stronger tendency to bark than others. This is because they were bred to use their voices for a specific purpose.

• Hounds, such as beagles, foxhounds, bloodhounds, and basset hounds, use their voices a lot because they were bred to call back to their masters during a hunt. The baying call of a beagle and the mournful howl of a bloodhound are particularly penetrating and persistent.

• Herding dogs like Australian kelpies and Shetland sheepdogs were bred to use barking as a way of controlling their flocks.

• Terriers, such as miniature schnauzers and Jack Russells, were bred to alert their owners to the presence of rodents by barking.

• Toy breeds such as Pomeranians, Pekingese, and toy poodles were bred to be lap dogs, so their propensity for barking is a little unusual. They're feisty little things, however, and they bark a lot to show they have big spirits.

"I'd better chase it—or at least bark at it." This type of bark is usually accompanied by confident body language, such as a raised tail or perked-up ears.

Some dogs give this kind of bark when they see something they don't recognize—anything from a person wearing a slicker or a vacuum cleaner in the living room to the sight of their own reflection in a mirror. "You might see the same pattern of lunging forward and then backing up that you would see if your dog were barking at an unfamiliar dog," says Dr. Jones.

High-Pitched

Dogs who want something will often ask for it with an ear-splitting yap. The usual pattern is to bark once, wait a moment to see what happens, then bark again if they're not satisfied. Or they'll give a whole series of high-pitched barks to get your attention. In either case, the barking will usually be accompanied by tail-wagging or other playful signs, says Terry Ryan, a trainer in Sequim, Washington, and author of *The Toolbox for Remodeling Your Problem Dog*.

High-Pitched and Urgent

Just as some people try to relieve anxiety by pacing, some dogs resort to rapid, high-pitched, desperate-sounding barks. "Barking is a definite tension reliever," says Dr. Jones. "It's like primal-scream therapy for dogs."

Some types of dog are especially likely to bark when they're feeling lonely, says Dr. Jones. These include sociable dogs such as beagles, herding dogs such as collies, and breeds that were designed solely to be companion dogs, like most of the toy breeds.

CHAPTER EIGHT

BARKING BACK

People aren't very good at dogspeak, but sometimes giving a growl or a yelp
conveys a clearer message than human speech can. And an occasional howl
tells your dog that you appreciate him.

No matter how hard they try, dogs will never be proficient in English. Most of what they hear from us comes across as just noise, which is why owners occasionally try to turn things around by communicating in barks, howls, or whines.

It's unlikely anyone will ever publish a *Berlitz Guide to Canine Chat*, if only because speaking dog is a lot more complicated than mastering a foreign language. For one thing, dogs really don't communicate with their voices very much. They depend instead on nonverbal language such as posture, gestures, and scent. Since they don't have a well-defined vocabulary the way humans do, there isn't a bark equivalent for "go outside" or "get your leash." In addition, human vocal cords can't accurately reproduce the sounds of canine speech. Even if you growled to warn your dog off the couch or barked to get his attention, the message wouldn't get through.

"Most dogs would laugh at us if we barked at them," adds Liz Palika, a dog trainer in Oceanside, California. "Their hearing is so much better than ours that we couldn't possibly do justice to their different barking tones."

This doesn't mean dogs won't respond when you imitate a bark. They may bark back or at least look interested for a moment—but it's not

because you accidentally delivered a decipherable message. It's because they're responding to your body language, the tone of your voice, and your overall level of enthusiasm, says Joanne Howl, D.V.M., a veterinarian in private practice in West River, Maryland. "Some people I know do bark, but it is not very effective," she says. "Our dog accent is so atrocious that we ruin their language."

All in the Tone

Even though barking, yelping, howling, whinning, or growling will never replace training or other forms of nonverbal communication, there are situations in

This golden retriever is responding to her owner's tone of voice and body language. Some people try barking at dogs, which gets their attention but doesn't mean much.

which speaking dog, however poorly, allows you to deliver messages that otherwise might get missed. The idea isn't to learn specific barks, but to use some of the same tones and inflections that dogs respond to, says John C. Wright, Ph.D., a certified applied animal behaviorist, professor of psychology at Mercer University in Macon, Georgia, and author of *The Dog Who Would Be King.*

Growling. Dogs that are angry will sometimes respond with a long, low growl. Among canines, it's mainly the high-ranking dogs who growl, while other, more subordinate dogs are less assertive. As a result, dogs are conditioned to equate growls with leadership.

People can take advantage of this when it's time to convey the voice of authority. When dogs are doing something they shouldn't,

Dogs howl to communicate over long distances, but this Labrador cross and his owner are having a howling session just for the fun of it.

giving a low, simmering growl will put them on notice that the "top dog"—meaning you—isn't pleased. You don't have to growl to get results, Dr. Wright adds. Dropping your voice and saying "heyyy" in a low, extended tone will give the same message. "They are prepared to hear a low pitch as a growl," he explains.

Avoid growling too often. Dogs with a tendency to be aggressive or dominant may perceive growls as a direct threat and respond with growls—or worse—of their own. It's also too severe a message for minor problems, like disagreements about getting on the furniture.

Growling is appropriate when you're dealing with puppies, Palika says. They know that their job is to obey their mother or other adults, and a growl is immediately understood.

Howling. In the days when dogs lived far apart, howling was the equivalent of sending up smoke signals. "Where are you?" might be answered by "We're over here." Experts aren't sure if howls actually mean anything or if they're just a convenient way to communicate over long distances. And there's no way to tell if howling at a dog does anything more than get his attention. But dogs may appreciate a howl from their owners, if only because they may view it as a valiant effort to be social, says Dr. Wright.

Yelping. Puppies quickly learn to soften their bites during play-fights when a littermate responds with a yelp. Yelping is a very effective way to help a pup understand that he's biting too much or too hard. "It means, 'Stop, you're hurting me, you're being too rough,'" Dr. Wright explains.

CHAPTER NINE

WORDS EVERY DOG SHOULD KNOW

Dogs will never be gifted linguists but they can learn more than we give them credit for.

Apart from knowing their names, a few basic commands, and really exciting words like "walk" or "biscuit," most dogs are at a loss when it comes to humanspeak. It's not that they're not capable of learning more words. It's just that most people don't feel it's important enough to teach them. But teaching your dog a range of commands has advantages for both of you—your dog will be better to live with, and he'll get a real kick out of doing things that please you.

"Your dog's ability to learn vocabulary is unlimited," says Liz Palika, a dog trainer in Oceanside, California. Her Australian shepherd Ursa learned more than 150 words during her 13 years. When pulling a wagon, Ursa even understood how to follow directions, such as "pull easy," "pull hard," "pull fast," "go left," "turn right," and "make a U-turn."

"Since I was often behind her or had my hands full, she couldn't see me or read my hand gestures," Palika says. "She had to rely on my voice and words."

Ursa was more than just a good wagon dog. She also knew commands like "find the car keys," "take this screwdriver to Paul," and "give me the TV remote."

With patience, dogs can be taught almost any word. This Labrador has learned what "football" means.

Basic Vocabulary

Most dogs, of course, are never going to be Scrabble champions, and while many owners would be thrilled to expand their dogs' vocabu-

laries, they'd settle for a modest six or eight words rather than hundreds. Which words you choose are up to you, although every dog should know the basic five: "sit," "stay," "come," "heel," and "down."

Dogs who know basic obedience commands are a lot easier to be around, Palika says. They feel more secure because they know exactly what you're saying, and they're less likely to steamroll over you the second you open the door or ignore you because they're chasing a squirrel down the block.

The words themselves aren't really important, Palika adds, as long as your dog gets the same message. One of her students, for example, owned an Italian restaurant and used variations of pasta words as commands. Lasagna meant "heel," for example, and linguine meant "stay." "It's a neat trick as long as he doesn't forget what pasta dish meant what command," says Palika. "If his dog zipped out the front gate, he would have to remember to shout 'spaghetti', or the dog wouldn't stop."

Beyond the Basics

Dogs are both attentive and eager to please. They're capable of learning new words very quickly, and many owners decide to keep teaching them new ones. It's satisfying when a dog sits or lies down on command, but it's a lot more fun when he understands expressions such as "wave goodbye."

Teaching words isn't difficult as long as you're patient and take the time to clearly link words with actions, Palika says. Here are some tips for effective training.

Train when he's relaxed. Do your training when your dog is relaxed, but not sleepy—after a good walk, for example.

Use some treats. Start your training by holding in your hand something your dog loves. It can be a dog biscuit, a tennis ball, or anything else that will get his attention. Use the reward to draw his attention where you want it to be. Suppose you're teaching your dog to retrieve the remote control. Put it on the floor in front of him, then use the treat to guide his nose downward while saying "get the remote." When he gives the remote a sniff or nudge, praise him and give him the reward. Then repeat it four or five times.

Make it fun. Dogs learn best when they're having fun, so make training sessions seem like play rather than work. As long as your dog understands that doing something gets you excited, he'll want to keep doing it. Once he's

With a vocabulary that contains more than just the basic words, dogs like this golden retriever can enjoy advanced activities such as agility exercises.

EXTRA CREDIT

Some dogs pick up new words as readily as they pick up bones. If your dog is unusually gifted, you may want try some serious vocabulary-building. For example:

- *Scratch my back.* Nothing soothes a middle-of-the-back itch like a friendly clawed paw. Encourage your dog to paw your back while saying "scratch." When he does, reward him with a treat and hearty praise.
- *Take out the trash.* Most dogs want jobs, and how many people actually jump at this task? Buy plastic trash bags with a handle. Use food to encourage your dog to grab the handle, then give him a lot of praise. Once he gets the hang of grabbing the bag, start escorting him to the curb and praising him some more.
- *Find the sports section.* A newspaper's sections appear in the same order every day. Lay out the sections in their usual order, then point to the sports section. He'll learn to ignore national and local news and go straight to the scores.
- *Find ESPN.* Give your index finger a rest from the remote and let your dog channel-surf. Get him to paw at the control, again by encouraging him with food. If he gets lucky enough to paw the right channel, praise the heck of out of him.
- *Tell them I'm not interested.* Having your dog bark on command is a great way to stop spiels from insistent phone solicitors. See page 117 for information on teaching dogs to bark.
- *Wake me up at 6:00 A.M.* Who needs a bone-jarring alarm clock when a face-licking tail-wagger is available? Dogs crave routine, and they have clocks in their brains that tell them when to wake up. Giving your dog a treat when he comes to the bed and licks your face almost guarantees a repeat performance.

learned the words, your tone of voice won't matter all that much, says John C. Wright, Ph.D., a certified applied animal behaviorist, professor of psychology at Mercer University in Macon, Georgia, and author of *The Dog Who Would Be King.*

Praise the good, ignore the bad. Dogs learn best when they're praised for doing things right. They tune out when they're punished for doing things wrong, says Dr. Wright.

Be consistent. Some dogs learn difficult commands in a few hours, while others may take weeks. But all dogs learn best with repetition. If you practice the commands a few times a day, they'll gradually begin to link the words with the action and the action with the reward. "Anything rewarded consistently with a dog will get done consistently," says Jeff Nichol, D.V.M., a veterinarian in private practice in Albuquerque, New Mexico.

PART THREE

READING BODY LANGUAGE

Dogs depend on body language to an amazing extent.
How they stand, the inclination of their heads, the degree of eye contact,
the set of their ears, and the movements of their tails all speak volumes.
Once you start looking at body language, you'll have a much
better sense for what dogs are saying or feeling.

CHAPTER TEN

WHAT HIS BODY IS TELLING YOU

From their mobile faces to their expressive tails, dogs use
body language to communicate with people and other dogs. You can tell
at a glance what dogs are thinking and feeling.

People often think that if a dog isn't wagging his tail, then he's probably not saying much. But dogs use their whole bodies to express themselves. It's worth taking some time to watch your dog, and to pay attention to how he moves and how he looks when reacting to different situations. When you become familiar with his signals—a crouch, flattened ears, or an attentive, cocked head, for example—you'll understand him better, and that will make living together more harmonious for both of you.

Dogs use body language to convey a full range of emotions, wants, and needs, and to express their place within their society. A dog's society is his pack. In the wild, a pack consists of other dogs, but a pet dog's pack comprises his human owners and any other dogs in the family.

Although a particular body part often signals one meaning—for instance, a wagging tail is usually interpreted as a sign of happiness—you need to see what else is going on to understand the full message. For example, when a dog is bowing down and his tail is wagging, then his whirling tail is a clear signal of happiness. But if he's lying on his back, with his eyes and head averted and his front paws folded close to his chest, a moving tail is definitely not a sign that he's happy. Instead, he's showing submission and probably some fear, and is asking for a little kindness and consideration.

Dogs use their whole bodies, from their tongues to the tips of their tails, to express their feelings. This golden retriever is alert and interested in what's going on.

READING THE SIGNS

When someone gets lost in Alaska's millions of acres of wilderness or caught in an avalanche, the Alaska Search and Rescue Dogs are called in. It's not just the dogs' superior senses that help save lives; their handlers need to be able to tell what their dogs are thinking and feeling and to develop an almost symbiotic level of communication with them. It's one time when a human is watching and reading his dog's body language as closely as his dog is watching his.

"The dogs are all trained to give us an alert by barking or digging when they find something," says Corey Aist, who works with his Labrador retriever, Bean. When the teams have been out there for several hours, the conditions are rough, and the dogs are tired, their handlers need to watch carefully for more subtle clues. Some of these clues would be imperceptible to less well trained eyes, but when dogs and humans work so closely together, small signals can have an importance out of proportion to their size. The set of a dog's tail or a minute change in the curvature of his nose, for example, can be enough to tell a handler that his dog thinks there's something worth investigating further.

The other important element in the relationship is trust. "You must completely trust your dog to do the work you've asked him to do," says Paul Stoklos, who searches with his German shepherd, Arrow. "Even if you feel sure he's headed in the wrong direction, follow him anyway."

That's how Stoklos and Arrow once found a man who had become separated from his family in the Alaskan wilderness. Hours of searching with dogs and four-wheel-drive vehicles proved futile—until Arrow became interested in an old poacher's trail. The man's family said he would never have made the mistake of going in that direction, but Arrow was clearly determined to check. Stoklos followed him, and far down the trail, they heard the man's shouts for help. "If I hadn't trusted Arrow, we might never have saved the man's life," says Stoklos.

Some dogs are worse at signaling than other breeds. Tails are invaluable for signaling, so any dog without one is at a disadvantage. Rottweilers, for example, have docked tails. They've also been bred to have big shoulders and an imposing posture. They have trouble showing submission because cringing and making themselves look small isn't an option.

By contrast to their domesticated cousins, all species of wild dogs have shapes and colorings that are well-adapted to signaling. They have short hair that doesn't mask their body language, stiff guard hairs along their backs that they can raise in warning, reasonably distinct facial markings that highlight their expressions, and white underbellies that emphasize their submissive pose when they roll onto their backs.

Reading Your Dog's Emotions

Many canine expressions and gestures such as a hard stare or a nudge are easy to interpret and give us a very straightforward insight into how dogs are feeling, says Ian Dunbar, Ph.D., a behaviorist and the author of *Dog Behavior*. Other gestures, such as tongue-flicking, scratching, shaking, or yawning, have meanings that aren't so obvious. The more you learn about body language, the more you will understand about what your dog is feeling.

Dogs use body language as a natural part of daily life. They don't stop to think about what they're saying and how they're saying it. Their body language happens spontaneously—and it's happening much of the time.

POOCH ?? PUZZLER

Do dogs dream?

When a sleeping dog suddenly yips loudly and starts running in place, it's a fair bet he's having a dream. But none of those anxious, giving-a-speech-in-your-underwear dreams for dogs. From their movements and expressions, it appears that they dream of their favorite activities.

It will probably be a long time before scientists know exactly what they dream about. Based on what we know about them when they're awake, however, we can make an educated guess. "I think dogs dream smells," says Jeffrey Masson, Ph.D., author of *Dogs Never Lie about Love*. "This is their dominant sense, just like sight is ours, and we dream visually."

Old English sheepdogs have difficulty sending clear messages. They can't raise their hackles because their hair is too soft to stand on end, and their stares are invisible.

BODY POSITIONS

Dogs do nearly all of their communicating with body language. Some of the messages are easier to understand than others, but with a little practice, you'll soon be able to translate all your dog's messages.

▶ Saying hello

When dogs greet their owners or another human friend, they often bark happily, hold their tails high and wag them, and race toward the person. Often, as a dog nears his owner, he'll begin to signal his lower status by crouching, lowering his wagging tail, or rolling over, says Michael W. Fox, Ph.D., author of *Understanding Your Dog.*

When greeting each other, dogs use a slightly different approach. They posture to each other as they approach sideways and begin circling. They'll usually stand erect, on tiptoes, with upright ears and tails held high. They'll sniff each other's faces and rear ends to gain vital information about each other's sex, status, and mood. Familiar dogs spend less time sniffing than do dogs who are strangers. If one dog is obviously more dominant, that dog will appear to grow larger, while the subordinate dog will seem to shrink. One dog might put his head or paw on the other's shoulder in an attempt to establish dominance.

If it's not obvious which dog is dominant, they'll jostle side by side, with one trying to place his chin on the other's shoulder. Often the posturing will continue until they accept each other as equals. Dog friends who consider themselves equals will greet each other using quick motions, moving fast, spinning in circles, and jumping up on each other. Acquaintances (but not friends) will sniff each other, and the subordinate dog will lower himself to the other. Sometimes he'll lick the dominant dog's muzzle and raise a front paw to him in an appeasing gesture. Once the posturing is over and accepted, the dogs may sniff and jump on each other before getting down to the fun stuff of romping.

(continued)

49

BODY POSITIONS—Continued

▼ Happy, calm, and relaxed

When dogs feel relaxed and contented, their whole bodies radiate their happiness. Relaxed dogs stand with all four feet placed evenly on the ground. If they're sitting or lying down, their bodies will assume an easy posture, their muscles free of tension. Dogs with pricked ears will let them relax and fall slightly outwards. Those with floppy ears will let them hang gently or allow the tips of their ears to flop forward. Their heads will be at a comfortable height, neither high nor low, and their foreheads will be smooth. Their mouths will be relaxed at the corners, and either closed or partly open, as though they're smiling. Their tails may be still or wagging slowly. The position of the tail will depend on the breed. Some dogs, such as Afghans, hold their tails very low when they're relaxed, while others, like fox terriers and Airedales, hold them high.

▶ Playful

When dogs want to play with their owners, or when they're asking another dog to play, they'll lower the front halves of their bodies to the ground. Their rear ends will be left pointing in the air, so that it looks as though they're bowing, and their tails will be waving madly in anticipation. They may lower their heads, with their mouths and lips relaxed, and they may pant. Sometimes they'll give a high-pitched bark. They'll prick their ears up alertly and point them forward or, if they have hanging ears, they'll hold them as high and far forward as they can manage.

When their play invitation is answered, dogs will bounce up and down and may bark in excitement. Once play is under way, their exuberant body language, from their pricked-up ears to the jaunty set of their tails, expresses their happiness.

◀ Interested and alert

When dogs go from being calm and relaxed to being interested in something, all parts of their bodies move up and forward. They'll raise their heads and prick their ears up and forward. They'll lean forward slightly, and their mouths may open a little. Their eyes will be bright and intent. A front paw may come up, as though they're getting ready for action.

(continued)

51

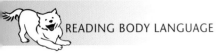

Body Positions—Continued

◀ Bored

Dogs who are confined in restricted spaces without any mental stimulation will soon become bored. They'll look uninterested and morose, with their ears drooping and their eyes set in blank, glassy stares. They'll usually be flat out on the floor, often with their heads resting on their front legs, and their tails limp. Dogs can shake off their boredom and gloomy demeanor the instant they're presented with something fun or interesting to do.

▶ Excited

Dogs usually get excited when they're playing with another dog, greeting a human friend, or it's time to go for a walk or play a game. Excited dogs often show their feelings very clearly by jumping about, or they may stand quivering, with their tails wagging furiously. Often their ears will be held forward in anticipation of something enjoyable, and their eyes will shine with happiness.

When they're greeting their owners, they'll likely rush toward them with their heads held up and their tails wagging, and start nudging them. They may hold their ears back, not as a sign of fear, but as a mark of respectful submission to their leaders.

▶ Sad

A sad dog has the body language of submission. Much like a sad person, he looks thoroughly dejected. He'll hang his head and his tail will be limp.

Dogs rarely become sad unless they're left alone for long periods. Once they're given some attention, exercise, or mental stimulation, they'll usually become relaxed and happy again.

▲ Stalking

When dogs become actively interested in something and decide to hunt, stalk, or play with it, they may lower their heads slightly as they watch it. This is particularly common in hunting or herding breeds, who are bred for this kind of activity. The front halves of their bodies will also be lowered as they stalk, while their rear ends will remain up. They'll watch the object of their interest with a sharp and unwavering gaze. Even when they're standing still, their feet will be positioned so that they can take off suddenly if need be.

(continued)

BODY POSITIONS—Continued

◀ Protective

When dogs take it upon themselves to guard and protect what they see as theirs, their body language will start out looking much the same as that of alert and dominant dogs. If they're challenged, though, they'll begin giving out some unmistakably aggressive signals—baring their teeth, thrusting their heads up and forward, and staring boldly to show that they're equal to and ready for the challenge. They'll lean forward to make themselves look bigger than they really are, and their legs will be placed firmly to make it clear that they're standing their ground.

▶ Aggressive

Dogs who are feeling aggressive or who are on the offensive will make their whole bodies rise and move forward so that they look larger, stronger, and more formidable. They'll lean forward on tiptoes and raise their hackles (the hair on their shoulders and back), which is another effective way of appearing bigger. Their tails will be up and held still, and the hair on the tail may bristle. Their ears will be up and forward. They may be snarling, with their noses wrinkled, the corners of their mouths pushed forward, and their lips tight and tense. Their eyes will be staring—direct and hard. As the aggression escalates, they'll pull their lips back to bare their teeth and will spread their back feet slightly to brace themselves so that they can leap up to fight.

▶ Seeking attention

Dogs are very gregarious animals. They like to be touched, played with, and just hang out with their owners. They enjoy walks immensely, not only for the exercise and the stimulation of the various sights and smells they encounter but also for the human companionship. And because dogs are so sociable, they spend quite a bit of time asking their owners for attention.

A paw on a person's knee can sometimes be a dominant gesture from an assertive dog or an appeasing gesture from a more submissive one—but most of the time, it's just a way of saying, "I'd like some attention, please!" Pawing the air in front of someone serves the same purpose, as does sliding a head under his hand and jostling it or standing up and leaning on his leg.

Other common attention-seeking tactics that dogs employ include nudging aside a newspaper or book that a person is reading, scrabbling noisily on the floor as though they're digging, and nudging or headbutting someone.

(continued)

55

BODY POSITIONS—Continued

▼ Dominant

Dominant dogs stand tall. When dogs meet, they'll raise their heads and lift their tails. They'll make themselves look larger by raising the hair along their spines and on their shoulders. They may stand on the tips of their front toes and take one or two small, stiff-legged steps forward. Their ears will be forward and as upright as their natural shape and position allow. One dog may put his paw on the shoulder of the other to reinforce his dominance. Unless the other dog begins to show submissive signals, the two dogs may resolve the power struggle with a fight.

Mounting or other sexual behaviors aren't always associated with reproduction. Dogs will sometimes mount other dogs to express dominance. Both the mounter and the mountee can be either male or female. Mounting and other sexual behaviors are the ultimate in disrespect when dogs try to perform them on their owners.

It's common for dogs to greet people by jumping up on them and trying to lick their faces. Dogs who jump on their owners and also have erect tails and stiff ears are trying to convey dominance.

▶ Submissive

Submissive dogs always try to make themselves appear smaller. It's a way of saying, "I'm no challenge, so please don't hurt me." They'll crouch or cower, with their backs arched and their heads pulled in and lowered. Their ears will be pulled down and back, and their foreheads smooth. They won't make eye contact and may in fact avert their eyes. They'll pull back the corners of their mouths and may look to be smiling, although this isn't a smile as we know it. They may also lick their noses. Their tails will be down and perhaps pulled up tightly between their back legs. And the tips of their tails may be wagging or twitching. They may make pawing movements with their front feet.

When they're with a more dominant dog, they'll sometimes lick his muzzle, or lift a front paw to him to show that they acknowledge who's in charge. Other times they'll show their acceptance of the status quo by licking their own noses and putting their ears back—either slightly or flat to their skulls. If their ears are flat to their skulls, they're accepting a reprimand; if their ears waver back and forth, or one is higher than the other, they're also accepting it, but with a fair degree of reluctance. If they're totally obedient, they'll also tuck their tails between their legs.

In extreme submission, dogs lie down, roll over, and bare their bellies. They'll pull their legs in against their bodies, and their front paws will be tucked in close, too. Their tails will be pulled in between their back legs and tucked against their bellies, and the tips of their tails may be twitching. Some dogs will dribble a little urine.

Not all submissive behavior indicates a fearful mood, though. A dog may bare his belly to his owner yet maintain direct, soft eye contact, which shows that he's not afraid. His posture is one of deference and trust. He could also, of course, be angling for a tummy rub.

(continued)

BODY POSITIONS—Continued

▼ Fearful

Dogs who feel frightened but are not moved to behave aggressively will try to make themselves look smaller than they really are. Frightened dogs will lower their heads and lay their ears back. If they're very fearful, their ears will be plastered tight to their heads, and they'll usually avert their gaze from whatever it is that's scared them. Their pupils may be dilated, and they'll sometimes even close their eyes completely in their attempt to cope with the situation. Their mouths will probably be closed, too. The skin on their muzzles may be wrinkled and the corners of their mouths pulled back and down in a tense expression.

Sometimes dogs find themselves in situations where they're afraid, but they feel that they have something to protect—themselves, their humans, or property—and they're prepared to take a stand. When this happens, their body language will convey both fear and aggression. Their bodies will probably be lowered, legs bent, and their heads held forward but low. Their ears may be back, showing fear, or may go back and forth, signaling their conflicting emotions. Some dogs will gaze at what's frightening them, others will look away, and some will show the whites of their eyes. They'll bare their teeth and wrinkle their muzzles—all signs of aggression. Their hackles will be up, their tails low but bristling. A fearful dog who is cornered and is also showing aggressive body language should be taken seriously. He's saying that he's quite prepared to bite.

► Anxious

When dogs are stressed, they'll lower their heads and pant in a desperate effort to relieve their anxiety. Their pupils will be dilated and they won't be able to look at the person or thing that's causing their distress. Their ears will be down and back, and their lips will also be pulled well back and creased at the corners. They'll hold their bodies low and their tails will be tucked between their back legs. Often their paws will be sweating. Sometimes they'll roll over and bare their bellies, and even express a few drops of urine. Dogs who are sitting still with one paw raised are usually worried or anxious.

▼ Relieving anxiety

Dogs use a number of body language signals to soothe themselves, other dogs, or people they're interacting with, says Terry Ryan, a dog trainer and author of *The Toolbox for*

Remodeling Your Problem Dog. These actions, called calming signals, look to be irrelevant to what's happening at the time, and they're the canine equivalent of the way people will change the subject of a conversation if an argument seems likely to erupt. Some common calming signals include yawning, tongue-flicking, turning away, breaking eye contact, sniffing, scratching, or shaking themselves as though they're wet.

The way to tell that dogs are using calming signals is to look for an action that's out of context. During an obedience-training session, a dog may suddenly scratch at his collar. If he doesn't have fleas and hasn't been scratching during the rest of the session, he's probably trying to relieve stress. He could be saying, "Hey, I need a break from concentrating."

CHAPTER ELEVEN

What Your Body Is Telling Him

Dogs watch people more closely than people ever watch them.
You need to pay close attention to your body language so you don't
accidentally send your dog the wrong message.

Had a bad day at the office? Your dog knows as soon as you walk in the door. Just as you can tell what dogs are feeling by their postures and the ways they move their tails, your body language—the hundreds of poses, gestures, and facial expressions you unconsciously use all the time—tells them a lot about your moods and intentions.

Some of these clues are pretty obvious. When you walk into the kitchen or pick up the leash, it doesn't take a canine Einstein to figure out that something good is about to happen. But dogs are also capable of tremendous discrimination. Things people would never notice, like minute shifts in posture or a flicker at the corner of an eye, are instantly noticed and evaluated. Dogs can tell at a glance when you're happy or sad, when you want to play, and when you're annoyed by the tipped-over trash.

"Humans have a wonderful spoken vocabulary that's very extensive, but most of it is a closed book to dogs, so they attach a great deal of importance to physical signs," says Steve Aiken, an animal behaviorist in Wichita, Kansas. They're so attuned to body language, in fact, that they often pick up messages where none

When this Labrador's owner gets down on all fours, she mimics the pose a dog uses to invite play. Her dog knows right away that a game is afoot.

were intended. Many household misunderstandings could be avoided if people were a little more conscious of the signals they send.

Here's a common scenario: You're down on all fours, desperately searching for a dropped wedding band or an essential screw, and your dog is driving you crazy by jumping on your

60

back, running in circles, and barking his head off. Play is the last thing you have in mind, so you snap and shove him away, and he slinks off looking disappointed. He misinterpreted your mood, but there's a good reason for it. When a dog wants another dog to play, he'll often crouch down and put his tail in the air. It's called a play-bow, and that's exactly what he thought you were doing, says Melissa Shyan, Ph.D., an animal behaviorist and associate professor of psychology at Butler University in Indianapolis, Indiana.

Here's another example: When people have difficult conversations on the telephone, their voices get a little raspy, or their breathing gets labored or shallow. Dogs recognize the signs of stress and will sometimes get a little anxious themselves, especially if they think their owners are stressed because of them. If this happens a few times, they may begin to associate the telephone itself with anxiety and will start getting upset whenever their owners pick it up.

It isn't practical (or necessary) to constantly worry about how your dog is interpreting your facial expressions or body language. Most dogs roll with the punches just like people do, and a little misunderstanding isn't likely to bother them for long. But if you suspect that your dog's behavior has changed because of something you've done, it's worth paying attention to the types of signals you've been sending out. "It's up to you to give your dog feedback if you think he's misunderstood your body language," says Deena Case-Pall, Ph.D., a psychologist and animal behaviorist in Camarillo, California. "Otherwise he'll keep associating the same act with his first impression."

Canine on Patrol

There are few dogs more highly trained than those that accompany police officers on duty. The National K-9 Training School in Columbus, Ohio, trains many dogs for police work every year. K-9 units have been established in police departments throughout the United States.

It's not just the intense training that makes these dogs so effective, though. It's also the focus on their owners. Many police dogs live with their police officer handlers around the clock.

Curt Larsen, a K-9 officer for the City of Poughkeepsie, New York, spends as much or more time with his German shepherd, CheeBee, than he does with his family—and CheeBee's good work is the proof.

"When we're out patrolling the streets, he acts just like any other dog, looking out of the window, enjoying the view," explains Larsen. "But he can tell when something is about to happen just by the way I hold myself and the way I drive. If I speed up and reach for the lights, CheeBee is ready for action. He looks straight ahead, he gets more rigid, and his ears go up."

CheeBee can also tell when Larsen's interactions with people on the street are likely to be friendly or not. "He can tell by my demeanor whether or not he needs to worry," says Larsen. "He knows hand-shaking and pats on the back are okay. But once, when I found drugs on a guy, the guy pushed me, and CheeBee flew out of the car and grabbed hold of him."

PUPPY DOG TALES

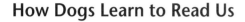

How Dogs Learn to Read Us

Just as children quickly learn to pick up clues from their parents, dogs understand the wisdom of watching their owners. After all, people are the ones who dole out food. They control the door that leads to the backyard. They're the ones who decide when it's time to play and when to be stern. Dogs enjoy life best when it's predictable, and there's no surer way to predict what's about to happen than by watching their owners' silent signals. Over time, dogs get remarkably adept at reading and interpreting these signals. They have an almost uncanny ability to know what's coming. In some cases, in fact, they know what you're about to do even before you do.

Since this type of "mind-reading" can only enhance the bond between people and pets, Aiken recommends encouraging it whenever you can. The next time your dog quickly moves out of the way when you make the slightest turn in his direction, reward him for his skill in anticipating your movement, he advises. This will make him even more determined to scrutinize you closely. He'll gradually sharpen his powers of observation and will seldom be taken by surprise.

Observation comes naturally to dogs. They used to live in large groups called packs, and it was essential for every dog in the pack to know what the others were doing and what their movements signified. In the thousands of years that dogs have been domesticated, they've undoubtedly lost many of their survival instincts—but not the power of observation because it's a skill that continues to be helpful today.

BREED SPECIFIC

Some breeds are better at reading body signals than others. Herding breeds, such as Border collies, corgis (below), and Australian kelpies, were bred to pay close attention to cattle and sheep so they could predict their movements. These dogs got many of their instructions from hand signals, so they always paid careful attention to body language. These instincts remain so strong that even their nonherding contemporaries feel compelled to keep an eye on what's happening.

Dogs' senses are incredibly sharp but their interpretations of human movements and facial expressions are somewhat limited. No matter how attentive dogs are, it's impossible for them to truly think like a person. They have to draw on their skills in communicating within their own species to interpret our movements and patterns of behavior, explains Barbara Simpson, Ph.D., a veterinary behaviorist in Southern Pines, North Carolina. As a result, they focus mainly on signals that are similar to those used by dogs or those that they think may play a role in survival. "Dogs remember situations in which they've been hurt, and they watch out to make sure that they don't happen again," says Dr. Shyan. "But mostly they just want to have a great time, so they watch us for signs that something's going to happen that will make their lives happier."

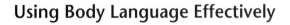

Using Body Language Effectively

Dogs will never be adept at learning English or sign language, and humans will never learn to communicate as expressively as dogs using body language. But it's generally not that difficult to use your body, face, and hand movements to communicate messages a little more clearly—or at least to avoid sending the wrong signals that dogs are sure to misunderstand.

Posture

People who stand proudly with their shoulders back and their heads erect are sending the world a silent message that says "I'm confident."

This golden retriever is enjoying a pat on the head from his owner, but if a stranger did the same thing, he might feel uneasy.

People respect those who are self-assured and confident, and so do dogs.

Combine a confident posture with a brisk, self-assured walk, and dogs quickly assume that this person is powerful and in charge and will take care of everything. They respond immediately because they've seen confident dogs—who have tremendous status among their peers—act in a similar way.

Hand and Arm Movements

People use their hands and arms a lot when they're talking or feeling emotional, and we intuitively understand what different movements mean. Holding your hand over the top of someone's head, for example, makes that person feels vaguely threatened, while standing with your arms opened wide makes you appear friendly and inviting. Dogs react to both types of gestures in a similar way. They dislike it when people they don't know reach down to pet their heads. Among dogs, this type of reaching down is considered provocative, even an invitation to fight. Open arms, on the other hand, are similar to the spread-eagled, flat-on-the-back position dogs assume when they're playing or feeling relaxed. People with an "open" position are seen as being friendly and unthreatening.

Quick hand movements may scare or aggravate dogs. In centuries past, fast-moving objects were either dinner or aggressors, says Dr. Shyan. This is why dogs instantly get alert when we move our bodies quickly. They feel much more relaxed when we move our hands slowly and deliberately.

Some people go a bit overboard with body language when they're greeting dogs they don't

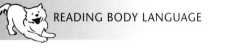

This collie sees his owner's open arms as offering a big welcome, so he's eager to come on command.

know. They'll shove their hands out for dogs to sniff or wave their arms around to show they're happy and enthusiastic. It's not the movements themselves that are the problem so much as the speed and force with which they occur. Dogs are naturally a little nervous around strangers, and forceful gestures may be interpreted as threatening—and dogs may react accordingly.

Quick or Jerky Movements

When two dogs are squaring off for a confrontation, they'll stiffen and stand tall, and their movements will be jerky and nervous. "Dogs pick up on anything that seems abnormal or worrying in our movements, too," says Aiken. "If someone is at the front door and you make jerky motions because you're uneasy, your dog will pick up on that and think right away something is wrong." When you move slowly, however, they know you're calm and relaxed, and they'll relax too.

"Every dog reacts differently depending on his personality, but most dogs will be startled if their owner suddenly launches into an exercise routine or has a wrestling game with

someone else," says Bill Wolden, an instructor at the exotic animal training and management program at Moorpark College in Moorpark, California. "Many dogs feel threatened and become alarmed until they've had a chance to figure out what's happening. They feel much more comfortable when you're going at a slow speed."

Facial Expressions

Happy dogs and happy people have smooth foreheads and give easy eye contact. Angry dogs and angry people have furrowed brows and sometimes a hard, fixed stare. But that's where the similarities end: A human smile and a canine smile mean entirely different things.

People smile when they're happy. Dogs, on the other hand, smile—it's really more like a grin—when they're afraid. They'll raise their upper lip and bare their teeth, which looks very menacing. It's their way of scaring off whatever it is they're afraid of. Trainers recommend keeping your mouth closed, or at least being careful not to show too many teeth, when you're greeting a strange dog who looks tense and alert. Smiling may make him think you're being threatening, and he may get aggressive in return.

"Most dogs learn very quickly that a human smile is a good thing," adds Mary Welther, a dog trainer in San Diego. "The body language that goes with a human smile helps them understand this, and they learn to react in a positive manner. If a dog is unsure about something and you smile at him, he'll come to understand that you approve of what he's doing."

Move as Dogs Do

Miscommunication is most common among strangers. Once you've spent a few years with a dog, the two of you have pretty much figured out each other's body language and there aren't too many surprises. When a new or unfamiliar dog comes along, however, body language that speaks volumes to your own dog may be greeted with confusion, blank stares, or worse. It's worth knowing a little universal dog language to make the introductions more friendly.

PAY ATTENTION

Every dog can be taught to be more attentive. Herding dogs need little encouragement, but most dogs lose their focus fairly easily. One way to keep them alert and attentive is by teaching the "watch me" command.

1 Hold a treat in one hand. Have your dog sit in front of you and let him sniff the treat. Tell him "Watch me!" and raise the treat from his nose to your chin. As he watches the treat, watch his eyes.

2 When his eyes flick to your face, tell him "Good dog to watch me!" and give him the treat. Practice two or three more times and then take a break. Repeat the exercise several times. As he progresses, make it more challenging. Have him watch for longer periods or move about as he watches you. Then, when you want to teach him something new, you can use the "watch me" command first to make sure he's paying attention.

Get down to their level. Since dogs sometimes use their height, which they exaggerate by stretching their legs and craning their necks upward, in order to intimidate other dogs, they assume that people do the same thing, and may get affronted when you approach and loom over them.

A friendlier greeting is one in which you get down to their level, either by kneeling or by slowly bending over. The lower you go, the bigger dogs feel, and that can make them feel more secure and less threatened. It's also a good idea to extend your hand slightly so they can give a quick sniff without getting too close. "Dogs will sniff a stranger to figure out what he is all about," Wolden explains.

Take care with a stare. Dogs certainly don't mind looking into their owners' eyes, but a direct stare, especially from a stranger, is considered very offensive as well as aggressive. It's okay to look at a strange dog's eyes to see how he reacts, but don't hold your gaze for more than a second. (If a dog is growling or otherwise acting aggressively, avoid eye contact entirely.) It's better to avert your gaze and look just past him when you meet for the first time. Or you can lower your eyes when he tries to make eye contact, which is a way of saying "I'm not a threat, so you can relax."

Approach him sideways. Dogs greet one another by sniffing hindquarters, which involves a sideways approach. You certainly don't want to imitate the greeting, but approaching sideways is a good way to make friends because among dogs it's considered good manners. Walking straight toward a dog will make him uncomfortable, and he may mis-

take your friendly attentions for something more threatening.

Leave your emotions at the office. There's no avoiding bad days, but the same emotions that rile you can make dogs extremely nervous. When you bang open the door and stomp into the house, your dog will quickly assume that he's in for a tense evening. Worse, he'll likely assume that you're mad because of something he did. "You'd be just as keyed up if someone came rushing into your domain," says Aiken. You can't force yourself into a good mood, but it's worth pausing in the driveway to imagine your home-coming from your dog's point of view.

The owner of this Labrador cross tries to leave her worries at the door so that she gives him a warm and friendly greeting.

CHAPTER TWELVE

FACE

Dogs can't put on a happy face when they're feeling blue.
And they can't change the natural look of their breed either.
So their state of mind is usually easy to ascertain.

We can read people's moods to a certain extent from the set of their facial features. But people have the ability to consciously mask their feelings, composing their faces to say one thing when their minds are saying something different. Dogs have many distinct facial expressions and usually it's pretty clear whether they're happy or sad, angry or content. Though they don't deliberately set out to deceive or dissemble in the way humans do, the natural appearance of their breed, or their mix of breeds, can cause confusion. Markings, coloring, the shape of the head or the eyes are something a dog can do nothing about. But because we persist in associating a mood with these immutable looks, miscommunications can occur.

Many dog owners choose a breed of dog entirely on the strength of a perceived personality that is related to the breed's natural expression. "Golden retrievers always look like they're very happy, and I wanted a happy dog, not a serious one," says Nancy Hoffman of Oceanside, California. Labrador retrievers, Alaskan malamutes, and Samoyeds also always seem to have cheerful facial expressions.

Other breeds give different impressions. Australian cattle dogs and Border collies have

Everything about this golden retriever's face says he hasn't a care in the world.

upright ears and an intense gaze, and people think they're always on red alert, ready for action. Pugs, with their short muzzles, black facial coloring, and large eyes, seem anxious or studious. Although these expressions do portray something of each breed's natural personality, it's not always the whole picture. Not all pugs are permanently on the brink of an anxiety attack, just as not all golden retrievers are always sublimely happy.

The positioning of dogs' heads and ears works in tandem with facial expressions to give us helpful clues about what state of mind our dogs are in. When dogs hear or see something they find unusual, they'll move their ears up and forward and cock their heads to the side. Combined with the alert and intent look on their faces, this makes their expressions appear even more quizzical. "There are nuances in facial expressions that must be watched carefully if we're to understand our dogs as best we can," says Mary Stout, a trainer in San Diego, California. "A twitch of an ear, the lifting of the lip, the tilt of the head, and the furrowing of the forehead all have significance and something to say."

Structural Variations

Although most dogs' facial features play a very important part in their ability to communicate, not all dogs are created equal when it comes to having the tools to express themselves easily or clearly. Sometimes a dog's body type or breed characteristics limit his facial repertoire.

Nearly all facial expressions, for example, include some kind of movement of a dog's mouth or lips. Breeds like bloodhounds with their long, thick, pendulous lips, called flews, have much more difficulty making some of these expressions. Although they can snarl—pulling their lips back and baring their front

teeth—other expressions that require more subtle lip movements (especially at the corners of the mouth) are virtually beyond their capabilities, try as they may. And even if they can achieve some of these movements, they can be very hard for the onlooker to discern. Calming gestures such as licking may be particularly hard to see. Also, dogs with long flews have difficulty drawing up the back of the lips to make what people take to be a happy expression. Because of this, we often think these dogs are feeling sad, even when they're not.

EMOTIONS UNDER WRAPS

The facial expressions of short-haired dogs are generally easy to read. But other breeds, such as Old English sheepdogs and Lhasa apsos (below), have luxuriant locks that hide their expressions. Perhaps the most extravagantly hairy dog is the puli, a Hungarian sheepdog whose floor-length dreadlocks can make it difficult to tell front from rear.

So how do these dogs show what they're feeling? Most of them, like Maltese and Shih Tzus, get artificial help—their owners tie their hair back out of their eyes. But pulis don't like direct sunlight in their eyes, so their hair is usually left loose to shield them. Fortunately their eyes and their characteristically happy faces are still visible through their corded coats. And, as pulis are lively and outgoing, they're usually bouncing about enough to flick the hair out of their eyes anyway.

When a dog's repertoire of expressions is restricted, it's important to watch his overall body language to understand what it is he's trying to communicate. Shar-peis, in particular, drew the short straw here. Bred to have meatier, fleshier faces than other breeds, the shar-pei's multitudinous skin folds severely restrict lip expressions and the movement of skin on the muzzle, brow, and around the eyes.

Hair covering can also obscure dogs' facial expressions. Old English sheepdogs, who have thick coats and shaggy hair in their faces, are at a distinct disadvantage here. Almost all their expressions, subtle or obvious, are difficult to see. "When working with a long-coated breed such as the Old English, I watch coat movement," says Stout. "If the hair moves over the eyes, or around the mouth, I assume that the dog is making some kind of an expression. I then watch the rest of his body language to see if I can understand what he's trying to say."

By understanding what your dog's facial expressions signify, you can combine this information with what else his body is telling you. That way you get a complete picture of what he's feeling and trying to say.

Facial Markings and Colorings

Some breeds, such as Doberman pinschers, Australian shepherds, Bernese mountain dogs, Rottweilers, and Japanese chins, have distinctive colorings or markings that draw attention to certain facial features. Tan markings above their eyes and dark lips against a pale muzzle help make their expressions more visible.

Picture a dog with a white muzzle and black lips and eyes surrounded by white fur, with perhaps a touch of tan around or above them. When the dog snarls—lifting his lips, wrinkling his nose, and furrowing his forehead—his coloring makes this expression more pronounced. His black lips are offset by the white muzzle, and his white teeth are outlined by black lips. The lighter colors around his eyes and the tan markings where eyebrows would be also make his intense eyes more obvious.

Even all-white breeds, such as Samoyeds or Great Pyrenees, or pale-faced ones, like Alaskan malamutes, often have dark-rimmed eyes, black noses, and black lips, which make their expressions more visible.

POOCH PUZZLER

Is your dog smiling?

When dogs seem to be smiling, you can't always take their expressions at face value. Some dogs have what's known as a submissive grin, says Ian Dunbar, Ph.D., author of *Dog Behavior*. This grin is actually a snarl, but some dogs do it when they are expressing high emotions—usually aggression, but often happiness and excitement. This expression seems to be breed-related and is often seen in Australian shepherds, Doberman pinschers, Dalmatians, and Border collies.

There's obviously room for confusion when a snarl can be misinterpreted as a smile. The key is to look at the rest of the dog's body language. A smiling dog's body language will be happy, with a wagging tail, while a snarling dog will be tense and aggressive.

A Guide to Facial Features

Dogs' facial features work together, and the message they're combining to send isn't hard to understand once you know what to look for. Here's what each feature may be saying.

Ears. Unlike people, dogs have mobile ears that can swivel, lay back, or tilt forward. They also move independently of each other. This range of movement makes their ears very expressive. When a dog's ears are held forward, he's alert; when they're back and relaxed, he's relaxed, too. Forward-facing, tensely erect ears show aggression. Ears folded back tightly show a dog who's afraid and maybe aggressive.

Eyes. A soft and loving look shows affection and trust, and an absence of fear and tension. A direct, eager look indicates interest and alertness. A sideways glance means submission or uncertainty. Rapidly blinking eyes are a reaction to stress and can be a dog's attempt to calm himself down. Direct, hard eye contact sends a message of dominance or aggression.

When the whites of a dog's eyes show, you need to look at other body language clues to work out the cause. When a dog is afraid and his ears are pulled way back, the stretching of the skin may cause the whites to show. However, if a dog is lying on his back for a tummy rub, the whites of his eyes may show simply because gravity is pulling his eyelids back.

Forehead. When the skin on a dog's forehead is relaxed, so is he. When it's smooth and drawn back tightly, that means his ears have been pulled down and back because he's afraid or perhaps aggressive. A dog who's feeling anxious will furrow his forehead over his eyes, just like a knitted human brow.

Mouth. A mouth partly open is a relaxed, normal position for many dogs. It doesn't always signify an emotion, but when it does, the emotion is generally happiness. A panting dog may be nervous or stressed, or maybe he's just hot. If he's licking—another dog, a person, or his own muzzle—that's a sign of greeting or submission. Licking can also be a gesture meant to calm himself, a person, or another dog.

When a dog's teeth are chattering, this isn't a sign that he's cold, but generally indicates happy anticipation. A dog who's expecting an especially good toy or who's in the middle of an exciting play session may chatter his teeth.

Lips. Relaxed lips indicate a relaxed dog. An aggressive dog will pull his lips back tightly in a snarl. A stressed dog will pull his lips way back, creasing the corners of his mouth. In many dogs, the black lips contrast with the color of the muzzle, emphasizing their expressions and the size and whiteness of their teeth.

The contrasting colors on this Bernese mountain dog's face, such as his tan eyebrows and black lips against a white muzzle, draw attention to his expressions and also make them very easy to read.

FACIAL EXPRESSIONS

It's easy to read your dog's face once you understand the subtleties of his expressions. And you can marry this information with other body language clues to gain a deeper understanding of what he's thinking.

◀ Relaxed, happy, and comfortable

Everyone likes to see this expression and, in fact, dogs usually look pretty contented and at peace with the world. A dog who's feeling comfortable and unworried, lying by the fire or out on the porch, will look serene and untroubled. His brow will be smooth and his mouth may be either closed or open in a relaxed position, perhaps with his tongue lolling out.

Playful

When a dog's asking someone to romp with him, he'll make it pretty obvious that he's got fun in mind. "A dog who wants to play will have his eyes wide open, his ears will either be cocked forward or flat, and he may pant or salivate," says Melissa Shyan, Ph.D., an animal behaviorist and associate professor of psychology at Butler University in Indianapolis, Indiana. "He'll look just like a puppy."

▶ Excited and welcoming

A dog who is happily greeting his owner or another human friend, or a puppy who's saying hello to a friendly older dog, will open his mouth slightly and flick his tongue rapidly in and out. He may try to lick the other person or dog, which is a clear sign of respect and affection, or he may lick at the corners of his own mouth.

(continued)

71

FACIAL EXPRESSIONS—CONTINUED

▶ Submissive and worried

A dog who's slightly submissive and a little worried may look indirectly at whatever's worrying him, but he's more likely to look away. That's his way of saying "Please ignore me, I'm no threat." His mouth will usually be closed, but sometimes it will be open and his tongue will appear. It may flick out between his front teeth, which is a sign of nervousness or anxiety. He may also try to lick. This gesture is designed to appease and to assure the other person or dog that he knows his place and respects the other's superior status.

◀ Interested and curious

When a dog's interest picks up, so do his facial features. They'll all move up and forward a little. "A curious dog will aim his ears at what he's looking at, and he'll be sniffing the air, hoping to figure out what that unusual scent is," says Dr. Shyan. He may be nudging something with his nose and his mouth may be closed, unless it's a hot day, in which case his mouth will be open all the time. The skin on his forehead may have a tiny wrinkle, but most of the time it will be smooth.

When a dog starts stalking whatever has caught his attention, his facial features will remain up, forward, and intent. He may squint a little, his mouth will be closed, and his ears will be pricked up.

◀ Worried or anxious

Dogs who are worried or stressed will have dilated pupils, open mouths, and they'll pull their lips right back, creasing them at the corners. They may also be panting, which is a sign that they're stressed.

Frightened

Dogs who are frightened don't just pull back with their bodies—they do so with their faces. They'll pull their ears back tightly against their heads and pull their lips down and back. They'll also usually lower their heads and look away from whatever is bothering them.

▶ Watchful and alert

Dogs who are watchful and alert will do the opposite of frightened dogs—their facial features will move up and forward in their eagerness to study what it is that's interesting them. Their eyes will be intense and watchful, and their brow may be furrowed in concentration. The skin around their eyes may be creased, and their mouths slightly agape. The nose will be twitching and their neck muscles will be taut.

(continued)

Facial Expressions—Continued

▶ Aggressive

Aggressive facial expressions start out looking much the same as those of an alert dog. However, when a dog starts feeling that aggression might be called for, his features will become more distorted. He'll begin by lifting his lips at the side of his mouth, to show his sharp canine teeth. If he then thinks the situation calls for a sterner warning, he'll pull his lips right up and bare all his teeth. His forehead will be furrowed, and the skin around his eyes will be deeply creased. His mouth will be open, and he'll probably be growling or barking. He'll also wrinkle the skin over his muzzle—sometimes so much that his nose changes shape.

◀ Conflicting emotions

Dogs are sometimes of mixed minds about things. When a dog's feeling both protective and a little afraid, as a timid dog might when a stranger intrudes on his turf, his facial features will show his conflicting feelings. His ears may be halfway up, showing a degree of boldness, yet held back against his skull, indicating fear. Sometimes his ears end up in a position between the two extremes, which shows his confusion. While drawing his lips up and baring his teeth—a sign of aggression—he may also signal fear by pulling his lips back so that their corners crease. As he bares his teeth, his mouth may be open, not in a tense, aggressive position, but open almost fully. This is what a distressed puppy would do, and adult dogs commonly revert to puppylike actions when they're perturbed.

CHAPTER THIRTEEN

EYES

Dogs don't see the world in the same way people do,
but their eyes are just as expressive, and you can tell a lot about
their state of mind just by looking at their eyes.

Sight is our most important sense, and it's the one we rely on most. But dogs don't depend on their vision that much. They mostly use it to confirm what their other senses tell them, says Craig Larson, D.V.M., a veterinarian in private practice in Santa Barbara, California. For example, dogs may hear their owner's car and dash to the front gate. They're familiar with the sound, so seeing the car simply proves what they already knew. The same thing happens with scent. Dogs smell a scent, know

it's that of a squirrel, and follow the trail. When they flush the squirrel, the sight of it stimulates them to chase it, but doesn't give them any new information. It just confirms what their noses already told them.

When you're trying to communicate with dogs, you need to know how their vision works and how they use it. Once you know this, you'll be able to use visual communication in a way they understand. You'll also realize that if your dog seems to misunderstand you, it may be because he doesn't see things the same way you do.

POOCH PUZZLER

Why do their eyes shine in the dark?

Catch a dog's eyes in the glare of a flashlight or the headlights of your car at night, and you'll see them shining back at you.

Their eyes glow in the dark because they have a structure behind the retina called the tapetum lucidum. This is a highly reflective layer of cells that gives the eyes a second chance to absorb all the available light, says D. Caroline Coile, Ph.D., a neuroscientist in Ochlocknee, Georgia. The tapetum in dogs is usually greenish yellow, and that's the color you'll see at night.

Canine Eyesight

Dogs' eyes are more sensitive to light and movement than people's are, but they can't focus on things as well. That's why dogs can see very slight movements in dim light, but they sometimes can't see balls a foot away in broad daylight. Even brightly colored balls that contrast vividly with the surroundings won't be much easier for them to see because dogs have poor color vision.

People and dogs have different numbers of receptor cells—called rods and cones—in their eyes. Rods pick up very low levels of light, but only in black and white. Dogs have more rods than we do, which means that in dim light their sight is keener than ours. This is a throwback to their wild days. Prey such as deer are most active at dawn and dusk, so wild dogs needed to be able to see in dim light to have any chance of catching their next meal, says D. Caroline Coile, Ph.D., a neuroscientist in Ochlocknee, Georgia. Cones, on the other hand, are needed to see in daylight and to pick up color. Dogs have fewer of these than people do.

While it used to be thought that dogs saw the world in black and white and shades of gray, like a black and white television set, researchers now know that dogs have some color vision. But recognizing color isn't very important for their daily lives. "They've managed to survive all these years without recognizing all the world's colors," says Wayne Hunthausen, D.V.M., an animal behaviorist and past president of the American Veterinary Society of Animal Behavior in Westwood, Kansas.

BREED SPECIFIC

Greyhounds, whippets, salukis, and borzois are called sighthounds because they hunt by sight rather than scent. They're very attracted to movement, have a strong instinct to chase moving prey, and have better distance vision than other dogs, which means they watch their prey during the hunt.

What does matter to dogs is detecting movement, says Dr. Coile. When dogs were predators, movement was the trigger that made them pay attention because it meant that dinner was nearby. Today's dogs don't need to hunt, but they retain their ancestors' skills and instincts.

Dogs also have a wider field of vision than people do. Their eyes are set wider apart than those of humans, which means dogs can see

Color Combinations

While dogs' eyes mostly come in various shades of brown, it's not uncommon to see other colors or mixtures of colors. Some dogs have mismatched eyes: One eye may be blue and one brown, or one may be brown and the other half brown, half blue. This is common in Siberian huskies, Dalmatians, Australian shepherds, collies, and other breeds with white or merle coats.

Dogs with blue eyes have a missing layer of pigment in the iris. It gives the dogs an unusual look and makes their eyes a little more sensitive to light. But it has no effect on their eyesight. Dogs with blue eyes, however, are more likely to be born deaf: Blue eyes are caused by the same genes that result in white and merle coat colors, and these genes are linked to hearing defects.

more to each side of them. Their field of vision ranges from 190 degrees for flat-faced dogs such as Pekingese to 270 degrees for greyhounds, says Janice da Silva, Ph.D., a veterinary ophthalmologist in La Puente, California. By contrast, humans can only see 180 degrees.

One thing that doesn't vary much between breeds is the size of their eyes. The variation in eyeball volume between Chihuahuas and mastiffs, for example, is a surprisingly tiny 11 percent, which is why toy dogs' eyes tend to bulge.

Some breeds are more prone than others to eye problems. Rough collies, Border collies, and Shetland sheepdogs are sometimes born blind because of a genetic mutation, and breeds with prominent eyes may suffer from exposure keratitis, or wear and tear on the cornea.

The Meaning of Eye Contact

Dogs communicate with their eyes. For example, if one dog tries to take liberties, such as attempting to steal another dog's toy or bone, he may receive a long stare. Dogs use staring as a threat, and the would-be thief will recognize the danger and back down. Dogs also stare to tell other dogs who's boss, as Betty Fisher, a trainer and author of *So Your Dog's Not Lassie*, discovered when she introduced a new Newfoundland to her pack leader. "She turned her head, looked back over her shoulder, and stopped him dead in his tracks," Fisher says.

A stare helps in saving face as well. When he's playing, a dog may roll over onto his back—normally a submissive position—but he'll still make direct eye contact with the dog standing over him to show that he's not being cowardly.

Between people and dogs, eye contact doesn't usually mean a challenge or a threat. Dogs get used to humans looking directly at them, and they realize that our intentions are normally good. When dogs lock eyes with people, they're generally just fooling around or inviting them to play.

Blinking is another way dogs communicate with their eyes. When they meet for the first time, they'll sometimes give an exaggerated blink. This doesn't mean they're distracted or not interested. It's their way of saying that there's no problem or threat.

When It's Okay to Disobey

PUPPY DOG TALES

Guide dogs are trained to aid people who are blind in all sorts of ways. They take them on public transport and help them get safely through crowds. But sometimes it's what dogs won't do that matters.

Jim Hughes, a high school history teacher in Farmingdale, New York, owes his life to his guide dog, Ronny. Jim was walking with Ronny across a construction site. Suddenly Ronny stopped and refused to go any farther, despite Jim's increasingly exasperated commands to do so. "He wouldn't move," Jim says. "It was as though he was saying, 'No, I won't!'"

Finally, Jim carefully moved one foot forward—and encountered nothing but air. The reason for Ronny's refusal became clear: Obeying Jim would have meant falling into a huge pit. Ronny's good judgment saved Jim from serious injury.

The Seeing Eye guide dog school in Morristown, New Jersey, calls this kind of refusal "intelligent disobedience," and, as Jim can attest, it's the smartest thing a dog can do.

EYES AND EMOTIONS

You can tell a lot about what dogs are thinking and feeling by looking at their eyes. They use their eyes to express love and contentment, anxiety, and anger. Here's a guide to the most common expressions.

▶ Direct eye contact

Dogs who give you a keen and alert look are feeling happy and confident. The skin around their eyes will be smooth, with perhaps a small crease at the outside corners. This is how dogs look when they're greeting someone or inviting them to play, or when their owners have just given them something very desirable—like permission to snuggle up on the bed.

▼ Hard stare

Dogs stare when they've seen something that warrants closer attention, like an intruding cat. When they decide that further action is needed, they'll lower their heads a little and squint slightly. It's the same expression wolves use when they're watching their prey for weakness. Shepherds call this expression "the eye" and treasure it in herding dogs.

Dogs adopt a similar expression when they're feeling defensive, threatened, or aggressive. They'll raise their eyebrows, and the skin above their eyes will crinkle a little. Depending on what other emotions they're feeling, their foreheads may be furrowed. If they're aggressive, yet also feeling a bit fearful, their foreheads will be heavily furrowed. This is the expression some dogs show when, for example, the vacuum cleaner comes out of the closet. This look basically says, "I'm not sure if you're friend or foe."

Averted gaze

Avoiding eye contact or looking away is how dogs try to keep the peace, says Steve Aiken, an animal behaviorist in Wichita, Kansas. It's how timid or submissive dogs say, "I don't want to cause any trouble. I know you're the boss." Dogs look this way when they meet other, more dominant dogs or when they sense they've done something to displease their owners.

Oblique stare

Sometimes, a stare isn't a sign of aggression. For example, dogs who are staring but trying hard not to show it, and whose eyes are almost closed, are planning something. Lying on the floor, supposedly snoozing, they're probably watching the cat but want to fool the cat into thinking they're asleep. Once the cat turns away, they'll probably pounce, hoping to entice the cat into a game.

Looking sideways

Dogs look out of the corners of their eyes when they're being coy or asking to play. It's a polite way of expressing interest without being pushy.

(continued)

EYES AND EMOTIONS—CONTINUED

◀ Eyes opened wide

Wide eyes signify astonishment and surprise, and sometimes fear. A sudden noise can cause dogs to jump, turn around, and look wide-eyed at the source of the sound. Dogs who are frightened may open their eyes so wide that the whites show more than usual.

Blank stare

Blank stares don't need much interpretation—they mean bored dogs. If they're awake and their eyes are open but no one appears to be home, then they're in a bored-stiff trance. This can happen when dogs are forced to control themselves—for example, when their owners have told them to sit and stay while they're talking to a neighbor. Dogs may do as they're asked in such cases, but their blank stares express their boredom eloquently.

▶ Narrowed or half-closed eyes

Dogs who are happy and relaxed will narrow their eyes or half-close them. This is how dogs will look when they're enjoying something like a tummy rub or a long session of stroking from their owner. These half-closed eyes convey total bliss, and there's no misunderstanding that emotion.

CHAPTER FOURTEEN

EARS

Dogs use their ears for a lot more than hearing.
Their ears are mobile and expressive and they use them
to signal emotions to people and other dogs.

Dogs have excellent hearing, in part because their ears are wonderfully mobile. Controlled by about 15 different muscles, their ears swivel, twitch, rise up, and fall back. All of these movements allow dogs to detect faint sounds and pinpoint their direction. At the same time, their ear movements telegraph their moods and intentions, in the same way that our changing expressions and gestures tell others what we're feeling.

You can't gauge a dog's feelings by ear movements alone, any more than you can tell what people are thinking just by looking at their eyes, says Jacque Schultz, director of special projects for the Association for the Society and Preservation of Animals in New York City. You have to look at the ears in relation to other forms of body language, like the position of the tail or a dog's overall posture. This is especially true when you're dealing with dogs who have less-than-expressive ears, such as cropped or very long ones. "Dogs with cropped ears are limited in the amount of signals they can give," Schultz says. "They've been purposely made to look fierce and stoic so that they don't look to be showing pain or backing down in a fight."

All the positions of a dog's ears should be gauged in comparison to the way that a dog

PICK OF THE CROP

Breeds such as Doberman pinschers, boxers, Great Danes (below), and schnauzers have traditionally had cropped ears. These breeds naturally have hanging or folded ears, but cropping turns them into erect, pricked ears. This changes their look from gentle and placid to intent and aggressive, and that can change how people and other dogs perceive them. "Many crop-eared dogs unwittingly send the wrong message to other dogs," says D. Caroline Coile, Ph.D., a neuroscientist in Ochlocknee, Georgia. "They can't express a full range of emotions because they look perpetually aggressive and dominant."

normally carries his ears when he's relaxed, says Stanley Coren. Ph.D., professor of psychology at the University of British Columbia in Vancouver, Canada, and author of *The Intelligence of Dogs*. "Dogs with severely cropped ears will be harder to read," he says.

Some breeds are better at expressing certain emotions because of the shape of their ears. German shepherds, for example, have erect, triangular ears that make them look attentive and alert all the time, even when they're just casually looking around or dreaming about dinner. When they're focused and alert, their ears will become even more erect.

A basset hound, on the other hand, may be just as attentive as the German shepherd, but he can't convey the same degree of intensity. His heavy, pendulous ears simply aren't constructed for the task.

When you're watching dogs to see what their ears are saying, you need to take their ear types into consideration. You also need to look closely to interpret their ear language correctly. Some of the messages can be quite subtle, and positions that look very similar can mean different things, says D. Caroline Coile, a neuroscientist in with a special interest in canine sensory systems in Ochlocknee, Georgia.

BREED SPECIFIC

Some of the long-haired breeds, including cocker spaniels, poodles, Schnauzers and Lhasa apsos, grow hair in their ears. The combination of hair and ear wax sometimes makes an almost impregnable plug that blocks the ear canal. Hanging ears are also prone to health problems because of poor ventilation: Humidity builds up inside the ears and encourages the growth of fungi and bacteria. Hanging ears tend to trap grass seeds, as well. This is a perennial problem for cocker spaniels, who sometimes need surgery to remove the seeds. Floppy-eared dogs that enjoy playing in water, such as Labrador retrievers, golden retrievers, Chesapeake Bay retrievers, and Irish setters, are particularly vulnerable to ear problems, especially if care isn't taken to keep their ear canals clean and dry.

Prick-eared breeds have different health problems. Their ears seem to be a favorite target of biting insects, they're prone to sunburn, and they also run the risk of aural hematomas, a type of blood blister that causes the canine equivalent of "cauliflower ears".

Butterfly ears
Chinese crested dog

Semi-prick ears
Wire fox terrier

Judging Dogs by Their Ears

Even if you don't know a thing about reading ears, their shape and position can influence your perceptions of a dog's personality or temperament. Dogs with erect ears, such as corgis and Alaskan malamutes, always appear alert, intelligent, and assertive. Those with semi-erect ears, like collies, Shetland sheepdogs, and fox terriers, also look alert, but a little friendlier than those with fully erect ears. And dogs with hanging ears, such as basset hounds, beagles, Afghans, and Labradors, appear very friendly and placid. People are naturally attracted to these dogs because their hanging ears give them an appealingly docile, puppyish look.

It's unfortunate that very stylized ears can project confusing messages, at least to human eyes. Basset hounds, for example, usually have lively, sociable dispositions, but their floppy, long ears give them a mournful look. Cocker spaniels, on the other hand, have long, lavishly furred ears that make them look mellow, yet the reality is that they tend to be high-strung and excitable. And huskies have erect, triangular ears, which, along with their wolflike shape and coloring, don't convey their friendly, often docile natures.

POOCH PUZZLER

Why do some dogs have floppy ears?

Most human ears are pretty much the same size and shape, but dogs have an amazing range of styles, from the neat, pricked ears of Samoyeds to the long, pendulous ones of bloodhounds. It wasn't always this way. Dogs are descended from wolves, and wolves don't have floppy ears. So what made some breeds' ears go from erect to floppy?

The answer is breeding. Tracking breeds such as beagles and bloodhounds were bred to track by scent alone, and their long ears help by dragging on the ground and stirring up air currents that make the scent molecules move around, says Anne Legge, a breeder of champion bloodhounds and judge of mantrailing trials in Winchester, Virginia.

Another reason for breeding dogs with floppy ears is that people simply like the docile, submissive look that long ears give. "Long ears set dogs' faces off in the same way that human hair does ours," says Jacque Schultz, director of special projects for the Association for the Society and Preservation of Animals in New York City. "They make their faces seem softer and more human-looking."

Hanging ears
Saluki

Folded ears
Whippet

Prick ears
Alaskan malamute

EAR POSITIONS

Although their ears come in a wondrous array of shapes and sizes, all dogs move them in similar ways to express what they're thinking and feeling. When you marry dogs' ear movements with what the rest of their bodies are telling you, you'll get a pretty clear picture of their state of mind.

▶ Neutral

Every dog, whether his ears are big, small, pricked, or floppy, has a neutral ear position that indicates he's relaxed and isn't thinking much about anything. The skin around the base of the ears will be smooth because he isn't making an effort to move the muscles. Dogs who are happy usually put their ears in the neutral position.

◀ Pricked up

Dogs who are stimulated by something they see or hear will prick their ears right up and point them in the direction of their interest. Dogs who are feeling aggressive will raise their ears, too. This is easiest to see in dogs that have prick ears, such as German shepherds. Dogs with folded or hanging ears, such as greyhounds or Labradors, aren't able to raise their ears as much, so the pricked-up response is harder to see. A clue to look for is creases around the base of the ear, which indicate that the muscles are active. "Watch the top of a dog's floppy ears," says John Hamil, D.V.M, a veterinarian and breeder of champion bloodhounds in Laguna Beach, California. "Floppy-eared dogs will pull their ears up toward the top of their heads when they're excited or interested in something."

The amount of tension in a dog's ears will tell you how strong his feelings are. There's more tension in an aggressive dog's ears than in those of a playfully alert dog.

◀ Pulled down and back

When a dog's brow and skull muscles are tight and tense, and his ears are pulled down and back, he's probably feeling frightened, anxious, or submissive. The more intense his feelings, the more extreme the ear position will be. Dogs also assume this position when they're wondering what's going to happen next or when they're play-fighting with other dogs. Putting the ears back seems to say, "This is just a game. I don't mean you any harm."

▶ Limp

Ears that droop like wet laundry are a dog's way of saying, "I'm bored stiff—not much action around here." Dogs with prick ears can't manage the full droop, but they'll let their ears sag sideways a bit. Those with naturally hanging ears will let them hang even lower.

◀ Multiple positions

Dogs are sometimes of two minds about things and this will show in the way they hold their ears. It's not unusual to see one ear pricked up while the other is partially pulled back. Or one ear may be folded while the other is flat against the skull. In some cases, the ears keep changing position as a dog's emotions change. You'll often see this when someone your dog doesn't know comes to the house. He's not sure whether to be excited or nervous, and his ears reflect his confusion.

CHAPTER FIFTEEN

TAIL

Dogs' tails are one of the most talkative parts of their bodies.
They can express happiness, aggression, stress,
and all the emotions in between.

Whether they're stately plumes, scruffy tangles, lively whips, or wagging stubs, dogs' tails are often moving and always talking. You can tell a lot about what dogs are feeling by the action of their tails. And the messages are often more complex than "Great, it's time to eat." Different wags show that dogs are nervous, shy, happy, or aggressive. Once you know what to look for, you'll know what they're feeling and even what they plan to do next.

When dogs are alone, they usually don't wag their tails, even when they're having a great time

UNNECESSARY SURGERY

Rottweilers, Dobermans, and boxers (right) are known for their stubby, assertive little tails, which zip back and forth like hyperactive metronomes. But these tails, common as they are, are artificially short, thanks to breed standards and a technique known as docking.

The various national breed clubs are responsible for defining the "ideal" look for different breeds. These looks are mainly achieved by selective breeding, but for some breeds, the natural tail doesn't meet the standard and is customarily docked, or cut short, a few days after birth.

Even though docking is common and many veterinarians don't see any harm in it, it does interfere with a dog's ability to communicate, says Barbara Simpson, Ph.D., a veterinary behaviorist in Southern Pines, North Carolina.

"He doesn't have as many components to let him express what he's feeling, but if the other dogs are well-socialized, they can pick up enough information from the other signals that dogs with docked tails send."

Most dogs have tails that are the same color as the rest of their coat. But some dogs, including beagles, basset hounds, and Tibetan terriers, have tails of a different color, especially at the tip. This allows their tails to act as attention-getting flags, making it much easier for them to signal their intentions to other dogs.

excavating the garden or barking at birds that are flying overhead. The reason for this is that tail-wagging is mainly used for social communication, much as people trade small talk at office parties. Once a dog gets around people or other dogs, the tail really goes into action.

How fast and vigorously it moves depends on the breed and the dog's personality. Some dogs, such as Cavalier King Charles spaniels, tend to wag wildly at the slightest provocation. Other breeds, such as Rottweilers, don't wag anywhere near as much.

Among all breeds, a slight wag, when just the end of the tail moves, is considered a casual greeting. The happier and more excited dogs get, the more vigorously they wag. Tails that are stiff and not wagging are a signal that dogs are feeling defensive, protective, or aggressive.

"One trick that a dog doesn't need to learn is how to wag his tail," writes Marjorie Garber, author of *Dog Love*. "A wagging tail is the spontaneous sign of joyful recognition, and dog owners usually respond to it with a joyful recognition of their own. For the dog wears his heart on his tail."

Different Tails, Different Tales

Not every dog is adept in tail-speak. Just as some people are less articulate than others, some dogs don't communicate very well with their tails. This has less to do with ability than genetics: Some breeds have tails that are less mobile than others. Others have tails that are held close to their rumps. No matter how much they try to communicate, their tails won't cooperate.

Tightly curled
Basenji

This can be a real problem for dogs like French bulldogs, basenjis, and pugs, whose tails are small and tightly curled. They tend to rely on other types of body language when they need to express their emotions, says Shirley Thomas, an American Kennel Club judge and champion pug breeder in Flushing, New York, and author of *The New Pug*. When they're happy, they wiggle their bodies back and forth and shake their tails from side to side.

Docked
Doberman

"They also use their heads a lot. They'll wrinkle their foreheads when they're curious, and they can move their ears into many different positions," she says.

Bushy
Alaskan malamute

Short and upright
West Highland white terrier

High and stiff
Airedale

Between legs
Greyhound

Australian shepherds are born with very short tails, or, in some cases, with no tails at all. Boxers, schnauzers, Rottweilers, and Doberman pinschers customarily have their tails docked, or cut short. These dogs use their stubby tails as much as they can, but their ability to express themselves is quite restricted.

Some tails, on the other hand, are made for communication because they're easy to see. Dogs with long, bushy, eye-catching tails, such as German shepherds, Samoyeds, and Siberian huskies, don't have any trouble expressing their emotions. Not only do their tails move freely, but the luxuriant masses of hair can be made to rise at a moment's notice, giving them charisma and an air of authority.

Scottish terriers and West Highland white terriers are between these two extremes. While their tails are quite short, and short-haired, they're still very expressive because what they lack in size they make up for in mobility and upright positioning, says Mary Warzecha, a columnist for the *American Kennel Club Gazette* in Windsor, Connecticut.

While a hairy tail can make it easier to communicate by exaggerating dogs' normal tail movements, it can also be a problem for dogs with very short tails, like Old English sheepdogs. Their thick, hairy coats can cover their tails like a comforter. No matter how much they move their tails, the movements may be invisible. To compensate, these dogs will often move their entire rumps back and forth.

Judging Dogs by Their Tails

Dogs are rarely standoffish and they're never prejudiced. A German shepherd won't make judgments about a Labrador, and a poodle is perfectly happy playing with a golden retriever. People, on the other hand, are quick to form judgments not only about each other but also about dogs. And to a large extent these judgments are shaped by a dog's tail.

Consider Welsh terriers. They have wildly wagging, jaunty tails that ride high on the rump, and they make people smile just to see them. Great Danes, on the other hand, have tails that attach to the body lower on the rump. To human eyes, this can make them seem a little moody or aloof. No matter how happy or friendly they actually are, their low-set tails don't seem quite as welcoming as the high-flying tails of some other dogs.

Different breeds carry their tails in different positions as well. Fox terriers and Airedales, for example, naturally carry their tails high and rather stiffly. This can make them look assertive or even aggressive—not only to people but also to other dogs. Vizslas and golden retrievers carry their tails in a more relaxed fashion, and

this makes them look mellow and unthreatening. Greyhounds, whippets, borzois, and Afghan hounds usually carry their tails between their legs. People often think they're timid, frightened, or unhappy, but they're not. It's just how their tails are.

Tails and Scent Communication

Dogs' tails have one other vital role in communicating: Every time a dog moves his tail, it acts like a fan and spreads his natural *eau de dog* around him, just as a woman walking through a crowd may leave a lingering aroma of perfume.

Dogs use their sense of smell much more than people do, and one odor that always gets their attention comes from the anal glands, two sacs under the tail that contain an odoriferous liquid that's as unique among dogs as fingerprints are among people. By smelling this scent, dogs can determine many interesting facts, such as each other's sex, age, and status, says Deena Case-Pall, Ph.D., a psychologist and animal behaviorist in Camarillo, California.

P O O C H   P U Z Z L E R

Why do dogs chase their tails?

Dogs look like they're having a great time when they're spinning in circles and trying to catch their tails. But sometimes it's not any fun at all. "They may have an irritation on their backs, an itchy bottom, or a flea allergy," says Dick Schumacher, D.V.M., a veterinarian and executive director of the California Veterinary Medical Association in Davis, California.

If a trip to the veterinarian doesn't reveal any problems, and your dog is still chasing his rear end, then he really is doing it for fun. "Some dogs just see their tails and want to know all about them," says Steve Aiken, an animal behaviorist in Wichita, Kansas.

While dogs with long tails tend to chase them more often than do those with very short tails, it's not a very common activity. "And some dogs never chase their tails at all," says Dr. Schumacher.

It's the dog equivalent of reading someone's driver's license and finding out all their pertinent information," she says. From the details they glean, dogs can tell whether to be respectful or disdainful, lustful or indifferent.

Every time a dog wags his tail, the muscles around his anus contract, pressing on the glands and releasing the scent. A dominant dog who carries his tail high will release much more scent

Tail-wagging helps distribute a dog's unique odor so others can learn more about him.

than a submissive dog who holds his tail lower. And the wagging of his tail, of course, helps to distribute the scent.

One of the reasons that nervous, frightened, or submissive dogs hold their tails between their legs is to prevent other dogs from sniffing them. It's their way of trying to fade into the background and not draw attention to themselves.

Tails in Action

When dogs aren't communicating with their tails, they can find plenty of other useful things to do with them. For a start, the tail is a vital part of a dog's balance system. Some breeds, like Afghans, Irish wolfhounds, and greyhounds, were bred to chase fast-moving prey. Their tails are thin and very long in proportion to the rest of them. They can run at great speeds, and they use their tails as a counterbalance when turning. Their long tails give them agility and the ability to turn quickly in response to the movements of their prey, says Lou Gerrero, a breeder of champion Afghans and an American Kennel Club judge in Simi Valley, California. "These dogs' tails are long, tapered, and low-set, and when

When greyhounds run, they use their long, thin tails as rudders to help them turn quickly.

combined with their sloping rumps, there's a powerful rudder effect."

Dogs also use their tails as rudders when they're swimming. Chesapeake Bay retrievers and Labrador retrievers have tails that are thick and strong, which helps them move easily through the water. Their tails are also very flexible and this helps them make quick turns in the water, explains Janet Horn, a breeder of champion Chesapeake Bay retrievers in Frenchtown, New Jersey.

Other dogs use their tails as convenient form of insulation. Nordic breeds such as Siberian huskies, Samoyeds, Alaskan malamutes, and keeshonds have brushy or plumed tails with long, dense fur. When they're lying down, they can pull their tails over their faces to keep out the cold, says Vicky Jones, a breeder of Alaskan malamutes in Sharpsburg, Georgia.

"These dogs also use their tails to help them move a bit faster when they're pulling a sled across ice because their tails act like a rudder," Jones says.

Tail Positions and Movements

You can tell a lot about dogs by the ways they move their tails. Tail-wagging is just part of their repertoire. The position of the tail is also significant. By looking at the position and movement of dogs' tails, you can get a pretty good idea of what they're trying to say.

▶ Sweeping from side to side

Dogs often wag their tails in broad sweeps when they're playing or anticipating something good, like food. But they also use this wag when they're throwing their weight around or getting ready to launch an attack, says Petra Horn, a trainer in Mira Mesa, California. The only way to know the difference is to look at other cues, such as the way they're standing, to tell what their intentions are.

◀ High and wagging

Dogs are always in good moods when their tails are held high and are wagging back and forth. The speed of the wag will increase dramatically when they get a good response from whomever they're hoping to engage in play.

(continued)

TAIL POSITIONS AND MOVEMENTS—Continued

◀ Horizontal

You can tell a dog is interested in something when his tail is horizontal to the ground. This signal is only evident in dogs with long tails, of course. Those with short or docked tails will express the same message by holding the tail slightly higher than usual, says Kathy Marmack, a supervisor of animal training at the San Diego Zoo in California.

▶ Tucked

Submissive, anxious, or frightened dogs invariably tuck their tails between their legs. The farther a dog tucks his tail, the stronger his feelings. A dog who's extremely frightened will tuck his tail so much that it may reach all the way to his stomach. Even when the tail is tucked, however, the tip will wag a bit, which displays his stress.

A tucked tail isn't always a sad sight. It's normal for puppies, for example, to tuck their tails when they're greeting adult dogs. It's their way of showing respectful submission. Once the adult accepts a young dog's greeting, the tail will uncoil and start moving more naturally again.

▶ High and rigid

When a dog's tail goes from being horizontal to upright and rigid, you can be pretty sure that an interesting situation has turned into a potentially challenging or threatening one, says Janice DeMello, an obedience trainer in Somis, California. Dogs who are trying to assert their authority will usually raise their tails slightly above the horizontal. To make themselves appear even stronger and more dominant, they'll raise the tail even more and wag it slightly back and forth. You can tell a dog is truly annoyed or angry when the tail goes almost rigid. If anger gives way to actual aggression, the tail will go higher still and it

won't move at all. However, the hair will bristle and rise on end. This is how dogs make themselves appear bigger than they really are. Hair on the shoulders and back, called the hackles, will start to bristle, too.

▶ Low and moving slightly

While dogs experiencing anger or other "high" emotions will raise their tails, those feeling a little low will make them droop. A tail held below horizontal and wagging very slightly means a lowering of spirits. Such a dog is slightly worried or a bit insecure. Or he may be feeling a little sick.

CHAPTER SIXTEEN

HOW TO PREVENT CONFUSION

Dogs are often mystified by our body language and tone of voice.
Understanding what they do respond to makes it
easier for us to send the right messages in the right way.

Even though dogs can recognize and understand some human words and body language, most of the ways we behave and communicate seem a little foreign to them. They try to understand what they see and hear by translating human behavior into canine terms, and that's when confusion sets in.

People move their hands a lot when they get excited, for example, and dogs have seen us do it a hundred times. They know from our energy and expressions that we're happy, and yet they can't help suspecting that we're angry because in the animal world, quick, exuberant movements usually mean aggression or danger rather than fun and happiness.

Confusion is also an issue when we tell dogs to do things and they don't do them. Maybe you yell at a dog to stop barking, and he keeps barking. Or you say "heel," and your dog forges ahead. It often seems as though the more insistent people get, the worse their dogs behave, and so frustration levels rise. "People think that their dogs are stubborn, but there's no such thing as a stubborn dog, just a dog who's been given confusing signals," says Chuck Tompkins, an animal behaviorist and vice

Dogs respond best when our words and body language convey the same message. This miniature poodle is ignoring the command to come because she interprets her owner's exuberance as anger.

president of animal training at Sea World International in Orlando, Florida.

When you consider that dogs and people are different species with entirely different ways of communicating and viewing the world, it makes sense that a certain amount of confusion is unavoidable. Dogs don't have the capacity to understand humans, but we do have the capacity to understand them. Once you understand how dogs perceive you—your tone of voice, your body language, and the many ways in which you express yourself—the communication barriers become less insurmountable.

Vocal Barriers

People's speaking voices can throw dogs into a quandary. They're familiar with the range and volume of their owners' voices, of course, but voices that they don't know can be confusing. Dogs don't listen to words that much, but they are attentive to such things as tone and laughter, and they're very good at comparing voices with body language. That's why people can be saying one thing while their dogs are hearing something entirely different.

Tone of voice. Dogs are very sensitive to the tone of people's voices. In their world, young or submissive dogs are the ones with high-pitched barks or yelps, while more dominant dogs are the ones most likely to give a low growl.

It's not uncommon for dogs to get slightly nervous around men with deep voices because they associate that pitch with authority—or, in some cases, with the reprimands their mothers gave them when they were young. The men, of course, don't understand any of this, or why they're getting such a negative reaction.

People don't have to disguise their voices to communicate with dogs, but raising the pitch a little can help. To a dog's ears a higher voice sounds less threatening and happier. Trainers often recommend using an energetic, slightly high-pitched tone with all dogs, not just those who get nervous around deep voices, because it can help dogs respond with more enthusiasm.

While low-pitched voices cause the most confusion for dogs, high-pitched voices cause problems of their own, especially when they're used for discipline. Suppose you're leash-training your dog, and he's forging head, zigzagging across your path and generally doing just about everything except heeling. If you have a high voice and give a reprimand—and people's voices usually get higher when they're tense—your dog may act as he would with a young or subservient dog and just ignore you.

Whether your voice is naturally high or low, it's worth lowering it a notch when giving reprimands. Even if you don't sound angry, the deep, gruff tone will spark your dog's memories of early authority figures, and he'll be more likely to do as you tell him.

Words and actions. Dogs are experts at reading all kinds of body language, which means that they can quickly tell when your

This toy poodle is very sensitive to his owner's tone of voice. Men with deep voices often get better results when they raise the pitch while praising their dogs.

words or tone of voice aren't telling the whole story. This often happens in vets' offices, where anxious owners try to soothe nervous dogs by telling them that everything's okay. The dogs know perfectly well that everything's not okay, and their owners' attempts to give comfort may have the opposite effect. It's as though the dogs are thinking, "Things must be pretty bad if she's going to lie like that."

Things get even worse when dogs start growling because they're scared. It's natural to want to reassure a frightened dog, but doing so will probably increase his tension because he'll interpret soothing words as support for what he's doing, says Moira Cornell, an obedience trainer in Canoga Park, California. This type of confusion can be a problem because your dog simply won't understand that what he's doing isn't appropriate, she explains.

A better approach is to tell your dog in no uncertain terms to cut it out, she advises. He'll respect the firmness in your voice, and the clarity of the message will take some of the pressure off him. He'll realize that you're in charge and will be able to handle things from then on.

Laughter. It takes almost superhuman willpower not to laugh when dogs are acting silly or when they're trying to do something serious but wind up looking silly anyway. It's important to refrain from laughing when dogs have done something wrong, because dogs interpret laughter as a happy sound that means they have your full approval. Laughing when they do something wrong makes them think you approve—and to keep getting your approval in the future, they're sure to do the same thing wrong again.

Body Language Barriers

When dogs want to learn more about other dogs, they focus on posture. From a distance, a dog can figure out what another dog is thinking by looking at how he holds his body and tail. An alert pose means that he's attentive. When he's standing stiffly, with his tail straight out and wagging rhythmically, it means that he's cautious and on guard.

Dog-to-dog messages are pretty clear-cut because both dogs are speaking the same language. But dogs are in foreign territory when they try to decipher human body language, especially because our bodies sometimes contradict our voices or expressions.

It's important when dealing with dogs to be aware of your body language and to make sure that it's communicating the same thing as your voice. Your voice and body language are likely to be at odds when you're cross with your dog but are trying not to show it. No matter what you're saying, your dog will see that your face, arms, and shoulders are stiff. They're all signs that you're on edge, and he'll be confused because you haven't sent him a clear message about what you're feeling. Your voice may be saying that everything's fine, but if your body is saying that it's not, your dog won't know which signal he's supposed to believe.

The trick is to keep your posture as relaxed as you can when you're interacting with your dog, says Cornell. If your shoulders and arms are rigid and your expression stern, your dog will sense that you're angry because he pays more attention to your body than to the words that you say.

ACTING THE PART

Dogs in the movies look natural, but what's on the screen represents hours of training. Scripts often call for dogs to do things that are contrary to their natural behavior. It's up to a trainer to ensure that the dogs understand exactly what they're supposed to do.

To successfully train a dog to "act," trainers must have a dog's total attention no matter what comes up, says Mary Kay Snyder, who trained the Dalmatian puppies in the movie *101 Dalmatians*. Most trainers use a clicker to let dogs know that a treat is coming when they do their jobs correctly.

"An actor dog is conditioned to pay attention and perform the command. Then he expects to hear the clicker go off. Once the scene is over, the dog is rewarded with a treat," says Snyder.

Since dogs in the movies are often shown running, they have to learn to run on a treadmill. It's the only way to film scenes that are shot in a studio.

"It's a pretty boring activity, yet we want a dog to look excited and not get confused," Snyder says. "I condition him to watch me running in front of him."

Dog actors also have to learn to run in one direction, then suddenly stop and run the other way. "With this trick we have someone call a dog to come one way, then his trainer calls him from the other direction," Snyder says.

It often takes three or four months to train dogs for film sequences. A vital part of the preparation is to take the dogs to a variety of places before they put a paw on the set. "I want to accustom them to hearing different sounds and meeting different people so that nothing surprises or confuses them," Snyder says. This will help them act calmly around the loud noises, strange people, and large equipment found in a movie studio or on location. They also have to be comfortable on set with creatures they don't see every day, such as chickens or pigs.

Dog actors, like this miniature schnauzer, are trained to focus intently on their trainers and to stay calm in all sorts of unusual situations.

Mental Barriers

It's normal for us to interpret dogs' behavior in human terms, but our judgments usually aren't very accurate. Dogs have rich emotional lives, but their emotions aren't the same as ours. People often swear that their dogs look guilty when they've done something wrong. But dogs don't feel guilt—at least, not in the same way we do. That means that when you come home and find the trash on the floor and your dog cowering in the corner, you can't assume that he knows he did something wrong. In all likelihood he's responding to the look on your face, and he knows it doesn't look good. As for the trash at his feet, he's probably forgotten it was his doing in the first place.

Staffordshire bull terriers often have a dominant streak. Indulging them with rough play, which they adore, will only reinforce their dominant tendencies.

More confusion may arise when you start cleaning up the mess. You're in a bad mood and angry, and you get even angrier when your dog, rather than looking abashed, starts rooting around in the trash for extra tidbits. He's not being disrespectful, says Jayme Evans, a dog trainer and founder of Canine College in Middleburg, Virginia. In his mind, since you're touching the mess, it must be okay for him to touch it, too. He's just following the leader, which is what dogs do naturally.

The important thing is to always make your reaction match the situation. Your dog needs to be able to make a logical connection between what he did and your response if he's to understand what you really mean. He may not like being corrected, but at least he'll see that as a logical response. But starting to scold your dog, then suddenly relenting and indulgently giving his ears a scratch will seem inconsistent and illogical—and that will leave him baffled and confused.

Mistaking who's in charge. Dogs like to know who's in charge, and mostly they're very happy for their owners to take on that role. But sometimes people give the wrong message, making dogs think the role has passed to them. And that can cause all sorts of problems.

Questions of leadership often occur during play. When dogs play with one another, the action is rough-and-tumble. They're fast and athletic, and they use every part of their bodies to prove they're rougher and tougher than their opponents. The goal of their games is often to see who backs down first. It's all in fun, but underneath the fun is a genuine contest for control and dominance.

The same motivations can underlie their play with humans. People who play roughly with their dogs by wrestling or pulling on a rope are creating a situation in which dogs feel they have to win. This usually isn't a problem because whether dogs win or lose, they had a great time. But some dogs are naturally more dominant than others, and there's no way they'll willingly lose without putting up a fight.

"With dogs that have a tendency to be aggressive, it's not a good idea to wrestle or play tug games," says Evans. If they're losing, they may get increasingly rough until they think they are winning. If you deliberately let them win, they'll come away feeling as though they have the upper hand. This can cause all kinds of problems, not just during play but also during the rest of your time together.

Even with dogs that aren't aggressive, rough-and-tumble romping can get out of hand quickly. Dogs play with people the same way they play with dogs—by play-biting. But they don't take into account that while dogs have protective layers of fur and loose skin that can withstand a certain amount of playful mauling, people don't. That means that people can't take the same level of rough stuff that another dog can—so an owner who's having fun one minute can be in pain and angry the next. The result is canine confusion.

Appearance Barriers

Dogs watch people much more closely than we ever watch them. Should our facial expressions not match the other signals that we're giving, dogs get confused. When you're trying to act

This woman's upbeat tone of voice, happy facial expression, and relaxed posture are all sending the same message, so her Belgian shepherd knows for sure that she's happy with him.

stern, for example, but your eyes are twinkling or your mouth is curving into a smile, dogs aren't sure which to believe—your stern voice or your happy facial expression.

Likewise, if you use a serious voice to tell your dog to stay but a few seconds later give him a wink, he'll think that you're giving him permission to get up and move around.

Putting on a happy face does come in handy when you want to congratulate a dog for following orders. But don't try to fool dogs with "false" expressions, and try not to mix the signals you're giving. Dogs only feel secure when they know what you're feeling; mixed signals make them nervous and uncertain.

PART FOUR

FAILURE TO COMMUNICATE

Many communication problems begin when a dog is
unsure of who's the boss. To establish leadership and avoid
communication breakdowns, you need to use your body language,
facial expressions, and voice effectively. At the same time,
you need to read your dog's signals correctly.

CHAPTER SEVENTEEN

WHO'S IN CHARGE?

Every dog will be happier if he knows who's in charge.
By letting your dog know you're the boss, you'll
make life easier for both of you.

Children learn from their parents and teachers to share their toys, to play fair, and, above all, not to be bossy. And if they don't learn from their parents, they quickly learn on the playground that other children don't like being bossed around.

Dogs see things differently. They love to be bossed around. In fact, dogs *need* to be bossed around, especially by the people in their lives.

Dogs are pack animals. What this means is that when they lived in the wild they lived in highly structured societies. They relied on a leader in order to survive. Dogs today don't have the same survival imperatives, but the old instincts remain. Dogs think of their human family as their pack, and they look to their owner to be the leader of the pack.

"Dogs feel more secure when they know who's the leader," says Sandy Myers, director of Narnia Pet Training in Naperville, Illinois. "Their packs are linear, with one member at the top. If we humans don't take on that role, our dogs will take it."

Most dogs don't want to be the leader. They'd much rather let you call the shots. But if you have a live-and-let-live philosophy, they'll often get uneasy because they're not sure where to turn for leadership. So they step in, however reluctantly, to fill the void.

When a dog does attempt to become the family's leader, problems can follow. Rather than taking orders from you, he'll become increasingly dominant, says Yody Blass, an animal behaviorist and director of Companion Animal Behavior in Ashburn, Virginia. "He may start growling, nipping, or even biting whenever he feels the need," Blass says.

It's important to teach your puppy early in life to respect your leadership and your rules.

Once a dog starts taking charge, he may be reluctant to give up his new-found power. This means he'll keep biting and growling and pushing you around until someone—it could be you or a member of your family—finally steps in to take control.

That's why you need to establish your authority, to make sure that your dog realizes that you're in charge, not him. "You need to be a benevolent leader," says Robin Kovary, director of the American Dog Trainers Network in New York City. "A good leader is never abusive. Dominance doesn't mean being harsh."

How to Lead Your Dog

Leadership comes from clear communication and consistency. Dogs can't reason, second-guess you, or ask questions when they're confused, so you need to make it absolutely clear what you want from them. And because they don't appreciate a wishy-washy leader, you need to lay—and then stick to—a few firm ground rules. That way, they'll know what's expected of them and will respond better. Here are some tips on becoming and staying your dog's most-trusted leader.

Be consistent. When your dog gets different messages from different people, he'll become confused. Worse, he may decide that since there are two (or more) sets of rules, any rules that come from humans are made to be challenged. "It's important to develop reasonable guidelines for your dog, and then make sure that everyone in your family agrees to them," says Kovary. For example, if you don't want your dog jumping on the sofa or beds, the whole family has to go

When he hears the command "off!" given consistently and clearly, this kelpie-Labrador cross will soon learn not to jump on people.

along with this—and that means keeping him off the tables and chairs, as well.

It's also important to enforce your rules consistently. When you boot your dog off the sofa on Monday, but let him hop up on Tuesday, he'll soon learn to not take your rules seriously.

Take a firm stand. "Never allow or encourage aggressive or bratty behavior in a puppy," says Kovary. It's cute when puppies mouth your hands or jump on you while you're playing. But that behavior won't be so cute once your puppy becomes a full-grown dog.

Reinforce good behavior. Parents encourage their children to do the right thing by rewarding them for good behavior. Dogs respond to compliments, too. In fact, your dog will learn what you want him to learn much more quickly when he gets positive reinforcement—a word of praise when he sits right away, for example, or a treat when he comes running when you call.

Instill a work ethic. Some dogs are never required to do anything. They come when they want, lie where it pleases them, and feel free to ignore you when it suits their fancy. Not surprisingly, these are usually dogs with attitude problems. To keep your dog honest, it's always a good idea to make him work for some of his rewards. That way your dog will quickly learn that the way to happiness comes through pleasing you, his leader.

For example, have your dog sit at the front door before you let him walk out. Tell him to sit and wait while you place his food bowl in front of him. Make him sit or lie down before being petted, or before greeting you or any visitors. And always reward his obedience with praise, a pat, or a treat. Your dog will soon learn that service and obedience are the keys to making both of you happy.

Defusing Dominance

Most dogs are happy to have a human leader. Sometimes, though, a dog will challenge you for leadership. He may do this with subtle signals—

MAKING THE INTRODUCTION

Dogs are territorial, so they get nervous when others invade their turf. That's why trainers recommend introducing dogs away from home, when they don't have territory to defend.

"Always introduce two dogs on neutral ground, such as in a park," says Wendy Volhard, a dog trainer in Phoenix, New York. "You don't want to put your dog in a position of having to defend his territory." Once the dogs have been properly introduced, it's fine to take them both home, but you'll still need to respect the resident dog's status, Volhard says. That means letting the "main" dog through the door first when you arrive home. He'll probably turn around and look at the newcomer. Then, in some subtle way, he'll let him know that it's okay to follow. And once they're friends, you won't have to worry about conflicts later on.

---

like lying on your feet and refusing to move when you try to stand up—or by actually acting aggressive. When this happens, you need to take serious steps to manage him. The key is to let him know that you're the one in charge, but without provoking a confrontation. This is one situation in which you don't want to move too fast because once a dog has started asserting his dominance, he'll perceive any opposition as a challenge and will be more likely to stand his ground. Your goal is to gradually assert your leadership while reducing your dog's tendency towards aggressiveness.

Give him less protein. Many dogs get too much protein in their diets. Extra protein means extra energy—and in dogs that have strong,

dominant personalities, extra energy can lead to further contests of wills. Look for dog food with protein levels of under 20 percent, says Ilana Reisner, D.V.M., a veterinarian and animal behaviorist at Cornell University in Ithaca, New York.

Get him moving. Exercise siphons off a dog's excess energy, which in turn can dampen his desire to be boss. It also releases endorphins, calming chemicals in the brain that can help put your dog in a better mood. Try to get him walking, jogging, or doing other strenuous exercise for at least 20 minutes a day. Large dogs or dogs that are unusually active, like Border collies, can use a lot more.

Avoid confrontations. There are two situations that often trigger confrontations from dogs with dominant tendencies. The first is competition over a prized object. Until your dog has started to learn his proper place in the family, don't take away his toys or anything else that he considers to be his. (At least, avoid doing it when he's looking; it's fine to spirit away "trouble" objects when he's not around.) The second main cause of confrontations is a reac-

This Yorkshire terrier has learned to sit and wait for permission before eating his dinner.

tion to a perceived threat. Dominant dogs may react badly to being surprised, so try not to disturb him when he's resting, or come up suddenly from behind.

Even though it's your job as the leader to call the shots, there's nothing wrong with cutting your dog some slack while you're teaching him to be subordinate. A face-to-face confrontation will only stiffen his resolve, whereas making gradual adjustments in your relationship is more likely to lead to lasting changes.

Practice obedience commands. This is a good way to reinforce your leadership and teach your dog to respect it. You don't need to be a master trainer or to spend hours every day having formal, parade-ground drill sessions. The idea is to get your dog used to following simple commands—such as sit, down, stay, or come—and to repeat the lessons twice a day for 5 to 10 minutes. Once your dog is following your commands during these training sessions, he'll be more likely to follow them the rest of the time. You can use these commands to make him earn whatever it is that he wants, whether it's toys, treats, or time with you.

Set the pace. Being a leader is a full-time job. Even when you and your dog are playing, you need to be the

105

These German shepherds follow their owner's lead and let her set the pace in the games that they play.

best to avoid rough games, like wrestling and tug-of-war. These activities encourage aggression by pitting your dog against you. When a naturally dominant dog wins such a game, he'll think he's one step closer to knocking you off the leader's rung.

Outsmart him. No matter how dominant your dog has been acting, you have a tremendous advantage: You're a lot smarter than he is. This means you don't always have to resort to confrontation—sometimes a little sneakiness will do the trick. Suppose, for example, your dog makes off with something he's not supposed to, like your shoe, and then acts aggressive when you try to get it back. You don't have to force the issue. Instead, offer him something he wants more, like a favorite toy or treat. Then when your dog drops your shoe, discreetly kick it away from him and out of sight. Then you can retrieve it later.

one in charge. This means that you, not he, decide when playtime starts and when it stops. You decide whether he should play vigorously or whether he should take it easy. And when you're done playing, simply take your ball and go home. He'll learn to follow your lead instead of trying to make you follow his.

You should also be the one who decides which games to play. The best games are those in which you give commands and so reinforce your leadership. When you're throwing a ball, for example, you call the shots by making your dog drop the ball every time he retrieves it. It's

Leading a Multi-Dog Household

The best relationships between people and dogs are those in which the people are the leaders and the dogs know it. This is especially true in a multi-dog household.

In any group of dogs, no matter how large or small, there's a very strict order. There's one dog who's the leader, and every other dog knows his place in the group and what's expected of him. Usually, the individual dogs will sort out the

hierarchy on their own without help from you. But owners sometimes make it harder for dogs to work things out because they try to make everything equal between their dogs. "This causes stress among the dogs, and that results in a battle for leadership," says Myers. "Each dog has his place and if we disrupt that, the lead dog will try to set things right. There's no equality in a group of dogs."

You can help to keep things stable in a multi-dog household by working out which is the lead dog and then respecting his rank. "To see who the lead dog is, figure out what each dog values," suggests Myers. "It's different for each dog—say, petting for one dog, food for another. Then watch to see which dog will leave his most valued item when the other approaches. Usually, the one that doesn't move away is the leader."

Once you figure out which dog is the canine leader, make sure you respect the pecking order. This means paying attention to the lead dog first in all things. For example, feed him before the other dogs, greet him first when you get home, and let

This miniature schnauzer is the top dog in the family, so he gets fed first. The toy poodle, as his follower, eats a little later.

him go through the door before the others. He'll take these extra privileges as his due, and the other dogs won't resent him at all because it's the way they expect things to be.

However, when two dogs aren't getting along, you'll need to step in. Lindsley Cross of Carmichael, California, learned this first-hand when she brought home Rosie, a six-month-old terrier-pointer mix. Cross's other dog, a two-year-old kelpie mix named B. G., was happy to share Cross with the newcomer. Rosie, however, hated it when B. G. got any attention. She would push Cross away whenever she tried to pet the older dog. Rosie also started stealing B. G.'s rest spots and playing roughly with her, sometimes making her yelp with pain.

B. G. never stood up to Rosie, and Cross didn't intervene, so the situation didn't improve. After five months of bullying and pushy behavior, Cross had had enough, and asked experienced dog owners for advice. They told her to deep-six her laissez-faire approach and to stop Rosie's rough play the minute it starts—by telling Rosie "no," for example, and by holding her away from B. G. when she started muscling in.

And that's all it took. Rosie is still a little pushy, Cross says, but she's learned she can't get away with being too aggressive. In addition, B. G. naturally got more assertive once Cross started acting as a backup. The dogs will always compete, but now it's more of a friendly contest than a battle for control.

CHAPTER EIGHTEEN

SENDING MIXED MESSAGES

What dogs hear is not always what people say.
Knowing how such misunderstandings occur is one step toward
communicating more clearly with our dogs.

We spend a lot of time with our dogs and get to know them pretty well. But it's worth remembering that we're a completely different species, with very different ways of communicating. That's why, despite our best intentions, we occasionally send mixed signals, telling our dogs one thing when what we mean is something else entirely.

Suppose your dog is merrily barking away in the backyard. If you're like most people, you'll eventually respond by sticking your head out the door and yelling "quiet"—at which point your dog starts barking even more loudly. This is a classic case of mixed signals. You thought your message was perfectly clear. But your dog interpreted your yelling differently. "Great," she

Volume doesn't mean the same thing to dogs as it does to people. That's why yelling at your dog to stop barking can sometimes encourage her to bark more.

probably thought. "She's barking too, and now we can do it together."

These sorts of misunderstandings don't have to happen. Once you understand how your dog thinks, you'll discover how to communicate in ways that she can clearly understand.

Differences in Body Language

People and dogs often get their wires crossed because they have different interpretations of body language. Hand movements, posture, and even facial expressions have entirely different meanings for people and dogs. Take a smile. Among humans it's a sign of friendship and pleasure. But dogs mostly "smile" when they're acting aggressively—and they assume that others do it for the same reason, says Sandy Myers, director of Narnia Pet Training in Naperville, Illinois. So your good-hearted greeting, meant to put a dog at ease, may get a cool reception.

This doesn't mean you should greet your dog with a frozen face. Dogs understand their owners better than we often think, and they learn to read human signals even when they're different from their own. But when you're dealing with an unfamiliar dog on the street or in someone's home, you might want to save the smile for later, when the dog has a better sense of who you are and feels comfortable with you.

The same goes for eye contact. Among people it's a sign of courtesy and confidence. We respect people who look us in the eye. Those who avoid eye contact, on the other hand, often appear distracted or even shifty. But among dogs, the opposite is true. Direct eye contact is often perceived as a challenge or a sign of aggression. A dog who stares directly at another dog is saying, "I want to be in charge here." The second dog, if she's a peaceful sort, will avert her eyes. Or, if she's not feeling peaceable, she'll stare right back, which means she's not backing down and is ready for trouble.

Dogs can certainly learn that eye contact from humans is perfectly acceptable, but this level of understanding takes time. When you're greeting a dog you don't know very well, the last thing you want is to unintentionally challenge her. At the very least, she'll have a hard time trusting you; at worst, you could get bitten. A better way to greet dogs is to look away, says Robin Kovary, director of the American Dog Trainers Network in New York City. This gives them a chance to approach and give you a sniff without feeling threatened. Once you get to know each other, it's fine to make eye contact because they'll recognize that humans don't know all the rules and will make allowances for this type of social faux pas.

Posture is another way in which we occasionally send the wrong signals. People move their hands a lot when they talk, or they stand tall and open their arms in an embracing gesture. From a dog's point of view, these expansive gestures and quick hand movements

This Irish wolfhound prefers being greeted with indirect eye contact and slow, calm movements.

can be unnerving because that's simply not how dogs greet each other. They're much less direct: They sidle up to strangers, moving slowly so as not to arouse suspicion. This is why dogs often shy away when someone approaches too quickly or with a lot of energy. Your hearty good-will and glad-to-see-you exuberance can seem vaguely threatening, at least until they get to know you better.

Personal Space

When it's time to stretch out and get comfortable, dogs aren't shy about picking choice locations. A soft carpet in the middle of the room will work nicely. So will a comfortable

109

leather couch or, on really cold nights, the warm comfort of a queen-size bed. And once they get settled, they're extremely reluctant to move. That's why owners often spend their days stepping gingerly over or around their recumbent canines, and their nights huddled on the edge of the bed while their indolent dogs spread out in dreamy comfort.

There's nothing wrong with letting sleeping dogs lie, but allowing them to dominate the family's space is one of the most common forms of miscommunication, says Yody Blass, director of Companion Animal Behavior in Ashburn, Virginia. You may feel it's simple courtesy to let your dog lounge in peace or to step back when she pushes her way past you in the hall. But to your dog, these are signals that she, more than you, is worthy of respect.

Dogs are extremely class-conscious. In the distant past, when dogs lived only with other dogs, their society was strictly hierarchical. Some dogs were leaders, others were followers. Each dog knew her place. The top dogs got the best places to sleep. They ate and drank first. And they expected other dogs to defer to them.

Most dogs don't live in canine packs any more, but they're still concerned about status. They're happy to obey those whom they perceive as holding a higher status. However, they're less likely to be quite so accommodating when they feel that the balance of power is shifting their way.

That means that when you step around your dog instead of telling her to move, or when you allow her to sleep in the bed or push past you on her way out the door, she'll begin thinking of

It's not only large dogs that occasionally try to rule the roost. Small dogs like this pug can also try to dominate the humans in their family, especially when they're allowed to take over the furniture.

herself as the top dog, Blass says. That could mean that she'll view you as her second banana. What began as a courtesy, in your mind, will be interpreted by your dog as a hint to take charge.

This can occur even in families where dogs don't sleep on the furniture. A dog who sleeps in a doorway and doesn't move when you approach is quietly testing the boundaries. You probably don't think twice of stepping around her, but over time she'll take this to mean that you're deferring to her and that her star is rising in the family hierarchy.

It's important to recognize this difference in perspective because dogs that start dominating space may try to dominate in other ways, as well. It all comes down to respect: You wouldn't stand in the President's way if he were approaching, and your dog shouldn't stand in your way, either, Myers says.

Vocal Signals

Dogs often misinterpret the way people speak to them. They don't find it easy to understand words alone, so they listen for other things, like the pitch and tone of your voice, to help them understand your meaning. This means you need to match these things to the content of your message to ensure that your dog knows what you mean. For example, people with high voices may need to make a special effort to sound forceful enough when they're giving a dog a command, says Greg Strong, a trainer in Easton, Maryland. If they don't, a dog may think that she doesn't really have to do what she's told—and respond accordingly. And people with deep voices may have difficulty pitching their voices high enough to convey pleasure and approval when they're praising a dog.

Words are most effective when they're said in the right tone of voice. This boxer knows that his owner's serious tone means a reprimand.

Dogs can also be confused when people use the wrong tone. For example, if you put a kind of question mark on the end of a command, your dog may not realize that you expect her to do something. Similarly, if you speak to her in too stern a tone, she may think you're unhappy with her, and so be reluctant to respond to you.

Another common source of confusion is a lack of expression in a person's voice. For example, if you praise your dog in the same brisk, no-nonsense tone that you use to give commands, she probably won't know that she's done something right, says Kovary. Instead, praise her in a high, happy, enthusiastic voice that will tell her clearly that she has pleased you.

Sending Clear Messages

Once you understand how dogs think, it's usually not difficult to speak and act in ways they can understand. It's worth making the effort because no matter how hard your dog tries to get along, human society is a lot different—and a lot more confusing—to her than it is to you. By communicating clearly and telling her exactly what's expected, she'll feel confident and will be more comfortable looking to you for direction.

Be consistent. If you were trying to learn Spanish, you'd be thoroughly befuddled if one day you were told adios means "hello" and the next day you were told it means "goodbye." Dogs run into this lack of consistency all the time. One day we shoo them from the table when they're begging for a hand-out, and the next day we say "just this once." Giving mixed signals creates a lot of confusion—along with a lot of mooching dogs.

Because she is praised the moment she drops the ball, this shiba inu understands that she's done the right thing.

The best way to avoid communication breakdowns is to be totally consistent, says Kovary. If you don't want your dog begging from the table, don't slip her food. Ever. If you don't want her on the couch, say "off," and be prepared to enforce it. Use exactly the same commands all the time. In learning to live with humans, dogs are essentially learning a new language, and giving consistent messages will make it easier for them to know what's expected.

Praise often. Dogs don't understand much human language and they can't read a list of rules. It's difficult for them to know what they are and aren't supposed to do. That's why it's crucial to give dogs a lot of praise when they do things right, says Kovary. When your dog steps out of your way when you walk to the door, tell her she's a good girl. Rub her head when she comes to your call, and give her a treat if she stops barking when you tell her to. No matter what form praise takes—a kind word, a stroke, or a biscuit—it makes it very clear to your dog

that she read your message loud and clear. It also tells her that you appreciate her efforts— and every dog loves to hear that.

Praise immediately. It's not always easy for dogs to make a mental connection between what you're telling them and what it relates to. "You've got about a three-second window in which your dog connects what you're doing or saying with what she's done," Blass explains. For praise to be effective, it has to be immediate.

Show her what you want. Few things are more frustrating than being told to do something, but not understanding what, exactly, you're supposed to do. Dogs go through this all the time. Like tourists who don't speak the language, they can tell from your tone of voice that you want something, but they haven't the slightest idea what it might be.

One of the quickest ways to get around communication barriers is to show your dog what you want, says Kovary. In other words, if you see your dog about to do something wrong, show her how to do something right.

For example, lead your dog outside when it looks as though she's going to make a pit stop on the carpet, and then praise her for going in the right place. If she doesn't move when you tell her to, nudge her out of the way. When she sniffs you where she shouldn't, step forward to make her back off, or give her the command "off." Combining commands with this type of direct reinforcement—along with praise when they do what you want—makes it much easier for dogs to understand what you're telling them.

CHAPTER NINETEEN

TEN COMMON COMMUNICATION PROBLEMS

Most of our dogs' behavior problems are simply a result of miscommunication. Once you work out what dogs are saying and find better ways to communicate with them, most behavior problems are easy to fix.

Dogs and people have been living together for thousands of years, and for the most part we understand each other pretty well. But every now and then we encounter situations in which communication breaks down. Our dogs don't understand what we want them to do, or, just as often, we give them messages we didn't intend.

When you consider that people and dogs speak entirely different languages, it's surprising that failures to communicate don't occur more often. "It's hard enough to communicate clearly and effectively with people," says Liz Thomas, a dog trainer in Alexandria, Virginia. "But when we try to communicate with our dogs, we have the added difficulty of working with a different species that doesn't talk and doesn't think the same way people do."

Communication problems sometimes take surprising forms, and it's not always easy to recognize them for what they are, Thomas says. Suppose your dog has been chewing on your shoes. She isn't merely misbehaving. She's trying to tell you something. What that something is depends on the dog and the situation. Dogs who spend a lot of time alone will sometimes chew as a way of dispelling feelings of loneliness or frustration. Other dogs chew because they don't understand the difference between their possessions and yours. Others may chew for the simple reason that it feels good to do it.

In other words, people and dogs speak different languages—and until we each learn the other's language at least a little bit, we're bound

Consistent rules are necessary to avoid confusion. If you don't want your dog on some of the furniture, don't let her on any of it, including the beds.

to have communication problems. Often, these problems take surprising forms. You might not think that destructive chewing, leash-pulling, or housesoiling result from our failures to communicate with our dogs, or vice versa. In fact, communication may be at the heart of some of these difficulties.

In many cases, solving these problems gets a lot easier with a little bit of empathy on our part. Here are some ideas on how to better understand why your dog is doing something, and how to overcome some of the most frequently occurring—not to mention vexing—obstacles to human–canine harmony.

Aggression

Some dogs know what they want and will be very aggressive about getting it. They'll bump against their owners to demand attention. They'll take over certain spots in the house and nothing will induce them to move. They will insist on playing or being petted and won't take no for an answer. Essentially, they want to call all the shots.

Aggression can take more serious forms as well. It's not uncommon for dogs to growl or grumble—or in some cases, to bite—in order to have their own way. This type of aggression never goes away on its own. In fact, it's the most common behavior problem that sends owners to behaviorists and trainers looking for help.

Aggression is a complex problem because it can be caused by many different things. Some dogs simply have dominant personalities. Even if they never show signs of actual aggression, they'll always try to get their way. Other dogs may be insecure or angry. They're the ones most likely to growl or bite.

You can tell a lot about your dog's personality by the way she expresses her aggressive or dominant tendencies. Here's what the signals usually mean.

Hey, talk to me. It's fairly common for dogs to nudge or gently butt their owners simply because they want some attention. This type of behavior usually isn't a problem as long as dogs aren't acting pushy under other circumstances, says Pat Miller, a trainer in Salinas, California.

I want to be in control. Dogs that are always nudging people and who also play roughly, take over choice spots on the furniture, or refuse to move when their owners try to squeeze past are showing more serious forms of aggression. They want to be in charge, and they're taking steps to fortify their advantage. Unless you stop them quickly, they'll continue trying to be dominant and will get pushier and more difficult to be around.

CALL FOR HELP

Even though aggression isn't necessarily any harder to change than other behavior problems, there isn't as much room for error. A dog who doesn't learn her lessons quickly may bite or threaten people, and that can be dangerous. That's why experts recommend calling a trainer or behaviorist at the first sign of aggressive displays, says Myrna Milani, D.V.M., a veterinarian and behaviorist in Claremont, New Hampshire.

This Labrador mix loves a game of Frisbee, in which she cooperates rather than competes with her owner. This type of play will help prevent her from trying to become the dominant member of the family.

Since biting, growling, and other forms of aggression can be quite dangerous—not only to you, but to other people as well— you may want to call a trainer for help. But the basic principles of "demoting" a dog and making her more co-operative aren't very difficult to apply.

For example, play games in which you and your dog cooperate, like throwing a ball or going for walks. Games such as tug-of-war, however, create a mood of competition, which only reinforces a dog's desire to come out on top.

Territory and possession can mean a lot to dogs, which is why aggressive behavior often includes taking over the furniture and refusing to move. As long as your dog is showing signs of aggression, you should keep her off the furniture all the time. Dogs see the furniture as a "choice" location, and by keeping them off, they'll come to understand that their position in the family is subordinate to yours.

Doorways are another form of territory, and you should make sure that your dog always goes through after you and not before. In addition, don't let her lounge in front of a doorway or a flight of stairs, says Robin Kovary, director of the American Dog Trainers Network in New York

POOCH ??? PUZZLER

Why do dogs like to tug?

Pulling on one end of a rope toy while their owner pulls on the other is a favorite game for many dogs. Why do they like it so much?

"A tug-of-war triggers a dog's competitive instincts," says Steve Aiken, an animal behaviorist in Wichita, Kansas. "In the wild, the dominant animal gets first crack at every resource, including food," Aiken explains. However, animals are constantly competing with one another to see who that dominant animal should be. A lowly member of the pack that tries to grab a piece of food from the leader, for instance, will trigger a tug-of-war. The winner gets the food—and a position at the top of the pecking order.

"This is the reason why you hear dog trainers recommend that you don't play tug-of-war with your dog," says Aiken. "If you lose, it's a signal that perhaps you aren't the leader any more. This can cause behavior problems further down the track."

Still, lots of people and dogs do enjoy a good game of tug, and if it's done right, no harm will come of it. "Just make sure that you're the one who always wins," says Aiken. If your dog is likely, through strength and tenacity, to get the upper hand, you're much better off playing a game of fetch, where your dog is obliged to obey you but has fun at the same time.

115

City. Your dog should happily give way to you, not the other way around.

Taking your dog for long walks or doing regular obedience work are superb ways to control aggression. It strengthens the bond between you and reinforces your role as the leader. It also will tire her out, and a tired dog is less likely to be aggressive, says Kovary.

Let your dog know there's no such thing as a free lunch, that it's her job to earn your attention. Don't give her anything—food, petting, or anything else—unless she does something for you first. Make her sit before going outside, or practice other commands before putting her food on the floor.

Barking

No one objects to a little barking, but some dogs have an awful lot to say. They bark at everything—bicyclists, cats, or the sound of moving drapes. Or they'll bark by the hour, apparently for no other reason than to hear themselves speak.

Barking is one of the most common behavior problems. It's also among the most serious, not only because it drives owners crazy but because neighbors who run out of patience may wind up contacting local law enforcement authorities. Yelling doesn't help because dogs often think you're barking back, Kovary says.

Barking can be an intractable problem, not only because it's a natural behavior but because dogs have a lot of different reasons for doing it. Here's what they may be saying.

Someone's coming! Like their owners, dogs are territorial—but instead of building fences,

This Jack Russell terrier is barking because she wants her owner to check something out. When her call is answered, she'll stop barking on her own.

they bark. This can be helpful when you want to know if someone's on your property, but it can be a real nuisance when it's directed at everything from cats to the postal carrier.

If your dog's definition of intruders is too inclusive, you may want to resort to diversionary tactics, says Shirley Sullivan, president of PR Dog, a training and dog day care center in Falls Church, Virginia. For example, when you see the postal carrier coming, keep your dog busy and focused on you by having her repeatedly sit and lie down, a practice trainers refer to as "puppy pushups." The idea is to keep your dog busy until the distraction goes away.

Don't forget I'm here. Some dogs rev up their barking when their owners are on the telephone or engaged in another activity that shuts them out of the field of attention. Again, this is an easy problem to correct. Sullivan recommends snapping the leash on your dog when you're about to get busy. If she starts barking, tug on the leash to get her attention and quiet her down. Most dogs will get the hint fairly quickly. Eventually, just putting on the leash before you make a telephone call will guarantee you a little peace.

SPEAK NOW!

Barking is as natural to dogs as talking is to people. No matter how much you try to discourage barking, it's hard for dogs to figure out what the problem is. That's why trainers often take the opposite approach. Rather than teaching dogs not to bark, they teach them when to start. "Getting a dog to bark on command is the key to training a dog to stop barking," says Sandy Myers, a trainer and director of Narnia Pet Dog Training in Naperville, Illinois.

First, find out what you can do to start your dog barking. Speaking in an excited tone may do it. Or try jumping up and down, running in place and waving your arms up and down, or just acting excited. When your dog starts to bark, praise her by telling her "good bark" or "good speak" and give her a treat. Keep doing this until just giving the command will set her off.

Once she barks on command, it's time to teach her to stop on command, says Myers.

Use the command to get her barking. Then, when she pauses between barks, give her a treat and tell her "good quiet." Dogs can't bark and chew at the same time, and most dogs will eagerly swap one activity for the other. Keep practicing this until your dog consistently stops barking when you give the "quiet" command.

The idea isn't to stop the barking entirely, Myers says. "We want our dogs to let us know when something is out of the ordinary. And some dogs need to get barking out of their system. But they also need to respond to the 'quiet' command."

Myers recommends practicing once a day, both to start barking and to stop it. "Your dog will get to do the barking she naturally wants to do, and you'll be teaching her to control it at the same time."

Dogs such as this vizsla can be taught to bark on command. By controlling when your dog does and doesn't bark, you'll have a much better relationship with your dog and with your neighbors.

Listen to me. Dogs get bothered by all sorts of things, and they respond by calling their owners the only way they know—by barking. This type of barking is normal and you don't want to stop it, Kovary says. Take a moment to check out what's going on. Once your dog sees you're on the scene, she'll feel less responsible and will probably stop barking on her own.

Begging for Attention

Dogs can be real gluttons for attention. This often means they're a bit anxious and fearful and in frequent need of reassurance. Or they may simply be accustomed to getting a lot of attention, and the more they get, the more they want. It's gratifying when your dog pushes his head against your hand for the occasional rub or lies close to you when you're relaxing, but no one enjoys being hounded by a canine "shadow" who can't bear to be alone even for a minute.

It's not difficult to teach dogs to be less demanding, but first you need to understand what they're telling you with all their clinging.

I'm insecure. Even the most self-sufficient dog has certain fears—of thunderstorms, for example, or the sound of firecrackers—that will send her in search of attention. There's nothing wrong with giving a frightened dog a little reassurance, but you don't want to make too big a deal of it. If you do, she may get the idea that there really is something to be afraid of—or at least she'll get in the habit of turning to you whenever she gets nervous.

"Don't go overboard with affection because that tells your dog it's okay to be scared," says Kovary. "You're reinforcing her fear."

This Belgian shepherd puppy is jumping up on her owner to get attention. There's nothing wrong with the occasional request, but some dogs won't leave their owners alone. That's when you have to figure out what's causing them to be so demanding.

Rather than just giving comfort, she recommends a more proactive approach. Think about the things that scare your dog silly. It may be thunderstorms or fireworks, or even the sound of a newspaper rattling. Whatever it is, think about ways to expose her to small doses.

Dogs who are afraid of thunderstorms, for example, can learn to cope with them when their owners make tape recordings of storms and play them back at very low volumes, rewarding their dogs as long as they stay calm and relaxed. The idea is to gradually decrease the "fear factor" by playing the recording a little bit louder every day. If your dog starts getting nervous, reduce the volume. But as long as she stays relaxed, keep giving her praise and treats. If you do this slowly—and it may take months of daily "exposure"—she'll probably get a little better, and less demanding of your attention.

I want to be in charge. "If a dog tends to be pushy in all sorts of situations, demands for attention may indicate that she wants to be in control," says Miller. Your dog needs to be taught to earn any attention you give her. For example, if she's demanding to be petted, she should be told to sit or lie down before she gets those loving strokes. It's also better to keep the petting session brief. That way, she learns to relax and be less controlling.

I'm bored. Dogs who don't have a lot to do will sometimes beg for attention merely because they can't think of anything else to do. For example, if you're working on a computer project at home, and your dog begins to nudge you persistently after several hours, she may be saying that she's tired of just lying around while you're crunching spreadsheets.

You really can't expect dogs to entertain themselves all the time, Miller says. Dogs are social creatures and they want to spend time with you more than anything else. This doesn't mean you should give in to their every demand, but you will have to remember to schedule some time when they can have your undivided attention. As long as you take them for walks or play with them for 30 to 40 minutes a day, and don't let them con you into giving them attention in between, they'll learn to wait for "their" time, Miller says.

Begging for Food

There isn't a dog on the planet who doesn't lobby for extra goodies now and then. But dogs who persistently beg for food or steal it when no one is looking aren't merely being greedy—they have something to tell you.

I'm hungry. It's hard to believe that a dog who tucks into one or two good meals a day will devote so much energy to mooching. But every dog needs different amounts of food, and it's possible that your dog is merely hungry. You may want to try moving the usual dinner hour forward an hour or two. Or you can divide her usual amount of food into three or four servings and dish it out more often. Dogs will often feel more satisfied when they get several small meals instead of one big one.

Pay attention to me. Dogs, like people, sometimes develop a strange relationship with food. In their mind it's the symbol of love and companionship, and they'll beg for food when what they really want is attention. "Never give your dog food from the table," Thomas says. "You don't want her to learn that pestering you

Begging for food is often your dog's way of saying "I'm hungry for attention." Give her some petting instead of a treat, and she will probably stop begging.

while you're eating will result in her getting a morsel or two. Rewarding such behavior can be the start of an annoying habit."

There's a simple technique that will discourage dogs from staking out the dining table. Choose a single spot where you want your dog to stay when you're eating. It could be in a corner of the dining room or in another room. Just be sure that you can see her while you're eating. Put her on a long lead, lead her to the "place," and give her a treat. If you do this every day, she'll learn that the easiest way to get food is to go to this spot on her own, Thomas says.

"Once your dog consistently goes to her place on command, teach her to lie down and stay in that place," Thomas says. The "down" command can be tricky at first, but here's an easy way to teach it: Hold a treat level with her eyes, then draw it downward and along the ground away from her. She will follow the treat with her eyes and automatically lie down. Give her the treat, tell her to stay, then sit down and enjoy your dinner.

At first you'll want to get up a few times to reward her for staying put. Once she understands that food comes to her, she'll be perfectly content to stay in her place and will be less likely to hit you up for food while you're eating.

I'm bored with my diet. Most dogs happily feast on the same food every day, but some get tired of having the same old thing, especially when there are more interesting food aromas to check out.

There's nothing wrong with periodically giving dogs new foods, but to avoid dietary upsets, do it gradually by adding the new food or flavor to the current one in progressively greater proportions over a period of about one week. Try mixing some wet food in with the dry. Or add water to your dog's dry food to make a gravy. Even warming food slightly can stimulate a dog's tastebuds. Warm food releases more smells, and it's the smell of food more than the taste than gets dogs excited.

Climbing on the Furniture

Dogs enjoy getting comfortable, and a soft chair or comforter-topped bed is a much nicer place to catch 40 winks than the hard floor. But

Dogs love getting on furniture and they don't mind sharing it with the humans in the family. This Labrador mix finds the high vantage point makes it easy to see what's going on.

comfort isn't the only reason dogs take over the furniture. From their point of view, the human comfort zones are positions of power—more attractive by far than a bean bag on the floor. Which is why even dogs given the best accommodations will often sneak up on the couch or slip into your bed late at night. What are they trying to tell you?

I want to see what's going on. Nowhere is the realtor's mantra—"location, location, location"—more true than among dogs. They like to know what's happening around them and to be a part of things, even when they're only silent spectators. Unlike their own beds, which are usually tucked out of the way, couches and easy chairs are located in prime positions and offer great vantage points from which to see what's going on. In addition, furniture is relatively high off the ground, and high positions, among dogs, are considered prime status spots.

Once a dog appropriates a piece of furniture, it can be very difficult to persuade her to sleep elsewhere. Apart from using repellents, which often don't work very well, trainers recommend covering dogs' chosen spots with books or other impediments for a few days, while at the same time providing a more comfortable dog bed that's located in prime real estate—right next to the couch, for example, or near the center of the room, where she can see what's going on.

I thought it was okay! People don't always admit it, but trainers have found that furniture-

Canine Bed Testers

Dogs rely on their human friends to manufacture comfy sleeping places for them. But humans are at a distinct disadvantage: How can we tell which beds dogs like and which they don't?

Drs. Foster and Smith, a pet product manufacturing and catalog company based in Rhinelander, Wisconsin, has come up with a remarkably simple solution. They ask the dogs.

"Our employees take dog beds and fabric throws home with them and test them out on their own dogs," reports company spokesperson Candy Besaw. "That way they can see if the dog likes the item—especially the fabric that the bed is made from."

Candy's own dog, a wire-haired fox terrier named Linus, proved to be a legend because of his longevity at the company, bed-testing for most of his 21 years.

Linus and other senior dogs prefer thick foam beds that are easy to get into and out of. "Many older dogs have arthritis, and the foam beds are easy on their aches and pains," says Candy.

Other dogs have different choices. "Very small dogs seem to like oval-shaped cuddler-type beds, which are small and have high, soft sides," explains Candy. "But larger dogs prefer big cushions because they can stretch out on them."

hogging dogs are usually getting some surreptitious encouragement from someone in the family. No matter how often you tell your dog to get off the couch, she's going to keep getting up when someone else is encouraging her on the sly.

Dogs learn best when they get consistent messages from all the people in their lives. As long as everyone in the family takes a united stand—by warning them before they make their ascent onto the furniture, and immediately kicking them off on the occasions they get lucky—dogs will generally decide that it's not worth the bother and will cheerfully accept their own comfortable beds.

Destructive Behavior

Puppies will happily spend hours chewing shoes, wrecking table legs, or shredding jackets. Part of this is due to teething—chewing makes them feel better. And partly it's because chewing is fun, and they haven't yet learned to tell the difference between a rawhide bone and your new loafers. Most puppies go through teething between four and eight months of age.

What's normal behavior in puppies, however, is a sign of problems in older dogs. Here's what it probably means.

What else is there to do? Dogs will sometimes trash their owners' belongings simply because there's nothing better to do, says Kovary. It is especially common in dogs who spend a lot of time alone.

A Buster Cube keeps this vizsla occupied for hours. When he has a lot to do, he's less likely to look for other forms of entertainment— like destroying the house.

They get bored and start looking for excitement. And chewing is a fun diversion.

I'm scared to be alone. Dogs are social animals who don't like being alone. Most dogs learn to cope with it, but some get nearly frantic, and chewing and other forms of destructive behavior are their way of reducing feelings of loneliness and fear. "Your clothes and belongings have your scent on them," Kovary says. "Your dog will feel closer to you and less lonely if she chews on them and inhales some of that scent."

Regardless of what's causing your dog to chew, it's usually not that hard to make her stop, Thomas says. Probably the best solution is to buy a few chew toys—assuming, of course, that the toys are more appealing than your possessions. "The Kong toy is one of the best toys you can buy," Thomas says. "It's made of hard rubber and is virtually indestructible. And it's hollow inside so that it can be stuffed with treats to make it even more attractive."

Another great toy is the Buster Cube. These are hollow toys with hidden compartments you can fill with food. As dogs mouth the toy and push it around, bits of food will occasionally fall out.

The promise of food can keep dogs happily engaged for hours—and when they're playing with their own toys, they're less likely to show an interest in yours.

Dogs need more than toys to burn off excess energy. Regular exercise is essential, Thomas says. Dogs who wear themselves out on walks or by running around are much less likely to get bored and lonely. "A tired dog is a well-behaved dog," Kovary says.

Greeting Disorders

Nearly every dog gets excited when people come to visit, but some go completely overboard. They run around in circles, bark their heads off, or jump as high as they can, leaving dusty little paw prints on skirts and jackets. Even people who love dogs don't enjoy being greeted with so much exuberance, and they don't appreciate the intrusion of inquisitive noses into embarrassing places.

Apart from walks and meal times, most dogs don't have a lot of high points in their days, so it's not surprising that they get worked up when visitors drop by and liven things up. It's easy to train puppies to greet people with decorum, but it's more difficult to teach older dogs to behave more soberly. Not only are they set in their ways but also there may be other reasons for their assertive hellos. Here's what they're probably thinking.

I'm just being myself. Among people, the most socially unacceptable kind of dog greeting is to have a cold nose pushed into a private place. But among dogs, this is simply the way they do things, and they can't figure out why people get so uncomfortable. This is one situation where dogs and people will never see eye to

This golden retriever has been taught to sit when her owner opens the door to visitors. She's rewarded for this good behavior by being allowed to sniff the visitor's hand when she enters the house.

LICKETY SPIT

While a peck on the cheek is a common and acceptable form of greeting between humans, a sloppy, wet lick from a dog can send guests and owners ducking for cover.

"Licking often signals submissive or solicitous behavior," explains Steve Aiken, an animal behaviorist in Wichita, Kansas. "When they lick us, they may be acknowledging that we're their leaders."

When adult dogs greet each other, the more submissive one may greet the other by nudging his muzzle and sometimes licking around his lips, explains Linda Goodloe, a certified animal behaviorist in New York City. "Lip-smacking and lip-licking are considered pacifying behaviors," says Goodloe.

Licking can sometimes be a way of begging for food, too. When wolf puppies greet their mother after she's been hunting, they lick her muzzle to encourage her to regurgitate the food for them. Fortunately, in domesticated dogs licking is more a sign of respect than a request for a meal.

eye without some training, Kovary says. You should never let your dog put her nose in people's crotches, she advises. When your dog makes her move, quickly tell her "off" or "no," and do it every time. "Once your dog has calmed down and is sitting quietly, you can let her satisfy her curiosity by sniffing your guests' hands," she says.

I'm ambivalent about this. Dogs tend to get most excited when they're of two minds about guests arriving, says Kovary. On the one hand, they're happy and eager to greet the person entering the house.

This Brittany spaniel always gets over-excited when visitors come. To keep her under control, her owner puts her on a short leash beforehand and gives her a treat when she behaves.

But they're also wondering how this new person will fit into the group, and they aren't quite sure how to respond. So they display a whole variety of behaviors—jumping up, barking, and so on—as a way of "testing" how this new person is going to react to them.

An easy solution is to distract your dog as soon as people arrive. One way to do this is to make her lie down straight away. By going into training mode, you will focus attention more on you than on the new arrivals. When she does what you tell her, give her a treat, Kovary adds. It won't take her long to learn that acting calmly and following commands gets her something good to eat. Of course, this will make your dog look forward to visitors even more, but she will also know that gracious greetings bring better rewards than rambunctious jumping.

Some dogs get the message right away, but others need more work. Thomas recommends putting dogs on a six-foot leash before people come over. As guests arrive, you can either stand on the leash or take up most of the slack in your hands. "She won't have enough leash to allow her

INTRODUCING YOURSELF

Most of us have learned to greet dogs by putting out our hand with the palm down, giving them a chance to sniff the back. There's nothing wrong with this approach, but some experts believe that it's better to greet dogs with your palm up.

"The palm of your hand emits a positive electric charge, whereas the back of your hand emits a negative electric charge," says Wendy Volhard, a professional trainer in Phoenix, New York. A positive charge attracts dogs and a negative one repels them, she explains.

CALL FOR HELP

No one enjoys finding spots on the carpet or puddles in the kitchen, but occasional "accidents" are a normal part of owning a dog. What isn't normal is when a dog who's always had control is suddenly making messes all the time.

Frequent housesoiling is often the first sign of physical problems, says Christine Wilford, D.V.M., a veterinarian in private practice in Seattle. Dogs with urinary tract infections, for example, may have to urinate several times an hour, and if you aren't there to let them out, they'll do what they have to do. Other conditions that can cause a loss of control include diabetes, bladder stones, or an intestinal problem. A few accidents are unlikely to be signs of serious problems, but you should call your vet if your dog isn't back to normal within a few days.

in. "Try placing a bag of treats outside your front door and put a sign on it that says, 'These treats are for our dog—but only if she is sitting when you come in,'" Thomas suggests. Most people will get a kick out of joining in, and your dog will learn more quickly as more and more people participate.

Housesoiling

Dogs are usually house-trained by the time they are a few months old, and once they know the rules, they'll do everything they can to reach their favorite spots in time. But even dogs with perfect track records will occasionally go where they shouldn't. These aren't really "accidents" because grown dogs know that they're supposed to go outside. Dogs who go in the house are invariably trying to tell you something.

I couldn't wait. Even dogs with fastidious manners and good training have certain limits. Unless you have a doggy door, they can't let themselves out when nature calls. When you're

feet to rise more than three inches off the floor," Thomas says. "There's no risk of her jumping around or sniffing your guests."

Greeting problems can be awkward because you can't deal with them in private—you have to get used to training your dog at a time you'd rather be concentrating on your guests. But the slight social awkwardness will pay off fairly quickly, especially if you ask your guests to join

Adult dogs rarely make messes in the house unless there's something wrong. But for puppies, waiting to go outside may be more than they can handle.

gone all day or working late, it's simply not realistic to expect them to wait, says Mike Richards, D.V.M., a veterinarian in private practice in Cobbs Creek, Virginia.

For most dogs, Richards says, 12 hours is about the limit. When you're going to be gone longer than that, the only solution is to make other arrangements—having a neighbor let your dog out, for example, or hiring a pet sitter to drop by once a day.

I'm in charge, and here's the proof. Among dogs, urinating represents more than a comfort stop. It's also their way of marking territory and establishing their status in the family. That's why people who get a second pet are often subjected to an outbreak of housesoiling as one of the dogs—usually the older resident—begins urinating in strategic spots.

It may take a few weeks or longer for both dogs to feel comfortable with the new arrangement, says Sandy Myers, a trainer and director of Narnia Pet Training in Naperville, Illinois. You can speed things up by reinforcing the natural pecking order. Give special preference to the "top dog"—which is usually, but not always, the one who's been there the longest. Try feeding this dog first, she advises. Let her go out the door first, and give her the most attention. Once your dog feels that her status in the family is secure, she'll be much less inclined to defend it on her own, Myers explains.

I worship the ground you walk on. When a dog rolls on her back the minute you come home and then urinates on the floor, she's not forgetting her housetraining and she's not being rude. In fact,

she's doing the opposite. "Such a dog is being superpolite," explains Kovary. "She's saying, 'I know that you are my leader and I will do anything you ask.'" Called submissive urination, this is very common among dogs, Kovary explains. But it's not a good sign in the family because it means a dog is overly anxious or intimidated. About all you can do is try to make sure that your dog is more secure. There are a lot of ways to do this. For example, don't stand over her and look down when you first get home—kneel down and greet her from a more "equal" level, Thomas suggests. It's also a good idea to avoid direct eye contact for a while because some dogs find it intimidating.

Extreme submissive behavior isn't easy to fix because it can be an intrinsic part of a dog's personality. If simple changes don't help, you may want to call your vet or a trainer for help.

This Labrador retriever gets plenty of praise from her owner when she responds quickly to his commands. This reinforces her obedient behavior.

Dogs easily get distracted by all the exciting things around them, and this makes it hard for them to pay attention.

Ignoring Commands

We all tune each other out sometimes, and dogs are no different. But sometimes they deliberately ignore their owners' requests. Here are some of the reasons why.

I don't understand. Giving a command the wrong way is a recipe for confusion. "Unless you're clear, brief, and consistent, your dog may not understand what you want of her," says Greg Strong, a trainer in Easton, Maryland.

"Some people tell a dog to sit, but then they put a kind of question mark at the end—like they're asking her to sit instead of telling her to. If you do that, your dog may not obey the command," says Strong.

Use brief, one- or two-word commands, he advises. "Be careful to use the same word or words every time, and be sure to use a distinctive, upbeat tone of voice."

What's in it for me? Dogs know they're supposed to obey, but sometimes there's no way they'll drop a bone or run back to their owners unless something good is going to come out of it. As far as they're concerned, the merits of ignoring their owners may outweigh the benefits of complying.

Owners who don't praise their dogs enough will soon find that their dogs "forget" to obey, says Kovary. Just like people, dogs need an incentive to continue doing their jobs. For most dogs, these jobs are to do what their owners tell them, and the reward should be enthusiastic, immediate praise—whether that praise comes in the form of a treat, a pat, or an exuberant "Good dog!" explains Kovary.

I'm afraid of what you'll do if I do what you tell me. If every command were followed by something exciting and fun, there would be a lot more attentive dogs. But in the real world, commands such as "come" or "down" can often indicate that something unpleasant, like a bath, is about to occur. Dogs have long memories, and the ability to put two and two together. Once a dog makes the connection between "come" and "bath," she will be likely to ignore you in the future.

It's a good idea to follow any command with an action that pleases your dog, Kovary says. This is important if you want her to come when you call her. In fact, it's a good idea to never call a dog to you when you know you're going to do something she'll dislike, like giving her a bath or crating her. In these cases, it's better to go to her rather than expect her to come to you.

Hey, things look interesting over there. Some dogs tune out their owners occasionally because there's too much else going on. Distractions, and maybe a bit of daydreaming, can result in some commands going unheeded.

I can't hear you. Dogs who have suddenly quit responding to commands or only respond to them occasionally may be going a little bit deaf. To see if your dog is hard of hearing, stand a few feet behind her and clap your hands. If she doesn't react, you'll need to get her to a vet.

I don't have to listen to you. Dogs are very status-conscious. They want to know who is the leader and who isn't. If they don't know, they'll assume that they are and will pay less and less attention to their owners.

You cannot have an effective relationship with your dog unless you are willing to take on the role of leader. That involves giving commands and following through on them. Make sure that you're consistent in the messages you give your dog. Don't let her be bratty or aggressive. And when she wants something, make sure she earns it first by doing something you've told her to do.

Dogs are a lot like children in that it doesn't take them long to discover your weaknesses. Many people, for example, tell their dogs "come," but they don't really expect them to come right away, and their dogs certainly don't feel like rushing over. So they tell them "come" again, and a third time, and their dogs still don't come—because their owners have inadvertently taught them that it's okay to ignore them. The only way to prevent this is to only give commands that you're able and willing to enforce, Thomas says.

Pulling on the Leash

We've all seen people flash past whose dogs were clearly taking them for a walk rather than the other way around. Dogs that pull constantly on the leash can turn an enjoyable stroll into a shoulder-wrenching marathon. As with other forms of misbehavior, bad leash manners are your dog's way of saying something. It's important to discover why your dog is pulling on the leash, so that you can find the right solution.

This schnauzer clearly feels that it's his duty to take his owner for a walk. One of the easiest ways to reverse the situation is to suddenly turn around and walk the other way. This will force the dog to follow rather than lead.

This German shepherd mix is given time to check things out when she goes on walks with her owner. Because she has time to investigate, she's less likely to pull ahead.

I'm in charge here. Dogs who pull on the leash have somehow gotten they idea that they, not you, are in control. This usually occurs in families where the people haven't firmly established that they—not their dog—are the ones calling the shots.

Gotta check this out. From a dog's point of view, anything new is intriguing, and anything intriguing is worth investigating. Sights and sounds that mean nothing to people serve as magnets to dogs.

Gotta get that squirrel. Some dogs strain at the leash whenever they see a smaller animal nearby. Dogs used to be predators, and their instincts tell them to respond to movements by going forward themselves.

Let's get where we're going as fast as we can. Enthusiasm isn't just a human emotion. When dogs know they're on the way to some-

thing exciting, they may pull on the leash in an attempt to get there sooner.

I'm so excited. Sometimes when a dog isn't taken out for a walk on a regular basis, she'll be so excited every time she does go for a walk that she'll always pull ahead. The best way to avoid this is to take your dog for a walk every day, even if you don't need to walk her for bathroom breaks.

When this isn't practical, arrange for a friend, neighbor, or professional dog walker to take your dog for a walk. This way your dog won't be so excited and will be less inclined to pull ahead.

Regardless of why dogs pull on the leash, the underlying message is the same: They feel that whatever is happening around them or what they're feeling at the moment is more important than worrying about you.

To curtail their penchant for pulling, you have to distract them from whatever it is that's grabbing their attention and get them to focus on you and you alone, says Shirley Sullivan, president of PR Dog, a training and dog day care center in Falls Church, Virginia.

There's an easy way to do this, says Sullivan. "If your dog lunges ahead of you while you're walking, immediately turn around and walk in the opposite direction. This will surprise your dog—and dogs generally don't like such surprises."

After a few weeks of subjecting your dog to these unexpected turns of events, she will begin watching you so she won't be surprised the next time. And the more she watches and keeps pace with you, the more pleasant your walks are going to be.

PART FIVE

PUTTING IT TO WORK

Knowing how dogs communicate—with other dogs as
well as people—provides a tremendous edge in understanding
what they're trying to say. You can use their language, which includes
not only sounds, but also touch and smells, to form a deeper
bond and help them behave a little better.

CHAPTER TWENTY

TEACHING YOUR DOG

Dogs love to learn new things, so teaching your dog
not only makes him easier to live with, it also keeps
him busy and makes him feel useful.

Dogs can do some truly amazing things. They find people who are lost, guide those who are blind, and act as the ears of people who are deaf. They can detect drugs and explosives. They've even been used to help prevent plane crashes.

Unfortunately, some dogs have abilities that aren't so useful. Like the bearded collie who thinks it's great fun to bark at delivery trucks. Or the German shepherd who builds towers in the backyard, using cans of cat food he's filched from the kitchen cupboard. Or the springer spaniel who's learned to open the refrigerator and eat all the food inside.

Both groups of dogs are intelligent and talented, capable of carrying out complex tasks. The difference is that the first group of dogs has been taught by people to do things that people find useful. Those in the second group, however, lacking human guidance, have taught themselves to do things *they* think are useful. Their owners, of course, may have a somewhat different opinion about what is and isn't helpful.

Dogs need to be busy, and this golden retriever mix gets a lot of satisfaction from fetching the newspaper every morning.

Why Dogs Need to be Taught

When you see your dog snoozing away the better part of the day, it's hard to believe that dogs like to be busy. But inside every dog is an instinctive need to do a good day's work. "Dogs were never bred to just be our pals," says Deborah Loven Gray, of Washington, D.C.,

author of *Your Dog's Life.* On the contrary, dogs have been bred for thousands of years to perform specific tasks, such as hunting, guarding, herding, or retrieving. "And if he's a mixed breed, a dog can combine more than one of these purposes," says Robin Kovary, director of the American Dog Trainers Network in New York City.

Whatever their breed, dogs have a genetic need to be busy all day, every day. When they're not busy doing something—anything—they easily become bored. When that happens they look for whatever kind of entertainment they can find, and their idea of fun—chewing on furniture, digging up the yard, or barking out the window all day—is unlikely to be the same as yours.

Even though most dogs will never be trained for police work or to do search and rescue, basic training gives them a purpose. Doing something as simple as teaching your dog to sit or walk on a leash will give him a sense of direction. Rather than being bored and frustrated, he'll be excited and fulfilled because he has a job to do, and he'll do his best to please you.

Dogs also need training because they see the world in ways humans can hardly understand. What comes naturally to them is totally out of

The $58,000 Dog

Of all the extraordinary things that dogs can do, perhaps none is as amazing as preventing airplane crashes. Yet that's precisely what Jackie, a five-year-old Border collie, does every day.

Jackie lives and works at the Willow Grove Naval Air Station Joint Reserve Base near Philadelphia, Pennsylvania. Before she arrived, the base was struggling with a problem common to many airports: close encounters between aircraft and birds. At Willow Grove, the bothersome birds were Canada geese. Repeated collisions between planes and geese had caused $58,000 in damage to the expensive military aircraft over a five-year period. Despite some very creative attempts to solve the problem, including such things as setting off fireworks, shooting water cannons at the geese, and playing tapes of birds in distress, the Willow Grove geese proved difficult to evict—until Jackie was recruited.

Border collies were originally bred to herd sheep, but Jackie's mission is to herd geese away from the base's runways. Every time someone in the base control tower spots geese in the neighborhood, an air traffic controller radios the firehouse where Jackie lives. Then the real action begins.

Jackie is driven to where the geese are and set loose. "Jackie tries to corral the geese, the way she would with sheep," says Dave Bumm, one of Jackie's handlers. But the geese, unlike sheep, fly away. This is perfect for protecting the planes, but always leaves Jackie a bit unsatisfied. So to keep her happy, Bumm and the other handlers give her plenty of praise and play ball with her back at the firehouse.

Jackie's been on the job for over a year, and in that time there have been no collisions on her watch, compared with three bird strikes in the 18 months before she arrived.

place among the humans in their lives. Among dogs, for example, it's accepted, even expected, for one dog to defend his food by snarling at or biting an interloper, says Pat Miller, a trainer in

Salinas, California. Among humans, however, the same behavior won't be tolerated. Training is the only way to help dogs understand what's expected of them and to give them clear guidelines for what they should and shouldn't do.

Giving Clear Signals

Most dogs enjoy learning new things, so there's no reason to settle for dry-as-dust backyard drill sessions once or twice a day. Dogs, like people, learn quickly and have the most fun when they bring all their senses into play.

By using a combination of words, sounds, hand signals, touch, and other forms of communication, you can teach your dog all the basics, and more, in a relatively short time. After that you can take advantage of his new-found skills to find other ways in which the two of you can communicate more clearly and so build a better relationship.

Words. Dogs may not be gifted linguists, but they can still learn a variety of words. Not surprisingly, the words they remember best are those that they associate with positive, pleasurable things. That's why trainers recommend rewarding dogs lavishly, with praise or tidbits to eat, when they first start responding to spoken commands. You don't have to give them treats every time, but when your dog's first starting out, linking words and treats will help him learn more quickly.

Sounds. Dogs respond to more than just words. They have much better hearing than humans do, and they also depend on their hearing more than we do. This means that sounds we tend to ignore—like the tone of someone's voice

A gentle touch on this vizsla's rump, combined with a verbal command, is his signal to stand still.

or a throat clearing—come through loud and clear for them. You can use these and other sounds, like clapping your hands, to reinforce spoken commands or merely to let your dog know he's done something right.

Hands. Dogs are a lot more responsive to body language than they are to words, which means that hand signals are a very effective way to convey messages. These silent, visual signals are helpful for adding emphasis or extra meaning when you're teaching your dog to understand certain words. In fact, you can train your dog to respond entirely to hand signals. This is particularly helpful for communicating across long distances, or if your dog becomes deaf as he gets older.

Touch. Dogs are extremely responsive to touch—whether they're doing the touching or being touched. You can use touch simply to keep your dog calm and relaxed, which will help him enjoy learning even more. Getting him used to some touches that he may not normally like will make him a lot easier for the vet or groomer to deal with. Touch will also help reinforce verbal commands, such as stand. Or you can use touch to teach your dog the sorts of touches that you do and don't like.

Touch works both ways, of course, and part of training is learning your dog's touch vocabulary. Every dog uses touch differently, but there are a few general rules. A muzzle that nuzzles into your hand, for example, can be a request for affection or an invitation to play. A dog that brushes against you may be asking for a loving touch—or he may be saying "Step aside, I have the right of way."

Scent. Dogs have a phenomenally sharp sense of smell, and smell is their primary means of communication, at least when they're with other dogs. That's why it makes sense for us to use scent as a way of communicating with them. Using scents that dogs don't like is a good way to tell them to leave certain things—like the furniture or the trash can—alone. Unpleasant scents can also tell them to stop barking. And we can use scents that dogs do like to help them deal with new situations, to introduce new people, and to provide comfort when we can't be with them.

A Nose for Diagnosis

Many retirees use the end of one career to pursue a second line of work. That's how George, a schnauzer who started out as a bomb-sniffing dog in Tallahassee, Florida, found himself using his sniffing skills to detect a different kind of danger.

George's second career began when a dermatologist in Tallahassee, Florida, Armand Cognetta, read a medical news report about a British woman whose dog persistently sniffed a mole on her skin, which later turned out to be cancer. Dr. Cognetta found himself wondering if dogs really could smell cancer, and if they could, whether they could be trained to detect it. So he teamed up with a trainer named Duane Pickel to see if Pickel's prize-winning dog, George, could be as successful at sniffing out skin cancer as he'd been at sniffing out bombs for the Tallahassee Police Department.

"Dogs need to have a purpose in life, and George loves to go to work and do new things," says Pickel. To train George, Pickel took him through a series of increasingly difficult tests, from retrieving melanoma samples stored in test tubes to detecting a cancer sample that had been placed under one of many band-aids on a volunteer's body. Finally, he put George to the true test by allowing him to sniff real cancer patients. On Pickel's command "show me," George would place a paw on the spot that he'd sniffed out. In most cases George was able to identify suspicious spots that doctors had believed to be cancerous, but hadn't yet been tested by biopsies.

COMMANDS EVERY DOG SHOULD KNOW

Dogs have an amazing capacity to learn commands. Highly trained show, working, and service dogs often know dozens of commands, including words, sounds, and signals. Most pet dogs are taught with vocal commands, but hand signals or nonvocal sounds are also effective. Whatever method you choose, most dogs only need to know 11 simple commands to get along happily with you and the rest of the world.

Wait. Some dogs have a way of pushing their way to the front of the line when they want to go through doors or down narrow hallways. Telling them "wait" lets them know they're not supposed to go until you tell them to.

Sit. This is one of the easiest commands to teach, and also one of the most useful. Dogs who know how to sit are less likely to be jumping on you or anyone else, fighting with other dogs, or dragging you across the street at a red light.

This German shepherd–Labrador cross has been trained to sit and stay, so his owner can trust him to wait patiently until she comes out of the shop.

A dog who knows how to heel correctly, like this shiba inu, will always walk nicely at his owner's side, rather than pulling her down the street.

Down. Like "sit," the "down" command is an essential part of doggy etiquette. It's also more comfortable than a sitting position when your dog is going to be hanging out for more than a minute or two.

Stay. Often paired with "sit" or "down," the "stay" command tells dogs to cool their jets for a while. It's not the easiest command for many dogs to learn because they'd rather be moving around than staying still.

Heel. Unless you live in the country and your dog never sees a busy road or walks on a leash, he has to understand this command. "Heel," or a variation such as "let's go," simply means that your dog will walk by your left side without lagging behind or lunging ahead. It's especially important for large dogs to understand "heel" because otherwise their relentless tugging on the leash will make going for walks seem too much like work.

Come. This is a crucial command in your dog's repertoire. Dogs who understand "come" will turn on a dime and head back to you as soon as you say it. It's a command you can use to keep them from running into the street or knocking into people in the park. It will tell them to come back when they'd just as soon keep running.

Stand. This command tells your dog to quit fidgeting and be still. It's useful for when you're grooming him, bathing him, checking him over, or drying him off on a wet day.

Off. Rare is the dog that doesn't prefer an expensive sofa or a goose-down comforter to his own bed. Dogs that understand "off" won't necessarily stay off the furniture, but at least they'll get off quickly when they know the command. "Off" also tells them not to jump up on you or other people.

Okay. Dogs love this command. "Okay" means they've done a good job. It means you're done giving orders and they can just act silly for a while. It may even mean it's time for dinner.

Out. Dogs know a good thing when they see it (and taste it), and getting them to relinquish such delicacies as a bone from the trash or your leather loafers can be a challenge when they haven't properly learned "out." This command means they should drop whatever it is that's in their mouth. They won't necessarily like it, but they'll do it as long as you start teaching them "out" when they're young.

Bed. This command, or a variation such as "crate," tells your dog that it's time to head for his sleeping place. It's useful not only at bedtime, but also when you want him to quiet down for a while.

This Australian kelpie mix knows that when his owner says "off," it's time to surrender his place on the sofa.

CHAPTER TWENTY-ONE

CHOOSING THE RIGHT NAME

What you call your dog is a very personal choice. You'll have to live
with the name for 10 or 15 years, so it pays to choose one you both like and
that your dog will find easy to learn and a pleasure to respond to.

When President Clinton welcomed his new chocolate Labrador into the White House in late 1997, thousands of Americans offered him ideas on what to name his dog. The president found himself sifting through proposals ranging from "Arkin-paws" to "Shoes" before he made his choice.

Like countless other dog owners, the president found that there's much more to naming a new dog than polling people for ideas. A range of factors, from personal associations to your dog's own response, should be considered when deciding on a name.

Ultimately, that's just what President Clinton did. The name he eventually chose for his new dog—Buddy—not only reflected his special memories of his late and much-loved Uncle Buddy, but it was also the name he felt his dog responded best to.

Most experts think the president was on the right track. In choosing a name for his dog, President Clinton made a lot of the right moves.

When to Use Human Names

Many people like to give human names to their dogs. President Clinton is just one case in point; a look at dog license registrations in any city,

*Each of these chocolate Labrador puppies deserves a
name that reflects his individuality and uniqueness.*

town, or county provides countless others. Human names bestowed on dogs include Max, Maggie, Molly, Pepper, Brandy, Ginger, Sam, and Jake.

Trainers are divided on whether dogs should be given human names. The Monks of New Skete, who breed and train dogs at their monastery in Cambridge, New York, and are the authors of *How to Be Your Dog's Best Friend*, don't favor human names for dogs. The monks believe that giving dogs human names makes owners think of their dogs as people rather than animals, says Father Marc of New Skete.

But most trainers feel it doesn't really matter what you name your dog as long as the two of you are comfortable with it. "Your relationship with your dog is more important than his name," says Robin Kovary, director of the American Dog Trainers Network in New York City.

But whatever name you choose—human or not—the most important thing is to make sure it's appropriate to your dog's breed, gender, and size. By doing so, you recognize your dog's uniqueness and his distinctive personality, says Father Marc.

How to Make the Right Choice

Many people look for names that reflect their own expectations rather than their dog's personality, says Myrna Milani, D.V.M., a veterinarian and animal behaviorist in Claremont, New Hampshire, and author of *The Weekend Dog* and *Dog-Smart*. That can lead to poor name choices, such as a joke name or one that will cause people to react inappropriately to the dog, either with laughter or fear.

For example, Rambo is a poor choice for a pit bull terrier because it plays up the breed's aggressive image, and so may make another person fear the dog, no matter how friendly he

NAMES YOU SHOULD NEVER CHOOSE FOR YOUR DOG

Dogs are remarkably adaptable, so it's pretty hard to choose a name that will warp them for life. But there are some names, trainers say, that simply don't work—those that make fun of the dog, that could be confused with other words or commands, or that contain a sound dogs simply don't like. For example:

Moe. Sounds too much like "no!"

Helen. A dog may confuse it with "hello."

Sassy. Dogs dislike "s" sounds, probably because they resemble a snake's hiss.

Killer. For large dogs with tough reputations, a macho name will make them seem more frightening to other people. For small dogs like toy poodles or Chihuahuas, it will just sound silly.

Tiny. Every dog, whether he's big as a horse or small enough to fit in a teacup, thinks of himself as a big dog. Why hurt his feelings?

really is. And Tiny is a bad choice for a large breed such as a Great Dane because it makes fun of the dog's size.

It's also important to make your dog's name easy for him to learn. Father Marc suggests choosing a two-syllable name that begins with a strong consonant, such as Kirka or Jilly. Your pup or dog will learn this type of name more quickly. That's because a long name, with three or more syllables, may be too complicated for a dog to learn easily, while a one-syllable name may sound too similar to parts of words that are used in everyday speech. This can cause confusion and make the name difficult for a dog to learn. A two-syllable name, however, will be easier for him to distinguish from all the other words he hears.

And avoid using names that sound too much like commands, advises Kovary. A good example is "Juno," which a dog could easily confuse with the word "no."

There are many names to choose from, from the commonplace to the exotic. Here are a few other things to consider before you decide.

Watch your dog for ideas. It's always good to look to your dog himself for ideas on a name, says Dr. Milani. If he's constantly sniffing out his environment, a name like Sherlock might be a good choice for your canine detective. For a dog who likes to run, Dasher could be the perfect moniker.

There's one exception to this principle, though. If your dog is a Rottweiler, Doberman, pit bull, or other breed with an aggressive reputation, you should avoid giving him an equally aggressive name. "The name could end up being a self-fulfilling prophecy," Kovary says. For example, a Rottweiler named Terminator who runs up to greet people may get a fearful reaction when they hear his name. When he senses their fear, his own response may be

more negative than it would be if he had a less aggressive-sounding name.

Choose a name that feels good to your dog. It's also important to consider a dog's preferences when deciding on his name. For example, most dogs dislike hearing an "s" sound, because it's like an unpleasant hiss, says Dr. Milani. She recommends trying out a few different names and sounds on your dog to find out which ones he responds best to.

Choose a name that feels good to you. It's important to give your dog a name that you like a lot. Dogs pay attention to your body language and the tone of your voice. If your dog can tell you feel good when you say his name, he'll be more likely to respond happily when he hears it.

Whether your dog is a dachshund or a Great Dane, his name should be appropriate to his breed and size. Giving him a name that pokes fun at his physical features might upset him by causing people to laugh at him.

Make it dignified. Naming a dog isn't a time to get funny or cute. "To use excessively sweet or joke names demeans both the dog and the relationship," says Father Marc. Dubbing your dachshund Frank or Weiner may seem funny at first, but the laughter that will follow whenever you call him could lead to problems. A dog who feels he's being laughed at may act aloof or uncertain around the person who's laughing. To him, the laughter appears mystifying or even hostile.

Overly cute or sentimental names can also cause problems. A German shepherd named Cuddles might pull his ears back or look away when he hears his name because he dislikes the laughter that it sometimes prompts.

Using Your Dog's Name for the Best Effect

After you've christened your pooch, you need to make sure you use his name effectively and appropriately. A frequent mistake people make is to use their dog's name not only to call him, but also in ordinary conversation with friends and family. When that happens too often, your dog may tune you out and stop responding when you call his name, says Dr. Milani. The solution is to find more than one way to refer to your pet, especially if he's within earshot. For example, if you're talking about your dog while he's lying at your feet, it's better to refer to him as "my guy" or "my pal" instead of by name.

It's also important to make sure you don't use your dog's name when correcting him.

This miniature schnauzer responds happily to his name because it's only used for pleasant things, like praise or to go for a walk, never for correcting him.

That's because your dog will respond more happily and promptly to his name if it always means that something wonderful is about to happen, like a walk or something to eat.

When you catch your dog doing something he shouldn't, it's best to use a simple, concise command such as "off!" or "leave it!" to correct him, rather than using his name in a stern tone as a kind of reprimand.

The most important thing is to use your dog's name in ways that make your high regard for him clear to him and to others. "A dog is sharply aware of changes in your voice tonality, facial expression, and body language," says Father Marc. "The more intelligent a dog is, the more sensitive he'll be to his owner's attitudes."

CHAPTER TWENTY-TWO

CHOOSING THE RIGHT COMMANDS

A well-behaved dog is a pleasure to have around. But before
you can train your dog to be a model canine citizen, you need to know
which commands are the right ones to use—and why.

Few people enjoy getting bossed around or being told to do something right away. We prefer a system where everyone is equal and every opinion carries the same weight.

If we lived in a world ruled by dogs, however, we'd have a very different perspective. Dogs aren't concerned with being autonomous. In fact, that's the last thing they want. What they care most about is being part of a family, whether that family consists of other dogs or the people in their lives. Taking orders, from a dog's point of view, is part and parcel of belonging; it makes them feel secure because it lets them know exactly where they stand.

This four-month-old Labrador–Scottish terrier cross is learning good manners while she's young—the best time for learning.

That's why you're doing your dog a favor when you teach her to obey commands. You may feel you're cramping her style at times, but she really wants you to tell her what to do. Giving orders—whether they're a simple "sit" or "down" command or a demand to get off the couch—makes it possible for her to know exactly what's expected, and she'll find a lot of reassurance in that.

Paradoxically, dogs that are comfortable obeying commands generally have more freedom than those without any training at all, says Pat Miller, a trainer in Salinas, California. A dog who comes reliably when you call will be able to enjoy more off-leash playtime than her less obedient friends. When she doesn't jump on people, she's more likely to be invited to join the crowd when you have visitors over. And when she's well behaved, she'll be allowed to spend more of her time with you, rather than being exiled to the backyard.

Every dog needs to know a few basic commands. But there's more to giving orders than saying "come" or "down." Some commands are a lot more effective than others. In order to choose the best commands, you have to think like a dog for a moment, because your dog's idea of a good command is going to be a little different from yours.

Clear Commands

Most dogs have good intentions. They want to please their owners and are unhappy when they don't. So why are there so many disobedient dogs? Most of the time it's because their owners haven't learned to communicate very well. The dogs want to obey; they just can't figure out what they're supposed to do. Here are a few ways to customize your commands in ways your dog will understand.

Get her attention. One reason dogs sometimes misbehave and ignore commands is that they don't realize they're being talked to. When you're playing in the park, your dog will be having such a good time running and sniffing that a shouted "come" may not enter her consciousness—which is why trainers advise coupling a command with a word that's guaranteed to get your dog's attention. A sure

A dog who can be trusted always to come when she's called, like this vizsla, will be able to have much more freedom than a dog who's not so reliable.

attention-getter is to use your dog's name, as in "Maggie! Come!"

Keep it short. Dogs aren't fluent in people-speak. They don't understand involved explanations or multi-sentence pleas because they can't pick out the one relevant word in a long stream of sound. That's why a command like "Maggie, will you please come here for once?" is likely to get you nothing more than a blank stare. What dogs do understand are short, quick commands, like "come" or "sit."

Make it firm. Our instincts are always to be polite, even when giving a command. But this doesn't work with dogs because what should sound like a command—"Maggie, sit!"—often sounds more like a question. In your dog's mind, you're asking, not telling, her to do something, and she won't see any reason to respond because in her mind she's not being told to.

Making commands short and terse is the best way to let your dog know that you want something, and you want it now. Dogs don't

This toy poodle understands he's done something wrong because his owner is using a firm tone of voice to correct him.

resent this tone of voice. On the contrary, they're always grateful when we make our expectations clear.

Be positive. Dogs are the Norman Vincent Peales of the animal kingdom—they thrive on positive thinking. More importantly, it's easier for them to understand positive commands—telling them what you want them to do—than negative ones, in which you simply say "no!" Suppose, for example, your dog is barking at the mailman. Yelling "no!" will get her attention, but she may not be sure what the "no" refers to. A better approach when she's barking is to say "come!" and reward her when she does. The positive command is as effective—and probably more so—than the negative one because it gives your dog a clearer sense of what you want her to do.

Use the right tone of voice. Dogs are extremely sensitive to even the smallest sounds or variations in sound. This means that the tone of your voice can make all the difference between whether a command is right or wrong.

In most situations, a firm, matter-of-fact tone is best because it sounds authoritative without being harsh or stern. However, sometimes dogs may be reluctant to obey. For instance, when they're tearing around the park with other dogs, they may not want to come to you. You need to persuade them that coming to you is as much fun as frolicking with their friends—so use a high-pitched, enthusiastic tone of voice that makes them really want to leave their friends for you.

There's one sure-fire method for recalling lagging pooches, says Shirley Sullivan, president of PR Dog, a training and dog day care center in Falls Church, Virginia. The formula is to say your dog's name, then tell her, "come here!" The word "here" should be said in a high-pitched, even falsetto tone of voice. Dogs called in this way respond eagerly. They hurry to their owners—and their tails are wagging.

Be consistent. Even though dogs can recognize the sounds of certain words, they don't necessarily understand their meaning. Using the same commands all the time is the only way to avoid confusion. When you tell your dog "off the chair" today and "get down" tomorrow, she won't have the slightest idea what you're trying to say.

No matter what commands you use—and ultimately the words themselves don't matter all that much—using them consistently will make them much more effective.

CHAPTER TWENTY-THREE

TALKING WITH HAND SIGNALS

Dogs take many of their cues from watching people and
responding to their body language. That's why hand signals
are a very effective way to communicate.

Three-year-old Cory, a Shetland sheepdog from Vienna, Virginia, loved it when the people in his family used the telephone. As soon as they got on the horn, Cory would bark, yodel, whine, and generally add his two cents' worth to the conversation.

Unfortunately for Cory, his owners didn't appreciate his ear-splitting contributions. So they figured out how to stop his interruptions—without saying a word to him. Their secret: Hand signals.

These days, when Cory comes running at the sound of the telephone, whoever answers it responds with a hand signal that tells him to sit, a signal Cory instantly responds to. If he opens his mouth to start barking, a finger to the person's lips quiets him immediately.

Cory's family has discovered one use for hand signals. However, there are plenty of other reasons why it's a good idea to use your hands to communicate with your dog.

The Benefits of Hand Signals

It's often easier to teach a dog to respond to hand signals than to verbal commands. "Dogs are much more tuned in to body language than to verbal communication," explains Pat Miller,

a trainer in Salinas, California. "It's actually more challenging to teach a dog a word than body language when training him."

For example, it doesn't take Miller much time to use a treat and a hand signal to teach a dog to lie down. "But even though you've been

Hand signals are useful in noisy situations, such as when this Staffordshire bull terrier and her owner are pausing at a busy city street.

145

using the word 'down' to teach the behavior, when you try using the word without the hand, your dog may not lie down. It takes a concerted effort to make a dog understand that the word alone is his cue to lie down," she says.

There are other situations in which a dog who responds to hand signals has a distinct advantage over one trained solely with verbal commands. For example:

• **When there's too much noise.** You can use hand signals to communicate with your dog in situations where it's not easy for him to hear you. For example, when your dog is within sight, but too far away for you to call him, a large, sweeping hand signal can tell him that it's time to head back to you.

Similarly, when you're on a noisy city street or on a beach with a booming surf, your dog's ability to understand your silent signals can help the two of you communicate. And when you want to communicate with your dog without making any noise—near someone who's asleep, for example—hand signals are just the ticket.

For dogs who are born deaf, like this blue merle Shetland sheepdog, hand signals can completely replace verbal commands.

• **When your dog is deaf.** Many dogs lose their hearing as they get older, says Shirley Sullivan, president of PR Dog, a training and dog day care center in Falls Church, Virginia. "By teaching your dog hand signals when he's young, he'll be accustomed to responding to hand signals if he goes deaf later in life. You won't have to start training him all over again."

Stan Chappell of Vienna, Virginia, has firsthand knowledge of how hand signals can help an aging dog. His poodle mix, Molly, lost her hearing when she was 14 years old. Because Chappell's wife had trained Molly with both voice and hand signals, Molly continued to obey commands and even learned new ones, despite her advanced age.

"I think Molly's ability to understand hand signals gave her more confidence," Chappell

BREED SPECIFIC

Some breeds are prone to being born deaf. The two genes that produce white or blue merle coloring in some dogs, such as collies, Australian shepherds, and bull terriers, are linked to a higher rate of deafness. Dalmatians have both these genes and also the highest rate of deafness: 30 percent are totally deaf.

says. "And because we could still communicate with her, I think the hand signals actually helped prolong her life."

When Hands Give the Wrong Message

Although there aren't any human hand signals or motions that are likely to rile a dog, like a canine equivalent of a rude gesture, some things people do with their hands can trigger negative reactions, especially from dogs who are shy, aggressive, or nervous.

For example, approaching a strange dog and reaching down to pet the top of his head may cause him to shy away or snap. In human terms, it's like having a stranger grab the back of your

This Rottweiler is more likely to accept a new person if she lets him sniff her outstretched arm and hand before she tries to pet him.

neck. Just as a person would find that upsetting and invasive, so does a dog.

Miller suggests letting a dog sniff your outstretched arm and hand before trying to pet him. "It's just proper canine etiquette," she explains. "When strange dogs greet each other, they sniff first before they romp and play. The socially inept dog who tries to run up and pounce playfully on another dog before a proper greeting often gets roundly trounced. It's like meeting a total stranger and hugging him instead of shaking hands."

In fact, any sudden moves with your hands or other parts of your body can startle or scare a dog, Miller says, even when they're not directed at him. "Dogs interpret everything around them in relation to themselves. Any motion that you make in the vicinity of a dog has meaning to that dog, such as slapping your buddy on the back or hugging your girlfriend. A dog may misinterpret such an action as a threat to his owner, and so think that he needs to protect her."

Training with Hand Signals

You can reinforce training with hand signals, especially if you're using treats or rewards to train your dog, says Miller. With a combination of hand signals and treats, you can coax the behavior you want from your dog, and then reward him for it. "And the more often a dog is rewarded for a particular behavior, the sooner he'll choose to offer that behavior," Miller says.

Hand signals also reinforce verbal commands—and when a dog learns to link a hand signal with a particular action, he'll soon respond to the hand signal alone.

COMMON HAND SIGNALS AND HOW TO TEACH THEM

Your dog doesn't need to be fluent in sign language to learn how to respond to common hand signals. Most dogs can learn basic signals in a matter of minutes.

Teach Your Dog to Stay

1 While your dog's sitting or lying down, show him the flat of your palm, with your fingertips pointed up. Move back one step, return immediately, praise your dog, and give a reward.

2 Repeat, but move two steps back this time. Slowly increase your distance away from your dog, and the length of time he must stay. Slowly increase the distractions in his environment, too, such as background noise and people moving around.

Teach Your Dog to Lie Down

1 Put your dog in a sitting position. Hold a treat in front of his face. Move your hand down to the ground and back toward you a few inches. The path your hand follows should be an L–shape.

2 As your dog follows your hand with his eyes, he will lie down. When he does, reward him with the treat and lots of praise.

Teach Your Dog to Sit

1 Find a reward for your dog, such as a small treat. After getting his attention and showing him the reward in your hand, move your hand up and over his head.

2 As he follows your hand with his eyes, his rear will drift toward the ground and he will automatically sit. When he has completed the sit, praise him lavishly and give him the reward.

Teach Your Dog to Come

1 Start by facing your dog, who should be a few feet away. Have your hands at your sides and a treat in your hand. Say your dog's name and the word "come." As you say "come," sweep your arm up and out to the side.

2 Then sweep your arm forward and into your chest. If your dog doesn't respond to the hand signal and verbal command, use the treat to lure him to you.

CHAPTER TWENTY-FOUR

TALKING WITH TOUCH

Dogs are experts at using their sense of touch to communicate with other dogs and people. Once we learn the different ways dogs like to be touched and what they mean, we, too, can be fluent in the language of touch.

Dogs depend on touch to a degree humans can barely comprehend. More than vision, scent, and hearing, touching allows them to form emotional bonds and communicate their most basic needs. Newborn puppies nudge their mom's nipples with their noses and paws to stimulate the flow of milk. Even when they're dozing, they get uneasy when she moves away and will only relax when they're touching once again.

Just as humans develop language skills early in life, dogs quickly become adept in the language of touch. Throughout their lives, in fact, their interactions with other dogs and with people resemble a contact sport. To us, it all looks like play. But to dogs, a hip nudge, nose bump, or paw push speaks as clearly as a shout.

The Meaning of Touch

Dogs spend a lot of time sorting out their respective roles, and they use touch as a way of establishing control or subordinance. When two dogs meet, one dog may push the other with his shoulder. It looks like a playful nudge—and in some cases it is—but it's also a way of saying, "I can push you around so you'd better toe the line." A push with the nose is another way of communicating authority. Dogs who are shy and retiring will rarely use these types of touch, while dogs who are naturally dominant use them all the time.

Their social interactions aren't all about status, of course. Dogs love to play, and once the "Who's in charge?" preliminaries are out of the

From the moment they're born, puppies, such as these Saint Bernards, begin to communicate by touch. The mother and the young pups only relax when they're touching.

way, they'll use a variety of touches to communicate their willingness—or their reluctance—to have a good time.

Some of the signals a dog uses to establish status, like putting his paws on another dog's shoulders or banging him with his hips, are also friendly overtures. A dog who pushes with his nose, for example, and is also wagging his tail or bowing his front end, is saying he'd like to play. Even touches that look ominous, like grabbing the fur around the neck, may be friendly as long as the dogs know each other and they're displaying other play signals at the same time.

There's no way to know for sure what a dog is trying to communicate just by looking at touch signals. You have to look at the whole picture: how he's moving, whether he has a smile on his face, how his tail is wagging, and so on. By licking, a dog can be asking for attention, showing affection, or being submissive, says Robin Kovary, director of the American Dog Trainers Network in New York City. If in the past your dog's nuzzling of your hand has brought him friendly pats from you, he's likely to nuzzle you whenever he wants affection. If you give your dog a treat whenever he nuzzles your hand, you can bet that future nuzzles will be your dog's way of hitting you up for a snack.

Touching Back

Dogs grow up "speaking" touch, but for people, learning to communicate with touch is like mastering a second language. Fortunately, dogs are patient. They understand that people are a little slow sometimes, and they will execute an entire chorus of touches to make their point.

This retriever mix is using a signal of dominance by putting his legs on the shoulders of his companion, but his wagging tail shows that he's only playing.

Suppose a dog is in the mood for attention. Were he with another dog, he'd nudge him a few times and wag his tail, and all would be understood. But he knows from experience that the subtleties of touch get lost in the translation from dog to human. So he'll do the canine equivalent of talking louder. A hand lick may be followed by a nose nudge. Or he'll rub against your legs and put his head on your knee. He knows that sooner or later you'll look up from the paper, notice he's there, and give him a pleasant rubdown, or, if he's really lucky, something to eat. Over time, he'll learn which types of touch you're most likely to understand and will start with those. He'll also learn that different people in the family respond to different kinds of touches.

While dogs are pretty good at telling their owners what they want, people aren't as fluent. They assume that touches that mean something to them, like a head rub or a big hug, will also mean something to their dogs. Most of the time, however, the result is pure confusion. People shake hands when they meet, for example, but dogs hate having their feet touched. We put our hands on each other's shoulders to express affection, while dogs may view this type of touch as a threat.

It's not difficult to learn the language of touch. Even though dogs respond to dozens of touches, you can communicate most messages with just a few different kinds. Here are the main ones.

• **Don't be afraid.** Dogs usually greet each other by ducking their heads and keeping their bodies fairly low to the ground. They do this because a dog who stands tall may be issuing a

challenge. This is where confusion sets in. People are a lot taller than dogs. In their eyes, we look pretty formidable. And because we're tall, we tend to reach down and pet their highest part, the top of the head. Among dogs, touching the top of the head is a clear signal that they're being challenged.

The best way to reassure dogs is to change our greetings. In addition to stooping down, it's a good idea to touch them under the chin or on the chest instead of on the head. "It's less intimidating than a pat on the head, which some dogs dislike," says Kovary.

• **Take it easy.** Whenever your dog is showing signs of stress—because he's being groomed, for example, or he's figured out that you and he are headed for the vet—make him lie down, then place your hand on his groin, which will calm him down, advises Kovary. Stroking a dog's side or chest slowly and firmly is also calming—in mature dogs, it's known to reduce heart rate and lower blood pressure.

• **I like what you're doing.** Since dogs crave physical contact, virtually any touch will let them know that you're happy with what they're doing. "When my dog is lying down quietly and not barking, I use touch as a form of praise to reinforce a behavior I like," says Sandy Myers, director of Narnia Pet Training in Naperville, Illinois. Gently pulling your dog's ears or rubbing his belly will let him know that you're pretty happy with him.

This German shepherd knows that he's not being issued a challenge when his owner gets down to his level to greet him. He is also reassured by the strokes under the chin.

Most dogs dislike being touched on the paws and will try to pull away. You can get them used to it by touching their paws when they're young.

Touches to Avoid

It's pretty hard to annoy a dog who spends his whole life looking up to you and who enjoys nothing more than some of your attention. But owners often forget that what feels good to them doesn't necessarily feel good to their dogs. Dogs view some kinds of touch, no matter how gentle or kindly intended, in all the wrong ways.

Most dogs hate having their feet touched. Experts aren't sure why it bothers them. It's possible they have ticklish feet and the touching makes them uncomfortable. Dogs rarely touch each other's feet, and in the canine book of manners, it's probably considered an unacceptable liberty, says Pat Miller, a dog trainer and behaviorist in Salinas, California.

Hugging is another kind of touch dogs wish humans would keep to themselves. The closest dogs come to hugging is when mothers carry puppies around in their mouths. Apart from that, dogs don't use clingy behavior to express affection. In fact, hugging probably reminds them, unconsciously, of the days when a close "embrace" meant they were being attacked. It's also possible that dogs associate hugging with being mounted by a dominant dog. Hugs restrict a dog's ability to move or escape, and they're not happy about that, says Kovary.

That's why you shouldn't discipline your dog by holding your hands on either side of his head—it's a gesture that makes him uncomfortable because he feels locked in.

A HAIRY BUSINESS

The sense of touch is very important to dogs, but they lose some of that sensitivity because their hairy coats essentially insulate them from things in the environment. To compensate, they're equipped with specialized touch receptors that allow them to pick up subtle messages.

These receptors are sensory hairs, called vibrissae, which are embedded in areas of the skin that have concentrated blood supplies and numerous nerve endings. The vibrissae are located above the eyes, below the jaws, and on the muzzle. Dogs use these touch-sensitive hairs to find out more about their environment, such as the strength and direction of air currents and the texture and shape of objects.

CHAPTER TWENTY-FIVE

TALKING WITH SCENTS

A dog's most powerful sense is the sense of smell. They use it to
find out all manner of fascinating things about the world and
to communicate with other dogs they encounter.

Dogs have an astonishing sense of smell. Researchers have found, in fact, that dogs are up to a million times more sensitive to certain scents, such as sweat, than humans are. So it's not surprising that they do much of their communicating by scent. Watch your dog closely the next time you take a walk. You'll see he spends relatively little time looking around because most of his attention is, quite literally, right in front of his nose.

This explains why even well-trained dogs will sometimes lunge, nose-first, toward a fire hydrant, tree, or other object of interest. Your dog's nose is so sensitive he can smell traces of other dogs that are hours or even days old, and he can discover their sex, their attitude, even their seniority just by taking a sniff. Essentially, he can "talk" to other dogs simply by smelling their scent—or by leaving his own.

A dog's instinctive need to sniff and be sniffed can be irritating for dog-walkers in a hurry, but it provides a valuable teaching tool. Since dogs use scent to talk to each other, it's possible for humans to use scents to talk to their dogs.

Putting Them at Ease

Dogs are creatures of habit who don't always like changes in their routine or lifestyle. You can use scents to help them deal with new or difficult situations more easily, says Robin Kovary, director of the American Dog Trainers Network in New York City. When you board your dog, for example, you can help him adjust by leaving one of your old, unwashed T-shirts or other

*When his owner goes away and leaves this beagle
with friends, he also leaves behind a piece of his
clothing. A familiar scent helps comfort dogs and
makes them feel more secure.*

garments. He will feel less frightened and insecure because your scent will keep him company.

Just as dogs get nervous about new situations, they're sometimes nervous about new people, too. That's why trainers recommend introducing dogs to new arrivals in the family—a new baby, for example—by letting them sniff a blanket or an article of clothing belonging to the person before they meet face to face. Dogs who "meet" people by first getting to know their scent will feel as though they've been properly introduced and will be more likely to accept them and will not be alarmed when they meet.

Teaching with Scents

Just as dogs use their noses to discover good things—like cookies on a counter—they also depend on scent to warn them away from things that aren't so good. You can combine scents with other training techniques to help dogs learn what they shouldn't do, says Shirley Sullivan, president of PR Dog, a training and dog day care center in Falls Church, Virginia.

For instance, you can discourage your dog from pilfering food off the counter by sprinkling the area with a distinctive scent such as anise oil, while also booby-trapping the area by lining tin cans along the edge of the counter. The next time he makes a raid, the cans will tumble down and startle him. Because dogs depend so much on smell, he'll associate the smell of the anise oil with the frightening noise. After a while, the oil alone will be enough to deter him, Sullivan says.

Smells that dogs find unpleasant can also help them learn. For example, citronella collars can help to stop dogs barking. The quick burst of citronella that's released with the first or second woof will soon persuade a dog that being quiet is better than getting a noseful of a nasty smell. You can also use citronella to keep dogs off the furniture or out of the trash.

It's not only smells that send messages, but also the lack of smells. For example, dogs that have urinated in the house will sometimes return to the same place, drawn by the lingering odor. That's why you need to remove not only the stain, but also the odor. Odor neutralizers, available in pet supply stores, do the job quickly and easily. Once the smell is gone, he'll be much less likely to return to that spot in the future.

CHAPTER TWENTY-SIX

TALKING WITH SOUND

Even when they're sound asleep, dogs always keep one ear open.
They rely on their hearing much more than humans do, so using sound
is a very effective way to communicate.

Dogs hear much better than we do. They can hear sounds from four times farther away, and they can also hear high-pitched sounds that are way beyond our range of hearing. Their sensitivity to sounds is important because they rely on their hearing more than we do. When we talk to our dogs, they don't merely listen to our words. They also focus on the way our voices sound.

And they listen to a lot more than just our voices. The rattle of kibble in the bag, the creak of a step outside the front door, or the opening of the drawer where the leash is kept are just a few of the sounds that tell dogs that something's about to happen. "Most of the time we're teaching our dogs things whether we realize it or not, because dogs are always looking for and interpreting clues about what's happening in their environment," says Pat Miller, a trainer in Salinas, California.

Because dogs are inquisitive creatures who like to learn, we can take advantage of their curiosity by using their keen hearing to communicate the messages we want them to hear.

This Australian shepherd fetches her leash whenever her owner jingles her house keys because she knows that's the signal that she's going for a walk.

Basic Vocabulary

Nearly all dog owners talk with their pets—not just when they're giving commands or praise, but also to share their feelings or to point out an exciting sight, such as "Do you see the ball over there?"

No one knows for sure how much human language dogs really understand. Highly trained show dogs understand dozens of commands,

and nearly every dog knows at least a few key words, like "walk" and "dinner," as well as a few more complex phrases. "Most people can teach their dogs 5 to 10 words, or more if they try hard enough," says Sharon Crowell-Davis, D.V.M, coordinator of the Applied Animal Behavior program at the University of Georgia in Athens.

Five or 10 words may not sound like a lot, but they pretty much cover the commands most dogs need to know—like "sit," "come," "down," and "stay." However, dogs focus on more than just commands. They listen and make associations every time we speak. And they're pretty good at putting things together.

Even though a dog may not completely understand a relatively complex (to her) phrase such as "get the ball," experience will teach her what you're trying to communicate and soon she won't have any trouble catching your drift. It won't be long before she responds by rooting through her toy basket in search of her ball.

Dogs also tune into sounds that we don't think twice about. Miller's computer, for example, says "good-bye" whenever she logs off. Her dogs may not understand the words, but they've learned that "good-bye" means that Miller's finished working and will soon let them go outside to play.

Dogs don't attach meanings to words in the same way that people do, so you can't expect

This shiba inu can tell from her owner's happy tone of voice that she's pleased with her.

them to expand their vocabulary right away, says Robin Kovary, director of the American Dog Trainers Network in New York City. They have to hear the same word or phrase at least a few times before it takes on meaning. However, if that word or phrase becomes associated with something they like, such as a walk, they'll make the connection fairly quickly.

Suppose you want your dog to know what "walk" means. Once or twice a day, say "walk!" as you pick up the leash before going outside, and make sure your dog sees and hears what you're doing. It won't take her long to learn exactly what "walk!" means—and she'll demonstrate her knowledge with tail-wagging, jumping-around excitement. You can do the same thing with words and phrases like "eat," "ball," or "come here." As school teachers can attest, repetition followed by fun is the best way to teach the basics.

Of course, no matter how many words your dog learns, she'll never understand their "meaning" in the same way that you do. But she'll understand other aspects of words, like their sound and inflection. In other words, to talk effectively with dogs, we need to focus not just on what we say, but also on how we say it.

Talking with Tone

Since dogs are acutely aware of the subtlest of sounds, they're very sensitive to your tone of voice. In fact, trainers believe that your tone of voice is more important than the words you use when you're communicating with dogs.

You can put this to the test simply by telling your dog that she's the most miserable, good-for-nothing cur that ever walked the earth. As long as you talk in a happy-sounding tone of voice, she'll wag her tail and wriggle her body in delight.

Conversely, telling a dog how wonderful she is while using a stern, low-pitched voice will make her a little nervous. Her ears may go back, her tail will curl downward, and she'll try to make herself as small as possible. She'll be unhappy and worried that she's displeased you because she recognizes the tone you use when you're unhappy with her.

Most trainers recommend using three different tones of voice when working with dogs. For commands, use a firm but even tone of voice. For praise, a happy, relatively high-pitched tone works best. For corrections, use a low-pitched, disapproving tone.

These tones are effective because they mimic the tones that dogs make when communicating with each other. Speaking in an even voice, for example, is similar to the pitch of a dog's everyday bark, which is why it's ideal for commands and other matter-of-fact messages. A high-pitched tone of voice resembles a dog's excited bark, so it's a good way to convey happiness and pleasure. And low-pitched, stern voices resemble the growl of disapproval from a mother dog, and that's why it's the best tone for giving corrections.

It's not always easy, of course, for people to vary their voices enough to capture the full range of dog attention. Men with deep voices may have trouble raising their voices high enough to convey praise and pleasure in a way that dogs can easily understand, says Greg Strong, a trainer in Easton, Maryland. Women with high voices may have the opposite challenge: Lowering their pitch sufficiently to correct their pets. Not surprisingly, many men are better at giving corrections, and many women are better at giving praise.

For both men and women, the most important thing is to make sure that your tone of voice matches the message you're trying to convey. "I've heard people tell a dog to sit, but then they put a kind of question mark at the end, like they're asking the dog to sit instead of telling her to," says Strong. If you do that, your dog may not obey—because she may not realize you've given her a command.

Beyond Words

The fact that dogs depend on sounds and not merely words to understand the world around them is something you can use to your advantage, both for training and simply to communicate a little more effectively.

Suppose you don't want your dog to beg while you're eating dinner. One way to send that message to your dog is to tell her "off!" or "no

Listening for a Living

For some dogs, tuning in to everyday sounds isn't just an adventure—it's their job, and they can make a world of difference for people who have lost some or all of their hearing.

Called hearing dogs, these are intelligent, eager-to-please canines who have been trained to alert their owners when they hear door bells, smoke alarms, telephones, and alarm clocks. The dogs can even be trained to alert parents that their baby is crying, says Joyce Fehl, director of development at National Education for Assistance Dog Services in Princeton, Massachusetts.

Most of the dogs trained by her organization are adopted from animal shelters, and they're screened to determine how well they can recognize and react to certain sounds, Fehl explains. A standard test is to set off an alarm clock. If a dog runs to the clock, proving she can identify where the sound is coming from, she's a good candidate for further training.

All the dogs are taught to recognize certain sounds, but they're also capable of learning new sounds once they've been adopted by their new owners. Barbara Spano of Carteret, New Jersey, discovered this for herself one morning when her hearing dog, a poodle named Lilly, pawed insistently at her face to wake her up.

When Barbara got out of bed she felt the floor vibrating. She looked out the window and saw that a truck had crashed into the utility pole by her house. She called 911, and the emergency officers later said she was lucky that her house hadn't caught fire—all of the electrical lines had been pulled away from the wall.

Hearing dogs are encouraged to think independently and they receive extensive training. But the one trait that makes them special is that they have very deep attachments to their owners and will do everything possible to keep them safe. "They also need to sleep with one ear open," Fehl adds.

message—and eventually she'll learn that throat-clearing means hand-outs won't be forthcoming and that it's time to go away.

The fact that dogs can learn to attach meanings to all kinds of verbal sounds has also led to the use of a technique called clicker training.

A clicker is a small plastic box with a metal strip that makes a clicking sound when pushed and released. When a dog obeys a command, the trainer or owner clicks the clicker instead of saying, "Good dog!" Immediately after the click, the dog gets a treat. "Clicker training is a good idea because it works with the dog's mind rather than against it," says Miller. That's because it uses positive reinforcement and rewards a dog instantly for obeying.

You can achieve the same effect on your dog with other sounds, too. Any sound that dogs associate with praise and pleasure, such as an enthusiastic "yes!" or a quick hand clap, will work just as well.

The idea is to use sounds that your dog recognizes that tell her that she's done something right the instant that she's done so. This will help your dog learn faster, and you'll both enjoy being able to communicate a little bit better.

begging." Or you can simply clear your throat and look directly at her. The noise will get her attention, and your stare will tell her that you're not pleased. It won't take her long to get the

159

CHAPTER TWENTY-SEVEN

TALKING WITH TREATS

Just like humans, dogs enjoy good things to eat.
But treats aren't just for fun—they can also help you
communicate better with your dog.

Dogs are distractable creatures with short attention spans, which is why it's not always easy to get them to notice what you're saying. But they're also capable of intense concentration, especially when food is involved. That's why many trainers recommend using treats to help us communicate better with our dogs. Whether you're training your dog, distracting him from bad behavior, or looking for ways to keep him amused, nothing speaks louder than food.

Trainers often use treats, such as cheese, freeze-dried liver, or other tasty goodies, as incentives for good behavior and to keep dogs focused during training sessions, says Robin Kovary, director of the American Dog Trainers Network in New York City. More is involved than the fact that most dogs have insatiable appetites. Of all your dog's senses, the sense of smell is the most powerful— more powerful by far than his sense of hearing or eyesight. When you're teaching basic obedi-

During training, a tasty treat helps keep this fox terrier's attention focused.

ence, words like "come" or "sit" don't have a lot of meaning, at least at first. But an odoriferous dog biscuit sends a message they can understand right away. Combining two messages—a verbal command coupled with a more compelling scent—makes training a whole lot easier.

Suppose, for example, that you're teaching your dog to come when you call. At first he won't understand the word "come." And he'll have a hard time paying attention to what you're saying because he'll probably be distracted by everything else that's going on around him, from the smell of the grass to a fly buzzing past. But when you're holding a treat, his attention will be riveted. Just as important, he'll be intensely motivated to do whatever it takes to gain that treat. So the treat helps in two ways: It helps him focus, and it rewards him when he comes galloping over.

The same technique works when you're trying to teach your dog to stay. The "stay" command is one of the hardest to teach because it involves leaving your dog in one place while you go someplace else. After about five seconds, dogs start getting bored just sitting or lying there, and they start looking around for distractions. That's usually when training sessions turn into chasing sessions.

Everything changes when you put a tasty treat on the ground a few feet in front of him, says Shirley Sullivan, president of PR Dog, a training and dog day care center in Falls Church, Virginia. It's as though all of the distractions were suddenly obliterated. Rather than desperately wanting to get out of school, your dog can hardly wait to do what you want—as long as he gets something to eat when he does it.

Of course, if you give your dog a treat every time he does something right, you'll not only have a well-behaved dog, but also a fat one. When you're training a puppy or giving a refresher course to an adult, treats are a great way to keep him focused and motivated. But good things should be given in moderation. "You don't want your dog to become fixated on food," Kovary says. Once your dog has learned the basics, he really doesn't need the extra incentives. Of course, humans don't need ice cream, either, but we appreciate having treats now and then—and your dog does, too.

The Power of Distraction

Treats send other messages besides "sit" or "stay." You can also use them to distract your dog from doing things you'd rather he didn't, like struggling when you brush his coat or barking out the window at butterflies. Treats are especially good for problem behaviors such as barking, if only because dogs can't eat and bark at the same time.

Or suppose you're trying to stop your dog from chasing cars. While walking your dog on a leash, have a treat ready when you hear a car approach. Quickly use the treat to coax your dog into a sitting position—and keep him focused on the treat so that he holds that position as the car goes by. You're helping your dog replace a bad habit with the behavior you want, and treats can help speed up that process, Sullivan says. After a while, he'll be so used to ignoring cars that he'll do it automatically, even when you've phased out the treats.

You can also use treats to keep your dog happy when you're away from home. This is important because dogs who are left alone often get bored or anxious and express their feelings by barking constantly, digging, or chewing. Something as simple as giving your dog a treat-stuffed toy, using a Kong, a Buster Cube, or a hollow bone, can often be enough to solve the problem. Because when a dog has a job to do—ferreting out tasty goodies—he will be too occupied to be anxious or bored.

A rubber toy filled with treats provides this Samoyed with a lot of fun and mental stimulation.

Credits and Acknowledgments

(t=top, b=bottom, l=left, r=right, c=center, F=front, C=cover, B=back).
All photographs are copyright to the sources listed below.

PHOTOGRAPH CREDITS

Ad-Libitum: Stuart Bowey, ic, vib, viic, 5t, 9c, 13b, 20t, 20b, 26t, 30b, 35tl, 38t, 40b, 42b, 48b, 49b, 50b, 51b, 51tr, 52br, 55b, 57t, 59tr, 62t, 66b, 68t, 70b, 71br, 72tr, 73br, 78tr, 79b, 80b, 82bl, 82br, 83bl, 83bc, 83br, 84bl, 85tl, 86b, 87t, 87c, 87b, 88t, 88c, 88b, 92b, 93br, 95b, 97b, 98b, 103t, 107bl, 107br, 109t, 111b, 112t, 116t, 117b, 120b, 122b, 124t, 128b, 134t, 136bl, 137br, 140bl, 140br, 141t, 142b, 144t, 145b, 147b, 150b, 157t, 160t, BCb.

Auscape International: Français-COGIS, 27b, 53tr, 110t, 118t; Gissey/COGIS, 56b; Hermeline/COGIS, 71tl, 94t, 108b, 153t; Jean-Michel Labat, 25t; Labat-COGIS, 17b, 32c, 54tl, 90t; Labat/Lanceau, 60t, 93tr; Labat/Lanceau/COGIS, 64t; Lanceau-COGIS, 47t, 89b, 152b; Varin/Cogis, 44c.

André Martin: 91tr.

Australian Picture Library: Philip Reeson 39c.

Behling & Johnson: Norvia Behling, 12t, 24b, 58b, 72bl, 80tl, 156b.

Bill Bachman and Associates: 85bl, 102b.

Bruce Coleman Ltd: Adriano Bacchella, 23b, 99tr; Jorg and Petra Wegner, 74b, 106t.

Dale C. Spartas: 10t, 14t, 37tr, 59bl, 63b, 78bl, 91bl, 115t, 130c, 138t, BCcl.

FLPA: Gerard Lacz, 54bl, 79tl.

Foto Natura: Klein/Hubert, 74tr.

Graham Meadows Photography: viiib, 2t, 53bl, 73tl, 127t, 129t, 136tr.

Judith E. Strom: 6b, 146t.

Kent and Donna Dannen: 37b, 46b, 52tl, 105b, 123t, 132b, 161b, BCtr.

NHPA: Susanne Danegger, 125b.

Oxford Scientific Film: John Mitchell, 35br.

R. T. Wilbie Animal Photography: 34t.

Rodale Images: Mitch Mandel, iic, 41t, 85c, 126b, BCcr.

Ron Kimball Photography: xc, 28b, 74b, 81b, 84t, 100c, BCtl, FC © 1993.

Ron Levy: 29c.

Stock Photos: Anthony Edgeworth, 113b.

The Image Bank: Vikki Hart, 15b. Dag Sundberg, 39c; Sobel/Klonsh, 151t.

The Photo Library: 119b, Brian Stablyk, 67t; Gordon E Smith, 154b; Lorentz Gullachsen, 92tl; Tim Davis, 143t.

Yves Lanceau/Auscape: 8t.

ILLUSTRATION CREDITS

Chris Wilson, 65b, 148,149

The publisher would like to thank the following people for their assistance in the preparation of this book:
Trudie Craig, Peta Gorman, Tracey Jackson.

Special thanks to the following people who kindly brought their dogs in for photo shoots:
Len Antcliff and "Bozie"; Kathy Ash and "Max"; Leigh Audette and "Boss"; Tim and Andrea Barnard and "Sam", "Rigel", "Tessa", and "Molly"; Anne Bateman and "Bonnie"; Esther Blank and "Max"; Corinne Braye and "Minne"; Sophie and Joel Cape and "Max" and "Millie"; Matt Gavin-Wear and "Amber"; Robyn Hayes and "Patsy"; Anne Holmes and "Marli"; Sophie Holsman and "Zane"; Fran Johnston and "Tess"; Suzie Kennedy and "Eddie"; Natalie Kidd and "Cisco"; Michael Lenton and "Jasper"; Gish Lesh and "Twister"; Lubasha Macdonald and "Tigra"; David McGregor and "Kelly"; Cameron McFarlane and "Donald"; Chris Wilson and "Julia".

Index

Underscored page references indicate boxed text. *Italic* references indicate illustrations.

The Well-Mannered Dog

DOG CARE
Companions™

The Well-Mannered Dog

From Dealing with Cats to Staying in Hotels, a Total Guide to Good Manners

From the Editors of

part of the family™

Edited by Matthew Hoffman

Rodale Press, Inc.
Emmaus, Pennsylvania

© 1999 by Weldon Owen, Inc.

Printed in the United States of America
Rodale Inc. makes every effort to use acid-free ∞, recycled paper ♻ .

Library of Congress Cataloging-in-Publication Data

The well-mannered dog : from dealing with cats to staying in hotels :
a total guide to good manners / from the editors of Pets, part of the
family ; edited by Matthew Hoffman.
       p.   cm. — (Dog care companions)
  Includes index.
  ISBN 1–57954–115–1 hardcover
  ISBN 1–57954–260–3 paperback
    1. Dogs—Behavior.   2. Dogs—Training.   I. Hoffman, Matthew.
II. Pets, part of the family.   III. Series.
SF433.W45   1999
636.7'0887—dc21   99–39662

Distributed to the book trade by St. Martin's Press

  4 6 8 10 9 7 5 3   hardcover
              10 9   paperback

Visit us on the Web at www.petspartofthefamily.com, or call us toll-free at (800) 848-4735.

OUR PURPOSE

To explore, celebrate, and stand in awe
before the special relationship between us
and the animals who share our lives.

Pets
part of the family™

The Well–Mannered Dog

Contributing Writers
Sheree Crute, Susan Easterly, Tony Farrell,
Susan McCullough, Christian Millman, Jana Murphy, Amy D. Shojai

Rodale Books
Editor: Matthew Hoffman
Publisher: Neil Wertheimer
Editorial Director: Michael Ward
Research Manager: Ann Gossy Yermish
Copy Manager: Lisa D. Andruscavage
Copy Editor: Kathryn A. Cressman
Cover Designer and Design Coordinator: Joanna Reinhart
Associate Studio Manager: Thomas P. Aczel
Book Manufacturing Director: Helen Clogston
Manufacturing Manager: Mark Krahforst

Weldon Owen Pty Ltd
Chief Executive Officer: John Owen
President: Terry Newell
Publisher: Sheena Coupe
Associate Publisher: Lynn Humphries
Senior Editor: Janine Flew
Senior Designer: Kylie Mulquin
Designer: Jacqueline Richards
Illustrator: Chris Wilson/Merilake
Icons: Matt Graif, Chris Wilson/Merilake
Production Manager: Caroline Webber
Production Assistant: Kylie Lawson

Film separation by Colourscan Co. Pte. Ltd., Singapore

CONTENTS

PART FIVE

MEETING THE NEIGHBORS

PART FOUR

THE WELL-TRAVELED DOG

Introduction

Every winter, thousands of dogs representing more than 150 breeds arrive at Madison Square Garden in New York City for the annual Westminster Kennel Club dog show. This prestigious event admits only dogs who are champions of record—meaning they've blown away all the local, state, and regional competition. If dogs were allowed to get college degrees, these dogs would all have *bark*-alaureates.

I go to the Westminster dog show every year because I love watching these canine Einsteins at work. And yet, I can't help thinking that all of this precision training isn't very practical. Sure, it would be nice if our dogs obeyed the command "sit" perfectly and looked both ways before crossing the street. But most of us would rather our dogs did the things that really matter. Like greeting the mailman with a quiet woof instead of tearing at the door, or politely sniffing cats instead of chasing them.

Molly, my Labrador, is a case in point. She's mostly well-behaved, although she occasionally interprets "come" as "run the other way." As I've discovered, however, obedience isn't the same as good manners. For example, no matter where I take her for walks, she invariably does her business on someone else's lawn, as if her own yard just isn't good enough. At home, she's an incor-

rigible garbage thief. She steals whatever leftovers she can find, then gets sick on the carpet.

Molly doesn't need more training. She needs an etiquette coach.

That's exactly what *The Well-Mannered Dog* is. The only etiquette book for dogs, it tells exactly how to help them behave in real-life situations. Forget about perfect sitting or heeling like a pro. It tells how to stop dogs from dribbling their breakfasts on the floor. How to teach them to respect your personal space. Even how to go to bed when you tell them.

Dogs do need to know the basics, of course, and it's up to us to teach them. That's why we've included a ton of useful tips on providing discipline, the best and most effective commands, and handling a leash without getting tangled.

Dogs will always be dogs, of course. They're always doing things that come naturally to them but that people consider unmannerly or merely gross. Take chewing. You'll discover the real reasons that dogs put their teeth to work, and what you can do to make them stop. Or cat chasing. Appearances to the contrary, dogs and cats aren't natural enemies. Most cat chasing, in fact, is really a case of mistaken identity (cats resemble the small, furry prey that dogs used to eat). You'll learn a number of useful ways to help dogs and cats get along.

All dogs want to be polite—not because bad manners get them sent to bed without their suppers, but because they want to please the people in their lives. Here you'll find hundreds of ways to help them learn more quickly and to remember what they learned. When to say "yes" instead of "no." When to be firm and when to turn your back. The best times to practice manners

and the best places. (One trainer recommends practicing in beer store parking lots on Saturday afternoons.)

To shine on the social scene, dogs need to know more than basic good manners. So we talked to Liz Palika of Oceanside, California, one of the country's best-known trainers and author of *All Dogs Need Some Training*. She gave us step-by-step plans for teaching dogs special skills, such as bringing your slippers, turning on light switches, and waving goodbye. The tricks look fancy, but they're easy to teach in just a few lessons.

Just as some dogs always seem to be on their best behavior, others do things that are truly, well, a little strange. Like Stormy, a Labrador retriever who doesn't drink his water, but plays with it. Maggie, who insists on depositing her 78 pounds on people's laps. Lady, who steals the children's toys from the toy box. You'll be amazed by their exploits—and by the creative solutions that helped them behave a little better.

Whether your dog is a social embarrassment, a domestic terror, or simply a little rough around the edges, it's easy to give him the social polish that he deserves. You'll both appreciate the difference.

Matthew Hoffman

Matthew Hoffman
Editor, *Pets: Part of the Family* books

PART ONE

Good Dogs Do Bad Things

All dogs do things we wish they wouldn't. It's not that they're stubborn or willful—though sometimes they are—but that their ideas about manners are different from ours. We shake hands; they sniff. We sit on furniture; they sprawl all over it. But despite these and many other differences of opinion, dogs are always eager to please. This makes it easy to teach them what we want them to do.

CHAPTER ONE

WHY MANNERS MATTER

Dogs with good manners are welcome anywhere.
Whether or not they sit on command or bring in the newspaper,
proper doggy etiquette gets them the love and attention they deserve.

Chooch is the kind of dog that people dream about. A reddish-brown Chow Chow, he has an adorable face and a heart of gold. He valiantly protects his family by keeping watch over the front door, and he's patient enough to allow kids to use him as a pillow as well as a play toy. And on the rare occasions when his owners skip a walk or two, he carefully positions his 85-pound body over the cat's litter box and takes care of business.

This Samoyed always drops what he's doing and comes immediately when he's called. That's the essence of good manners.

Chooch's owner, Janis Aquirre of Milton, Massachusetts, appreciates this dainty touch, although she has no idea how he learned it. Cassie, the cat, is less impressed. She clearly believes that Chooch is the rudest thing she's ever seen—after all, it is *her* litter box. This just goes to show that a dog's well-mannered gestures can become another family member's problem.

What Are Good Manners?

Dogs are always doing things that people (and cats) don't understand because their cultural backgrounds are so different. This difference in perspective makes the business of defining good manners an inexact science, at best. "What we call a behavior problem is most often a problem for us, not for our dogs," says Karen L. Overall, V.M.D., Ph.D., a certified animal behaviorist and director of the behavior clinic at the University of Pennsylvania School of Veterinary Medicine in Philadelphia.

A dog who chews shoes, for example, is just doing what dogs do. He may be confused in his choice of objects, but he doesn't intend any harm. A tough Rottweiler who growls at strangers through the door probably isn't mean; he's only displaying the protective talents common to his breed. And a dog who acts as though the living room is his very own Indy 500 track is probably blowing off steam and doesn't mean to drive you crazy.

But regardless of their individual backgrounds, breeding, and personal concerns, all dogs should know a few mannerly basics, says Joanne Howl, D.V.M., a veterinarian in West River, Maryland. At a minimum, they need to know the following rules.

- They shouldn't destroy the furniture.
- They should do their business outside and not in the house.
- They should come whenever you call.
- They should always walk politely on the leash, without pulling.
- They should respect people enough not to get aggressive.

Everyone would probably add a few personal concerns to the list, Dr. Howl adds. If you live with other animals or walk your dog in public, for example, you certainly want him to be calm around dogs and cats. Other people want their dogs to stop barking on request. To resist jumping on people. To not give wet kisses to people who don't appreciate them. Dogs are adaptable and eager to please, so they usually don't have too much trouble learning what they're supposed to do, says Dr. Howl.

Good for People, Good for Dogs

The benefits of dogs being well-mannered are pretty obvious from the human point of view. Dogs who behave well and respect the rules become much appreciated members of the family, and other people like them, too.

Dogs get similar benefits, says Dr. Howl. They are very social. They feel best when others are happy with them and when they know what they're supposed to do and how they're supposed to act. "Dogs feel insecure when there are no guidelines for their behavior," she says. "They need structure because they come from a culture, known as the pack, that has regulations and hierarchies like our own."

Dogs who stay home most of the time can get away with knowing just the rudiments of etiquette. But those who travel—on vacations, shopping trips, or nice long walks around the neighborhood—need to know a little more. The better they behave in public, the more opportunities they'll have to be with their owners—and for dogs, that's the greatest reward of all.

The Key to Good Manners

Whether or not you give your dog a formal education—by taking him to obedience school, for example—he should understand that he always needs to look to you for direction. The easiest way to teach him this is to control—and

---

BREED SPECIFIC

Dalmatians are mighty cute in the movies, but in real life they can be a handful because they have an inherited tendency to be nervous and somewhat unsociable. They're great dogs, but they do best with people who are knowledgeable about training and who have an abundance of patience.

One Classy Dog

PUPPY DOG TALES

Greyhounds are known as intelligent, elegant dogs of superior breeding. Then there's Hattie. She has the intelligence all right, but her manners aren't exactly what you'd expect from a doggy debutante—especially one who lives with Karen L. Overall, V.M.D., Ph.D., a certified animal behaviorist and director of the behavior clinic at the University of Pennsylvania School of Veterinary Medicine in Philadelphia.

Hattie, who lives near a farm, loves nothing better than rolling in cow manure. Horse manure is good, too, but she prefers the bovine kind. And she really rubs it in, getting as much of the redolent stuff next to her skin as she possibly can. The smell can linger for days or weeks, until Dr. Overall can't take it anymore and gives her a bath. Hattie, of course, simply goes in search of more cow dung.

Experts have a lot of theories as to why dogs roll in dung, but Dr. Overall suspects that it's not very complicated. Hattie probably rolls in manure for the same reason that humans wear cologne. "She's just coating herself in her favorite scent and having a great time," she says.

doesn't matter what: sitting, lying down, coming to you, whatever. When he obeys—and when food is on the line, dogs are very cooperative—give him his meal.

He will have just learned an important rule: When he does what you ask, he gets fed. To really nail down this point, Dr. Howl recommends teaching it in all sorts of situations. Have your dog sit before you let him outside—and reward him when he does it. Practice a few obedience commands, and reward him when he gets them right. If you do this all the time, he'll always look to you for directions, and that's the secret to teaching good manners.

Dogs vary widely in their abilities, Dr. Overall says. Some learn quickly, while others need more time. Some dogs are stubborn and willful. Others are shy and high-strung. "People often choose dogs because they have certain ideas about breeds," she points out. "That's not a good idea. All collies aren't Lassie, and all shepherds aren't Rin Tin Tin."

let him know that you control— the one thing he loves best.

"Your dog has to understand that you hold the key to the food box," Dr. Howl says. Food is a powerful motivator, and dogs will do just about anything to get a little more. To clearly establish the link between food and manners, Dr. Howl recommends teaching dogs one simple rule: Nothing in life is free.

Before giving your dog food, have him do something for you. It

One way to establish leadership over your dog is to let him know that you control the food. This English springer spaniel knows that she must sit politely to earn her dinner.

CHAPTER TWO

THE MISCHIEF MAKER

Call it a culture collision. Even dogs with the best intentions will get into trouble because their idea of proper behavior is totally different from their owners'. Every breed—and every dog—has a slightly different agenda. Confusion and mischief are inevitable.

Shakti loves laundry, especially when it is fresh, neatly folded, and put away in a basket. When the moment is right, the 6-year-old Yorkie dives in headfirst and begins rooting around until she finds the prize—a tightly rolled pair of socks. Once she nabs the fuzzy toy, she embarks on a fun game of show-and-tell. She trots over to her owner, shows him the socks neatly clenched in her teeth, and then waits, her eyes glistening with anticipation. Her owner, predictably, leaps to his feet and lunges forward, trying to rescue the socks.

Not a chance. Shakti instantly takes off, with her sockless owner in hot pursuit. The game doesn't end until the socks have been retrieved or shredded beyond recognition.

Shakti is definitely a mischief maker, but not because she is bad or poorly trained. Quite the contrary. She is doing what her owner has inadvertently taught her to do, says Karen L. Overall, V.M.D., Ph.D., a certified animal behaviorist and director of the behavior clinic at the University of Pennsylvania School of Veterinary Medicine in Philadelphia. People chase dogs when they want to get things back. Dogs chase each other when they want to play. Shakti, interpreting her owner's behavior according to her rules, gleefully continues the game.

The Meaning of Mischief

Dogs certainly aren't saints. They do a lot of things that people wish they wouldn't. Stealing socks is hardly the worst offense. There are dogs who chew table legs. Who steal chicken bones from the trash and steaks from the counter. Who stand still as their owners approach with their leashes—then tear off with mischievous looks and amazing flurries of speed.

This mixed-breed puppy's idea of a good time is destroying rolls of toilet paper. His owner would certainly call it mischief.

One thing that dogs never do is cause trouble because of bad intentions. Most of the time, they're just doing things that dogs have always done. But that same behavior, put into a human environment, looks an awful lot like mischief.

"Most behaviors that we consider bad are just natural for most dogs," says Nicholas Dodman, professor of behavioral pharmacology and director of the Animal Behavior Clinic at Tufts University School of Veterinary Medicine in North Grafton, Massachusetts, and author of *Dogs Behaving Badly*. "Barking and digging up the yard certainly qualify. And any greyhound worth his salt, for example, will go after a rabbit."

Don't Blame Me, I'm Just a Puppy

If you ever get a chance to see dogs in the wild, you'll be amazed by the extent to which their doglike appearance belies their undoglike behavior. Dogs (and wolves) who have never been domesticated are suspicious, aloof, and fiercely independent. They don't crave affection from people. They don't need handouts. And they certainly don't listen to anything you have to say. They're opposite in every way from the dogs who share our lives.

For thousands of years, people have deliberately bred out of dogs their original independence and spirit, and bred in such traits as gentleness, soft features, and a desire to please. "Dogs have been selected for puppylike looks and behavior," says Joanne Howl, D.V.M., a veterinarian in West River, Maryland. "We like dogs who are perpetual puppies." With that

Most dogs have been bred to be puppylike into adulthood. A few, like basenjis, retain some of the independence of their wild forebears.

playfulness, however, comes a certain amount of youthful, immature behavior. Like it or not, we've essentially bred the little rascal into our dogs, Dr. Howl explains.

A few breeds have retained their original spirit, she adds. Basenjis, for example, which have become increasingly popular, are prized for their intelligence, gorgeous coats, and unusual voices. (They're known as barkless dogs because they make a curious yodeling sound.) Basenjis are wonderful dogs, but only if you're prepared to deal with their very strong independent streaks. They won't make a lot of mischief, because they aren't like puppies. But then, they probably won't be as affectionate as other dogs.

My Genes Made Me Do It

Every dog is an individual, but dogs also belong to breeds (or mixes of breeds), and breeds have different personalities—and get into different types of mischief, says Melissa R. Shyan, Ph.D., a certified applied animal behaviorist and associate professor of psychology at Butler University in Indianapolis. For example:

Australian shepherds. Bred to manage herds of sheep, these hard-working dogs have tremendous amounts of energy. This helps them do their jobs in the fields, but at home in the living room, it puts them in a perpetual state of excitement. If they can't burn off their energy in an authorized fashion, they find other ways to do it, like zipping in circles around the couch for 10 minutes or herding wayward children and adults. And if they happen to topple a vase or two along the way, you can be sure it wasn't intentional.

Basset hounds. These warmhearted little hunting dogs are generally well-behaved, except for one thing: They love to bay, producing a mournful-sounding *arrrooowww*. It's not a bid for attention, just a throwback to their pasts, when they bayed to alert their humans that they'd cornered their prey.

Corgis. These dogs have received a lot of attention in the media because they're the dogs that Queen Elizabeth favors. For all their royal connections, however, these rough-and-tumble little dogs were bred to be hard workers. Owners sometimes complain that their corgis nip at their ankles or dodge between their feet when they walk—vestiges of their days as herders who had the job of rounding up livestock.

Irish setters. These happy, exuberant dogs can barely contain their enthusiasm for life. Along with their zest comes a certain amount of zany and impulsive behavior. But you have to consider their pasts. Generations of breeding have made them superb hunting dogs. An intriguing scent or a movement in the bushes is sure to arouse their curiosity and send them off in search of prey. This is considered talent when they're on the hunt. In the house or at the park, it looks like pure mischief.

Jack Russell terriers. Spunky, pint-sized, and full of energy, Jack Russell terriers can't depend on size to get what they want. What they do have is persistence, which they use to pester their owners into submission. They may lick hands until they get petted, for example, or jump up and tap their owners a few times—hard, when necessary—to get attention.

Labrador retrievers. No one is sure why they do it, but these sweet-natured dogs love to dig. They rarely bury things, but they turn yards into minefields of holes.

Lhasa apsos. These loyal, smart dogs are known for making a heck of a lot of noise when anyone or anything comes near the door of their abode. They originated in Tibet, where they were called *abso seng kye*, or "bark lion sentinel dog"—a very impressive name for a very small pup.

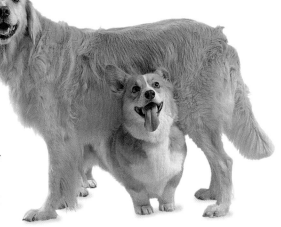

The mischief that dogs get into is partly determined by their breed. Corgis, bred to herd cattle, tend to nip at people's heels. Golden retrievers were bred to fetch game, so they like carrying things in their mouths.

Universal Mischief

A dog's breed is a big influence in his life, but it's not the only one or even the most important. Every dog, from the quietest springer spaniel to the rowdiest Labrador retriever, has to indulge his essential dogness from time to time. And dogs, regardless of their breeds, play by different rules than people.

Take chasing. Nearly all dogs do it, and they don't really care if the thing they're chasing is a tennis ball in the yard or a roll of toilet paper that they've knocked from its holder. Chewing, sniffing around for leftovers, and lifting their legs on vertical objects are just a few of the other ways that dogs express themselves. They can be taught not to do these things, but it's a challenge. These tendencies are just a part of who they are.

I Learned It from You

If you've ever wondered how smart dogs really are, try this experiment: Tip your plate one evening and let a scrap of steak slide to the floor. Your canine disposal unit will react to the arrival of this unexpected manna in two ways: First, he'll quickly grab the steak and scarf it down. Second, he'll return to the same spot just in case it happens again.

Dogs pay very close attention to the people in their lives. They try to understand what we're thinking and feeling, and to anticipate what we're going to do next. Even a dog who has never given a thought to human food can become a perpetual mooch if he tries it once and finds it good.

Some types of mischief, like mooching, may have their origins in things that occur accidentally. Many more occur because we inadvertently reward our dogs for the very things we'd like them to stop doing, says Dr. Shyan. Here are some examples.

Barking. Even small dogs can have very big voices, which is why barking is among the most common complaints that veterinarians—and neighbors—hear about. Barking is normal for dogs, but it drives people crazy. The usual response is to yell "Quiet!" But dogs don't understand that word. What they do understand is that you're barking along—and so they bark even louder.

Chasing. As Shakti the clothes hound can attest, nothing is more fun than running and

This Labrador mix loves to run and be chased. His owner may be desperate to get her laundry back, but to a dog, the chase is all a game.

Anything to Pass the Time

By the time he was 9 months old, Muttonhead had a very strong work ethic. One day when his family was gone, this industrious German shepherd decided to while away the time by doing a little housework.

He carried bedroom pillows downstairs and arranged them around the living room. He gently removed a set of delicate demitasse cups, one at a time, from the dining room sideboard and neatly lined them up on the couch. He finished his work by piling panty hose, socks, and other bits of clothing on the living room floor. On top of the pile went a single paperback book.

His owners were amused, but very surprised, by this strange behavior. So they talked to Melissa R. Shyan, Ph.D., a certified applied animal behaviorist and associate professor of psychology at Butler University in Indianapolis. It didn't take her long to figure out that Muttonhead had a surplus of energy and an uncommon amount of ingenuity. He was bored and needed something to do to occupy his time.

"As with many large young dogs who are left alone, Muttonhead found a few activities to entertain himself with," Dr. Shyan says. She recommended that Muttonhead's owners give him some fun toys to play with—preferably toys that required a little thinking on his part. This would keep his mind occupied and reduce his urges to redecorate.

tiny jaws around a size-10 sneaker. So we laugh. Now, flash-forward a year. Tiny puppy teeth have become adult molars and incisors, and discarded sneakers have been replaced with expensive Italian shoes. All of a sudden, it's not so cute. And the dogs can't figure out why they're getting yelled at.

No More Mischief

The great thing about dogs is how different they are from us. They're rarely serious and never grim. Their exuberance and puppylike behavior are the reasons we welcome them into our homes and hearts. A little mischief is a very small price to pay.

There's a difference, of course, between occasional misdeeds and serious misbehavior. Dogs who are destroying their owners' belongings aren't going to get a lot of love. Every dog needs to understand what is expected and what the rules are, says Dr. Overall. People, in turn, need to understand why their dogs do the things they do. It's the only way to help them behave a little better.

"You cannot completely eliminate an activity that's natural to a certain breed, but you may be able to reduce the intensity or frequency with which certain acts occur," says Dr. Shyan. Giving dogs toys they like, a lot of exercise, and a little bit of training and encouragement will keep most types of mischief in check. Your dog will still act silly, but he'll look to you for direction—and that's the biggest step of all.

being chased. Seems simple, but people have a hard time figuring this one out. When dogs don't come when their people tell them to or when they've picked up something that they shouldn't, their people take off after them—and dogs run away like it's all a game.

Chewing. Puppies love to chew, and people think it's pretty cute when they try to wrap their

STRANGE behavior

Name HANSOM

Breed JACK RUSSELL TERRIER

Age 2

The Behavior

Put Hansom on dirt, and he becomes a digging fiend. Once he gets going, the sky darkens with sprays of dirt thrown airborne by his whirring legs. For some reason, he does most of his digging at the fence. Some dogs tunnel in order to escape, but Hansom seems to do it just because he can. He chooses a spot, digs under the fence, then runs in and out through the hole, as though admiring his work. Over the years, the yard has taken on the appearance of a minefield; and flowers, plants, and grass rarely make it through the first season.

The Solution

Jack Russells are like merchant seamen: They just have to see what's over the horizon. Only instead of a boat, they have strong legs, tough paws, and inexhaustible amounts of energy. "This dog wants to see the world, and digging is one of the tools that Nature gave him to do it," says Betty Fisher, a trainer based in San Diego and co-author of *So Your Dog's Not Lassie*.

Dogs who dig digging won't give it up easily. Their ancestors did it, and they're going to do it, too. Hansom's owners will probably have to use tarps, boards, or other things he can't dig through to cover areas that he's attracted to, Fisher says. That's a start, but it's not a long-term solution because Hansom is clearly seething with steam and will find ways to dig anyway. What he really needs is something that will help him release all that energy, like taking long walks a few times a day.

Just chugging around the block won't keep this sailor in port, however. Calling Jack Russells "active" doesn't quite capture the type of seething energy that these dogs are born with. They need a *lot* of exercise.

Since Hansom craves a view of the world, Fisher recommends giving him one. A hole cut in the fence and covered with chicken wire would work. Better still would be to put the hole fairly high on the fence, with a small platform underneath. The platform doesn't have to be fancy, just some two-by-fours and a little plywood.

"Then he'd have a better vantage point than he could ever get from beneath the fence," Fisher says.

CHAPTER THREE

BEING THE DISCIPLINARIAN

Dogs crave direction in their lives. They used to get
this direction from other dogs. Today, they look to their
owners to tell them what to do and how to act.

No one wants to be the bad guy. You always feel that twinge of guilt whenever you push your dog out of your bed on a cold winter's night or tug the leash to the left when she so desperately wants to go right. Teaching obedience and giving reprimands are time-consuming and tiring, and they often seem to get in the way of dogs' good times. Who wants to tell man's best friend no?

Some people just aren't comfortable with wearing the sergeant's stripes. Dogs on the furniture? Nothing a vacuum cleaner can't take care of. Raiding the trash? Close the lid tighter and stash the can in the closet. Jumping on guests? Warn people ahead of time—and hope for the best.

The best never happens, of course. Unless dogs are shown what they should and shouldn't do, they're forced to make up rules as they go along, and their rules aren't going to be the same as yours. More important, dogs without discipline tend to be dogs without friends. When walking around the block is a perpetual tug-of-war, people are understandably reluctant to take the leash out of the closet. Dogs who jump on strangers don't get taken to public parks very much. And frenzies of barking can turn even the sweetest dogs into neighborhood pariahs.

Giving discipline isn't a lot of fun, but it pays off. Well-mannered dogs have advantages that their more unruly friends don't. These mixed-breed dogs know when they're allowed to play and when they should be quiet and out of the way. In return, they're allowed to spend more time indoors.

The Need for Leaders

Despite our natural reluctance to be taskmasters or scolds, dogs crave discipline. For 40 million years, they lived, played, hunted, and grew old within their family packs—carefully organized, close-knit groups of dogs who looked to their leaders, called alpha dogs, for instructions on how to behave and survive. Alpha dogs could be stern and demanding. But they always looked out for the welfare of the pack, and dogs understood and accepted this.

Good discipline is always friendly. Dogs form close bonds with people and want to please them. Most of the time, they need reminders more than reprimands.

Some dogs today have never seen a forest, much less lived in one, yet their need for leadership endures. Without other dogs to turn to, they look to us to take charge. Not because we're bigger or smarter, but because, just like the alpha dogs of old, we're the ones who control everything that they do. We control the food supply. We decide when they stay in and when they go out. We initiate play or insist on peace and quiet. In our dogs' eyes, we're very clearly the leaders of the pack, whether or not we take on the responsibilities that entails.

Being a leader involves more than giving orders and handing out discipline, says Suzanne Hetts, Ph.D., a certified applied animal behaviorist in Littleton, Colorado. Most of all, it requires giving clear directions about what is and isn't acceptable. Human society is incredibly confusing for dogs. They watch us closely for clues all the time. When someone comes to the door, for example, dogs aren't sure whether they're intruders or friends. Should they bark like crazy or wag their tails? They don't know unless their owners tell them.

"Dogs crave interaction, direction, and structure," says Ian Dunbar, Ph.D., a certified applied animal behaviorist in Berkeley, California. "They need rituals, and they like to know the status quo." In short, what they need most—indeed, what they crave—is guidance and a sense of what the rules are. They need discipline and won't be happy unless they get it.

Until fairly recently, most dogs got lots of discipline, mainly the wrong kind. Trainers and other animal experts (along with many human psychologists) believed that sparing the rod was spoiling the child. The goal of training was

Dogs don't regard discipline as cruel or unnatural. When dogs are together, older dogs will discipline the younger ones. Similarly, when dogs are with people, they expect to be told how to behave.

essentially to put dogs in their places, and some of the tactics used to achieve this could be very rough. Dogs certainly learned discipline. But they also learned to be afraid of punishment and even, in some cases, of their owners as well.

Teaching with Kindness

Most dog-training techniques originated with German or U.S. military trainers. Dogs essentially were treated as raw recruits who needed to be shouted down by tough drill sergeants or court-martialed into submission. Rather than getting praised for good behavior, they got a lot of criticism and punishment when they did something wrong.

Old-style training involved a lot of physical discipline. Trainers believed that humans should literally act like alpha dogs to enforce their rules.

CALL FOR HELP

Every person on Earth may belong to the same species, but our personalities are entirely different. You wouldn't expect the old man on the corner to act the same as the teenager next door, and even siblings are often so different that it's hard to believe they have the same parents.

Dogs are the same way. Far from being cut from the same furry cloth, every dog has a unique personality and temperament. The same types of discipline that work wonders with one dog may have no effect on another. It's not uncommon for people to diligently try to teach their dogs what they need to know, only to give up because they're convinced the dogs are incorrigible.

"I have seen owners tolerating terrible situations," says Ian Dunbar, Ph.D., a certified applied animal behaviorist in Berkeley, California. "They'll say things like, 'Well, he's just tricky with bones' or 'He doesn't really like kids.'"

It's fine to make allowances for dogs' individual differences and learning styles, but some types of misbehavior, such as aggression, are too serious to ignore—or handle on your own. "If you can't get the dog to stop what he's doing, it's time to call a behaviorist or find a proper trainer," says Dr. Dunbar. Some behavior problems will never get better without some help from a professional. In fact, they're almost certain to get worse, he adds.

Consider a technique called the alpha roll. People were often advised to reprimand their dogs by rolling them over onto their backs and forcing them to stay that way. It's a physically uncomfortable position. It's emotionally uncomfortable, as well, because it forces dogs into a submissive posture.

Choke collars are another way of meting out punishment. They're designed to pull tight when people pull on the leash. They put pressure on dogs' necks and immediately let them know when they're doing something wrong. There's nothing wrong with choke collars when they're properly used, and many trainers still recommend them. All too often, however, people were told to pull the collars very tight— tight enough to reduce or cut off the flow of air—whenever their dogs barked, jumped on people, tugged on the leash, or did anything else that "deserved" a swift correction.

Most experts today have a very dim view of these old-style training methods—not just because they were harsh but also because the theories that gave rise to them were largely wrong. It's true, for example, that dogs look up to their leaders; and those leaders, in traditional packs, could be tough disciplinarians. But alpha dogs weren't merely tough guys, says Dr. Dunbar. "Top-ranking dogs will often give gifts or share with lower-ranking dogs," he explains. "They most often rule by mental control, not physical aggression."

More important, experts came to realize what should have been obvious all along: Dogs are intelligent, sensitive animals who don't deserve physical punishment. In fact, they respond a lot better to praise and kindness.

Teaching dogs is easy because their natural inclination is to please. They just need to know what we want—and what we don't.

Gentle Discipline

Anyone who spends time around dogs knows how eager they are to please. They love food and adore going for walks, but what they crave most is the love and approval of their owners. Once they understand what people want, they'll do their best to deliver, says Dr. Hetts. Whether you're teaching basic obedience or correcting mistakes, you'll get the best results when you help your dog understand exactly what you want from her. Punishing bad behavior simply isn't necessary.

Teach what's good. Even though dogs have lived with humans for thousands of years, they have urges and agendas that are very different from ours. Their natural impulse is to do what they think is right, and they figure that everyone has the same idea as they do about what is "right." Once they understand that people expect something different, they're more than happy to oblige.

Suppose, for example, you're teaching your dog to walk on a leash. Rather than yanking the leash when she does the dog thing and goes the wrong way, help her understand that she's supposed to be following you. "Every 20 yards, stand still and ask your dog to sit," says Dr. Dunbar. "Don't move until she sits. Then say 'Good girl!' and perhaps give her a treat. Eventually, you will find that your dog sits whenever you stop walking because she understands that you're in control when she's on the leash."

Ignore what's bad. Dogs aren't angels. They're always doing things that they shouldn't, either because they don't know any better or because the temptation is too great to resist. Either way, punishment isn't necessary. In fact, you don't have to pay any attention to the misbehavior. What you should do is immediately encourage your dog to do something that's right.

Suppose your dog likes to jump on people when they walk in the door. Rather than yanking back on her collar every time she does it, plan ahead. Before opening the door, tell her to sit. Wait a few seconds to make sure she stays, then give her a lot of praise and something to eat. Dogs aren't foolish. They'll quickly learn that certain types of behavior—in this case, sitting when people come to the door—get your approval, and they'll want to keep doing them.

Teach with friendship. "Let go of the notion that you have to totally dominate your dog," Dr. Dunbar says. Unless you're planning to show your dog or enter her in competitions, there's no reason to demand clocklike precision or total obedience. Dogs respond very well to

kindness and patience as well as to fun, he says. As long as you're consistent in the things you ask them to do—never letting them on the couch, for example, as opposed to forbidding it sometimes, but not always—they'll try their best to do them. The rest of the time, you can pretty much relax.

FAST FIX Every dog has certain objects, treats, or even words that she loves better than anything else. Most dogs are passionate about food, of course. Some dogs love tennis balls. Others love rawhides or

It's never easy for dogs to concentrate when they're outside. Food is an excellent way to get their attention. This Samoyed has learned to focus on his owner because she gives him treats when he does what she asks.

chasing sticks or having their ears stroked. Make a list of all the things your dog truly loves. Then, when you want to teach her something new or reward her for doing a great job, bring out one of her favorite rewards, says Dr. Dunbar. The good thing about making a list of 10 or 20 items is that you'll be able to rotate through the list so that every reward, rather than being used all the time, becomes something rare and special—and worth working for.

You can even use the *idea* of rewards to help dogs behave better. Every dog has a favorite word, like "ball" or "cookie." When you want them to stop doing something, say their favorite words. They'll rivet their attention on you, knowing they're about to get something good. And that's when you give the reward.

Dogs learn very quickly when they anticipate getting something good. For many dogs, that's food. For this collie mix, it's a game of ball.

Love and Protection

PUPPY DOG TALES

Beagles were bred to hunt small game, but they're better known for their pleasant personalities and rather intense loyalties. Even among beagles, however, Jack was a standout. A 6-year-old beagle in South Bend, Indiana, Jack took it upon himself to be the guide, protector, and even the eyes of his less fortunate companion.

Jane Amos, a trainer and groomer as well as Jack's owner, is extremely knowledgeable about dogs. But even she was surprised when Jack took a personal interest in assisting Tina, a diminutive and elderly miniature poodle who had lost her sight because of a detached retina.

"I didn't train him to do it, but one day, I began noticing that he was taking care of Tina," Amos says. "Jack would periodically look around the house for Tina to check on her and make sure she was doing okay. He even developed a method of nudging her and guiding her so that she would walk around obstacles and avoid bumping into things."

Beagles are small dogs who don't weigh much more than a small sack of kibble, but what they lack in size they make up for in spunk. Jack didn't hesitate to protect Tina from other, bigger dogs in the neighborhood. During walks, in fact, he would quickly change position to put himself between Tina and other dogs they happened to meet, and he'd stay there until the coast was clear, Amos says.

Tina eventually passed away, but during her last years, Jack never quit looking out for her. He didn't need any encouragement at all. Tina was always grateful for the help—and that was the only reward Jack wanted.

STRANGE behavior

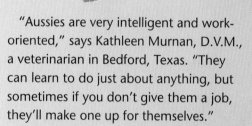

Name SHELBY

Breed AUSTRALIAN SHEPHERD

Age 4

The Behavior

Morning comes early in Shelby's home. At least, it does for Shelby. About 10 minutes before the first alarm clock buzzes—and a full hour before the last wake-up call—Shelby starts working her way through the house. She's awake, and she wants everyone else to be awake, too. Her technique isn't subtle. She jumps up, puts her front feet on the beds, and barks. And licks. And nudges. If none of these does the trick, a cold nose usually does. No one in the house is an early riser, so Shelby's attentions aren't appreciated at all. Especially because they spent a lot of money for a dog door so she could let herself out. She never uses it in the morning because she doesn't have to go out. She just wants everyone up. And she's creative in making sure they get up.

The Solution

Dogs have internal alarm clocks that are every bit as precise as the clocks that people use. Shelby's clock, unfortunately, is set unusually early, and for good reason: She was bred to work and herd—and herding dogs don't lie around until noon.

"Aussies are very intelligent and work-oriented," says Kathleen Murnan, D.V.M., a veterinarian in Bedford, Texas. "They can learn to do just about anything, but sometimes if you don't give them a job, they'll make one up for themselves."

Shelby knows that people need to get up and get going in the morning, and she just wants to pitch in and help. Somehow, she got the idea that her job was to be a four-legged alarm clock, and she's not about to lie down on the job.

In a way, Shelby's people are lucky, says Dr. Murnan. Her internal clock is set close to the time of the first alarm; it could have been much earlier. Either way, Shelby isn't going to sleep any later. The only solution will be to convince her that she has done her job—before she actually wakes everyone up.

"The first person up can keep Shelby with him by giving her a bone, a toy to play with, or even having her sit in the bathroom while he grabs a shower," says Dr. Murnan. "When it's time for the next member of the family to get up, then the early riser can release Shelby and let her do her thing."

PART TWO

THE CIVIL DOG

In choosing to cast their lots with humans, dogs were rewarded with
comfortable homes, great food, and the kind of pampering their wild
ancestors couldn't have dreamed of. The trade-off is that we expect
them to live by our rules—rules that are confusing and, well,
completely undoglike. They'll never learn not to bolt their food
or to abstain from sniffing strangers, but they can learn
to be a little graceful in their human homes.

CHAPTER FOUR
Setting Rules
pages 20–25

CHAPTER FIVE
Consistency Counts
pages 26–29

CHAPTER SIX
Reward the Good
pages 30–33

CHAPTER SEVEN
Ignore the Bad
pages 34–37

CHAPTER EIGHT
When to Practice Manners
pages 38–41

CHAPTER NINE
Where to Practice Manners
pages 42–45

SETTING RULES

When dogs do the wrong thing, it's often because they're not sure what
the right thing is. People easily adjust to changing situations, but
dogs don't. Consistent rules give them the chance to shine.

In 1998, syndicated newspaper columnist William Thomas wrote a piece about dog rules. With tongue firmly in cheek, he looked at how our efforts to set rules for our dogs often end up backfiring. The core of his column went something like this.

• The dog is not allowed in the house.

• Okay, the dog is allowed in the house, but only in certain rooms.

• The dog is allowed in all rooms, but has to stay off the furniture.

• All right, the dog can get on the old furniture only.

• Fine, the dog is allowed on all the furniture, but isn't allowed to sleep in the bed.

• Okay, the dog is allowed in bed, but only by invitation.

• The dog can sleep on the bed whenever he wants, but not under the covers.

• The dog can sleep under the covers by invitation only.

• The dog can sleep under the covers every night.

• Humans must ask permission to sleep under the covers with the dog.

Thanks to the speed of the Internet, various versions of Thomas's column flew around the world, appearing on dozens of Web sites and getting e-mailed to countless dog owners.

"It really hit a nerve," says Thomas, who writes from his home in Port Colborne, Ontario, Canada. "It rings so true in most people's experience."

Thomas's inspiration for the column came from his own dog, Jake, who was the first puppy he'd had since he was a kid. Having been a cat owner in the years between, Thomas learned anew how setting rules requires patience, dedication, and, above all, tenacity.

*Any dog with an ounce of common sense
will gravitate to a comfortable place. This
fox terrier was allowed on the furniture once.
Now she thinks she owns it.*

"At every juncture, if you're not careful, you surrender—and pretty soon he's driving the car," says Thomas.

Why Rules?

While it's amusing to ponder how our dogs tend to train us instead of the other way around, the reality is a little more serious. "How many dogs are a pain in the neck most of the time when they could be great friends almost all of the time?" says Jeff Nichol, D.V.M., a veterinarian at the Adobe Animal Medical Center in Albuquerque, New Mexico.

People value freedom in their lives, and they assume that freedom is good for their dogs, as well. But dogs don't do well with too much freedom. In fact, they crave discipline, says Joanne Howl, D.V.M., a veterinarian in West River, Maryland.

"It is vital to their basic nature as pack animals that they have rules," she explains.

When you set rules and enforce them, you're establishing a very important role for yourself— that of the leader. If you don't set rules, your dog will feel that she has no other choice but to move into the leadership void and start setting the rules herself. That's about the time when everyone stops getting along.

People tend to view their dogs as being equal members of the family. Dogs, on the other hand, never see people (or other dogs) as equals. There are always differences in the pack hierarchy. This means that if you're not at the top of

Labradors like to chew sticks, and this Lab mix is no exception. His owners encourage it, so he knows it's okay. Clear expectations make dogs happy—almost as happy as sticks do.

the family pack, your dog will see you as being below her—and her behavior will reflect this.

On the other hand, when you set rules and are firm about enforcing them, your dog's behavior will reflect this, too. "Dogs are not only comfortable with being subservient to the leader, that's a fundamental part of their nature," says Dr. Nichol.

The Canine Commandments

So what rules are important? One thing to remember is that what may be an important rule for one dog isn't necessarily important for another. And the same is true of owners. One person may not give a hoot when her dog

This Border collie pup is learning that she has to work before she can play. She'll happily sit—as long as she gets to run afterward.

climbs on the furniture; for someone else, this may be a major infraction.

Still, there are a few rules that every dog should be expected to follow. You can think of these as Canine Commandments. Other rules, which will vary among dogs and owners, are more along the lines of local ordinances.

Thou shalt come when called. It's not that big a deal if your dog doesn't roll over when you tell her to, but "come" is one command that should get an immediate, no-questions-asked response. Dogs who are running toward traffic—

or, more often, toward unsuspecting people—can get in a lot of trouble. "You have an obligation to be able to keep your dog under control," says Dr. Nichol.

Thou shalt honor thy grandmother. Experts in animal behavior often refer to a rule called Granny's rule. Also known as no free lunches, Granny's rule basically means that for every good thing you do for your dog, she has to do something to earn it. "This is a guiding principle of dog training," says Mark Plonsky, Ph.D., professor of psychology at the University of Wisconsin at Stevens Point and a canine behavioral consultant.

Granny's rule is critical because it establishes you as the person your dog needs to listen to. Dogs respond to Granny's rule because it also operates very strongly among dogs, where all good things came from the leader. What works among dogs also works when people enter the equation. When you give your dog her food, for example, she should always be required to sit and wait quietly until you let her know it's okay to eat. When you're getting ready to play catch or take her for a walk, have her perform a small trick or respond to a certain command.

Thou shalt not growl at thy leader. Sometimes it's hard to keep from laughing when dogs grumble at people who walk too close to their food bowls, or growl when people try to pry shoes from their mouths. But this type of behavior isn't cute, because it invariably leads to problems. A dog would never growl at her pack leader, Dr. Howl explains. Dogs only growl at people when they're challenging their leadership. "A leader needs to stand tall," she says. "If the leader is upset, a properly trained dog will

This shiba inu is acknowledging her owner's leadership by rolling over and showing her belly in a gesture of respectful submission.

drop lower to the ground. If a leader is really upset, a dog will roll over and show her belly."

One way to establish your role as the leader is to literally be the top dog—with the emphasis on top. Hold yourself high when you approach your dog, says Dr. Howl. When you're playing, make sure your dog is physically lower than you are. Dogs automatically respect size, and they'll pick up on the fact that your imposing stature is that of a leader.

Thou shalt follow the leader. How many times have you opened the door only to get shoved aside as your dog barrels out? And how many people try in vain to wedge their legs in front of their eager dogs when visitors come to the door? Dogs who rush past people are showing serious disrespect, says Dr. Howl. Once again, the reason for this can be traced to their days in packs. The leader was the one who left the den first; other, lower-ranking dogs followed.

What kept the peace in packs will also keep the peace in human families, explains Dr. Howl. Your job is to lead the way. Your dog's job is to follow close behind.

Enforcing the Rules

Dog are a lot like children in some ways. They test you. They push the boundaries of the rules you set, especially in the first 2 years of life. People need to see this time as their dogs' adolescence—and adolescents always need firm and consistent rules to follow.

Before setting rules, however, you have to decide which ones are actually important enough to enforce. There's not much point in laying down edicts if you're not prepared to back them up. In fact, rules that don't get enforced send a powerful message that it's okay for dogs to ignore more important rules.

Families aren't run like military units, of course. The idea isn't for people to be sergeants and dogs to be the raw recruits. But you do want to be consistent. Rather than setting dozens of rules that may be time-consuming and difficult

BREED SPECIFIC

All dogs need rules, but some breeds need them more than others. Border collies and Australian shepherds (left) have been bred to interact closely with the people in their lives. As a result, they're constantly asking for direction and feedback. More than most breeds, they need their owners to clearly communicate what is expected. When they don't get clear directions, they may feel as though they're failing.

23

to enforce, you may decide you only need two or three. The number isn't important; enforcing them consistently is.

Write them down. People make up rules all the time—and change them just as often. That's fine when you're dealing with other adults, but it's confusing as heck for dogs. Make a list of the rules you want your dog to know, Dr. Nichol recommends. So you don't forget—and to remind other people in the family—post the list somewhere obvious, like on the refrigerator door. "You need to be clear about what your dog is expected to do, especially if there is more than one person in the family," says Dr. Nichol.

Bring others to the bowl. It's common for dogs to listen to one person in the family and ignore everyone else. One solution is to have other people in the family feed your dog while the "top dog" stands by, suggests Dr. Plonsky. And before she gets the food, have her sit quietly or obey a command or two. When she gets the idea that all the people in the family have the power to control her food supply, she'll understand that all people need to be listened to.

The Dog Who Beat the Machines

Peaches, a nearly all-white beagle, earned her living by smelling wood-destroying termites. Her reputation as a bug-busting miracle spread, resulting in a challenge: She would be pitted against human pest inspectors as well as high-tech detection devices.

The contest was to be held at a building in State College, Pennsylvania, that had known termite activity, says Robert Snetsinger, Ph.D., professor emeritus of entomology at Pennsylvania State University in University Park. "We went to the Park Forest Village Community Church, which was a beautiful, older wooden building, and I checked it out carefully. I knew where we'd had recent swarms and where the termites were living."

While a dog's nose can't be patented as a new invention, it is a miracle device that boggles the modern mind. A beagle's nose has over 30 times as much skin devoted to scenting as does a human's. The olfactory bulb, the smell-center in the brain, is four times bigger than a person's.

"Peaches and I had been working together for about 2 years when I got a letter inviting us to the contest," says Mike Del Gaudio, former owner of a pest-control business in Scranton, Pennsylvania. "I knew she was good, but getting asked to prove it in front of all my peers was pretty scary."

He needn't have worried. At the command "termites," Peaches started to quiver. Her head cocked and her brown eyes glowed. As the machines slowly and mechanically combed the building, Peaches just kept finding bugs. "We hit on a couple of areas that were thought to be termite-free," Mike says. "Well, they weren't bug-free. When they opened the area to visual inspection later, there were nice infestations of destructive carpenter ants."

Peaches quickly found all the termites that the judges knew were there, plus an additional 12 sites that no one had known about. In short, she blew the doors off her competition.

Mike basked in the accolades for a few minutes, then slipped away to celebrate privately. "I took her to lunch, and she scarfed down three chili dogs," he says.

Dogs need to understand that all the people in the family are higher in status than they are, including the children.

Provide a place for time-outs. You can't be around your dog all the time. For puppies especially, time spent alone is often time spent acquiring bad habits. People are often reluctant to teach their dogs to stay in crates, but it's probably the best way to minimize problems while also making dogs feel safe and secure. "It's like a wolf's den," says Dr. Plonsky. "This is the den that your dog's wild ancestors would dig to take a nap. It's not a prison, but a very comfortable place to be."

FAST FIX People tend to underestimate how much exercise dogs really need. Whether you have a slothful Great Dane or a Border collie dynamo, regular exercise is the only way to help her burn off energy. Dogs who don't exercise enough tend to get restless and bored. Dogs who are bored tend to get stubborn and distracted.

Dogs need at least 20 minutes of exercise twice a day. Some breeds, like terriers and herding dogs, may need as much as a few hours. People who have been dealing with behavior problems are often amazed at how much their dogs improve once they get their paws moving. Walking around the park or chasing balls gives dogs the mental stimulation and social interaction they crave. Exercise also tires them out, and tired dogs are the best-behaved dogs.

Kelpies are working dogs who need tremendous amounts of exercise to feel—and act—good.

25

CHAPTER FIVE

CONSISTENCY COUNTS

Dogs want to please the people in their lives, but they get confused when
something that's allowed one day gets them into trouble the next. Giving clear and
consistent messages is the best way to help them understand what they're supposed to do.

We appreciate consistency in our lives. We demand it in our peanut butter. We treasure it when our paychecks arrive on time. And we like the fact that the supermarket always has what we're looking for when we stop by after work.

The consistency that we value for ourselves, however, doesn't always carry over to our dogs. "We complain about our dogs begging at the table, but then we turn around and slip them some food when we're in a generous mood," says Amy Marder, V.M.D., clinical assistant professor at Tufts University School of Veterinary Medicine in North Grafton, Massachusetts, and vice president of behavioral medicine and companion-animal services at the American Society for the Prevention of Cruelty to Animals in New York City. Or we encourage them to jump up and greet us when we're wearing old clothes, but then flip out when they do the same thing when we're wearing new suits.

Meanwhile, our dogs' feelings about all of these mixed messages can be summed up in one word: "Huh?"

A World That Makes Sense

Dogs are very smart animals who can understand and anticipate a lot of the things that we do. But unless you keep to a regular schedule and respond consistently to certain types of

A dog who scores at the supper table once is going to keep coming back for more.

behavior, you're asking them to learn things that their brains aren't built to deal with—mainly, the idea of appropriateness. Dogs can't understand that an action that's acceptable at one time isn't at another. They don't factor in things like your mood, your clothes, or the fact that Aunt Ruth has a morbid fear of dogs.

"We try to make dogs think like people, and it just doesn't work," says Norma C. Guy, D.V.M., a veterinary behaviorist with the Atlantic Veterinary College in Charlottetown, Prince Edward Island, Canada. People spend many years learning the nuances of appropriate behavior. Dogs don't and can't. Without clear and consistent guidelines, they have a hard time figuring out what they're supposed to do. This can lead to a huge amount of confusion, and the more confused dogs get, the harder it is for them to behave in ways we appreciate. This in turn makes them anxious, says Dr. Guy. Dogs crave predictability, and when things aren't predictable, they get tense and unhappy.

"It can be next to impossible to stop bad behavior if you're not being consistent," adds Joanne Howl, D.V.M., a veterinarian in West River, Maryland. It doesn't matter whether you're trying to stop your dog from begging at the table or encouraging him to be more sedate around visitors. Giving clear and consistent messages will help him learn more quickly and remember what he learned.

Get everyone with the program. If you live alone with your dog, it's pretty easy to be consistent. It's not so easy when there are other people in the family, each of whom may be giving a different message. "Dogs know how to manipulate the person who is most easily ma-

The same body clocks that tell dogs when their owners are coming home also make them sticklers for punctuality and routine.

nipulated," says Dr. Howl. No matter how strict you are about not feeding your dog from the table, for example, he's going to keep mooching if someone else is slipping him strips of bacon.

The easiest way to prevent mixed messages is to get everyone together and come up with a list of things that everyone agrees with, like certain types of behavior that will always be discouraged, says Karen L. Overall, V.M.D., Ph.D., a certified animal behaviorist and director of the behavior clinic at the University of Pennsylvania School of Veterinary Medicine in Philadelphia.

Live day to day. Dogs learn best when the same things happen at the same times every day, says Dr. Guy. Whereas people view weeks, months, and years as significant milestones, for

27

dogs, these long periods of time mean squat. They simply don't have long memories. On the other hand, their internal clocks are exceptionally accurate. That's why your dog goes to the door minutes before you come home from work. He knows that you'll be walking in soon because his inner alarm clock tells him so.

"A daily routine really helps relieve anxiety," says Dr. Guy. She recommends feeding dogs at the same time every day, going for walks at the same time, and setting up consistent training times. Dogs feel more confident when things are on schedule, and happy dogs are much less likely to do things that people don't like, such as chewing apart the couch cushions.

No means no. No one enjoys being the disciplinarian. When you're tired at the end of the day, it's not a lot of fun to struggle with an obstinate dog. This is why it's easy to let things slide. You may have told your dog a dozen times to get off the couch, but he keeps creeping up, and finally you give up.

Bad choice, says Dr. Overall. This type of inconsistency teaches dogs that it's okay to ignore commands. Like boorish suitors, they get the idea that when you say "no,"

they just have to try a little harder to get what they want.

Commands such as "no," "sit," and "get off the couch" shouldn't be negotiating points, says Dr. Overall. You have to be unfailingly consistent in enforcing them. "If you do this one simple thing, you won't have to be a disciplinarian all the time," she says. Your dog will understand what you want, and he'll accept your rules. And he'll be happier because there's less confusion in his life.

FAST FIX We spend so much time with our dogs that we often assume we're all speaking the same language. Research has shown, in fact, that 24 percent of owners believe that their dogs understand everything they say. But a lot of the time, dogs don't understand. Dogs are capable of learning dozens of words, but they have a hard time distinguishing words that are similar but not identical to the words that they do know. That's why a dog may respond beautifully to a word such as "come," but will look totally confused when he hears variations such as "c'mere" and "come on, boy."

"When you do that, your dog has to relearn the phrase," says Dr. Howl. That's why veterinarians recommend that you use exactly the same words all the time. When your dog doesn't have to guess what you're saying, he will be much more likely to respond quickly and with pleasure, she says.

BREED SPECIFIC

Every dog benefits from having a lot of consistency in his life, but large breeds with the most exuberance, like Labrador retrievers (right), absolutely require it in order to control their friendly, but sometimes over-the-top, energy.

STRANGE
behavior

Name STORMY

Breed LABRADOR RETRIEVER

Age 2

The Behavior

Stormy doesn't drink his water, he plays with it. Every time his owners fill his bowl, Stormy takes a few sips, then puts his front feet in the dish and begins splashing water all over the place, making one heck of a mess. His owners are facing a frustrating dilemma. They're sick and tired of cleaning up the spills after Stormy's perpetual water baths, but they don't want him to go thirsty because there isn't any water left in the bowl.

So far, they've decided to keep the bowl full, or at least try to, but the kitchen floor is starting to get waterlogged. They've tried using a weighted dish that's harder to tip over, but Stormy manages to spill all the water anyway.

The Solution

"This dog wants to swim," says Judith Halliburton, a trainer and behaviorist in Albuquerque, New Mexico, and author of *Raising Rover*. "He's a Labrador and it's in his blood, just like fetching. Labs have been bred for hundreds of years to work in the water, and they naturally enjoy it."

Even Labradors can learn to be a little neater, she adds—but the only way this is going to happen is if Stormy satisfies his water jones somewhere else. If they have a good-sized backyard, Stormy's owners could buy a small kiddie pool. "Stick it in the yard, fill it half-full, and let him have at it," Halliburton says. "Even in cooler weather, he may decide to go for a dip; and in warm weather, he'll probably live in it."

A more convenient solution would be for Stormy's owners to drop by a pet supply store and buy an elevated food-and-water stand. Usually made from stainless steel or plastic, this type of stand raises the bowls off the floor to about mouth level. Although they're mainly used to make eating easier for dogs with joint problems, raising the water 1 to 2 feet off the ground will ensure that Stormy doesn't stand in it.

"Lastly, when he's had his drink and starts messing around, take the bowl away," Halliburton says. "When he's calm and behaving again, put it back. He'll soon get the idea that the water in his dish is just a beverage, not a plaything."

CHAPTER SIX

REWARD THE GOOD

Dogs thrive on positive feedback. Rewarding them for doing the right thing works better than correcting them for causing trouble. Dogs are happiest and most confident when they get lots of praise—and know that they've earned it.

Ralph Waldo Emerson said, "The only re-ward of virtue is virtue." One thing is certain: He was not talking about dogs.

People who expect their dogs to naturally gravitate towards virtuous behavior, wearing nothing but a smile, are in for some disappointment. "It's not that dogs are selfish or inherently bad. It's just that they perceive things differently than we do," says Joanne Howl, D.V.M., a veterinarian in West River, Maryland. Dogs essentially see the world in one of three ways. Things are either good, bad, or indifferent, and these perceptions govern everything that they do.

• Things that are good are those that bear rewards, such as food, affection, and fun. Dogs naturally gravitate back to these things.

• Bad things are those that have unpleasant consequences, like a bitter taste or a porcupine quill in the nose. Dogs learn to avoid these things.

• Things that dogs are indifferent to, well, they just don't register on the radar, and dogs don't waste any brain space thinking about them.

For a long time, trainers and behaviorists believed that the best way to teach dogs good manners was to manipulate their instinct to avoid the bad. Dogs who ignored commands, rooted through the trash can, or otherwise got out of line were scolded or given a quick swat, says Norma C. Guy, D.V.M., a veterinary behaviorist with the Atlantic Veterinary College in Charlottetown, Prince Edward Island, Canada. The idea was that they'd associate the bad experience with the bad behavior, and this would put them on the path to righteousness.

There's certainly some truth to this. Imagine that you're a dog and you've just come across a skunk. Blam, you get a shot of staggering stink right in your snout. The next time you see a skunk, you'll be afraid that it will happen again, and you'll wisely take a detour because you now associate skunks with pain and misery.

But suppose you're lying quietly at home, happily munching on this great-tasting leather thing. You don't know that it cost $300 and came

BREED SPECIFIC

Dogs with dominant personalities, such as Rottweilers, sometimes perceive rewards as signs of weakness on the parts of their owners. These and other strong-willed dogs tend to learn best with a combination approach—being rewarded for good behavior and gently corrected for bad.

from Italy. All you know is that all of a sudden you got a tremendous wallop from your human. Sure, you now associate leather shoes with pain, but you also see your owner in a new, and not altogether pleasant, light.

"It's completely inappropriate to train an unwanted behavior out of a dog with punishment," says Dr. Guy. Dogs who are often punished may become anxious and fearful, and this causes them to act in anxious and fearful ways—which generates even more discipline. "It becomes a vicious cycle," she says.

I Like It When You Praise Me

Behaviorists have discovered that dogs learn better and faster when they're rewarded for good behavior rather than punished for bad. The good feelings that come from rewards last a long time, and the desire to repeat those feelings encourages dogs to keep doing well, says Dr. Howl. At the same time, dogs who are rewarded for doing good things feel closer to their owners and are less afraid than those who are always getting punished.

Rewarding good behavior doesn't mean pampering dogs or giving them crunchy biscuits just because they look cute when they're sleeping in the sun. It does mean giving them positive feedback when they do something that you want them to do. Suppose your dog is barking and you tell him to stop. He stops, and you give him a reward. It won't take him long to figure out that being quiet and listening to commands gets him a treat, while barking doesn't get him much of anything at all.

Dogs learn by associating actions with results. An action that brings pleasant results—such as a pat and some praise in return for not nosing visitors—is one that they will be eager to repeat.

Timing is everything. Dogs are natural Zen Buddhists in the sense that they live mainly in the moment. Their memories simply aren't very good. That's why it's no use giving them rewards for something they did in the past—and for dogs, the present becomes the past after a few seconds. They'll gladly gobble up the treat, but they won't have a clue what it's for, says Liz Palika, a trainer in Oceanside, California, and author of *All Dogs Need Some Training*. "If you even wait 10 seconds to reward them for doing something good, it's too late," she says.

Of course, dogs who are in the process of learning proper behavior don't have a lot of successes at first. You'll probably need to follow

31

them around just to catch them doing something right. Maybe your dog sniffs your slippers and walks on without touching them. Immediately praise him to high heaven and slip him a treat, says Palika. Does he look at the garbage can and decline to dig through it, or curl up on the carpet instead of on the couch? Let your voice be heard and the biscuit box be emptied.

Customize the rewards. Even though most dogs believe that food is the best reward they'll ever get, it's not the only reward or even the best one. For one thing, dogs tend to put on weight, and you don't want to beef them up, no matter how good they are. And some dogs are equally motivated by praise, toys, or other kinds of rewards. "You really need to take the personality and breed of the dog into consideration," says Palika.

Sight hounds such as Afghans and greyhounds were bred for hunting and chasing small animals, and they usually appreciate squeaky

Some dogs aren't motivated much by food. The promise of a game has this kelpie's attention and may be the most effective inducement to good behavior.

toys they can chew on. "Terriers go bonkers over fuzzy mouse toys," says Palika. Bred for hunting rodents, they like the feeling of furlike material in their mouths, she explains. Herding dogs such as Australian shepherds and Border collies won't say no to food, but a quick tear around the backyard, with you running behind and shouting praises, will have even more impact.

"If you're having trouble finding something, take your dog to the pet supply store and walk him up and down the aisles a few times," suggests Palika. Make the circuit through the cat section, too, since many dogs—especially digging dogs such as dachshunds—love toys that are shaped like rodents. Let your dog sniff the offerings. Hold toys in front of him and see what he likes. When he shows a lot of interest, you'll know you've found a special toy.

Reward little and well. Just as children who grow up having ice cream for supper may start feeling entitled to it, dogs lose the meaning behind treats when they get them too often, says Amy Marder, V.M.D., clinical assistant professor at Tufts University School of Veterinary Medicine in North Grafton, Massachusetts, and vice president of behavioral medicine and companion-animal services at the American Society for the Prevention of Cruelty to Animals in New York City. Overindulgence is fine at first, Dr. Marder adds. You want to reward your dog a lot when he's learning new things. After a few weeks, it's time to taper off. Rather than giving a reward every time he does something right, give it every second or third time, she suggests. Within a few months, the good behavior will become habitual. At that point, only hand over rewards occasionally.

You can tell if you're rewarding your dog too often by watching his reactions. The sight or smell of a treat should generate a lot of enthusiasm. If he gives you a ho-hum kind of look, you'll know you're being too generous. Or maybe it's time to switch to a reward that *does* get him excited.

Help him succeed. Some dogs just can't seem to get it right. Maybe you say "sit", and your dog gives the blankest look you've ever seen. You tell him to get off the couch, and he merely stretches and sighs. You wait eagerly, treat in hand, for him to do something—anything—right so that you can reward him. Meanwhile, he happily chews your shoes or lifts his leg on your rubber boots.

You can't wait forever, says Dr. Guy. Sometimes, it's better to be a role model and walk your dog through the proper behavior. "If you catch him in midstream, pick him up and take him outside and let him finish," she says. "Then reward him there." Try this technique anytime you find your dog doing something that he shouldn't.

Suppose you find him with his head buried in the trash. Take him by the collar and gently walk him past the trash a couple of times without letting him stop or sniff. Lead him to

On the Money

David Baca of Embudo, New Mexico, doesn't worry about rewarding his dog, Oliver. That's because Oliver, a Pekingese–pug mix, takes care of that all on his own. And if he's feeling particularly generous, he may reward his owner as well.

Oliver has a gift for ferreting out money. While other dogs dream of filet mignon or chasing rabbits, Oliver is most likely dreaming up his next big score. Baca discovered Oliver's affinity for greenbacks when a girlfriend began complaining that she was missing money. For three weeks, Baca kept getting blamed for her financial losses. But since he was broke at the time and was also short a few $5 bills himself, he couldn't figure out what was happening with the cash.

One day on a hunch, Baca set a $10 bill on the coffee table and stepped around a corner to watch. Sure enough, Oliver picked up the money. After following Oliver around for a while, Baca discovered an extra $45 stashed behind the refrigerator.

Oliver's heists made sense considering Baca's earlier days as a cattle rancher and his forays into town. When he and Oliver would walk past Zeller's General Store in town, he would occasionally slip Oliver some cash. Oliver would hold the bills in his mouth and walk into the store. Clerks in the store who knew Oliver would take the cash and give him a can of Vienna sausages, which he'd carry outside. Baca would open the can and give the frankfurters to Oliver—and that's a lesson no dog is going to forget.

another room, then reward and praise him there, says Dr. Guy. He'll begin to understand that certain types of behavior—walking past the trash, ignoring the shoes, staying off the couch—bring him the things he loves.

CHAPTER SEVEN

IGNORE THE BAD

Attention is a powerful reward. Dogs prefer positive, happy attention,
but they'll settle for the negative kind. That's why ignoring bad
behavior is often more effective than punishing it.

Every elementary school classroom has a kid who jumps up in the middle of a lesson and does an impromptu dance. Who makes grotesque faces. Who is always practicing armpit noises. "Ignore him," teachers say. "He's just looking for attention."

Animal behaviorists can relate to this. Some dogs are the canine equivalents of classroom cutups. And the solution is often the same, says Mary Lee Nitschke, Ph.D., an animal behavior therapist in Portland, Oregon. By ignoring some of your dog's less pleasing manners, you're taking away that which she holds most dear: your attention. "This is probably the most powerful tool people have in their training repertoires," says Dr. Nitschke.

Imagine dogs in the wild. In each pack, there's an alpha dog who is the leader. When a lower-ranking dog does something annoying or troublesome, the regal alpha dog doesn't even bother to look her way. It's only when a dog does something the alpha dog likes that she gets rewarded with his attention, says Karen L. Overall, V.M.D., Ph.D.,

a certified animal behaviorist and director of the behavior clinic at the University of Pennsylvania School of Veterinary Medicine in Philadelphia.

In human families, the alpha dog is you. And you can use your status as leader to help your dog behave better. "The way to correct a dog for poor behavior is not to punish her," Dr. Overall says. "You withdraw your attention."

When to Ignore

Ignoring bad behavior isn't a panacea, of course. It doesn't work at all when dogs are doing something aggressive or highly physical, if only because they're probably not paying attention to

BREED SPECIFIC

Ignoring bad behavior works best with dogs who have been bred to form very deep bonds with their owners, such as Siberian huskies and Alaskan malamutes (left). On the other hand, dogs who bond with everyone, like Labrador retrievers, are less likely to respond to this technique.

you when they're that worked up, says Bob Gutierrez, animal-behavior coordinator at the San Francisco Society for the Prevention of Cruelty to Animals.

It also doesn't work when dogs are doing something they enjoy quite a bit, such as barking at butterflies or chasing cats across the yard. Your approval won't add one whit to their pleasure because the activity itself is so much fun. "They're enjoying themselves and having a great time, and that's their reward," Gutierrez says.

The cold shoulder works best as a teaching tool when dogs are misbehaving in ways that demand your attention, such as jumping up, begging, barking, or hand-nudging. This technique doesn't work immediately, Dr. Nitschke adds. When you do it consistently, however, it will teach a lesson that dogs can remember.

How to Ignore

It's easy enough to turn your back on your dog when she's misbehaving. But there's a fine line between teaching and punishing. Ignoring dogs for too long or doing it too often won't make them better behaved. It will make them anxious. The idea is to withdraw your attention only until they have stopped doing whatever it is that you want them to stop. Then you can turn on the charm again.

But don't actually praise them at that point, Dr. Nitschke says. That would be telling them that their hijinks will get your attention—if they wait long enough.

Look away. Dogs are intensely aware of eye contact. In their natural world, a direct look can be either an invitation or a threat. Either way, it conveys strong emotional messages. Dogs who are being pushy or pestering you for attention will always be checking your eyes to gauge your reaction. You can send a message back by pointedly not looking at them, which tells them you don't approve, says Dr. Nitschke.

Ignore them immediately. Dogs don't need a lot of encouragement to continue doing things. Hesitating for a moment when they bark to get your attention or jump on you when you walk through the door gives them a window of interaction that they crave. And so they'll keep doing it.

"Immediately turn around, put your hands in your pockets, and stare at the ceiling," says Dr. Nitschke. Dogs can read body language, and they recognize the cold shoulder when they see it. It's an effective way to show your disapproval and take the fun out of whatever it is they're doing, she explains.

This whippet mix jumps up because she wants some face time with her owner. Turning away and ignoring the behavior takes away the one thing she wants most, forcing her to choose another type of greeting.

35

Be strong. Dogs are like children in that they're very persistent and quick to take advantage of moments of weakness. Ignoring them for 5 seconds—or even 5 minutes—sends a powerful signal, but that doesn't mean they'll quit pushing. In fact, they invariably whine louder or push with their noses a little more. Giving in at this point can set you back for weeks. "What you've done is reward the escalated response," says Dr. Nitschke. "You've just taught your dog to persist."

 **FAST FIX** A quick way to let dogs know that you don't approve of what they're doing is to leave them by themselves, says Dr. Overall. Suppose your dog walks into the kitchen while you're talking with a guest and plops a wet, dirty tennis ball on the clean linoleum—an invitation to play catch. The two of you should stop talking and leave the room. "Your dog will start thinking, 'Gee, I got a lot more interaction when I left the ball outside,'" says Dr. Overall.

Jealousy is clearly an issue for this Maltese, who will keep pestering his owner until he gets some attention. By refusing to acknowledge his entreaties, his owner is showing him that his techniques aren't working and he'll need to try something else.

Stay in the present. No one enjoys coming home after work and discovering that the contents of several garbage cans have been strewn all over the house. This is the type of situation when good intentions—"I will ignore bad behavior; I will not go crazy"—tend to break down. But ignoring the behavior is the only thing you can do. Yelling or punishing dogs for things that happened hours before doesn't work. Your dog simply won't understand what you're mad about. She'll just know you're mad—and she'll get anxious because she won't understand why.

POOCH PUZZLER

Why do small dogs take up so much room on the bed?

People who allow their dogs in the beds are often amazed by the amount of space they take up. Especially when it's 3:00 A.M. and they're freely lounging over a portion of the comforter that's well beyond what their body sizes seem to require. The people in the bed, of course, are invariably curled into compact little balls.

Small dogs do take up more room relative to their size, says Bob Gutierrez, animal-behavior coordinator at the San Francisco Society for the Prevention of Cruelty to Animals. Small dogs give birth to small litters of one or two pups, he explains. Big dogs, on the other hand, have litters of five or six pups. To make room in the den for all their siblings, big dogs learned to sleep tightly curled up. But small dogs get used to having the joint to themselves or sharing it with just one sibling. So they naturally sprawl out and take all the room that's available.

STRANGE behavior

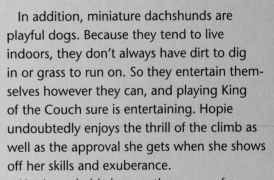

Name HOPIE

Breed MINIATURE DACHSHUND

Age 4

The Behavior

Hopie is into height. The baby of the family, she pretty much has the run of the house. The floor doesn't interest her much—even though, as a dachshund, that's the area she's closest to. What she really likes is to get as high as she can, which usually means climbing on the furniture. She has gotten pretty good at it, and that's fine with her owners. But as soon as they turn their backs, she scampers even higher—onto the backs of sofas and armchairs, for example—and perches. When she's caught and confronted, she gets frightened and pees. No one really minds her escalating habit, but the upholstery is taking a beating from the moisture.

The Solution

Quite a few dogs like perching in high spots. In the wild, dogs get up on rocks or banks so they can see what's going on around them and also to be safe from potential predators, says Betty Fisher, a trainer based in San Diego and co-author of *So Your Dog's Not Lassie*. "A lot of dogs, even much bigger ones, sit on the tops of furniture. It feels like a nice, safe place."

In addition, miniature dachshunds are playful dogs. Because they tend to live indoors, they don't always have dirt to dig in or grass to run on. So they entertain themselves however they can, and playing King of the Couch sure is entertaining. Hopie undoubtedly enjoys the thrill of the climb as well as the approval she gets when she shows off her skills and exuberance.

Hopie probably has another reason for getting up there, as well. Miniature dachshunds are quite small—you could tuck a few of them into a medium-size handbag. Getting on the top of the couch undoubtedly makes her feel taller and more confident. "I'd be willing to bet that Hopie is very sensitive and that she has accidents on the furniture only when she's getting yelled at and is afraid," says Fisher.

Since no one in the family seriously objects to Hopie's excursions, they should probably just relax and let her do it. Hopie doesn't shed a lot, and she's too small to cause much damage. Once she realizes that no one is going to yell at her, she'll quit watering the upholstery, Fisher says.

CHAPTER EIGHT

WHEN TO PRACTICE MANNERS

Education is a lifetime endeavor, which is why it has to be convenient
for people as well as dogs. Good timing is everything. Just try teaching
obedience after lunch—you'll both get failing grades.

There's one thing that explains the success of stock market moguls, stand-up comics, world-renowned watchmakers, and people who have the knack for boiling the perfect egg: They all have good timing.

Timing is equally important when you're teaching your dog to be a good citizen, says Quenten London, a training consultant with the National Institute of Dog Training in Los

Angeles. In fact, knowing when to work with your dog is often as important as knowing what to work on. "You're the one who's right there when problems occur," London says.

On the Clock

From a human point of view, good timing is mainly about convenience. Promising yourself that you'll give your dog lessons every morning isn't very realistic if you have three children to get off to school and you can hardly get to work on time. It doesn't matter if your dog wakes up alert and ready to go unless you're alert and ready to go at the same time. That's why the best time to work with your dog ultimately depends on your schedule.

From a dog's point of view, good timing is simply predictable timing. Dogs love regular schedules, says Norma C. Guy, D.V.M., veterinary behaviorist at the Atlantic Veterinary College in Charlottetown, Prince Edward Island, Canada. Predictability makes their world more understandable and less stressful. And the more

This golden retriever knows to the minute when it's time for her regular walk, and has learned to lie down politely and wait for her owner's signal.

confident and relaxed they feel, the better they're going to learn, she explains.

Follow the clock. Even though dogs have a hazy concept of time, their body clocks are exceptionally accurate—which is why they can predict to the minute when you're getting ready to fill their food bowls. You can take advantage of their internal clocks—and their eagerness preceding regularly scheduled events—by practicing lessons at the same times every day, says Robert L. DeFranco, executive director of the Animal Behavior Center of New York, a non-profit animal education and welfare organization in New York City. By the time you snap on their leashes and step outside, they'll be primed and ready to go, he explains.

Teach briefly and often. Dogs have very short attention spans, which is why long training sessions don't work, DeFranco says. They can stay alert and focused for about 20 minutes—and that's on a good day. Ten minutes is probably closer to the mark. Dogs can't learn a lot in 10 minutes, however, which is why most trainers recommend working with them two or three times a day, for 10 to 20 minutes each time.

When you miss a session, which happens all the time, don't bother making up for it by making the next session longer, DeFranco adds. Your dog will only lose interest—and, in most cases, so will you.

Teach first, feed later. Since food is such a powerful lure, the minutes before meals are

These dogs are learning that they can't start eating until their owner gives the command. The older dogs get full marks for trying, but the puppy in the foreground hasn't quite mastered the lesson.

often the best times to give quick lessons, says Dr. Guy. For example, have your dog sit and lie down a few times before you put his bowl on the floor. Practice a few "stay" and "come" commands. These short lessons can be very efficient. "Most people just dump the food in the bowl and leave, which is unfortunate because mealtime is one of the best times for training," says Dr. Guy.

FAST FIX If school boards had a diabolical urge to reduce test scores by 10 points or so, all they'd have to do is give the exams after a heavy lunch. Dogs wouldn't do any better. A full dog is a lazy dog—one who would really like to stretch out for awhile. Listening to you won't be a high priority right

after eating, says DeFranco. That's why you'll get the best results when you practice lessons before your dog has eaten.

Impromptu Teaching

Schedules are great when you're helping dogs learn the social fundamentals, but they're useless for dealing with breakdowns in behavior that are unanticipated or occur at random times. Suppose, for example, your dog has gotten into the habit of raiding the trash. Sure, you can scold him at 5:50 P.M. when you get home from work. He'll listen respectfully and maybe cock his head. The next day, he'll rummage through the trash again because he didn't have a clue what you were talking about.

Compared to people, dogs have very short attention spans. Punishing them hours after a particular misdeed has no effect because they can't possibly remember what they did. Your window of opportunity to instill good manners is only a few minutes long. "You have to modify the behavior as it's occurring," explains London.

The problem, of course, is that dogs are not stupid. Even though they probably don't plan their day's mischief ahead of time, they do recognize ripe opportunities when they see them. That's why they never tip over the trash can when you're standing in the kitchen with them, but they gleefully empty the contents and drag the can around the house when you're away at work. It's a Catch-22: Scolding them later doesn't work, and you're never around to catch them in the act.

There is a way around this: You have to lead them into temptation at a time when you're

Parks and outdoor areas are full of interesting distractions. This bull terrier mix needs to learn to ignore them and to focus on her owner instead.

going to be home and watching. Suppose your dog is an incorrigible trashmonger. On a day when you've thrown away some particularly redolent scraps, leave the lid off the can and leave the house—but don't go far. Walk around the block, water the flowers, and generally give your dog a little time to get ideas. Then quickly come back in. If you're lucky, you'll find him with his head neck-deep in the can. At that point, you can scold him and put him in a room by himself for a few minutes. He'll know exactly what he did and why you're angry, and that's a powerful combination for helping dogs behave a little better.

No More Distractions

Even dogs who have learned their lessons well— who heel nicely, come when you call, and go to bed when you ask—have moments when they simply can't focus on what you're saying. This usually occurs when they're in a new situation or out in public, where things are noisy and unpredictable—the opposite, in other words, of the environment in which they learned their lessons.

In real life, it's precisely in these unpredictable situations when good manners become so important. It's nice when your dog briskly comes running across the backyard when you call, but it's critical that he do the same when he's off the leash in a park or when his collar suddenly breaks on a busy sidewalk.

You can't anticipate everything that may happen, but you can look for situations that rattle your dog and break his concentration, and then look for ways to help him get used to them. Maybe your dog is skittish about traffic and street noises and gets so distracted or anxious that he ignores or doesn't notice your commands. Rather than avoiding these situations, seek them out, DeFranco says. With a lot of practice and a little bit of food, it's fairly easy to teach your dog to relax and stay focused in situations that used to scare him to death.

Here's how it works. Take your dog outside as you normally do. As soon as he encounters his first earful of noise, give him a small treat, DeFranco suggests. Give it to him right away, before he has a chance to get nervous. Keep looking for distractions—a noisy intersection, a crushing crowd of people, or whatever it is that makes him flighty or anxious—and reward him as soon as they occur.

Once he realizes that all those distracting sights and sounds signal treats, he'll focus less on what's going on around him and more on you—or at least on the good things he hopes you're holding in your hand.

HOT AND BOTHERED

Trainers often hear from owners who complain that their dogs are attentive and focused during their evening lessons, but then turn obstinate and cranky during the day. It's not their imaginations. In the summer, especially, dogs really may learn better in the evening or early in the morning, says Quenten London, a training consultant with the National Institute of Dog Training in Los Angeles. The reason why is not a big mystery. Here's how you can understand the classroom from your dog's point of view.

1. In July, go to the closet and put on the biggest, heaviest fur coat you own.

2. Go outside and practice some energetic heeling and sitting for 10 minutes.

3. Stagger inside, sponge off the sweat, and debate whether to call 911.

With their heavy fur coats and their relatively inefficient internal cooling systems, dogs are much more sensitive to heat than people are, London explains. During the warm months, even a few minutes of exercise or training can just about wear them out. This is why they usually learn best during the cooler times of day.

CHAPTER NINE

WHERE TO PRACTICE MANNERS

Where dogs learn makes a big difference in how well they learn.
Kitchens are nearly perfect, while yards are a little tricky. Choosing the
right place will make training quicker and easier for both of you.

Anyone who has ever bought real estate knows that the three most important things to consider are location, location, and location. Those who are teaching dogs, however, never hear much about location, and that's a mistake.

"It really is something that people need to take into consideration," says Barbara S. Simpson, D.V.M., Ph.D., diplomat for

The kitchen is a great place to train dogs. It has happy associations and tantalizing smells that concentrate their minds wonderfully.

the American College of Veterinary Behaviorists and adjunct assistant professor of veterinary medicine at North Carolina State College of Veterinary Medicine in Raleigh. Dogs are intensely aware of territory—areas where they live or visit often. When they learn new things, they associate those things with the places where they learned them, says Dr. Simpson.

People often discover this for themselves when their dogs return home after spending several weeks with a trainer. The trainer gives a glowing report and explains all the wonderful things the dogs have learned and how nicely they behave. So the owners give a few commands themselves—and their dogs just sit there. It may take a few weeks or even months for them to transfer those lessons to their new locations.

No Place like Home

Dogs do most of their learning at home. There are different rules in every part of the house. You may encourage your dog to sleep in the living room but not in the kitchen. A paw on the knee may be welcomed in the den but not in the dining room. Dogs learn most quickly when their lessons are tailored to and practiced in

different parts of the house, says Gillian Ridgeway, director of training for Who's Walking Who dog obedience center in Toronto. Here's what you can expect from each place.

The kitchen. The kitchen is an ideal spot to begin training, says Ridgeway. Dogs generally have good, cozy feelings about the kitchen, and that makes it a stress-free place to practice. And with the exception of families that include hungry teenagers, it's usually quiet and free from distractions.

"The best time to train a dog is when she's hungry," adds Ihor Basko, D.V.M., a veterinarian with practices in Honolulu and Kilauea, Hawaii. Dogs begin detecting food smells the instant they walk into the kitchen. They're going to be very motivated to learn what you have to teach—and even more motivated to get the reward that follows.

The living room. The living room is sort of an all-purpose training area. It's usually the biggest room in the house, which means there's plenty of room to practice commands such as "heel" and "come." It's also a good place to reinforce lessons learned in other parts of the house as well as to teach specific skills, like staying off the furniture, Ridgeway says.

The backyard. Only dogs who graduate magna cum laude from the indoor portion of their educations should attend graduate school in the yard. Otherwise, forget it. Yards are filled with intriguing smells, leaves to bark at, cats to chase, and a million other distractions. Whatever your dog has learned so far, putting it to work in the backyard is a tough test. It's here that you'll learn whether or not she's ready for the next big step.

POOCH PUZZLER

Why do dogs dig after pit stops?

Unlike cats, who thoroughly bury their waste, dogs usually just go and run. But sometimes, they complete their ablutions by giving the ground a few half-hearted digs. It looks as though they're imitating cats, and not doing a very good job of it.

Some experts believe that this pawing is a way for dogs to spread their personal scents, says Barbara S. Simpson, D.V.M., Ph.D., diplomat for the American College of Veterinary Behaviorists and adjunct assistant professor of veterinary medicine at the North Carolina State College of Veterinary Medicine in Raleigh. They don't actually scratch the waste, just the ground around it. Sebaceous glands between their toes leave an oily scent. Not every dog performs this ritual, Dr. Simpson adds. Dogs who are timid are reluctant to call attention to themselves. Dogs with dominant personalities, however, have a perpetual need to proclaim their superior status. Pawing the ground tells the world they were there.

The Real World

It's nice when dogs behave at home, but that's just the beginning. They also have to learn the ropes in the outside world. There's a lot of noise and confusion out there. They need to learn to listen and obey even when they're on crowded sidewalks or surrounded by traffic. "Dogs are very aware of home versus not home," Dr. Simpson says. "They will act very differently in unfamiliar locations."

Dogs who have made the grade in indoor training can graduate to the outdoors, where the distracting sights, smells, and sounds will really test their mettle.

It's in the real world that your dog will practice the most important skill of all. Veterinarians call this skill generalization. It's the ability to transfer all of her learnings from one environment to another.

Start with tennis lessons. Dogs who leave the familiar comforts of home sometimes feel like tourists in New York City: totally overwhelmed and distracted. They need a safe place to practice their initial out-and-about lessons. Dr. Simpson recommends tennis courts. "They're great places to do training," she says.

"They're out in the open with all the distractions, but they're still in confined areas."

You won't be practicing there long, she adds. Once dogs are past the initial rush of excitement, you can move to other venues to teach the basics. In the meantime, don't forget to pick up after your dog. "It's terrible to play tennis around piles of dog poop," Dr. Simpson says.

Go to a beer store. The next classroom is a lot more challenging than tennis courts because it's public, noisy, and packed with people. It's the parking lot at a beer store on a Saturday afternoon. "You have lots of foot traffic going in and out, but people are usually in a rush or have their hands full, so they don't stop too often to pet your dog," Ridgeway says.

It doesn't matter what lessons you're teaching, she adds. The point of training in a busy environment is that your dog will learn to pay attention to you no matter what else is going on. It's challenging. Any dog can learn "stay" in the living room when there's just the two of you and you're only standing a foot away. In a parking lot, there are tons of distractions, and you'll have room to move farther and farther away. This is an important part of training because it teaches your dog to watch you even when people come between the two of you.

There are limits to what dogs can learn at first in an environment like this, Ridgeway adds. During the first few tries, you'll probably lose your dog's attention as you step away. At that point, move closer or take your dog to a less distracting area. Too often, people don't do that.

"People tend to move farther away and insist that the dog do whatever they're telling her to do," Ridgeway says. "Don't stick to your guns on this." Training, she explains, always involves a few steps forward and an occasional step back. It's normal.

Go for a ride. Part of real-world training should also include riding in the car, says Dr. Basko. There's a pragmatic reason for this. Dogs who don't spend much time in cars tend to get sick on the upholstery. There's also a safety issue. Dogs have to go for rides sometimes, if only to go to the vet. They need to learn to stay in the backseat and not wedge themselves under the brake pedal.

Dr. Basko recommends periodically taking your dog's crate, cardboard box, or whatever she sleeps in and putting it in the backseat of the car. Put a few treats or toys in the crate and invite your dog in. Do it once a day. After awhile, you can forget the crate—your dog will naturally gravitate to the backseat. "Most dogs will learn this in a week, 2 weeks at most," says Dr. Basko.

SAVING FACE

Most people think of their dogs as somewhat short humans—until the dogs do something blatantly doggish, like shoving their noses in someone's privates. Dogs are always going to do embarrassing things, so it's worth having a few responses ready for those inevitable faux pas.

When Your Dog Does This...	Say This
Humps	"Sorry about that. He thought you were a flat tire."
Snacks from the litter box	"Did you know that's considered a breath freshener among dogs?"
Chases his tail	"He's been like that ever since we saw *Twister*."
Rolls in pond scum	"And to think that people pay big bucks for seaweed body wraps when they could have this for free."
Crotch-sniffs	"You could ask him to shake now, but you've already been introduced."
Jumps up	"Care to dance?"
Breaks wind	"He learned that from my husband."

45

PART THREE

MANNERS AT HOME

Human ways must seem mighty strange to dogs. We fill our houses
with furniture, then don't let them on it. We invite people over, but
object when dogs sniff their bottoms. We want them to be friendly,
but get annoyed when they follow us all around the house.
Despite some confusion, dogs can learn the basic manners they
need at home. Manners are necessary—not to spoil their fun,
but to help everyone get along a little better.

CHAPTER TEN

RESPECT FOR POSSESSIONS

Chew toys are dandy, but expensive leather is much more satisfying.
You can't reduce dogs' instinct to chew, but you can help them understand
that some things are always off-limits.

Everyone who lives with dogs has had the experience of discovering a soggy, chewed slipper on the living room floor or has watched with dismay as their dogs attempted to dig to China through the freshly shampooed carpet. Whether you have a puppy or an older dog, a certain amount of property destruction comes with the territory. It's what healthy, well-adjusted dogs sometimes do, says Sarah Wilson, a trainer in Gardiner, New York, and co-author of *Childproofing Your Dog*.

But there's a difference between occasional hijinks and systematic wreckage. Some dogs seem to have a natural tendency to destroy, and once they get started, it can be hard to make them stop. If you're going to preserve your possessions, you need to understand a little bit about how dogs think. Whether they've been chewing for years or are just getting started, you can teach them to show a little more respect—if not all the time, at least most of the time.

Five Types of Destruction

Every dog has different reasons for destroying possessions, but most of the reasons can be grouped into a few main categories, says Kimberly Barry, Ph.D., a certified applied animal behaviorist in Austin, Texas.

"I'm young and my teeth hurt." Puppies go through a teething stage from about 14 weeks to 6 months. Chewing on things helps ease the pain of sore gums, says Dr. Barry.

"I'm young and curious and I don't know any better." Just as children will pick up, poke, and dismantle things, young dogs take things apart with their mouths. In part, this is exploration. They're seeing what tastes good or has an appealing texture. But it's also inexperience. Puppies and young dogs naturally want to chew and don't yet understand that they're supposed to destroy their toys, not yours.

This Lhasa apso pup chews a lot, both out of curiosity and to help soothe the pain of teething. Chew toys will keep her jaws busy.

"It's fun." People often suspect that their dogs are chewing books, shoes, and furniture legs because they're angry or resentful about something. But their motivation is usually a lot simpler. Chewing feels good, and they like doing it, says Dr. Barry.

"I thought it was mine." By the time they're a year old, most dogs understand which objects they're supposed to play with and which they're supposed to leave alone. Unless, that is, no one took the time to teach them the difference. People often give dogs discarded shoes, baseballs, and other family items to play with. But dogs can't distinguish between a tennis shoe that they're allowed to chew and one that's supposed to be off-limits.

"I'm unhappy." The most destructive dogs of all are usually those who spend a lot of time alone and don't have a lot of excitement or stimulation in their lives. A bored dog will look for entertainment, and destroying the couch is certainly entertaining, says Dr. Barry. In addition, dogs need ways to relieve stress and anxiety, and an hour of shredding wallpaper helps them dispel bad feelings.

Giving Up Bad Habits

Chewing is a natural puppy stage, and it's almost impossible to make them stop, if only because their urges to chew can be a lot stronger than your desire to make them stop. Adult dogs who get destructive are harder to handle—not only because they're strong enough to do real damage very quickly but also because they become set in their ways, and habits are hard to change. "The problem with furniture ripping,

BREED SPECIFIC

The retriever breeds often destroy by chewing because they've been bred to work with their mouths. Dachshunds, beagles, and terriers such as Cairn terriers (right) tend to destroy by digging because they were bred to flush rabbits and other small game from their burrows.

linoleum pulling, wallpaper tearing, and chewing is that these activities are self-rewarding," says Wilson. Dogs like having fun, and destroying things, from their point of view, is a heck of a lot of fun. "It's not too hard to teach them not to do it while you're looking on, but most will continue to gleefully do it when they're alone," she says.

If you're willing to spend a little time teaching the basics, every dog can learn to control destructive impulses, Wilson adds. The only way to succeed, however, is to never let it happen. Just as an ex-smoker can't afford to take a single puff, a destructive dog has to go cold turkey. Three weeks of good behavior will be wiped out if he gets one afternoon of guilty pleasures. So you have to be vigilant. The idea is to make it impossible for dogs to indulge their destructive habits, while at the same time making destructive activities a little less pleasurable—and less necessary.

Out with the Bad

Regardless of why dogs chew, the one thing they have in common is that they don't understand that certain things in the house are completely and entirely yours, and that these things are not to be chewed, torn, scratched, or wrestled with. Even when they suspect that they're doing something wrong, they have a hard time linking specific actions, like eating the bedspread, with the displeasure that you show later on. That's why you have to catch them in the act. No one enjoys being on perpetual guard duty, but most dogs will start to get the idea within a few weeks—and the longer they go without destroying anything, the more the habit will start to fade.

Put temptation out of sight. The writer Oscar Wilde once said that he could resist everything except temptation. That's a sentiment that dogs can relate to. Since they aren't going to resist temptation on their own, you have to take temptation away from them. Before you go to bed, put shoes in the closet and close the door. Put stuffed animals out of reach. Keep expensive—and toothsome—valuables on higher shelves. The longer dogs are deprived of destructive opportunities, the less likely they'll be to resume the habit later on.

Keep them under wraps. You can't expect a dog to behave when you're not around, at least at first, Wilson says. You can't watch your dog every minute, but you can tuck him away in a safe place when you're occupied with other things, such as sleeping. Wilson recommends moving his bed into the laundry room or another comfortable place so that he won't get into mischief at night. Put him in the yard when

Dogs with destructive tendencies need to be supervised, but it's inconvenient to hold a leash all the time. This golden retriever has no choice but to stay put when her owner puts her foot on the leash.

you're cleaning the house or running errands. The idea isn't to banish him, but to make it impossible for him to destroy things when you're not around to catch him.

The one problem with this approach is that dogs crave human contact. Leaving them unsupervised and alone for more than about four hours will make them lonely and bored—and more likely to vent these feelings at the first opportunity. You'll have to plan on spending as much time with your dog as possible, Wilson says. Once he starts getting out of the destructive habit, you'll be able to relax a little more.

Use a leash indoors. It doesn't take long for dogs to get into trouble—2 or 3 minutes alone is plenty. "Sometimes, keeping them on leashes can help," says Inger Martens, a trainer and behaviorist in Beverly Hills, California. A quick tug when they start showing interest in something that they shouldn't is a great reminder, especially when a "No!" is thrown in. The leashes also allow you to keep them nearby and out of trouble.

It wouldn't be very comfortable to spend your days holding a leash, so you'll want to get creative, Martens says. When you're relaxing or reading, for example, put your foot on top of the loose end of the leash. Or thread the leash through a belt loop. At least you'll have your hands free while you do other things. And you won't have to do this indefinitely, Martens adds. Most dogs learn more quickly than people think they do, and a few weeks of close supervision is usually enough.

Cut them no slack. Dogs who get away with destructive behavior once are going to keep doing it. A half-hearted "no" or an angry look doesn't have a lot of impact, especially since the joys of destruction may outweigh the threat of a lukewarm reprimand. Take a stand and then follow up on it, Wilson says. When your dog starts chewing, scratching, or digging, immediately tell him "no." Make sure that he understands that you're not happy and aren't going to put up with it. Dogs respect authority and they want to please. When they understand absolutely and without confusion that you're

unhappy, they'll look for activities that you do approve of.

You can help them out by giving them an acceptable alternative, Wilson says. When you scold your dog and he stops what he's doing, quickly give him something else to play with. When he takes it, praise the heck out of him. This will help him make the obvious connection: "When I play with her things, she's unhappy. But when I play with my things, she's happy and gives me a tasty treat. I like this!"

Teach at the moment of destruction. Dogs have pretty hazy memories. Ten minutes after destroying a $100 pair of shoes, they won't even remember doing it. This is why it doesn't do any good to scold them or drag them to look at something after the fact. They may look guilty, but they're really just reacting to your mood—they won't have a clue what's going on,

A good way to stop dogs from chewing is to offer them something better, like a tennis ball.

says Rolan Tripp, D.V.M., a veterinarian in La Mirada, California, and affiliate professor of applied animal behavior at Colorado State University College of Veterinary Medicine and Biomedical Sciences in Fort Collins.

Also, yelling at them after the fact can make them nervous about your arrival, and that's the last thing you want. The only reprimand that works is one that's given right when they're in the act, Dr. Tripp says. If you miss the opportunity, about all you can do is take a deep breath, clean up the mess, and wait for the next time.

FAST FIX Some dogs are very selective about what they chew and will return to the same object again and again. A quick way to discourage them is to give the object a bad taste—by coating it with Grannick's Bitter Apple pet repellent, available in pet supply stores. Bitter Apple comes in a spray designed for plants, a generic spray, and a less acidic furniture cream. Another option is to coat objects with a diluted solution or paste containing alum, an extremely sour additive sometimes used to keep pickles crisp. "It's safe and it has a terrible taste," Wilson says.

In with the Good

Since dogs love to chew—and, in fact, they need to chew—it would be cruel to take away verboten objects without giving them some kind of alternative. Finding toys that dogs like can be a challenge because they generally prefer things that belong to their owners. A pair of shoes is redolent with your personal scent, and that makes dogs feel very satisfied as they

Hollow toys that can be loaded with tasty tidbits, such as Buster Cubes and treat balls, provide dogs with challenging alternatives to destructive behavior.

tear them apart. Socks, neckties, handbags—nothing is safe.

Every dog can be satisfied, however, if you shop around a bit. A lot of dogs adore tennis balls, for example, and will ignore everything else as long as one or two are lying around. Some dogs love stuffed toys, and others will happily work over rawhide bones. One toy that's worth trying is the Buster Cube, says Dr. Barry. This is a hollow toy that you fill with dry food. As your dog noses and bats it around, pieces of food will occasionally fall out, and this will hold almost any dog's interest.

No matter how much a dog loves a toy, however, he can't play with it all the time without getting bored. That's why experts recommend giving them a whole slew of toys—not all at once, but in rotation. Since dogs don't remember much from one day to the next, putting one toy away at night and giving them a "new" one in the morning makes every day seem like Christmas, says Dr. Barry.

The problem with toys, of course, is that they're not indestructible. Dogs have strong jaws and sharp teeth, and they're persistent. You're going to be buying a lot of toys. "When I give my dogs a fuzzy toy, I may as well hand them a $20 bill and let them chew that up," Wilson says. The ideal solution is to find a toy that your dog loves and that is also tough enough to withstand his attentions. Wilson recommends giving dogs chew toys called Nylabones, which are a lot tougher than balls or natural chews such as rawhide. Because they're made of synthetic material, however, Nylabones may not have the same attraction as your shoes. You can make them more tempting just by rubbing them between your hands. This will cover them with your scent. For most dogs, that makes toys worth chewing.

Dogs adore objects that carry their owners' scent, which is why they're so attracted to shoes. Adding your scent to your dog's toys by rubbing your hands on them will make them much more attractive.

CALL FOR HELP

Most dogs chew, dig, and destroy because they enjoy it. For some, however, it's really a cry for help because they can't bear to be alone.

Dogs traditionally lived in packs—tight-knit societies of dogs who slept together, played together, and ate together. Today, dogs consider people to be their packs, but the people are often gone for long periods of time. Some dogs get nearly frantic with loneliness, a condition called separation anxiety, says Kimberly Barry, Ph.D., a certified applied animal behaviorist in Austin, Texas.

Dogs with separation anxiety can be extraordinarily destructive, often destroying thousands of dollars worth of property and possessions. Dogs suffering from this condition aren't going to get better without some professional help, Dr. Barry says. Separation anxiety is easy to recognize, however. The signs include:

- The destruction occurs mainly when you're away from home—or at least, that's when it's most extensive.
- Your dog has hurt his mouth, cut his paws, or otherwise gotten injured while tearing things apart.
- He is most likely to damage objects when he's obviously upset or anxious.

CHAPTER ELEVEN

PROTECTING YOUR SPACE

Dogs always want to be close to their owners, which means they have a tendency to crowd their personal space. They need to learn that everyone has a zone of privacy that doesn't include them.

I f you're ever in the mood to make someone really uncomfortable, stand about 3 feet away—then move closer. We don't consciously think about it, but we have an area of personal space that surrounds us. When people invade this space and come closer, we start feeling a little crowded and claustrophobic.

Dogs have a rule governing social distance, too. For the most part, it can be summarized as, "The closer, the better." This is why people sometimes find themselves competing for bed space with a canine comforter. Or struggling to breathe when a 75-pound retriever climbs in their laps. Or trying to get a moment's peace while a four-footed shadow follows them from room to room.

"Imagine if your spouse, let alone anyone else, came up to you 20 times a day, bumped you, and said, 'Honey, touch me,'" says Sarah Wilson, a trainer in Gardiner, New York, and co-author of *Childproofing Your Dog*. "After about an hour, you'd say, 'Hey, go get a life.'"

Gimme Some Lovin'

To understand why dogs are so clingy, it helps to know their evolutionary history. Dogs are very social animals who have always lived in packs,

Dogs always crave companionship. Even when they can't have their owners' undivided attention, they're happy just to be near them.

which are the equivalent of canine communes. Dogs in packs ate, slept, hunted, and played together. They were happy when they were with each other and lonely when they weren't.

Our dogs don't live in packs anymore, but they have retained their craving for companionship. Most dogs learn to adjust to human styles. They know that people leave for work in the morning, come back in the evening, and everything is fine. They understand that people do things that don't involve them, like washing dishes and reading books. They're more than willing to sleep on the floor, chew a toy, and otherwise entertain themselves until the people in their lives are ready to give them attention.

Then there are dogs who never give up. They act as though a minute of separation were a lifetime. They follow people around, nudge their hands, and generally make pests of themselves in their bids for attention.

"They're constantly checking in for reassurance," says Rolan Tripp, D.V.M., a veterinarian in La Mirada, California, and affiliate professor of applied animal behavior at Colorado State University College of Veterinary Medicine and Biomedical Sciences in Fort Collins.

A Shot of Confidence

Whether dogs are begging for reassurance or are merely fond of attention, clingy behavior gets exhausting after a while. To help dogs be less demanding and more secure, here's what experts recommend.

Reward seldom, but well. Dogs would make perfect salesmen because when one bid for attention doesn't work, they're always ready to trot out another one, knowing that their owners will eventually give in.

"When you reach out and pet your dog every time he approaches, he's going to think, 'Aha, she obeys my every command,'" Wilson says. The only way to stop the pester-and-reward pattern is not to give in. Ignore the hand nudges and leg leans. Wait for your dog to do something that really deserves praise, such as going upstairs when you tell him to. Then give him plenty of attention and make him feel good, Wilson advises.

Reward mindfully. A character in the "Peanuts" comic strip once said, "Happiness is a warm puppy." We tend to give our dogs a lot of attention even when we aren't thinking about it—by rubbing their ears as we read or absentmindedly petting them when they lean against us. This affectionate give-and-take is the reason that dogs and people love each other. But for

BREED SPECIFIC

Nearly every dog will occasionally crowd his owner, but dogs who were bred to work closely with people, such as retrievers, are known for making it their life's work. Dogs such as Akitas and Rottweilers, on the other hand, were bred to work on their own, and they tend to maintain more personal space.

"For many golden retrievers, personal space is about 3 inches," says Sarah Wilson, a trainer in Gardiner, New York, and co-author of *Childproofing Your Dog*. "For salukis [left], it can be as much as 8 feet."

dogs who are already clingy, it nearly makes them desperate to push farther into your space, says Wilson.

Dogs are pretty smart about what works and what doesn't. If you make a conscious effort to only give strokes occasionally and to ignore your dog the rest of the time, he will realize that his crowding behavior isn't paying off and will start to back off, probably within a few days, says Kimberly Barry, Ph.D., a certified applied animal behaviorist in Austin, Texas. In the meantime, get ready for an increase in attention seeking, she adds. Dogs who are used to endless attention won't give it up right away. In fact, they may be more nervous and in-

This corgi is learning that a little distance from his owners isn't a disaster as long as he can see them. When he's calm, he won't need the leash anymore.

secure until they get used to the change and realize that everything is still fine.

Drop your voice. Researchers have found that people customarily raise their voices when they talk to dogs, just as they use higher voices when talking with children. There's nothing wrong with this except when you're trying to discourage certain types of behavior. Dogs don't understand many words, but they do understand tone. You may be saying, "Silly dog, don't climb on me," but if your voice is cheerful and high, what your dog hears is "C'mon up!" explains Suzanne Hetts, Ph.D., a certified applied animal behaviorist in Littleton, Colorado.

Dogs are very responsive to low-pitched voices, probably because "top dogs" who are annoyed will respond with low growls or warning grumbles. When you want your dog to give you some space, tell him so in a tone that he will respond to—low and gruff. Use his name first to get his attention, then say "off" or "down," Dr. Hetts advises.

Keep them close—but not too close. Dogs always keep a close eye on their people, but for some dogs, just watching isn't enough. They stand up when their people stand up. They follow them from one room to another. They even push their way into the bathroom. The reason they act this way is that they can't bear to be alone for even a moment. You can help them be more confident by teaching them that the world doesn't end just because you're out of sight, says Dr. Tripp.

• Put your dog on a leash and tie the leash to something across the room from where you'll be sitting. He won't be able to

POOCH PUZZLER

Why do dogs lick faces?

When two dogs meet, after they've gone through the sniffing preliminaries and are getting to be friends, one dog will invariably lick the other dog's face. They do the same thing with people—not just when they meet, but as a way of saying hi.

There's a reason for all this oral affection. In the days when dogs roamed wild, lower-ranking dogs in the pack would periodically lick the lead dog, says Kimberly Barry, Ph.D., a certified applied animal behaviorist in Austin, Texas. It was their way of conveying respect and affection.

A sloppy kiss isn't only about affection, however. Puppies quickly learn that they can get extra nourishment by licking their mother's face. Not only does this make her feel happy and more disposed to extend the dinner hour, but the puppies may get lucky enough to catch a stray bit of food from her last meal.

length of time that you're gone. You want to stay gone long enough that your dog notices, but not so long that he gets frantic.

- Dogs who are insecure don't get nervous only when their owners walk out the door or leave the room. They start getting anxious when they first detect the clues that a departure is imminent. As a final stage in the process, Dr. Tripp recommends helping your dog get used to all the signs and sounds that precede your departures. Pick up your keys, rattle them, and then put them down, he suggests. Do this periodically while you read a magazine or watch TV. Open and close the garage door a few times.

Rattling keys, opening and shutting doors, and other departure sounds don't faze this German shepherd. He has learned to stay calm when his owners are getting ready to leave.

come over and nudge you, but you'll still be in sight and close enough for him to stay calm. Do this several times a day until he starts to get used to the distance.

- Wait until your dog is relaxed and comfortable. Then get up and leave the room for a few seconds. He may look as though he's watching the Titanic depart, but he'll calm down quickly once you come back in and sit down again. Do this several times, keeping your absences very brief, Dr. Tripp advises. Over a period of days and weeks, gradually increase the

Dogs who take up a lot of space on the couch aren't just trying to get comfortable. They may be making a bid for "top dog" status in the household.

Your Space or Mine

Most dogs intrude on people's space because they're lonely or in need of reassurance. Some do it for the opposite reason: to put you off-balance. Dogs are very physical by nature, and they use physical contact not only to express affection but also to establish chains of command. A dog who shoves, hip slams, or leans against other dogs—or people—is establishing a position of authority. A dog who shoves past your legs when you open the door or who takes up increasing amounts of space on the couch by leaning against you is essentially saying that he's taking over, Wilson says.

Dogs give a similar message when they defend their food bowls or grumble when someone tries to move them off the couch. They're taking it upon themselves to claim their space and whatever (and whoever) happens to be in it. This type of attitude invariably gets more pronounced over time, which is why trainers recommend stopping it quickly.

"Your dog should know that everything in his world is yours, but that you are nice enough to share," Wilson says.

Give your dog a job. In the world of dogs, every dog occupies a certain place on the social ladder—top dogs, bottom dogs, and dogs in

Put on your jacket and take it off. The idea is to do all of these things so often that your dog begins to learn that these and other "leaving signals" don't mean much of anything. Then, when you really are leaving, he'll be less likely to work himself into a lather beforehand—and he'll be less likely to latch on to you when you're home as well.

• As long as your dog is sitting or lying quietly, walk over periodically and give him a reward—something to eat or just some attention, Dr. Tripp says. The idea is to reward him for not being nervous. What you don't want to do is reassure him when he's acting nervous. Giving dogs attention when they're frightened reinforces the emotion and will make them even more nervous, he explains.

If you keep doing this for a few weeks, your dog will come to understand that he actually does pretty well when you're not around—and, more important, that you'll always come back.

between. The same thing occurs in human families. Problems occur when dogs think that they're higher on that ladder than you. The best way to turn their thinking around is to make them understand that nothing in life is free and that all good things come from you. No matter what they want—their supper, a walk outside, or the biscuit you're holding in your hand—they should expect to work for it, says Dr. Tripp.

Have your dog sit before you put down his food. Require him to lie down before you open the door. Don't give him attention when he comes to you—he should wait until you offer it. The idea isn't to be a tyrant, but to make sure that your dog understands who is calling the shots. Once he understands that, he'll be much less likely to make demanding incursions on your personal space, says Dr. Tripp.

Mean what you say. It's human nature to be circumspect, out of politeness, if nothing else. But when dogs are pushing into your space, it's time to take a stand. Make a few basic rules and then follow through—not occasionally, but all the time. Suppose you've decided to keep your dog off the couch. Well, keep him off. Cut him no slack. No matter how cute he looks when he's sneaking up, tell him "off." Make sure that everyone else in the family does the same. For dogs no less than people, firm convictions and the willingness to follow through create respect, and even dominant dogs don't crowd the people they respect.

Show him the floor. Another way to protect personal space is to insist that dogs sleep on the floor and not on the bed. Some dogs view beds and other furniture as being status symbols as much as creature comforts.

"If your dog is making moves on your space, you don't want to confuse him by making him an equal at night," Wilson says.

FAST FIX Probably the easiest way to reclaim your personal space is to make your dog's spot of choice—on the couch, for example—unusable, says Dr. Tripp. Put a footstool where he sits. Cover that side of the couch with an uncomfortable sheet of plastic. Or keep a pile of books there. Once your dog loses access to his throne, he'll be less likely to lord it over you in other ways, he explains.

This kelpie-Labrador mix is learning that he must sit quietly and not push his way past his owner when she opens the door.

CHAPTER TWELVE

GREETING VISITORS

Dogs have their own ways of saying hi to each other. But their customary greetings to people need a little work. Most folks take a dim view of four-legged cannonballs with inquisitive noses.

Imagine a world in which dogs were the ones wearing suits, living in houses, and having dinner parties to meet the neighbors. Visitors arriving for a Sunday soirée wouldn't be greeted with handshakes or hugs. They'd get jumped on. They'd feel cold noses pressing into private places. They and their hosts would turn in circles and sniff each other's tails.

It's not our way of greeting visitors, but dogs have been doing it forever, and it works just fine. "All the usual greeting problems that people encounter are perfectly normal ways that dogs greet other dogs," says Brian Kilcommons, a trainer and behavioral expert in Gardiner, New York, and co-author of *Good Owners, Great Dogs*.

Dogs are a lot more physical than people. Puppies greet their mothers by jumping up and licking their faces. It's a gesture

This Lhasa apso jumps up to get closer to her owner's face. Jumping up is natural dog behavior, but unless they're discouraged from doing it at a young age, it can quickly get out of hand.

that means, "I'm glad you're my mom, and I'll always do what you say." Adult dogs also greet each other face-to-face, followed by a face-to-rear follow-up. It's their way of introducing themselves and determining who has the stronger, more dominant personality.

What works among dogs, however, is uncomfortable, impertinent, or rude when people enter the picture. No one looks forward to being on the receiving end of a probing nose or watching in dismay as their dogs leave muddy paw prints on their visitors' pants and jackets.

Jumping Up

It's cute when a puppy who weighs just a few pounds and barely reaches your ankle jumps up on her hind legs and reaches up with her paws. But that cute little puppy grows fast—some dogs put on 100 pounds in 6 months—and her cute little jumping won't be charming for long.

Dogs have a natural tendency to go airborne, says Wayne Hunthausen, D.V.M., a veterinarian in Westwood, Kansas, and co-author of *Handbook of Behavior Problems in Cats and Dogs.* For one thing, it's their way of greeting other dogs. More important, we inadvertently teach our dogs to do it, either by ignoring or encouraging it when they're young or by merely sighing and standing back when they do it later on.

"If you have people coming in and saying, 'Oh, it's okay, I don't mind it when your dog jumps up,' she's going to think it's fine to keep doing it—and she's going to jump on the next poor soul who shows up at your door," says Kilcommons. Dogs aren't always quick learners, he explains, and it's difficult for them to understand that while it may be acceptable to jump on one person, it's wrong to do it to someone else.

It's easy to teach puppies not to jump, but older dogs take more work because jumping is a habit and jumping is fun. "For some dogs, jumping up is more fun than eating," Dr. Hunthausen says.

Teach him with bribes. "Try walking in the door with a piece of food at nose-level," says Dr. Hunthausen. "Use a favorite food that smells great, and tell your dog to sit." You have to move quickly because you don't want your dog to have time to make her usual moves. As long as she sits and doesn't jump—and if she truly likes the food you're holding, she's going to do what you say—give her the snack. Then turn around and walk out the door. Come right back in and do the whole thing again.

Dogs are very good at linking actions with rewards, especially when the reward is food, Dr. Hunthausen explains. It won't be long before

Doggy Maître D'

At the Lake Sonoma Winery in Geyserville, California, the breads, cheeses, and wines are perfectly matched; there's a stunning view of the valley; and the service is tail-wagging friendly. Thunder, a 7-year-old Labrador–Great Dane mix, comes to the office every day with his owner, winery operations manager George Christie. Thunder meets arriving visitors at their cars and escorts them to their tables. Should someone drop a napkin or a purse, Thunder is right there, ready to pick it up and return it.

After 3 years of greeting up to 200 guests each day, Thunder has a lot of fans, Christie says. "People come back looking for Thunder, and they send us notes about him."

Thunder's manners are impeccable, but they aren't perfect, Christie adds. At 125 pounds, Thunder is very fond of food and has been known to cast a covetous eye at the guests' dinner plates. It's not that Thunder begs, Christie says. It's just that everyone enjoys feeding him.

your dog thinks to herself, "She walks in the door, I sit down, she gives me food. Cool!"

Admire the ceiling. "When your dog jumps on you, ignore it. Cross your arms and look at the ceiling," says Sarah Wilson, a trainer in Gardiner, New York, and co-author of *Childproofing Your Dog.* A jump is a dog's way of asking for attention, she explains. When she doesn't get what she's asking for, she'll start looking for something that works better.

Reward downward mobility. Physical techniques like giving your jumping dog a knee in the chest will certainly get his attention, but they're not as effective as other, gentler methods. Rather than criticizing bad behavior, trainers

Teaching "Off"

Every dog who aspires to social fitness needs to understand the word "off." This simple command can be used to keep dogs off doors, couches, and counters as well as off guests. It's an easy command to teach, and it works a lot better than opening the door and silently praying that your dog will stay down for a change.

Here are two ways to teach it.

1 When you're expecting company, put a leash on your dog and let it dangle behind her. When guests arrive and she jumps up to greet them, step on the leash. She won't achieve the height she's looking for, and her forward momentum will pull on her collar. In essence, she'll be correcting herself. When she quits jumping, praise her for being so smart and obedient.

2 Put a leash on your dog and hold the free end. When she jumps up to greet guests, firmly tell her, "Off!" and snap the leash to one side. A dog who is jumping is on two legs, which means her balance is off. Pulling the leash sideways will force your dog to put her feet back on the ground. Once she's down and relaxed, if only briefly, praise her for being so good.

say, it's more effective to reward good behavior. So ignore the jumping and praise your dog lavishly when she's sitting calmly or otherwise staying earthbound, Wilson says.

Of course, some dogs jump so often that it's hard to find an opportunity to praise them. The only way they're going to earn your praise is if you help them disrupt their usual habit. Carry a whistle and give a shrill blast as soon as your dog's front feet start to leave the ground, recommends Dr. Hunthausen. The noise will startle her, and she'll pause to think things over. That's precisely when you want to pet and praise her, he explains.

FAST FIX The next time you're expecting company, arm yourself beforehand with a spray bottle filled with a vinegar-and-water solution, mixed half-and-

Dogs who have been spritzed once or twice with a vinegar-water solution while jumping up tend to remember. Just showing them the bottle will remind them to keep their feet on the ground the next time company is over.

half. When your dog goes up for her usual greeting, spritz the solution in her mouth, says Julia Jones, an instructor and Northwest region program manager with Canine Companions for Independence in Santa Rosa, California. The solution is harmless, but it tastes yucky. "When your dog sits down to think about what just happened, praise and pet her," she says.

Rude Sniffing

It looks (and feels) strange to us, but there's a perfectly good reason that dogs stick their noses between people's legs or into their bottoms: communication. Unlike people, who depend mainly on senses such as speech and sight, dogs use smells to talk to each other. Their sense of smell is about 100 times more sensitive than ours, which means that they collect information that we don't even know exists. And private places, both in people and other dogs, are rich repositories of informative scents.

It's difficult to teach dogs not to sniff people—it's just what they do. What you can do, however, is make other, less invasive types of greetings even more interesting and rewarding for them. When people come over, for example, immediately tell your dog to sit and give her something to eat, says Dr. Hunthausen. "You want her to learn that sitting gets a better payoff than a nose full of a stranger's aroma."

As a last resort, you may want to try a more aggressive tactic. Some trainers recommend keeping an air horn (the kind used on a boat) near the front door. Encourage

guests to give a blast when your dog starts her routine. Dogs are accustomed to people putting up with their sniffing, so they always act surprised when someone responds negatively, says Judith Halliburton, a trainer and behaviorist in Albuquerque, New Mexico, and author of *Raising Rover.* Their usual reaction is likely to be, "Whoa, I've never had that happen before," and then they'll walk away. If they get the same reaction every time they try their sniff-and-greet routine, they'll start looking for other ways to introduce themselves, she explains.

I Pee Because I Love You

It's hard for people to relate to, but many dogs will urinate as a way of saying hi. In their world, a little splash of urine is the ultimate form of respect, a gesture that means they respect your authority, Kilcommons explains. That's why it doesn't help to scold them for doing it. They've just made a profound expression of submission, and they'll be crushed if you're unhappy and reject them. In fact, they will feel more submissive than before—and may urinate a little more.

"The more excited your dog gets, the less attention you should give her," Kilcommons says. Keeping greetings calm and low-key helps dogs stay calmer, and they're less likely to urinate when they're relaxed and secure. "When guests come over, ask them to not focus on your dog or lean over to touch her," he adds.

It's also possible to teach dogs to use drier greetings when people come in the door, Kilcommons says. Put a box of treats by the front door. When people come over—or when you come home yourself—take a treat and im-

mediately toss it on the floor before your dog has a chance to urinate. Then, walk on past and let your dog concentrate on finding and devouring the snack. "If your dog does the drill enough times, she'll learn to look for the treat rather than put on a show for your visitor," explains Kilcommons.

A Little Help from Your Friends

One reason that greeting problems are so hard to stop is that they occur at precisely those times when you don't want to think about training. It's hard to give your guests your full attention, for example, when you're opening the door with one hand and wrestling with your dog with the other.

Trainers agree that the only way your dog will quit jumping on, sniffing, or otherwise annoying visitors is if you stop her the minute she does it—and that may require keeping your guests waiting at the door for a minute or two. No matter how embarrassing it feels, it's probably not as bad as you think. After all, there are millions of dogs in this country. There's a very good chance that the people you're welcoming have dogs of their own. They'll understand exactly what you're trying to do.

One way to help people understand what you're trying to accomplish is to put a small sign on the front door, something like "Puppy training in progress. Please be prepared for anything!" Visitors will know beforehand what you're up to, and you won't feel as though you have to pretend that everything is fine when, for example, you open the door with one hand and haul back on your dog with the other.

STRANGE behavior

Name MAGGIE

Breed LABRADOR RETRIEVER

Age 8

The Behavior

Maggie is an old dowager of a dog with affection and good humor to spare. But she has an unfortunate habit. When people sit down, Maggie stealthily tries to slip all of her 78 pounds into their laps. And because Maggie loves everyone, no one escapes—not the visiting members of the Republican committee, deacons of the church, or her owner's 80-year-old mother-in-law, who barely weighs as much as Maggie. Her owner doesn't want to put her in a crate, but she doesn't know how else to control Maggie's relentless lap patrol.

The Solution

Maybe no one is admitting it, but someone is making Maggie feel really good about sitting on laps, says Brian Kilcommons, a trainer and behavioral expert in Gardiner, New York, and co-author of *Good Owners, Great Dogs*. Dogs love to be loved, and somewhere along the line, Maggie learned that laps are a great place to get all the love, hugs, and kisses that she ever wanted.

Guests are in a difficult situation when their host's dog insinuates her way into their laps, he adds. No one wants to be rude and take the chance of insulting the host. Even people who aren't very fond of dogs probably feel compelled to give her at least a little attention—and that's all the encouragement Maggie needs. It also seems likely that Maggie is a crowd-pleasing type who thrives on the cries of "Oh, Maggie" that her stunt provokes.

There are two things that Maggie's owner will have to do to teach her that lap scaling is not an acceptable sport. First, the family should hold a meeting in which each member swears to uphold the group's decision to not encourage Maggie—thus discouraging the one person (or more) who is secretly encouraging her and undermining the efforts of the rest.

Second, everyone has to vow to be vigilant in the presence of guests and quickly slip Maggie a little something as soon as she makes her move. "When she goes to sit in someone's lap, they should have her sit or lie down," says Kilcommons. "Then reward her for it. Give her a treat. Tell her what a good girl she is, and cheer and laugh while she's on the floor—instead of when she's sitting where she's not welcome."

CHAPTER THIRTEEN

GREETING THE MAILMAN

Mailmen spend a lot of their careers braving barking dogs. It shouldn't be part of their job, but it's an unfortunate reality. Dogs, on the other hand, see *their* job as protecting their territory. Reconciling these conflicting agendas can be a challenge.

For Molly, a 10-year-old Labrador retriever in Philadelphia, it's the best time of day. At 11:15 every morning, the hair on the back of her neck rises, her ears prick up and rotate forward, her tail starts swishing, and she lets loose with a cacophony of barks loud enough to be heard three doors down.

It's the mailman, same as yesterday. All he has in mind is dropping a few letters through the slot, but Molly sees things differently: He's a trespasser who, if he knows what's good for him, will get off her porch. Which he does, of course. At which point, Molly, feeling excited but self-assured, settles down for a rest. It's a stressful moment in her day—and in the mailman's—but tomorrow they'll do it all again.

Who Can Argue with Success?

Nearly every dog gets worked up when the mailman comes to the door. Partly, it's just excitement. "They think, 'There's someone out there, and I want to go, too,'" says Wayne Hunthausen, D.V.M., a veterinarian in Westwood, Kansas, and co-author of *Handbook of Behavior Problems in Cats and Dogs.*

More important, dogs want to protect their territory. They don't understand that strangers come into people's lives every day. They've been bred for thousands of years to be protective and loyal to their owners. In their minds, anyone who hasn't been personally introduced is a potential threat, and they're not about to sit back without kicking up a fuss.

Doberman pinschers have been bred as guard dogs, so they're more likely to bark at strangers than other breeds. They can learn to be quiet, but they rarely relax entirely.

Even though the arrival of the mailman is a daily event, dogs bark and carry on as though every visit is the first one. The reason for this, says Dr. Hunthausen, is that they're always successful. The mailman approaches, they bark, and he leaves—and dogs congratulate themselves for doing such a good job. And with every repetition, they get even more deeply rooted in their habits.

"If dogs were human, they'd all be in therapy because they'd be compulsive hand washers or chain-smokers," says Judith Halliburton, a trainer and behaviorist in Albuquerque, New Mexico, and author of *Raising Rover*. "Dogs are absolutely habit-driven, and the more they replay a reaction, the more ingrained it becomes."

If you don't have neighbors nearby, and if your mailman isn't the nervous type and the front door is more or less indestructible, this routine may not be a problem. But the furious barking, if it's loud enough and lasts long enough, can drive almost anyone crazy. Especially because it happens every single day—except, of course, on Sunday.

Restoring Quiet

It's never easy to teach dogs to greet mailmen graciously. For one thing, a lot of people work, so they aren't there to shush their dogs up. In addition, dogs have been barking at intruders for thousands of years, and they're unlikely to just give it up.

"Dogs with long-held habits need some kind of correction or distraction to get them off automatic pilot," says Dr. Hunthausen. "You have to do something to disrupt their pattern."

BREED SPECIFIC

Nearly all dogs bark when they hear someone approaching the house, but Doberman pinschers, German shepherds, and Rottweilers are among the loudest and most persistent because they've been bred to guard and protect their people.

• Pet supply stores and catalogs sell a product called the Super Barker Breaker. It's a relatively simple device with a sensor and an amplifier. When dogs bark, the machine barks back, loudly and at a high pitch that dogs dislike.

• Veterinarians sometimes recommend fitting dogs with special collars that emit bursts of citronella mist when they bark. Citronella is a natural substance that has a citrusy scent. Dogs dislike the smell, and the *pssst* sound of the mist distracts them from barking. Eventually, they figure out that it's their barking that causes that awful smell and noise, says Dr. Hunthausen.

• If you decide to get really serious, you may want to invest in a Scraminal detector. A hand-size motion detector available in pet supply stores, it makes a high-pitched beep when dogs get too close to windows or doors, which means they can't see the mailman arrive or leave.

• The lowest-tech strategy—and in some ways one of the most effective—is to drop a few pennies in an empty soda can and tape the opening closed. When your dog starts barking at the mailman, toss the can in his general direction while telling him, "Quiet!" says Dr. Hunthausen. At the very least, the clattering sound

will make him stop barking momentarily. If you do it often enough, your dog will perhaps be less likely to start barking in the first place.

Silence Ahead

Since dogs are creatures of habit, it's a lot easier to work with them before they discover how much fun it is to bark. "Prevention is the key to getting them to not go ballistic when they see the mailman," says Dr. Hunthausen. Here are a few ways to ensure that your mailman always gets a first-class reception.

Block the view. Many mailmen are just as quiet as dogs are noisy, which means the only way your dog knows the mail is coming may be when he sees the mailman coming up the walk. Pulling the blinds when you leave for work—or rearranging bookcases or other pieces of furniture so it's harder for your dog to see out windows—may be enough to keep him from getting started, says Dr. Hunthausen.

Increase their confidence. Dogs have a natural urge to protect their property, but they're also social animals who welcome friends. You can teach them to think of the mailman as a friend, says Dr. Hunthausen. He recommends staying home with your dog for a couple of days. "The minute your dog spies the mailman, tell him to sit and give him a reward," he says. Most dogs are more interested in eating food than in barking at the mailman. Once they get in the habit of sitting quietly—and eating—when someone approaches the door, they'll be more likely to be blasé about the arrival of unexpected visitors even when they're alone, Dr. Hunthausen explains.

Dogs can't eat and bark at the same time, as this German shepherd can attest. If you're home when the mailman arrives, give your dog a treat to keep his mind off the "intruder."

Keeping the Edge

One reason that mailmen have such a hard time of it is that many people are reluctant to curtail their dogs' protective urges. This shouldn't be an issue, Halliburton says. Dogs can be great watchdogs even when they know enough to be silent when the mail arrives.

"Dogs usually know the difference between a regular visitor and a threatening one," she explains. "You don't need your dog to defend your house against the mailman and the paperboy. Correcting him when he does that will make him more discriminating, but it won't diminish his instinct to protect."

CHAPTER FOURTEEN

MEALTIME MANNERS

Eating is one of life's great pleasures, and dogs make the most of it. But sometimes, their appetites lead them to unauthorized dining, such as stealing or mooching. That's when it's time to tame their appetites and teach them some etiquette.

Sometimes fate throws a dog a tempting morsel that can't be resisted. Take chicken breasts topped with ham and Swiss cheese, lined up neatly on the kitchen counter, with no sentry in sight. It was too much for Francine, a portly yellow Labrador, who managed to scarf down three of the four uncooked cordon bleus while her owner, John Murphy of Fort Worth, Texas, was busy answering the phone. Francine then walked to the back door, raced a few times around the yard, and vomited.

So much for social graces. In no more than 15 minutes, she committed the sins of grand theft poultry, gluttony, and unsightly purging. Worst of all, she wouldn't think twice about doing the same thing again if she got the chance.

Dogs and people have entirely different notions of etiquette, especially at mealtimes. People view eating as a social affair, and consideration for others is a high priority. But among dogs, getting as much as possible is on page one of the dining guide. They think that it's perfectly reasonable to be shameless beggars who steal food off the table, eat way more than their share, and spill a lot on the floor in the process,

says Judith Halliburton, a trainer and behaviorist in Albuquerque, New Mexico, and author of *Raising Rover*.

More Than a Meal

Your dog's manners, or lack of them, made sense in the evolutionary scheme of things. Dogs were hunters and scavengers who depended on their strength and resourcefulness to stay well-fed. Their first rule was, "If you can get it, it's yours." The second rule was, "Eat up because you may not get more anytime soon."

BREED SPECIFIC

Labradors aren't any more likely to raid the trash than other breeds, but they often get blamed anyway because they look as though they're guilty. Along with dachshunds, basset hounds (left), and beagles, Labradors have slow metabolisms that make them gain weight even when they haven't been foraging.

Nutrition aside, dogs make several assumptions about food that people don't share.

Food is scarce. Even though dogs today don't have to worry about where their next meal is coming from, they share the attitudes of their feral ancestors and cousins, who typically ate only once every two to three days. Naturally, they stuffed themselves silly whenever they had the chance.

Food is power. Dogs used to live in highly organized groups called packs. Within a pack, every dog had a social rank and knew who was above her and who was below her in status and power, says Nicholas Dodman, professor of behavioral pharmacology and director of the Animal Behavior Clinic at Tufts University School of Veterinary Medicine in North Grafton, Massachusetts, and author of *Dogs Behaving Badly.* When the pack made a kill, the dogs ate in order of rank. Your dog may not seem to care or even be aware of her place in the family, but on some level, power is very much on her mind.

Dogs have only been domesticated for about 10,000 years or so. Eventually, they may lose some of their old attitudes and start thinking about food more in the way that people do. But in the meantime, dogs will be dogs, and good manners are not going to come naturally. They have to be taught, coerced, or tricked to eat like civilized members of the family. How you approach the problem depends on your dog's personality and what, exactly, she's doing wrong.

Begging

In their perpetual quest for food, many dogs become accomplished beggars, and few people can enjoy a meal under their soulful, apparently starving gazes. No matter that your dog is 10 pounds overweight and ate an hour ago—she has your number. She knows that when she cocks her head, lowers her nose, raises her eyes—or whatever her usual tricks are—you're going to give in to guilt and fork something over.

Begging is a common mealtime faux pas, and it's one of the easiest to correct. Dogs tend to do things that work. When they've begged at the table and been rewarded, they're going to keep doing it, says Julia Jones, a service-dog instructor and Northwest region program manager for Canine Companions for Independence in Santa Rosa, California. On the other hand, when they realize that their old tricks don't work, they gradually give them up. Here's a three-part strategy that experts recommend.

1. "Only feed your dog out of her own dish," Jones says. Dogs go where the food is.

Dogs get emotional about food because it symbolizes power and status. This 5-year-old vizsla is getting ready to assert his authority by moving in.

If they're used to taking food out of your hand at the table, that's where they're going to go, she explains.

Some foods are meant to be given by hand, of course. It's fine to give your dog biscuits and other finger foods. But don't hand them over when you're in the kitchen or anywhere else where begging has been a problem, Jones says.

2. Only give them dog food. There's nothing unhealthy about giving dogs small amounts of human food, and any sensible dog prefers a juicy scrap of steak to a bowlful of dry kibble. Once your dog gets a taste for the good stuff off your plate, she'll be very reluctant to walk away empty-handed.

3. Don't give in to guilt, and don't hesitate to walk away. "You have to ignore the stares," says Halliburton. "As long as you pay attention to her when she's begging, she's going to hold out hope that you'll give in. But once there's no acknowledgment that she is even there, she'll know that she's just wasting her time."

Thieving

Some do it in plain sight. Others wait until their owners are out of the room or asleep. Then they make their moves. A ham-and-cheese sandwich on the counter disappears. The trash is tipped over and thoroughly sifted. A child is distracted for a moment—and her ice cream cone is gone.

If dogs sat on juries in criminal courts, charges of food stealing would never get a conviction because every dog steals food on occasion and some do it all the time. It all goes back to their days in the wild, when sneaky dogs tended to be long-lived dogs.

CALL FOR HELP

It's not unheard of for dogs to break into their food bags and gobble 5 to 10 pounds of food in just a few minutes. Or they will raid the counter and devour an entire ham. Beyond the obvious problem of thoroughly bad manners, this type of eating can trigger bloat, a life-threatening condition in which the stomach fills with gas, often within an hour.

Dogs with bloat will have an obviously swollen abdomen that is as taut as a balloon. They'll also be uncomfortable and may pace, breathe heavily, or try without success to vomit. Most common in large, deep-chested dogs such as German shepherds, Great Danes, and Doberman pinschers, bloat is always an emergency, and you'll need to get your dog to a veterinarian right away, says Wayne Hunthausen, D.V.M., a veterinarian in Westwood, Kansas, and co-author of *Handbook of Behavior Problems in Cats and Dogs.*

Training books invariably recommend "correcting" dogs when you catch them in acts of thievery. It's true that dogs want to please their owners, and a few disapproving "no's" may convince them to be more upstanding canine citizens. But food is a very powerful reward, whether it's given freely or pilfered, Halliburton says. "Lots of times, you can teach dogs not to steal food when you're standing there, but they'll go back to it when you turn your back."

Rather than depending on formal training to stop food stealing, many trainers prefer to use sneakier approaches. The idea isn't necessarily to convince dogs to do the right thing, but to make the act of stealing less rewarding.

Make the counters uncomfortable. When asked why he robbed banks, the notorious criminal Willie Sutton explained that that's where the money is. Dogs recognize this logic. They grab food from counters because that's where food usually is.

Since you can't guard the counters and their contents all the time, trainers have devised some ingenious ways to discourage unauthorized forays. Halliburton recommends buying a roll of two-sided carpet tape and putting a strip all along the edge of the counters. Then put some bait—a fresh piece of bread, for example—a few inches behind the tape. Carpet tape is tremendously sticky. When your dog jumps up and reaches for the bait, the tape will grab her probing paws and maybe pull out a few hairs. Dogs hate sticky sensations, Halliburton explains. If you do this for a few weeks, your dog may come to loathe the whole idea of counters and stay away entirely.

Bait the trash. From a dog's point of view, a trash can is like an all-night diner. It's always open, it's easy to get to, and it's full of wonderful rotten odors. Short of stashing the trash behind closed doors or buying an expensive can with a tight-fitting lid, the easiest way to keep dogs out of the trash is to make it an upsetting place to visit. Pet supply stores sell spring-loaded, mousetrap-like devices with large paddles that make a loud pop when they're jiggled. You can put them on top of the can or inside, on top of the trash.

"When your dog gets into the trash, the trap is going to pop, and she'll think the trash did it," Halliburton explains. "She'll think twice before she does it again, though it will probably take a few lessons."

Rattle their nerves. Dogs dislike loud, clattery noises. You can take advantage of this aversion to keep them off counters or away from the trash can. Jones recommends threading a string through the center of a hot dog and tying several empty soda cans to the other end. When your dog takes the wiener and runs, the resulting clatter will startle the heck out of her. Putting a few coins in the cans will make the clattering even worse. "This works especially well with dogs who are wise to the idea that they can get away with stuff when they're alone," says Jones.

Scraps of food sprinkled with hot-pepper sauce and dropped into the trash can will put a stop to dogs' trash-raiding tendencies.

FAST FIX A quick way to take the fun out of stealing is to season a few scraps of food with hot-pepper sauce or ground red pepper. You can put the food on the counter, in the trash, or wherever it is that your dog usually makes her raids.

The extra-hot sensation won't hurt her, but it will offend her tastebuds. Some dogs soon decide that human food is too spicy for their tastes and will stop their foraging, Jones says.

Gorging

Like people, dogs overindulge in foods that taste great. Unlike people, they think that just about every food tastes great. "Overeating is just sheer dog," says Wayne Hunthausen, D.V.M., a veterinarian in Westwood, Kansas, and co-author of *Handbook of Behavior Problems in Cats and Dogs.* "Many dogs don't start to feel satiated until they've gone miles beyond meeting their caloric needs."

This tendency to gluttony means that many dogs are perpetual moochers as well as overweight. And because their digestive systems can't always keep up, dogs who stuff themselves have a way of getting sick afterward—usually behind the back door or on your best carpet.

Since gluttony is part of a dog's evolutionary package, there's not much hope of teaching restraint. According to Dr. Hunthausen, you can slow her down so at least she doesn't get sick.

- Giving dogs more dietary fiber will help them feel full even when they eat a little less. Either use a high-fiber food, available from veterinarians and pet supply stores, or supplement their diets with such things as cooked oatmeal or lightly steamed vegetables.

- Giving dogs several small meals a day instead of one big meal is another way of helping them feel more satisfied. They'll still wolf down their portions, but at least they won't get indigestion afterward.

This golden retriever is eating at a sensible pace because the tennis ball in her bowl prevents her from gobbling.

- Veterinarians sometimes suggest putting a tennis ball or some other large object in the food bowl. This forces dogs to pick around the object and eat more slowly.

Guarding

Mealtime etiquette takes a dive when dogs feel as though they have to protect their food or even the empty dish. They don't do it because they're bad-tempered, Halliburton explains. They do it because their ancestors did it and because it's their way of reinforcing their status in the family pack. It's no big deal when a dog growls at another dog who's showing too much interest in her food. But dogs who get testy toward people are forgetting the rules—that the humans, not the dogs, are the leaders and they have the right to go anywhere they want, including near the food bowl.

Food aggression can be a problem because it invariably leads to other kinds of aggression. To

help your dog feel more relaxed and less defensive, here are a few tips you may want to try.

Feed the people first. From their days in packs, dogs understand that those who eat first are the leaders and aren't to be trifled with. This is why trainers recommend that the people in the family eat before the dogs do—and in a place where the dogs can see them. "This is a simple step, but it can make a big difference," says Sarah Wilson, a trainer in Gardiner, New York, and co-author of *Childproofing Your Dog.*

Watch him eat. "When you feed your dog, don't leave the room," says Halliburton. "She doesn't need privacy, and if you put her food down and hit the road, she may think that it's because she's entitled to have the room to herself while she eats."

Don't give food for free. A subtle way to teach dogs to be less aggressive about food is to remind them that they wouldn't be eating at

One way to curb food aggression is to reinforce your leadership by watching your dog eat her meals.

all if it weren't for you. "Make your dog do something for you before you do anything for her," says Wilson. Tell her to sit or to lie down before you put the dish down. If she doesn't do what you ask, put the dish out of sight. Then try again in a few minutes. Hunger will eventually prevail, and your dog will have a clearer understanding of the chain of command in the family, Wilson explains.

FAST FIX On those occasions when your dog is properly polite when you approach her food, drop a special treat into the dish, Wilson suggests. Not only will this reward her for being good but also she'll realize that good things happen when you're near her bowl, she says.

Being first in line at the supper table is a sign of status among dogs. This terrier mix doesn't like waiting her turn, but she's learning that people have higher status than she does—and that it doesn't pay to get pushy about food.

CHAPTER FIFTEEN

Bedtime Manners

Considering how much dogs like to sleep, it's surprising how
disruptive they can be at night. Here are a few tricks to ensure
that bedtime is the peaceful time that it should be.

Sleeping is something that dogs do very
well. They drop off with a speed that would
make a trucker jealous. "Most dogs sleep
more than half their day away, and some sleep
much more," says Kathleen Murnan, D.V.M., a
veterinarian in Bedford, Texas. "And most dogs
go right to bed when their owners turn out the
lights at night."

Dogs rarely get insomnia, in other words.
When they do, it's usually because they're not
feeling well or they have to go outside to water
the lawn. But despite this gift for slumber, nights
in some houses resonate with noisy sighs, perpetual pacing, and the click-clicking of hard
little claws on hardwood floors.

Some dogs need less sleep than others, which
means they spend some of their nights looking
for things to do. Others feel that it's their job to
act as security guards and pace through the
house every few hours. Still others accumulate
so much energy during the day that they simply
can't fall asleep at night. Regardless of the
reason, most of these dogs are perfectly happy
staying awake at night. Their owners, who may
spend hours with pillows clamped over their
heads, have a different opinion.

All-Night Dogs

Since the vast majority of dogs sleep so well—at
night, in the afternoon, and any other time they
lie down—people are always surprised when
they discover that they have a night owl in the
family. While some dogs have internal clocks
that are naturally a little skewed, most nighttime
perambulations occur when dogs aren't doing
a whole lot during the day. The combination
of boredom and stockpiled energy almost
guarantees that they'll do some pacing,
tossing, and turning.

Since their insomnia invariably becomes
your insomnia, you'll want to put some effort
into tuckering them out before they hit the hay,
says Marty Becker, D.V.M., a veterinarian in
Bonners Ferry, Idaho, and co-author of *Chicken
Soup for the Pet Lover's Soul.*

*This Norwegian elkhound puppy is just
doing what comes naturally. It's common for dogs to
sleep 14 hours a day or more.*

Dogs who lie around all day tend to be wakeful at night. This bull terrier mix is burning off energy and will be knocked out by bedtime.

evening, says Dr. Murnan. Some very energetic breeds, such as Labradors and Border collies, may need two or three times this amount, especially when they're young.

Since a dog's every instinct tells her to move, this isn't something you'll have to struggle with. Throwing a ball—or a rawhide, stick, or whatever it is your dog loves—around the yard for a half-hour will burn off a lot of energy. Walking is great exercise, and running is even better—not only because it helps blow off steam but also because it gets the two of you out of the house and into new worlds of sights and sounds. Mental stimulation as well as physical exercise almost guarantees that a dog will sleep soundly, says Dr. Becker.

Walk their little paws off. It was only in the past generation or so that dogs made the transition from the barnyard to the backyard. Before that, dogs were expected to work—as herders, hunting companions, and trackers. Dogs who were active all day didn't have much energy left at night, says Dr. Becker.

Modern dogs have a very different lifestyle. They spend as much as 80 percent of their time alone, and they pass the time by sleeping. Dogs who sleep all day long are not going to need as much sleep at night. More important, dogs have evolved as physically active animals. Those who sleep all day accumulate vast amounts of energy. The only way to burn it off is get them moving, preferably a lot. Nearly every dog needs a minimum of 20 minutes of exercise twice a day, once in the morning and again in the

CALL FOR HELP

It's rare for dogs to suffer from full-blown insomnia. However, older dogs may develop the canine equivalent of Alzheimer's disease. Called cognitive dysfunction, this condition can make dogs extremely restless as well as confused. Since insomnia is one of the first signs, you should call your veterinarian if your dog's usual sleeping habits take a sudden turn for the worse. There isn't a cure for cognitive dysfunction, but there are a number of medications that can help relieve the symptoms.

Teach them to play alone. Unlike cats, who have evolved as solitary animals and will happily play by themselves, dogs spent their evolutionary history in tight social groups called packs. Dogs in packs did everything together. Our dogs don't live in packs anymore, a change they haven't quite adjusted to. That's why suburban dogs with vast, fenced yards don't run around any more than their apartment-dwelling cousins. Unless someone is out there playing with them, they just sleep by the back door and wait for you to come outside.

Dogs may be reluctant to play alone, but they're perfectly happy to eat alone. Experts have found that it's possible to stimulate the former by forking over the latter. A toy called a Buster Cube, available in pet supply stores, uses food as a way to keep dogs entertained even when they're alone. This pushable toy has an inner compartment that holds bits of dry kibble. Dogs can smell the food inside, so they shove the toy around, releasing an occasional trickle of food. They eat the food, then shove the cube around some more. A fully loaded Buster Cube can keep them busy for hours, says Betty Fisher, a trainer based in San Diego and co-author of *So Your Dog's Not Lassie.*

Move back the dinner hour. Even dogs who sleep well at night may wake up early because their stomachs are growling—and dogs who want their breakfasts aren't about to amuse themselves while you sleep. Giving in to early-morning whines and nose nudges is a real mistake because dogs learn from success, says Dr. Murnan. What you can do, however, is feed them later in the evening, she suggests. Dogs with full stomachs are sleepy dogs.

Swap play for sleep. If your dog has been in the habit of waking you up early, Dr. Murnan suggests keeping something special—a rawhide or a favorite toy, for example—on the nightstand. When your canine alarm clock comes cruising, groggily hand over the treat. As long as it's interesting enough to occupy her for a half-hour or so, you'll buy a little extra snooze time.

FAST FIX Research has shown that supplements containing melatonin or chamomile can help people sleep, and they appear to work for dogs, as well, says Beth Brown, D.V.M., a veterinarian in Bradenton, Florida. Every dog will need a different amount, so ask your vet for advice.

A Place to Call Their Own

For more than 10,000 years, dogs have been bred to be companions for people. As a result, they depend on people's company and attention to be happy, says Dr. Becker. Many dogs, in fact, won't sleep well unless they're near—or even in bed with—their people. This is fine as long as you don't mind listening

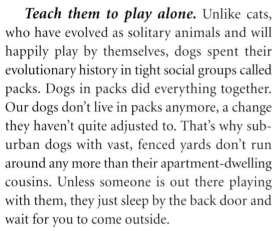

It's hard for dogs to sleep soundly when they're uncomfortable. A basket makes a snug bed for these two Maltese to share.

Dogs instinctively prefer enclosed areas to sleep in. This kelpie mix's bed, in a corner and hemmed in by sofas, creates a secure, denlike environment.

With their thick coats and wild backgrounds, dogs can make themselves comfortable in places where people can't. A carpeted floor is better than anything their ancestors had, but it's not ideal, if only because dogs have an instinctive need to dig into something soft and make themselves a cozy burrow. Pet supply stores sell a variety of well-stuffed beds, including beds filled with fragrant cedar chips, which most dogs love.

But you don't have to spend money. A thick blanket folded into a square and put in a shallow cardboard box makes a great dog bed. Dogs who are comfortable are much less likely to get up and pace around, says Dr. Becker.

Surround her with your scent. Just as people sleep better when they're in their own beds or wrapped around their favorite pillows, dogs sleep best when they're surrounded with familiar scents. For dogs, nothing is more comforting than the scents of their owners.

"Take the blanket you're giving your dog and sleep on it for one night," says Dr. Becker. "Your smell on it will comfort her when she's trying to sleep alone."

Make a sleeping den. Dogs invariably gravitate toward small, enclosed places—the very end of the couch near the armrest, for example, or in a tight spot in a corner. Once again, this instinct has its origins in their ancient pasts, when dogs kept themselves warm and safe from predators in cozy little dens. It's easy to make a den at home, and it doesn't have to be anything fancy, says Dr. Becker.

• If your dog's bed or blanket is in the middle of the room, move it to a corner—in the bedroom, living room, or wherever you want

to doggy snores and you're willing to share a double bed with a canine comforter. But this much closeness isn't always appreciated. Reconciling these different agendas—the human desire for a good night's sleep and the dog desire for closeness—sometimes requires creative solutions.

Provide the bed of her dreams. Dogs enjoy their creature comforts. When they don't have a soft, special place to sleep, they generally look around until they find one—and their pacing and complaining can be mighty hard to sleep through.

her to sleep, says Dr. Becker. Simply being "protected" on two sides makes dogs feel safer and more relaxed, he explains.

• Regardless of where your dog sleeps, you can make things cozier by rearranging the furniture a bit so that it creates an enclosed space that's large enough for her to sleep in easily, but not so large that it feels wide open. Small areas hold heat, and your dog will enjoy the added comfort.

• Many veterinarians recommend using crates to keep dogs comfortable and secure. Crates provide perfect enclosed spaces that dogs like, and they're convenient for people because they're easy to move and clean. Older dogs don't always take to crates, however, so it's best to begin while they're young. Once they're used to them, most dogs will automatically walk into their crates whenever they want a little rest.

Crates aren't cages. They're safe and cozy dens where dogs enjoy spending time even when they're not sleeping.

POOCH PUZZLER

Do dogs dream?

Dogs fall asleep in an instant, and judging from their kicks and yelps, there's a lot going on in the land of Nod. "If you've ever watched your dog sleep and seen her twitching and wriggling around, you've probably seen her dreaming," says Charles McPhee, director of the sleep apnea patient treatment program at the Sleep Disorders Center of Santa Barbara, California.

No one is sure what dogs dream about. Maybe they're chasing rabbits, herding sheep, or wandering in a canine paradise where dog biscuits grow on trees. Regardless of what dogs dream about, experts believe that their dreams are probably ripe with the scents of adventure. Unlike people, who depend on sight and have mainly visual dream images, dogs smell the world before they look, listen, taste, and touch it. A large percentage of their brains is dedicated to scent, so it's likely that smell is the foremost experience in doggy dreams.

Rumbles and Roars

If you have a Boston terrier, a pug, or a boxer, you've probably discovered that "quiet" and "sleep" don't always go together. These dogs sleep just fine. But along with other short-faced breeds, they have unusually narrow airways. They've essentially been bred to be persistent, sonorous snoring machines, says Dr. Murnan. They snore so loudly, in fact, that people in separate rooms can hear the rumbles, even with the doors closed. "If you have one of these breeds,

Dogs with short noses, such as Boston terriers and bulldogs, are among the loudest snorers because their airways are uncommonly narrow. They wheeze and snort, as well.

about all you can do is wear earplugs," Dr. Murnan says. "There's just nothing you can do to prevent it."

There are ways to reduce if not eliminate snoring in other breeds, she adds.

Keep their weight down. Dogs who are heavier than they should be accumulate fatty tissue around their necks and within their airways. As the air passages become narrower, they act almost like wind instruments, causing noisy snoring.

Ask your veterinarian about allergies. Even minor allergies—to pollen, fleas, or anything else—can cause tissues in the airways to swell. This, in addition to an increased production of mucus, causes congestion that leads to snoring. You can often treat allergies at home, either by keeping your dog away from whatever it is she's sensitive to or by giving an antihistamine such as diphenhydramine (Benadryl). Your veterinarian can tell you the precise dose you'll need to give.

Most allergies are easy enough to treat, but figuring out what is triggering them is a daunting task. Seasonal allergies are usually caused by mold or pollen, but food allergies or allergic reactions to carpet fibers or household chemicals can occur year-round. If your veterinarian can't figure out what the source of the snoring is, he may recommend that you take your dog to a specialist for a full-fledged allergy screening.

FAST FIX Just as people snore less when they flip from their backs to their stomachs, dogs also get a little quieter when you roll them over, says Dr. Becker. It won't solve the problem, but it will help you sleep a little better—until she rolls over again.

Dogs often snore when they sleep on their backs. Sleeping on their sides, like this kelpie is doing, usually reduces the noise.

STRANGE behavior

Name RUSS

Breed BOXER

Age 2

The Behavior

Russ is a big, fun-loving dog who relishes time with his family. He loves them so much, in fact, that one day he decided he wasn't going to go to bed anymore. When he hears the familiar command "go to bed," he stares at his owners as though they're speaking a foreign language. When someone gets impatient and tries to lead him by the collar, Russ rolls over on his back and lies there like a sack of potatoes. Sometimes, people resort to carrying him to his bed in the kitchen, but their backs can't take it anymore.

The Solution

Boxers are known for being fun-loving, childlike dogs—and like most children, they don't like going to bed when their parents are still up and having fun, says Marty Becker, D.V.M., a veterinarian in Bonners Ferry, Idaho, and co-author of *Chicken Soup for the Pet Lover's Soul*. "The secret to solving Russ's problem is to make bedtime a good time."

Russ's bed should be his cocoon, a special place where he likes to spend time, Dr. Becker says. It needs to be clean and comfortable, for starters. It would also help if there was always a toy waiting for him when he went to bed—a new one every week. The bed itself may be part of the problem. Even if it's fluffy, well-padded, and thoroughly imbued with Russ's personal scent, he may not be entirely comfortable with the size. People like big beds, but dogs don't. Dogs like beds that are just big enough for them to stretch out—anything more makes them feel out of sorts.

Surroundings are also important, says Dr. Becker. Maybe the dishwasher makes a terrible racket. Maybe his bed is too far from the people's bedrooms. Maybe he just doesn't like being in the kitchen. Moving the bed to another room or another spot in the kitchen may make it more attractive.

It's also possible, says Dr. Becker, that Russ's bedtime routine is just too boring. He recommends spicing things up a bit—by taking Russ for a walk just before he goes to bed, for example. Or they could lure him to bed by holding something tasty in front of his nose and leading the way. Dogs almost always follow their noses, and bed will seem like an attractive place when there's food waiting.

TURN ON THE LIGHT

Fumbling for the light switch can be a real pain, especially when you have to navigate a maze of couches, chairs, and bookcases to get there. Dogs have a natural advantage because they can find their way in the dark better than people can. Problem is, most people don't take the time to show them how to do it. If your dog is tall enough to reach the light switch, he can learn to turn it on and off—especially if it's a push-button switch rather than the up-and-down kind.

1 Stand near a wall, pat it, and encourage your dog to jump up and put his paws against the wall. When he does, slip him a biscuit for his efforts.

2 Once he has practiced a bit and is comfortable balancing against the wall, start patting the switch with one hand and guiding his foot to the switch with the other. When he turns it on, say, "Get the light!" and give him something to eat.

GET MY SLIPPERS

It's no fun getting out of bed on a February morning and walking on a frigid floor while you search for your slippers. Why not ask your dog for help? Any dog can learn to fetch slippers, and retrievers have a special knack for it. Be sure to start with an old pair because dogs don't always want to give them back at first.

1 Start by teaching your dog the word "slipper." Toss one of your slippers a few feet away and say, "Get my slipper." Eventually, he'll grab it and bring it over. Trade him the slipper for a biscuit.

2 Once he knows what slippers are, hide them in an easy place, like behind an open door or under the bed, and encourage him to find them and bring them over. Once he has this figured out, you'll never have frozen feet again.

EXCUSE ME

Dogs always crowd the door, either because they're excited or because they really think it matters that they get through first. To prevent traffic jams, it's worth teaching your dog to politely step back so people can go through first.

1 When your dog is crowding the door, don't open it. First, use your leg to block him, and urge him back, saying, "Excuse me."

2 As soon as he backs away a couple of steps, tell him how smart he is. Then open the door and walk through, letting him follow. As long as he stays behind you, praise him and reward him for his patience. If he tries to muscle in ahead of you, keep the treat and keep practicing.

☆ S P E C I A L   S K I L L S ☆

WIPE YOUR MOUTH

Dogs have lousy table manners. They put their whole heads in their bowls, swallow without chewing, and get food all over their faces. Every dog should know how to use a napkin to wipe his mouth when he's done.

1 Put a little food in your dog's dish—enough to get his interest, but not enough to dull his appetite for goodies. While he's eating, wrap a really good treat, like a piece of hot dog, in a towel.

When he is done eating and walks away from the dish, hold out the towel and say, "Wipe your mouth." As he sniffs around the towel for the hot dog, he'll wipe his mouth, more or less by accident. That's when you praise him and give him the treat.

2 With enough practice, your dog will understand that "Wipe your mouth" means he should rub his face on the towel. Hang the towel in a conspicuous place near his food dish. Even without the treat, he'll go to the towel and give his face a wipe.

☆ SPECIAL SKILLS ☆

RING THE BELL

Some dogs are too polite to bark or make a fuss when they need to go outside, which means you're always guessing. To clear up the confusion, you can teach them to ring a bell whenever they want to go outside.

1 Hang a string of bells near the door where your dog usually goes out. (Leather straps with jingle bells are available just about anywhere during the holiday season.) Rub one or two of the bells with a piece of hot dog.

2 Ask your dog, "Do you want to go out?" and invite him to sniff the bells. Once he smells "eau de hot dog," he'll take a lick—and the bells will ring. Quickly open the door, let him out, praise him, and give him the hot dog. While he's learning, stock up on hot dog bits. Let him out and reward him every time he rings the bells.

☆ S P E C I A L   S K I L L S ☆

WAVE BYE-BYE

This trick gives dogs something to do with their hands, so to speak. Instead of trying to push through the door when guests depart, they can offer a proper salute. Waving bye-bye is easiest for short dogs with low centers of gravity, because they're better able to maintain their balance while sitting up.

1 Teach your dog to sit up by holding a treat over his head. When he reaches up for it while keeping his hind end on the ground, give him the treat.

2 Once your dog is comfortable sitting up, reach out your hand as though to shake his paw. When he reaches his paw toward your hand, pull back, tell him, "Good wave!" and give him a reward. Every time you practice, raise your hand a little higher when reaching out. This will cause him to wave higher.

PART FOUR

THE WELL-TRAVELED DOG

All dogs travel a little, if only to the vet for their annual checkups. But their traveling needn't end there. Dogs who behave well in all sorts of situations—in the car, at other people's houses, in hotels, and in wilderness areas—get invited on all sorts of outings. And every dog appreciates that.

CHAPTER SIXTEEN

DRIVING IN COMFORT

Car travel is a breeze for some dogs and a bitter pill for others.
Driving shouldn't be scary and it shouldn't make dogs sick. Here are a few
ways to help dogs adjust to life on the road.

All dogs go riding in the car occasionally, and most of them love it—sometimes a little too much, in fact. It's a lot of fun taking dogs places, but not when they stand with their feet on top of the front seat and bark all the way.

Then there are those who loathe car trips. They're afraid or they get carsick. They fidget, cry, and drool, sometimes for 10 hours or more. More than a few drivers have secretly wished

they could put their dogs in the trunk along with the luggage in order to get a little peace.

Every dog, whether he's a seasoned traveler or a novice, can learn to be a better car companion, says Chris Walkowicz, a judge for the American Kennel Club, author of *The Perfect Match: A Dog Buyer's Guide*, and a frequent traveler who has logged thousands of miles with her various canine companions. Once dogs get comfortable and understand the etiquette, they'll enjoy—or at least rest easily for—every mile.

Making Good Memories

Dogs can't imagine the future, but they do remember the past. And for most dogs, past experiences in the car haven't always been pleasant—starting with that first trip when they left their litter mates. "The first ride in the car takes them away from the only family they've ever known," says Steve Dale, a radio host at WGN in Chicago, a syndicated columnist, and author of the book *Doggone Chicago*. "It can be heartbreaking."

Most dogs love going for rides, but even those who don't can learn to accept it and be more comfortable.

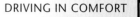

It doesn't get a whole lot better after that. Before dogs are 6 months old, they've taken several trips to the vet for examinations and shots. They may have gotten carsick a few times, and they've certainly gotten scared. And no matter how much reassurance their people give them, nothing changes the fact that they're riding in a machine that their ancestors never encountered.

People often forget how strange cars must seem to dogs, who can't really understand what they're all about. This is why veterinarians recommend taking the time to show dogs that cars are happy, exciting places. It doesn't happen overnight, but with a process called desensitization, dogs lose their fear and begin looking forward to life on four wheels.

- Since dogs like food better than just about anything, Dale recommends putting your dog's food bowl in the backseat or, if he's too scared even to climb inside, right next to the car. Feed him there every day for a week, he suggests.

- Several times a day, use the car in ways your dog can understand—by flipping treats onto the seats and encouraging him to go after them, or just by playing in the general area. "He should learn that good things in life happen when he's near the car," says Dale.

- Once your dog is comfortable in and around the car, slip into the front seat one day while he's eating in the back. You don't have to go anywhere. Let him get used to being in the backseat while you're in the front. Do this a few times, then actually start the car. Let the motor run for a minute, then shut it off. Do this three or four times a day for a few days.

- By this time, your dog will think that the car is a pretty cool place to hang out. So it's time

A full food bowl makes dogs very happy. This golden retriever is learning to associate the car with the thing he loves best.

to take a drive, maybe just to the end of the driveway and back. "If your dog whines or paces or shows other signs of stress, you may be moving too fast for him," says Dale.

- Every day or so after this, take your dog for a drive, gradually increasing the length of time you spend in the car. "Go somewhere you know your dog will enjoy," Dale says. "Get him french fries at the nearest fast-food restaurant. If you make every car trip upbeat and positive, your dog will learn to love the car. This process seems to take forever, but it does work."

Cruising in Comfort

Dogs get bored during long trips just as children do. And in fact, bored dogs act a lot like bored children—whining, pacing, and making a fuss. Of course, most dogs who have decent manners at home will have decent manners in the car as well. Those who don't may need extra help.

"I teach my dogs a vague kind of command, 'settle,' which means, 'You can pick where you lie down, but settle down,'" says Gina Spadafori, pet-care columnist for Universal Press Syndicate and author of the book *Dogs for Dummies*. It's an easy command to teach, she says, although you'll probably want to pick the place you want your dog to lie down, at least at first. Take your dog by the collar, say "Settle," lead him to the spot where you want him to lie down, and tell him "Settle" again. Then tell him "Good dog," and maybe give him a treat. Obviously, you need to teach the basics at home

Dogs who roam in the car are always a nuisance. Their wandering is dangerous, too. A useful command for them to know is "settle," which means "Find a comfortable spot to lie down—then stay there." It's also a helpful command to use at home.

before setting off on your trip, she adds. Most dogs pick it up quickly, sometimes in as little as a few days.

Home Away from Home

The main reason that dogs get uncomfortable on car trips is that they're in a new environment and they're feeling insecure, says Darlene Arden, author of *The Irrepressible Toy Dog*. Reassurance doesn't help; it can actually make them more insecure because they think, "Wow, she's nervous too, so I guess there really is something wrong."

The easiest way to help dogs relax is to keep them in a crate in the car, Arden says. Dogs in the wild always lived in dens, and dogs today still prefer small, enclosed places. Crates smell

A crate in the back of the car provides a cozy, denlike environment and helps keep dogs safe.

An alternative to a crate is a doggy seat belt. This helps keep your dog safe, of course, but it also keeps him in one place. This can make a difference on long trips because a cold, probing nose is distracting. And more than a few dogs have decided to find a new place to sleep—like under the brake pedal. "My sheltie, Andy, uses a seat belt, and he can either sit or stretch out," Spadafori says.

Another option is to set up a barrier that divides the people part of the car from the dog part. Pet supply stores sell a variety of dividers, from netting material and nylon screens to metal wire grills. "Barriers give dogs a bit more freedom and space of their own to move around in, and they work really well," says Spadafori.

like home and give comfort in the strange environment of a car.

They also provide protection, Dale adds. "The little guys can get bounced around really good in the car."

Carriers come in wire, soft-sided, and hard-plastic models. It doesn't matter what kind you buy, although soft-sided crates are easier to store when they're not in use. Dogs who use crates when they travel often sleep in them at home, so they're really very handy, Arden says.

Puppies take to crates right away, but older dogs are often a little reluctant to use them— and you don't want to wait until you're pulling out of the driveway to discover that your dog is going to howl nonstop unless you open the crate door. If he isn't used to a crate and you're planning a trip, see chapter twenty for advice on helping him make the transition.

A special dog harness that attaches to the regular seat belt keeps dogs safe and secure while traveling.

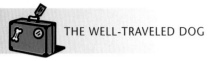

When you're traveling, let your dog out of the car every time you take a break. This will give him a comfort stop and a chance to have a sniff around.

Rest Stops

When a dog's gotta go, he's gotta go—and the jiggling of the car and the small bladder capacity of the average dog means you'll probably be stopping a lot more than you'd probably like. You can't fight nature, but you can help dogs be better car partners by making nature's call a little less urgent.

Give them a break when you take a break. Even if your dog is happily sleeping in the backseat, rouse him whenever you stop the car, says Spadafori. If you don't, he's sure to decide he has to go as soon as you've settled back into your driving.

"Generally speaking, as often as you need to take a break, so will your dog," she says. Dogs younger than 8 months usually need a pit stop about every 1½ to 2 hours. Older dogs can usually last 3 to 4 hours.

Make every stop count. Dogs get a real kick out of watering grass, trees, and highway signs—not because they're desperate to empty their bladders, but because they're leaving their calling cards for other dogs. If you pack your dog back in the car as soon as he anoints a roadside bush, you can be sure he'll shortly be whining because he needs some real relief. Dogs aren't going to change their habits just because they're on the road, but you can make trips go more smoothly by following what some people call the three-bush rule: Dogs aren't done until they've squatted or lifted their legs at least three times.

Remind them what they're there for. Thousands of dogs stop at highway rest stops every year. That means there are thousands of smells to distract your dog from the business at hand. To ensure he doesn't get so distracted that he neglects to do his business, it helps if he understands a command that means "go," says Spadafori.

Every time your dog squats or lifts a leg, give a command like "hurry up" or "potty." Use the same command every time, and try to use it every time he relieves himself. Then praise the dickens out of him by saying "good hurry up" or "good potty." Eventually, he will link the command with the action and be more than happy to oblige, Spadafori says.

Roadside Dining

One of the joys of traveling is sampling new foods along the way. At least, that's the human perspective. Dogs feel a little different. For all of their enthusiasm about exploring new places, they're distinctly conservative about what they eat. Buying whatever types of dog food you can find along the way isn't going to make your dog—or at least his digestive tract—happy. And no one has a good time when you're stopping every five miles because your dog has diarrhea or is throwing up on the backseat.

Since you may not be able to find your dog's usual food when you're in different parts of the country, Spadafori recommends packing food from home and giving it to him at the same times that he usually eats.

Water is less of an issue. Even though streams at rest stops may be contaminated, most traveler's diarrhea is caused by the stress of the trip and not by something your dog drank. Still, you'll probably want to pack water because

POOCH ?? PUZZLER

Why do dogs stick their heads out car windows?

It doesn't matter where you're driving or how cold out it is. Put a dog in a car, and the first thing he'll do is stick his head out the window, letting the wind blow his lips into a happy grin.

Even though dogs don't see as well as people do, they enjoy looking at the world around them—and they see a lot better when there isn't a thick piece of glass in front of them, says Steve Aiken, an animal behaviorist in Wichita, Kansas. More important, dogs "see" by smelling. "When they stick their heads out the window, perhaps they're getting a better picture of the world around them and enjoying it, " he says.

dogs get hot when they're traveling and will probably need to drink more often than you'll want to stop.

Walkowicz recommends filling a plastic bag with ice cubes and putting it in a cooler. When your dog is looking thirsty, let him lick the ice. It's a lot easier than filling a water bowl and watching the water slosh all over the floor mats. Some people get a little fancier and use water bottles that are made especially for pets. These work best for small dogs—large dogs tend to pull the tops off and make a mess, Walkowicz adds.

BREED SPECIFIC

Any dog can make a great car companion, but small breeds such as Chihuahuas, Yorkshire terriers, and toy poodles (left) are ideal because they're so portable. Very large dogs such as Great Danes and Irish wolfhounds are even better travelers because they are calm and will usually lie down and be happy.

95

Calming Upset Tummies

Dogs who aren't accustomed to car trips usually reveal their inexperience by getting carsick, sometimes before you've gotten out of town. Their stomachs usually get a lot sturdier by the time they're 9 months to 1 year old. But the excitement and stress of traveling, along with the rocking motion of the car, can cause nausea even in the most seasoned travelers, says Joanne Howl, D.V.M., a veterinarian in West River, Maryland.

Start on an empty stomach. Even though you want to keep your dog on his regular eating schedule, plan your trip so he hasn't stuffed himself just before you leave. "Give him a tiny portion an hour before you leave, just to settle his stomach," Dale says. "Then you can give tidbits spaced out during the trip that add up to the total meal."

Offer something sweet. "Give your dog a little bit of sugar on the ends of your fingers," suggests Walkowicz. "The sweetness seems to settle the stomach."

Peppermint is an old folk remedy for nausea, and it appears to work as well for dogs as it does for people. People who travel a lot with their dogs sometimes slip them peppermint candies every two to three hours.

Prevent nausea with ginger. Another time-tested remedy for carsickness is ginger, either in cookie or supplement form. People who take their dogs to shows and log thousands of miles a year use ginger all the time, mainly in the form of gingersnaps, says Walkowicz. If you want to give ginger supplements to your dog, use the human dose as a guide. For example, a

CALL FOR HELP

Cars trap enormous amounts of heat. When they're parked, the temperature inside can soar to 125°F in just a few minutes. This is uncomfortable for people, but it can be life-threatening for dogs because their internal coolers aren't very efficient. When they get too hot, they can suffer from heatstroke, a serious condition in which organs in the body essentially shut down.

Dogs with heatstroke will usually have bright red gums, glazed eyes, and very thick saliva. They will also pant heavily and may try to vomit.

Heatstroke is always an emergency that must be treated by a veterinarian. If you can't get to a veterinarian immediately, try to cool your dog quickly by soaking him with water, applying wet towels to his body, or by giving him ice cubes to lick.

50-pound dog should get about half of the human dose 1 hour before the trip.

Give them Dramamine. This over-the-counter remedy isn't as strong as some prescription medications, but it still may be helpful for preventing nausea. Veterinarians usually recommend giving 1 to 2 milligrams for every pound of weight, about an hour before traveling. Every dog is different, so you should talk to your veterinarian before giving it at home. Dramamine (dimenhydrinate) is better at preventing nausea than stopping it, however, so if your dog is already sick, it probably won't help much.

Dramamine is safe, but don't give it to dogs who have glaucoma or bladder problems unless you check with your veterinarian first.

Change the view. "Some dogs get sick in cars but not in vans," Walkowicz says. The reason for this is that the sight of scenery whizzing by can cause nausea even in regular travelers. She recommends keeping dogs in crates and turning them so the openings face away from the windows.

FAST FIX Driving with the car windows open gives dogs a blast of fresh air. Fresh air helps settle the stomach, and the windy sensation helps calm the part of the brain that causes vomiting, says Dr. Howl.

Travel Gear

People embarking on road trips always pack extra gear, such as maps, extra sunglasses, and good things to eat. The well-traveled dog needs to accessorize as well. Here are some essentials.

• Dogs who stick their heads out the windows need eye protection, such as sunglasses or goggles, available in pet supply stores. Even if you keep the windows closed, shades provide good protection from ultraviolet light and will prevent their eyes from getting irritated.

• Sunshine inside the car can get pretty intense, so you and your dog will want to wear a sunscreen with a sun protection factor (SPF) of

You need to plan when taking dogs on long trips. Taking a few travel acccessories will make the ride more comfortable for all the family.

15 or higher. Dogs with thin fur and white faces have the highest risk of getting sunburn. Be sure to buy a sunscreen that doesn't contain PABA (para-aminobenzoic acid) or zinc oxide, which can be harmful when dogs lick them off.

• You can buy seat covers and hatchback liners at pet supply stores. They come in colors and styles to fit every vehicle, and they'll protect your car from the inevitable doggy accidents.

• Travel is never risk-free, so you'll want to take along a first-aid kit, just in case. You can buy kits at pet supply stores, and they usually contain such things as tape, bandages, a thermometer, and over-the-counter medications like Kaopectate and Pepto-Bismol.

• Cars are usually pretty warm, so dogs need more water than usual. Take along a gallon of spring water, or fill a bottle with tap water. You'll also want to have a weighted water dish, which will be less likely to tip than a regular bowl. Some people travel with collapsible bowls, which are easy to store when not in use.

97

STRANGE
behavior

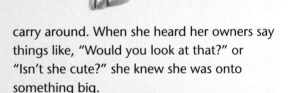

Name LADY

Breed PEKINGESE

Age 6

The Behavior

Lady is lovable and cuddly—and larcenous. For some reason, she is always stealing stuffed animals from the toy box and stashing them behind the couch. She isn't sneaky about it, either. She walks to the box, takes out a stuffed rabbit or seal, carries it through the bedroom and across the living room, then delicately deposits it between the couch and the wall. Lady's owners were charmed by this quirky behavior at first. Now they're not so sure, because her crimes are escalating. Lady has started boosting all sorts of soft things, including clothes, dish towels, and slippers. It's one thing when the grandchildren can't find a particular stuffed toy. It's another altogether when Lady's owners can't get dressed because their socks are missing.

The Solution

Appearances notwithstanding, Lady isn't in love with socks or stuffed animals, says Sarah Wilson, a trainer in Gardiner, New York, and co-author of *Childproofing Your Dog*. She's in love with attention. She probably picked up the first stuffed duck or bear because it felt nice to carry around. When she heard her owners say things like, "Would you look at that?" or "Isn't she cute?" she knew she was onto something big.

"Pekingese grasp concepts very easily," Wilson says. "They're quick to recognize a good gimmick. Lady's owners made a fuss over her for playing with stuffed animals, and she has just played it to the hilt."

Lady isn't going to change without help—the rewards have been too good. "If Lady doesn't get a response when she takes things, it won't be long before she decides that it's not worth it," says Wilson. This will require a little bit of fortitude on her owners' parts because there is something cute about a tiny Pekingese carrying a large bear. They'll just have to bite their lips and be firm.

Dogs can get very set in their ways, Wilson adds. A stony silence will help discourage Lady, but her owners will want to change her whole pattern. Wilson recommends rearranging the furniture to take away her hiding place. "They should clear out the treasures and move a chair, bookshelf, or potted plant in the way," she says.

CHAPTER SEVENTEEN

STAYING AT HOTELS

They don't use the weight room, elevators scare them, and they can't figure out why strangers—some pushing food carts—walk into their rooms. Dogs can be very polite guests, but only if they know what to expect.

Dogs are indifferent to maid service and the view from the 15th floor, and they certainly don't enjoy spending hours alone in hotel rooms while their owners are off sight-seeing. Taking dogs to hotels is always a challenge—not only for their human companions but also for the bellhops and concierges who have to field complaints about nonstop barking, or watch in dismay as canine visitors lift their legs on potted plants in the lobby.

"If dogs bark at home, they'll bark twice as much in a hotel; and if they chew on your couch, they'll do damage to a hotel room," says Steve Dale, a radio host at WGN in Chicago, a syndicated columnist, and author of the book *Doggone Chicago*. Even dogs who are perfectly behaved at home get nervous when they visit new places, he explains. Not only are they in strange surroundings but they are also spending quite a lot of time alone. When they get lonely or bored enough, they start looking for ways to vent their emotions, such as scratching at the door, barking, or chewing on table legs.

Dogs are sticklers for routines, Dale adds, and they have a hard time understanding that the rules they follow at home may not apply when they're in a hotel. A dog who always goes outside at 7:00 A.M. to do his business will want to do the same thing in a hotel—even when outside, in his mind, is the carpeted hallway just outside the room.

Staying at hotels doesn't come naturally to dogs, but they learn the ropes quick enough. A bit of planning will ensure that you and your dog can enjoy yourselves without upsetting the other guests.

Comfort Stops

Probably the biggest obstacle to social fitness is the fact that dogs are entirely casual in their bathroom habits. They don't require privacy, and it's easy for them to confuse a vast expanse of carpeting for the yard they use at home. Then there's all that foliage in the lobbies of hotels. It doesn't look any different from the ivy, shrubs, and trees that they visit at home, so they naturally get the wrong idea.

When you check in, you'll want to ask the clerk for directions to dog-friendly locations, Dale says. One hotel near O'Hare Airport in Chicago, for example, offers a garden facility where dogs can sniff and water the flowers— and, if they're interested, watch planes take off and land, as well.

But having a pleasant park nearby doesn't guarantee that dogs won't try to make pit stops somewhere between their rooms and the lobby. To avoid embarrassing breeches of etiquette, here are a few tips from travelers who have learned their lessons the hard way.

Keep moving. Dogs, especially males, rarely just stop and go. Rather, they do some preliminary sniffing—the canine equivalent of opening a magazine. Pausing for even a few seconds when you're taking your dog outside will give him a chance to launch the first part of his bathroom routine, and when that happens, the second part isn't far behind. Once you've put on the leash and are heading through the hotel to the outside, don't stop. Keep walking until you get there, says Gina Spadafori, pet-care columnist for Universal Press Syndicate and author of the book *Dogs for Dummies*.

Many hotels welcome dogs, but you don't want to show up unannounced. When you make reservations, let them know that you'll have company.

Move the leash back and forth. Walking through a hotel lobby isn't the same as walking down the sidewalk, and you'll probably encounter a number of time-eating obstacles, such as knots of people or closed elevator doors. Since every delay in your forward momentum will give your dog an opportunity to do what he shouldn't, you have to find another way to keep him moving. The easiest is to keep moving the leash from hand to hand. This forces him to keep moving even when you're not.

Keep the nose high. You can't teach dogs not to sniff, but you can teach them to keep their noses up—which, for male dogs, is the trick to keeping their rear legs in polite positions. "If they don't sniff, they're not going to lift," Spadafori says.

1. Keep one hand on your dog's collar or leash. As you're walking, be prepared to pull up his head when he starts to sniff.

2. As you lift his head, give a command like "don't touch," and keep walking.

3. When your dog looks up to see what you want, immediately praise him—and keep walking. With some practice, your dog will learn that the command "don't touch" means he should look up and keep moving. And the quicker you move, the fewer problems you'll have.

FAST FIX To prevent accidents in the hallway, elevator, or lobby, give your dog his favorite toy to carry when you leave the room. Dogs who are focused on their toys don't get distracted by their surroundings and are less likely to seek out their next leg-lifting or squatting target, says Spadafori.

Promoting Silence

Dogs take their jobs as family protectors very seriously, and barking comes with the package, says Chris Walkowicz, a judge for the American Kennel Club and author of *The Perfect Match: A Dog Buyer's Guide.* Dogs bark to alert their people to things that are new, scary, or interesting. This is fine at home, but in hotels, dogs find just about everything new, scary, or interesting. This means they bark a lot more than they usually do, and people in adjoining rooms won't be shy about complaining—either to you or to the desk manager. More than a few guests with vocal dogs have found themselves looking for a new hotel because their dogs made too much noise.

Dogs who aspire to social fitness need to understand that barky behavior isn't appropriate in public places. Yelling "Quiet!" usually doesn't help, because dogs interpret this to mean you're challenging them to a barking contest—and they'll bark louder to win. Here's a three-part strategy from Darlene Arden, author of *The Irrepressible Toy Dog*, that's much more effective.

1. When there's a noise outside or someone comes to the door and your dog starts barking, give him some praise after one or two barks. After all, a few barks are hardly unreasonable, and you want him to tell you about potential intruders. Your dog will know from the praise that you heard him and are pleased—and that he doesn't have to keep repeating himself.

2. As soon as you praise your dog, give the command "sit—no bark." The command forces your dog to focus on you instead of whatever it is outside that has his attention.

3. When he sits and stops barking, give him something to eat. The treat will keep his mouth occupied so he can't bark, and it will also reward him for his obedience as well as his silence.

Doing this exercise once or twice a day for a few weeks is usually enough to teach dogs to quit barking on command, Arden says. Dogs can't learn it overnight, however, so you'll want to practice before leaving home.

PLANNING YOUR TRIP

Some hotels cater to dogs and provide great walking trails, gourmet meals, and even grooming services. Many more, however, have closed their doors because too many canine visitors quite literally left their marks. To make sure there aren't any surprises, it's worth making a few calls before you leave home.

Make reservations and get confirmations in writing. "Some places don't have hard and fast rules, and things may change depending on who is at the front desk," says Steve Dale, a radio host at WGN in Chicago, a syndicated columnist, and author of the book *Doggone Chicago*. In addition, hotels sometimes change policies and may refuse to allow dogs, despite what it says in your travel guide.

Describe your dog honestly. Some hotels have size limits, Dale says. These limits will be expressed in different ways, such as, "only small dogs allowed," "only dogs under 30 pounds," or "no taller than your knee." Be sure your dog qualifies, whatever the going definition is.

Take his résumé. Some hotels may require copies of a dog's health certificate. Dale recommends that you take along other credentials, such as diplomas from obedience schools. Even if your dog doesn't look so great on paper, maybe he knows a flashy trick or two. "This may be enough to squeak your 40-pound dog into hotels that only allow 25-pound dogs and smaller."

Alert the staff. The check-in clerks will usually tell the staff, including housekeeping, that you have a dog. But it doesn't hurt to spread the word on your own, says Anne Marie DeStefano, director of sales for the Hotel Pennsylvania in New York City. "We can have extra towels and cleaning supplies available, and we will try to work around your schedule," she says.

Give a little extra. When you're passing out tips, don't forget to leave a few extra bucks when you check out of your room. Tipping is always optional, but it's a nice thing to do since dogs cause extra work for the hotel staff. Your dog may be bathed and coiffed, but he's still a dog, and all dogs shed. This immediately becomes apparent if the room has a white carpet and you have a black dog. Hotels use heavy-duty vacuums, but it still takes elbow grease to remove dog hairs. People don't mind doing extra work when they're getting something extra. You should definitely tip extra if someone has to clean up an accident or otherwise goes out of their way to make your stay comfortable. Any special courtesy performed for your dog surely deserves a bit of recognition.

Stick to the rules. More than a few travelers, desperate for lodging, have sneaked their dogs into no-dog hotels. It's understandable that people do it, but it's risky. You'll be charged extra if you're caught, especially if your dog causes damage.

Dogs who have spent all day in hotel rooms may find it hard to wait until they get outside to do their business. Giving them toys to carry distracts them until they reach the proper place.

Fighting Boredom

New sights and smells will keep dogs entertained for quite a while. Once their initial curiosity winds down, however, they start getting bored, especially when they're left alone for more than a few hours. And bored dogs, like bored children, start looking for things to do, and they're usually not good things.

Probably the most appealing way to pass the time, from a dog's point of view, is by chewing. In hotels, some of the most toothsome targets are remote controls, cushions, and table legs. It's difficult to stop dogs from chewing, because it's natural for them to do it when they're bored or anxious. Rather than trying to stop the behavior, about all you can do is give your dog something more appropriate to focus on, Dale says.

"Bring a favorite toy from home that already has your dog's smell on it," Dale advises. If your dog doesn't have a favorite toy, experiment a bit to see what passes the chew test. Some dogs will chew anything. Others prefer flavored synthetic chews, such as those made by NylaBone. Rawhide isn't a good choice when you're traveling, because many dogs swallow the pieces, which may give them diarrhea.

"You may want to try leaving on the radio or television, depending on your pet's preference," Arden adds. Dogs don't really listen to music or televised conversations, but the familiar sounds will remind them of home and help reduce

boredom and anxiety. In addition, the sounds will help mask outside noises, like doors slamming, that tend to raise canine blood pressures.

For dogs who are left alone, nothing beats the arrival of the housekeepers for a little afternoon excitement. For the housekeepers, however, encountering overly eager dogs is a little too much excitement. And more than a few dogs have taken advantage of their arrival to make a run for it. Arden recommends putting out the "Do not disturb" sign when you leave your dog alone. "You don't want him downstairs running up a bar tab while you're out seeing the sights," she says.

Sleeping in Comfort

Dogs are creatures of habit. They like to eat at the same times and go out at the same times. And at night, they like to sleep in the same places. "If your dog has a blanket or bed, take it with you," says Dale. Even if your dog doesn't have formal sleeping arrangements at home, you'll want to give him something that feels familiar, even if that means tossing one of your used shirts on the floor. Familiar smells relax dogs like nothing else does, and he'll probably curl up on the shirt and go to sleep right away.

"Hotels don't prefer it, but I have no problem with dogs sleeping on the beds as long as they're clean and well-mannered," Arden says. "Besides, if the housekeepers aren't changing the sheets in between guests, you shouldn't be staying there anyway."

Hotels that discourage doggy guests usually make the point that many dogs have fleas, and once fleas are in the room, they're very hard to get rid of. There's some truth to this, so make sure your dog is absolutely flea-free before checking in. These days there are some very safe, effective, and economical anti-flea medications that your veterinarian can recommend, so fleas don't have to be a problem.

A problem that's harder to control is shedding. Every dog sheds a little, and some dogs shed a lot. It's very difficult to remove dog hairs from carpets, furniture, and drapes. If you want your dog—and the thousands of other dogs who will follow—to be welcomed back, you'll want to take a few minutes every day to keep the fur from flying.

• "If your dog sheds big-time, brush him before you go inside the hotel," suggests Dale. "If you have a balcony, brush him every day out there."

Brushing your dog outside or on the hotel balcony will reduce the amount of hair he will shed on the carpets and furniture.

• Take along a blanket or sheet that you can spread over the areas where your dog will be sleeping.

• Before you leave the hotel, clean the room with a hair remover. Pet supply stores sell many different types. The Gonzo Pet Hair Lifter, for example, is a sponge that pulls hair off furniture. The Pet Hair Gatherer keeps carpets clean, and the Helmac Lint Brush easily removes hair from furniture, carpets, and drapes.

FAST FIX The easiest way to remove dog hair from carpets and upholstery is with a strip of masking tape. A small roll will remove tremendous amounts of hair very quickly.

His own basket. His own toys. Even his own blanket under the bed. All of these touches of familiarity are making this terrier feel right at home.

A Space of Their Own

Some of the best-behaved and most well-traveled dogs in America are those who are on the show circuit. Yet even these paragons of good manners, who wouldn't dream of barking at the housekeepers or stealing chocolates off the pillows, usually stay in crates that their handlers take along. It's not so much that they'll misbehave if given too much freedom, but that the crates provide them with comfortable and familiar places where they feel at home, says Arden. "Wouldn't you like to travel with your own private room and bed?" she adds.

People who travel a lot with small dogs usually prefer soft-sided crates because they're easy to carry around. Wire cages and fabric duffle carriers are also good because they take up very little space. Regardless of the crate you travel with, you have to give your dog time to get used to it before you travel, Arden says. Otherwise, that sparkling new "den" will feel just as scary as the strange hotel room. See chapter twenty for tips on getting your dog used to a crate.

Many hotels, incidentally, prefer that dogs be kept in crates, and some insist on it, says Anne Marie DeStefano, director of sales for the Hotel Pennsylvania in New York City, which hosts thousands of dogs when they arrive for the annual Westminster Kennel Club dog show. Dogs in kennels don't damage rooms, she explains, and the closed door reassures housekeeping folks, who may be afraid of dogs. "Of course, not everyone wants to cage dogs, and it's a hard rule to enforce."

There's one additional thing that everyone who travels with dogs should do, she adds. "The best time to walk dogs at hotels is very early in the morning, before 7:00 A.M." Taking your dog in and out early in the morning means that other guests won't be disturbed. "We also request that you use the service elevator so other guests

aren't uncomfortable riding next to a strange dog. People are especially nervous about big dogs," she adds.

Hotels are getting bigger all the time, and some include large expanses of gardens. It's natural for people on vacation to leave the pooper-scooper at home, and when it's 6:00 A.M. and you're the only one out, it's easy to "forget" to clean up what your dog left behind. Eventually, the hotel will be stuck with enough complaints—or shoe-cleaning bills—that dogs will no longer be welcome. So don't forget to put a few bags in your pocket before setting out.

FINDING DOG-FRIENDLY ACCOMMODATIONS

More than a few hotels and vacation spots have literally gone to the dogs and will do everything they can to make you and your canine companion welcome. Upscale hotels such as the Four Seasons, the Ritz Carlton, and Boston's Harbor Hotel offer such amenities as comfortable dog beds and dog-walking services. Some even provide monogrammed doggy-size bathrobes so that you and your dog can lounge in grand—and matching—style.

If you look, you'll find dog-friendly lodgings to fit every pocketbook. Here are a few guides that you can use to help you plan your next trip.

• The Dog Lovers Companion series of books provides the scoop on great—and not-so-great—hotels, parks, beaches, and other places where you can stay with dogs.

"The series is real insider-y about where you can take your dogs legally, where you can go with a wink and nudge, and where you better not try it," says Gina Spadafori, pet-care columnist for Universal Press Syndicate and author of the book *Dogs for Dummies*.

• The *Mobil 1999 Travel Guide on the Road with Your Pet* lists thousands of pet-friendly locations. You can also get information from the American Automobile Association.

• A bimonthly newsletter called "DogGone" publishes dog-friendly travel information based on its database of more than 23,000 pet-friendly destinations, from bed-and-breakfasts, inns, and campgrounds to hotels, ranches, and resorts. Contact editor Wendy Ballard at DogGone, P.O. Box 651155, Vero Beach, FL 32965-1155.

STRANGE
behavior

Name SALLY

Breed BEAGLE

Age 5

The Behavior
Sally has always been a barker. Her house is a long way from the nearest neighbor, however, and the noise never bothered her family much. What does bother them are Sally's responses to the grandfather clock they recently inherited. Starting at about noon and continuing until 8:00 or 10:00 at night, Sally howls at the clock when it chimes. And she does it every hour, day after day. Her owners have thought about having a clock maker disconnect the chimes, but they feel that would defeat the whole point of having the clock. They really want to keep the heirloom clock, but the racket is driving them crazy.

The Solution
There's no telling why Sally howls at the clock. Some dogs howl at other dogs. Some howl at sirens. And some apparently howl at clocks.

It's possible that the clock's chimes resemble a howl, and Sally feels the need to howl back, says Liz Palika, a trainer in Oceanside, California, and author of *All Dogs Need Some Training*. It's also possible that the chimes bother Sally's ears, and she howls as a kind of protest. But she doesn't appear to be uncomfortable when she does it, so she's probably just howling because, well, that's what some dogs do.

" 'Quiet' is a must-know command for loud dogs," says Palika. "And beagles are known for being loud. When Sally starts howling, her owners should tell her, 'Sally, quiet.' If she doesn't quiet down immediately, they should say, 'no,' in a low, growly tone of voice. And as soon as she stops howling, they should reward her with a treat." Sally will be faced with a choice. She'll either have to give in to her howling impulses or button up long enough to get the treat. Most dogs will choose the treat.

There is one little complication, however. Sally howls every time the clock chimes. This means her owners will have to be present, commands and treats at the ready, every hour on the hour, at least for a while. It's the only way Sally will make the connection between the command to be quiet and the sound of the clock. It may take a few weeks, but she'll eventually learn to lay off the Big Ben routine, Palika says.

CHAPTER EIGHTEEN

STAYING WITH FRIENDS

Even hosts who love dogs don't always love their behavior—especially when it's the type of behavior they'd never allow in their own dogs. Helping your dog be a proper guest will reduce the risk of social friction and ensure that everyone enjoys the visit.

Most dogs don't travel much. When they do, they probably feel like tourists who have stumbled into a fancy French restaurant with foreign menus and too many forks. Staying with friends is delicate even for people because the rules and expectations are always different than they are at home. The confusion is more pronounced for dogs, which means they're sure to commit all kinds of four-pawed faux pas, like climbing on the couch, complaining when they don't get their usual 5:00 A.M. walks, or, perish the thought, urinating on the corner of an expensive carpet.

This Shetland sheepdog doesn't love the water, but her hosts will appreciate her nice smell and will be more likely to invite her back.

Then there are the human issues you have to deal with. People who love you may not love your dog. And they certainly won't love the social limitations that dogs invariably impose. Their plans may call for a day of sight-seeing followed by a long night out on the town. Your dog, in the meantime, is expecting to be let out at certain times and to have plenty of company the rest of the time. These conflicting agendas can be compromised, but they can't be ignored, says Cheryl S. Smith, a trainer in Port Angeles, Washington, and author of *The Trick Is in the Training*.

There's also the question of whether your dog is truly welcome in your hosts' home, adds Darlene Arden, author of *The Irrepressible Toy Dog*. "If they are dog people, they'll likely be thrilled, but otherwise you could put quite a strain on the friendship," she says.

Arden, who has traveled extensively, has identified a few key areas where host-dog conflicts invariably arise. By anticipating these problems and planning ahead, you can keep your dog happy and keep your friends.

Neat Dogs Get Invited Back

People understand that rules change in different situations, but dogs don't know this. That's why trainers always emphasize consistency—dogs simply can't recognize gray areas. In their minds, nearly everything fits into one of two categories: allowed or forbidden. They can't make distinctions. At home, they drool on the kitchen floor and sprawl on the pillows. So why not in someone else's house?

Since dogs aren't going to change their habits for a 2-day trip, it's up to the people to make the necessary adjustments. Every dog has different habits, but the one thing that has the potential to cause the most conflicts is neatness. Taking care of your dog's personal hygiene is the easiest way to keep everyone happy.

Brush the heck out of her. Even people who love dogs don't love dog hair. The idea of having to vacuum all day after you've gone isn't going to make any host happy. It's worth spending an hour brushing your dog before leaving home, Arden says. While you're at it, give her a bath, too.

Control the slobber. Nature made dogs a little moist around the mouth. They drool when they eat, when they sleep, and when they're getting their bellies rubbed. A little bit of slobber probably won't rub anyone the wrong way, but sloppy splashes on the hardwood floors aren't going to warm your hosts' hearts. You may want to pick up a bib at a pet supply store. Or tie a bandanna around your dog's neck. It shows that your dog is aware of her limitations and is trying to be accommodating. People will appreciate the effort.

Dogs who shed a lot, such as German shepherds, should be brushed thoroughly before they go visiting. You won't get rid of all the loose hair, but grooming will prevent visible messes.

FAST FIX "If you allow your dog on the bed when you're at home, take your own sheet or bedspread for her to lie on," says Smith. Better yet, if she usually uses her own pet bed, take it along. You can put it on the floor next to your bed. She'll feel secure, and you won't have to worry about paying the dry-cleaning bills.

Making the Introductions

Travel is easy when you visit a pet-free family. Things get more complicated when you introduce your dog into someone else's menagerie. Cats aren't a problem because they usually just disappear until you and your pet leave. But dogs will have to deal with the new arrival.

"Dogs are social animals, and for the most part, they really enjoy meeting other dogs," says Norm Costello, D.V.M., a veterinarian in Rancho Sante Fe, California, and owner of Animal Keepers, a chain of upscale kennels in San Diego. But sometimes they don't. That's when people change their plans and start looking for a nearby hotel.

Rather than throwing dogs together and hoping that everyone gets along, Arden recommends starting off with a three-part ritual.

1. Dogs need to meet outside in the yard. This is because they are territorial, and the resident dog may feel as though she has to defend her property from strangers. Once dogs have met and gotten along, it's fine to go inside.

2. Put the dogs on leashes before introducing them. Fights don't occur very often, but even a quick outburst can do a lot of damage—to your nerves as well as to the dogs. Be prepared for a little bit of blustering, which usually gives way to friendship or at least acceptance. If it turns out that the dogs simply can't stand the sight of each other, you'll have to make other plans. They aren't going to get over it in a few days.

3. Stand back while they do their customary sniffing. It's the equivalent of a handshake, and you'll know in a minute or two if the introduction went smoothly. Once the preliminaries are over and the dogs relax, they're probably ready to be friends.

LIVING THE GOOD LIFE

There comes a time in every dog's life when traveling with the family isn't an option. Dog-sitting services are one possibility. Another is to check your dog into a kennel. Kennels have a bad reputation because, for a long time, they tended to be nothing more than outdoor runs with concrete floors. But an increasing number of kennel owners have realized that people aren't satisfied with such rudimentary accommodations. They want their dogs to be comfortable—indeed, pampered.

Enter Animal Keepers, a chain of upscale kennels in San Diego. Each dog has his own suite, and there's a wide range of exercise and play activities, including scheduled romps with other dogs. Water-loving dogs have their choice of kiddie pools in the courtyard. And there are many extras, including toys stuffed with treats and the "yappy hour," in which dogs get their own Frosty Paws ice cream treats.

"It's a change of pace for dogs, and they break down the doors to get in," says Norm Costello, D.V.M., a veterinarian in Rancho Santa Fe, California, and owner of Animal Keepers. "Sometimes, the owners are embarrassed because when it's time to go home, they have a hard time getting them out the door."

All of this opulence isn't free, of course. Traditional kennels typically charge $5 to $10 dollars a day, while the rates at Animal Keepers range from $18 to $21. Clearly, a lot of people don't mind paying a little extra. The upscale kennels have been so successful that Dr. Costello is building an even fancier facility in Orange County, with 15,000 square feet and individual suites that are the size of small living rooms and include raised beds and color televisions. Some rooms will also have video cameras with online hookups that will allow people to periodically check in via the Internet.

A Place to Call Home

Even dogs who are excited by the adventure of staying with new people will often conk out and stay asleep—and out of trouble—for a good part of the trip. That's the best scenario. The worst is when your dog paces, whines, chews the table legs, or has an accident in the corner.

Dogs don't calm down easily, so you'll want to get them settled in first. Take a minute or two to find a place where your dog can hang out when you're gone for the day, if nothing else. Having a place of her own will reduce the risk of household damage, and dogs generally feel happier and more secure when they're tucked into smallish spaces.

People who travel a lot with their dogs often pack baby gates in their cars. These fit in almost any doorway and can be used to cordon off parts of the house. Unlike solid doors, they allow your dog to see where you are and watch what's going on, which helps keep her anxiety to manageable levels.

Your friends may encourage you to confine the dogs—yours and theirs—in the same place. Don't do it, advises Dr. Costello. It's not uncommon for dogs to get along fine when people are around, then terrorize each other when the people are gone. Even if the dogs remain friendly, size differences can be a real issue. You don't want to be in the position of having to explain what happened when your great horse of a dog accidentally sat on her thimble-size companion.

Mary Monteith, a retired school teacher in Bristol, Indiana, discovered for herself the danger of using her host's accommodations for

A baby gate allows dogs to see where everyone is, while keeping them out from underfoot.

her own dog, a Shetland sheepdog named Skye. "During one visit, we fastened Skye to the dog tether in the yard," she says. No one thought about it, but Skye was a lot shorter than the resident dog—so much so that the tether pulled his collar right off his head. "We found Skye up on the highway, headed for home."

Mealtime Etiquette

Dogs don't worry about forks, napkins, or chewing with their mouths open. And because they eat just about anything, no one has to worry about serving them the right foods.

111

Meals away from home would seem like a no-brainer: Put some food in their bowls, and watch them go.

When dogs are by themselves, eating is easy. It gets more complicated when there are other pets around. Problems that you're likely to see may include:

Competition. Dogs consider eating to be a social activity, but they define "social" as merely being in the same place. Otherwise, it's every dog for herself, and they don't hesitate to defend their food.

Theft. In human culture, it's polite to take small servings and make sure that everyone gets their share. Among dogs, however, the rule is to gobble as quickly as possible—and then steal someone else's.

Cat incursions. Given a choice between stealing another dog's food or going for the cat's, dogs always choose the feline fare. For one thing, they won't get beaten up should they get caught in the act. And besides, they think cat food is very tasty.

Ugly messes. The combination of anxiety, excitement, and eating new foods often makes dogs sick. Diarrhea on the carpet isn't any fun at home, and it's mortifying when it happens at someone else's house. Experienced travelers always take a supply of their dog's regular food, says Steve Dale, a radio host at WGN in Chicago, a syndicated columnist, and author of the book *Doggone Chicago*. It's also wise to feed your dog away from where the resident pets are eating, no matter how much your host encourages you to do otherwise. Sure, they'll probably get along, but maybe they won't. Why take the chance?

Nature's Call

You would think that fire hydrants are the same everywhere, but dogs know better. And the idea of making pit stops in unaccustomed places—using this hydrant instead of that one—can be a little too much.

"I live in the country, and my dogs grew up on grass," Smith says. "When I visited people in the city, the dogs would refuse to go to the bathroom. I had to teach them to go on concrete." It works the other way, too—dogs who live in cities may be extremely reluctant to use dirt or grass. They can only hold it for so long, of course. Lost opportunities for pit stops on a morning walk can mean accidents in the house in the afternoon.

Unless your dog has truly remarkable holding power, you're going to have to be patient—and a little creative—to make sure there are no mistakes. Here are a few tips you may want to try.

Multiply by two. If you normally take your dog out twice a day, go four times when you're staying with friends. This will give your a dog a chance to get used to the neighborhood and get over her initial reluctance. The extra exercise will help get things moving, too.

Identify the best places. Just as people travel with itineraries of things to do, your dog needs an itinerary, too. Rather than showing her something different, however, find something similar to what she knows. If you live in the suburbs or the country, for example, find out where the parks are, Smith says. It's not that dogs insist on perfection, but anything that reminds them of home is going to be appreciated.

GETTING ALONG WITH KIDS

Dogs and children go together like peanut butter and jelly—or like oil and vinegar, depending on the mix. Your dog may just want to say, "Hello, hello, I love you," but for children who aren't used to dogs, all of this friendly noise can scare the living hooey out of them, says Steve Dale, a radio host at WGN in Chicago, a syndicated columnist, and author of the book *Doggone Chicago*. Here are a few ways to reduce the potential for social friction.

Tell children to move slowly and speak deeply. An unfortunate consequence of dogs' wild pasts is that they view fast-moving, squeaky things as being eminently chaseable. Young children, with their high voices and high energy levels, can find themselves getting more attention than they want. Unless your dog is used to children or is very well trained, children need to understand that they should move slowly and lower their voices to prevent her from getting too excited.

Stand tall. From a dog's point of view, children, with their small sizes and yippy voices, can easily be confused with puppies, who aren't to be respected. Until everyone gets to know each other, children should be encouraged to stand up when they're around dogs. This makes them appear taller and gives them more status, from the canine point of view. It's hard for children to resist the temptation to get down on all fours to play, but it makes them appear smaller and weaker, and some dogs will instinctively take advantage of the opportunity to push them around.

Pet them under the chin. Unless they know you, dogs don't like being patted on top of their heads. They see this as an act of dominance, and often they won't welcome it, especially from children.

Establish a chain of command. Obedience drills aren't a lot of fun, but they're the best way to teach dogs that they have to listen to all people, including the small ones. It's worth spending 5 to 10 minutes helping the children in the family to give some simple "sit" or "stay" commands. Your dog will figure out that she has to take the kids seriously, and this will reduce the friction later on.

CHAPTER NINETEEN

HIKING

When dogs take to the trail, the most sedate sidewalk strollers can turn into leash-straining bundles of trouble. A little pre-hike training and a few tricks will ensure that jaunts in the woods are a pleasure for everyone.

Even dogs who have spent their entire lives in cities, sniffing the same few blocks of sidewalk, undergo a transformation when they take to the trail. They revel in the fresh air and open land and nearly go out of their minds as they discover for themselves the thousands of intriguing smells that their ancestors smelled every day.

It's difficult for even the best-trained dogs to control themselves, and many don't even try. As soon as they're out of the car, it's as though they forget every command they ever knew. They bark wildly at squirrels, butterflies, and falling leaves. They surge up the trail, scattering hikers left and right. They run so much and get so excited that they're overwhelmed before they top the first hill. That's about when they plop down and seem to say, "You go ahead. I'll just wait for the first cab right here."

There's a lot more freedom on the trail than on a crowded city street, which is why people take their dogs hiking in the first place. But even in the wilderness, there are a few basic rules of doggy comportment, says Cheryl S. Smith, a trainer in Port Angeles, Washington, and author of *On the Trail with Your Canine Companion*. Rangers get complaints every year about barking, menacing, or merely overexuberant dogs. And hundreds of owners find themselves apologizing for their dogs' unruly behavior—and vowing never to take them hiking again.

BREED SPECIFIC

Dalmatians are among the best hiking dogs because they've been bred to travel far and fast—which is why they were the dogs of choice for early fire companies. Pekingese and other short-nosed breeds often have a hard time on the trail because their breathing isn't very efficient and they get winded easily.

Under Control

Nearly all of the behavior problems that occur on the trail could be prevented by the simple expedient of putting dogs on leashes, Smith says. Unless you do your hiking out of season or in extremely remote places, your dog is going to meet other hikers. Even people who own dogs themselves can't be sure if this 40-pound bundle of excitement rocketing toward them is friendly or not. And *their* dogs may not be sure, either.

Keeping dogs on leashes is the rule on most public lands—not only for the comfort of other hikers, but for the health of the dogs themselves. "Dogs have been shot for chasing wildlife; and since a lot of public hiking areas are also grazing areas, you have to be careful all the time," Smith says.

Dogs on leashes still get to enjoy the outdoors, she adds. They have innumerable opportunities to sniff and be sniffed, and they receive a lot of compliments for their impressive manners. This is assuming, of course, that your dog is used to a leash in the first place. If she's not, a pleasant hike has a way of deteriorating into a shoulder-wrenching afternoon as you try to go one way while your dog is determined to go the other.

Dogs don't need formal obedience training to get trail-ready, Smith says. Here's a crash course that you can start—and complete—a day or two before setting out.

• Before leaving home, take your dog for two or three walks a day. Put on the leash like you always do and head down the street.

• When your dog surges ahead, brace your feet and pull your arms in close to your body for support. "You don't have to say anything," Smith says. "Just stand there like a post." Dogs don't like the sensation of straining without making progress and will quickly back off a bit.

• When your dog relaxes and there's slack in the leash, say, "Good close," Smith says. Then continue your walk.

Dogs who are set in their ways will strain forward and hit the ends of their leashes repeatedly. "You'll have to stop again and repeat the process until she gets the idea," Smith explains. A few

Dogs should be expected to lighten the load for their human companions by carrying their own food and water in doggy backpacks.

115

Dogs usually walk on the left of their owners. But when you're hiking, it's useful to teach them to swap sides on command so that they can get out of the way of oncoming hikers.

whom, it seemed, had been coached in the finer points of etiquette. "I'd been looking forward to spending a few days just listening to the silence," she says. "But the barking never stopped, and twice I got hit in the knees by dogs zooming up from behind."

There aren't a lot of rules that dogs need to know to be good outdoor citizens, Smith explains. The basics include:

Keep the noise down. You can't expect dogs in the wilderness to act like librarians, but no one wants to listen to cacophonies of canine choruses. Dogs need to understand that while some barking is acceptable, too much is a problem. "Dogs will stop barking when you place your hand on top of their muzzles," Smith says. "After a while, they learn that this is the signal to be quiet."

Walk side by side. Wilderness trails are often too narrow for people and dogs to pass in comfort. Even dogs who stick by their owners will block passersby who approach on the left—the side on which dogs are trained to walk. To avoid collisions, Smith says, it's helpful to teach dogs to move to either side. Use the leash to direct your dog to the side that you want her on, then tell her, "Side," while motioning to your thigh. Most dogs will quickly learn to associate the word with the gesture and will happily move to the required side, Smith says.

Make the introductions. Trail life is filled with uncertainties, and for many hikers, a big unknown is whether approaching dogs are friendly or not. You have to help your dog understand that she needs to wait for your signal

days of practice aren't going to make your dog a candidate for the Westminster dog show, but they're enough to get her comfortable with the leash and will allow both of you to enjoy the outdoors a little more.

Manners on the Trail

Nearly every hiker can tell stories about weekends that literally went to the dogs. Molly Hopkins, a landscape architect in Albuquerque, New Mexico, remembers a hike in New Mexico's Pecos National Historical Park when nearly everyone she encountered had dogs—none of before approaching other people or dogs. "When I see people with dogs coming my way, I usually ask them if their dogs would like to meet mine," Smith says. "Sometimes, the dogs really enjoy it, and you never know, you may make a friend."

Let strangers pass. Since the narrowness of wilderness trails makes it difficult for people to keep their distance, the social thing for dogs to do is step aside when people approach, Smith says. This is especially helpful when you're on a trail with bicyclists or runners, because they can trigger a dog's chase instinct. "I always have the dogs sit when bicyclists approach or when other people have dogs that they aren't controlling very well," Smith says.

Canine Outfitters

Just as you expect people you hike with to carry their own belongings, your dog should pull her weight, too. As more and more dogs take to the woods, pet supply and hiking stores have begun stocking quite an array of canine hiking gear. You'll want to add a few extra items to your pack as well. Here's a rundown of what every trail dog needs.

A nylon collar and cloth leash. Metal choke collars tend to snag on brush; and because leather leashes absorb sweat, they act like magnets for porcupines and other critters, Smith says. She recommends using a flat nylon quick-release collar and a nylon or cloth leash.

Bug protection. When one dog is scratching because of fleas, it won't be long before every dog that she encounters is scratching, too. Smith recommends spritzing dogs with a flea spray before you hit the trail. Veterinarians often recommend sprays containing pyrethrins, which are safer than some chemical sprays. "I spray some onto a rag and then wipe the dog with it so I can control where the spray goes," Smith says.

Boots. A dog with sore feet isn't going to walk very far, which means that the people in the party will either have to stop before they're ready or carry her to the camp. To ensure that your dog keeps up, you may want to fit her with protective boots, available in pet supply stores. Most dogs don't like wearing boots, so you may want to borrow a set from someone to see if your dog will put up with them.

Many wilderness trails are narrow, so it's courteous to step aside with your dog and let others pass.

Food pack. Since your dog won't cook dinner or set up the tent, the least she can do is carry her own food, along with collapsible food and water dishes. Many pet supply and camping stores sell sidesaddle packs that are contoured to fit around a dog's rib cage. "Even a little dog is capable of carrying her own food," Smith says.

Packs take some getting used to because they make dogs a little wider than usual, Smith adds. This can confuse dogs when they're walking off-trail. "Some dogs are always surprised when they don't fit through the usual spaces."

Dotting the I's

Most hikes don't require a lot of preparation beyond packing food, fresh water, and perhaps some Dramamine for the drive to the trail. But your dog will have a much better time if you take care of a few additional details.

• If your dog's only exercise lately has been walking around the block, you'll want to spend some time getting her into shape for the trek, says Smith. She recommends taking longer walks than usual in the weeks before leaving, preferably walks that involve going up and down hills. Long walks are good because you'll be taking them on your trip.

• Ask your veterinarian to make sure that your dog is up for the trip. While you're

Pet supply stores sell I.D. capsules that attach to your dog's collar and contain information on where you're staying and how to contact you should your dog become lost.

POOCH PUZZLER

Why do dogs eat dung?

Even dogs who are picky about food will eagerly sample the droppings that other animals leave behind. Veterinarians aren't sure why they do it, but they suspect that it's one of three things.

1. Early training. Mother dogs often keep their nests clean by eating the stools of the pups, and dogs learn by watching.

2. Nutrition. Some dogs may not get all of the nutrients that they need from their food, and dung is filled with usable proteins, vitamins, and minerals.

3. Taste. Dogs have 215 million more scent receptors than people, and it's possible that the scent and flavor of dung provides a taste sensation that people can't—or don't want to—imagine.

at the vet's office, get a copy of your dog's health certificate and proof of vaccinations. Some campgrounds and border crossings won't let dogs pass unless they have the proper documentation, Smith says.

• Your dog's usual identification tags won't do you a whole lot of good if she gets lost, because you won't be home to get the call. Smith recommends equipping your dog with temporary identification—something that tells people where you're staying or what the campground number is. Pet supply stores sell small containers that hook on to pets' collars and contain papers that list your current location, your destination, and your contact information.

STRANGE behavior

Name RICKI

Breed BORDER COLLIE

Age 3

The Behavior

Ricki and her family go camping several times a year. While the adults are hiking or cooking supper, the children collect sticks, which they use for swordplay, building forts, and roasting marshmallows. Ricki, unfortunately, likes sticks even more than the kids do. So she steals them. When the children try to take them back, Ricki resorts to tug-of-war. Her attitude seems to be that the winner takes all—or at least half. The children get mad, Ricki gets yelled at, and the adults are sick of the whole thing. Except for her stick-athons, Ricki is a gentle dog and careful around the kids. No one understands why she has this grabby side or what they can do to stop it.

The Solution

Dogs act in mysterious ways. No one will ever know why Ricki focuses all of her attention on sticks. But her single-minded pursuit isn't unusual, especially among Border collies, who tend to be a little obsessive, says Betty Fisher, a trainer based in San Diego and co-author of *So Your Dog's Not Lassie.* "They have intense personalities and a very single-minded nature."

It's likely that Ricki will never give up her passion for sticks, Fisher explains. The challenge for the family is to make her more discriminating in her choice of sticks. She recommends that the adults (not the children, who won't have enough authority or control) practice a simple obedience drill: They should have Ricki sit and stay, then throw a stick for her to chase—and praise her when she chews or runs around with it. With practice, Ricki will learn that only sticks that are thrown are hers. Sticks that are on the ground or being used as marshmallow skewers are someone else's.

At first, Ricki will try to extend her privilege to all sticks, Fisher says. She may even get pretty pushy about it. She should be ignored. Praise should only be given when she plays with her stick. She'll have a hard time telling the difference at first. So she should probably stay on a leash so she doesn't get a chance to rediscover the joy of stick grabbing. If Ricki is successful at grabbing even one stick that she shouldn't, she may decide that that's the best way to get them after all.

CHAPTER TWENTY

AIRLINE ETIQUETTE

Flying is stressful even for seasoned travelers. It's worse for dogs.
They can't wander the aisles or watch in-flight videos. They need a little extra
help to stay comfortable and calm.

Most dogs are required by airlines to travel in the cargo hold, but small dogs may qualify as carry-on luggage. This means that they get to fly in comfort in the cabin, and they make great portable companions—unless they happen to get frustrated when their canine urges to explore and sniff are thwarted or when they're simply scared to death. That's when they start panting, barking, or whining. That's no fun for you, for them, or for the other people on the plane.

Dogs aren't like laptop computers, which can be pushed under a seat when you want a break. But they can be taught to relax and enjoy the flight. In fact, show dogs log more frequent-flier miles than most people and quickly get used to the routine, says Alan Resnick, editor in chief of *Dogs in Canada* magazine.

Working with Instincts

Dogs who ride in the cabin must be small enough to fit in a container that will fit under the seat. In most cases, the upper limit is about 19 inches high. You can buy airline-approved carriers at pet supply stores. Carriers made from hard plastic, such as the Vari-Kennel (size 100), will fit under most airline seats. So will soft-sided bags such as the Sherpa Bag.

People cringe at the idea of spending hours in such tight quarters, but dogs feel differently because they have an instinct called denning. They're most comfortable in small, cozy spaces. Once dogs understand that their carriers are dens, they view them as wonderful retreats and

He'll never love flying, but planning and preparation have turned this Belgian sheepdog into a seasoned traveler.

look forward to spending time there—not only at 30,000 feet but back home as well, says Resnick.

Dogs don't automatically take to new dens, however. It takes a little work to make a house a home.

- A few weeks before your trip, leave the carrier in the living room or bedroom so that your dog can explore it at his leisure. Putting a few treats or a favorite toy inside will pique his interest and help him associate the carrier with nice things.

- Once your dog is happily climbing in and out of the carrier—or, better yet, is taking little naps inside it—close it for a while. He may get a little nervous at first, but if you encourage him and make it all seem like fun, he'll start to relax. Keep him in the carrier for 10 to 15 minutes, then give him a great treat when you let him out. Do this two or three times a day, gradually increasing the crate time in half-hour increments.

- Keep practicing until he can stay in the crate for about 3 hours without getting upset. This is about the length of many plane trips. "Dogs have no concept of time," says Alan Alford, owner of Fresh Pond Travel in Marlborough, Massachusetts, a

Rules and Regulations

Whether your dog will ride in the cabin or in the belly of the plane, plan on spending about $50 each way. You also need a current health certificate and rabies vaccination record. And since most dogs fly belowdecks, you need to plan for their comfort and safety.

- Only a few dogs are allowed on each flight, usually on a first-come, first-served basis. So plan on arriving at least 2 hours before departure. Be sure to check your dog in with your regular luggage as "excess baggage." Don't send him "freight" because freight may not travel on the same flight as you.

- The flight crew can monitor the atmosphere in the cargo hold, so it's worth asking them to watch out for your dog while you're in the air.

- Airline crates have containers for water, but this usually gets spilled fairly quickly. "I put a doggy treat in one cup and fill the other cup with water and freeze it," says Chris Walkowicz, a judge for the American Kennel Club and author of *The Perfect Match: A Dog Buyer's Guide*. "The dog has ice to lick, but water won't slosh out and make a mess."

- Lining the crate with layers of newspaper and putting cedar shavings on top will help keep dogs comfortable. "It smells good and also contains any mess if the dog uses the bathroom or gets sick," Walkowicz says.

Dogs who are going to fly need to get used to traveling in crates. When they're introduced to the crates gradually, they'll come to see them as safe, secure dens.

121

company that specializes in booking travel arrangements for show dogs. "They don't recognize the difference between 2 hours and 12 hours."

In-Flight Manners

Some dogs take to air travel as easily as they sneak up on the couch, but others start getting nervous even before they leave home—and the sounds and smells of a busy airport can just about put them over the edge. The only way to keep them calm (and quiet) in the air is to keep them occupied, Resnick says.

Treat them little and often. Dogs who have big meals before flying are likely to deposit most of the food on the floor of the crate. But their stomachs won't object to small amounts of food, and the excitement of getting treats will keep their minds occupied. Resnick recommends taking along a hollow toy that's loaded with sticky cheese or peanut butter. Most dogs forget their fears when they're given something good to play with and eat—and dogs who are eating can't bark or whine, he explains.

Be nonchalant. Dogs are very good at picking up signals from their owners. When you're tense and nervous about how they're feeling, they get even more anxious. It's fine to reassure a nervous dog, but you should keep your voice low and calm and act as though nothing is out of the ordinary, Resnick says.

Make friends with your neighbor. Even though airline regulations don't permit dogs to

The Parachuting Pooch

Brutus loves to fly. In fact, this 10-pound miniature dachshund loves it so much that he does it without a plane. That's okay because his owner, Ron Sirull of Phoenix, Arizona, flies without a plane, too. A parachutist who promotes special events, Sirull has discovered that parachuting with Brutus really makes people notice.

Brutus doesn't have his own parachute (he can't pull a rip cord), but he doesn't need one, because Sirull hooks him up to a harness, puts on his special goggles, and tucks him inside a chest pouch on his jumpsuit. On the way down, Brutus's lips flap into a grin with the rushing wind.

Despite the thrill of hurtling downward at 35 miles an hour, parachuting is a very safe sport—although Sirull thinks it may have had some effect on Brutus's diminutive stature. "He used to be taller," Sirull jokes, "but we had a couple of hard landings."

step out of their carriers, there may be some unofficial leeway, especially if the people who are sitting around you don't mind a little canine company. "Whether you follow the rule is a matter of your conscience and the patience of the person you're sitting next to," says Alford. As long as your dog is quiet and keeps a low profile, many travelers won't object.

FAST FIX The quickest way to calm a puppy who's leaving home and flying for the first time is to surround him with a familiar scent. Resneck recommends lining the crate with a blanket from home. "Rub the blanket over Mom dog and the other puppies so you have a nice reminder of home that your new puppy can curl up in," he suggests.

STRANGE behavior

Name GORDY

Breed DALMATIAN

Age 6

The Behavior

Gordy has a one-way mind. His bed and food dish are on the lower level of a split-level home, and he eagerly runs downstairs when it's time to eat or go to bed. But for some reason, he doesn't realize that the stairs are exactly the same going up as coming down. When it's time to climb up, he freezes and starts trembling. Eventually, he makes the climb, but he never likes to do it. His owners suspect that he's remembering the time when he fell down the stairs several years before. They've tried yelling, cajoling, and dragging him up the stairs, but no dice. He's still terrified.

The Solution

"Dalmatians are the elephants of the dog world," says Judith Halliburton, a trainer and behaviorist in Albuquerque, New Mexico, and author of *Raising Rover*. "They have incredible memories and rarely forget a traumatic incident like a fall."

Actually, any dog can develop a phobia, and the fear often makes even less sense than Gordy's. Some dogs are terrified of lampposts or curbs. Some are afraid of hats or run away from men with beards or cower when they see people in uniform. Even the rustling of paper will put some dogs into a panic. In some ways, Gordy's owners are lucky. His fear does have some basis in reality, which gives them something specific to overcome.

"The way to solve this dog's problem is, literally, one step at a time," says Halliburton. "They should have him sit at the bottom of the stairs. Just that little command is going to lessen his anxiety because he'll think, 'Good, something I can do.'"

After Gordy sits, they'll need to tempt him upward with something very special. Halliburton recommends putting a bit of dried liver—Gordy's favorite food—on the first step. He may hesitate, but sooner or later, his tastebuds will urge him upward. When he climbs up to grab the food, he should be made to sit again. At this point, his owners will want to reward and praise the heck out of him, then give it up for the day.

Each day, they should help Gordy climb another step, lured by liver. "It's going to take at least as many days as there are steps," Halliburton says.

FIND THE CAR

It's not a trick that you can use at the mall, but when you're out in the country and far from the nearest road, you can depend on your dog to find his way back to the car. With a little training, he'll even be able to pick out your car among dozens of nearly identical makes and models.

1 Put your dog on a leash and walk him to the car several times a day for a few days. Touch the metal, say "car," and give him a treat. When he starts perking up when he hears "car," have him touch the car with his nose or paw, and give him a reward.

    Starting from the yard or the end of the block, tell your dog, "Find the car," and walk him to it. When he touches the car, give him a treat. Keep practicing for several days.

2 Rub the bottom of your shoe with a piece of hot dog and walk toward your car. Encourage your dog when he sniffs around your feet, and keep encouraging him as he follows your trail to the car. Give him a great reward when he makes it to the car and touches it with his nose or paw.

GET THE PAPER

Dogs love to carry things in their mouths, and sometimes they'll even bring them back. They especially love retrieving newspapers because they're easy to carry. And because the paper arrives every day, your dog will always have something to look forward to.

1 Make a "training paper" by rolling the newspaper tightly and wrapping it with tape. Toss it a few feet away, and say, "Get the paper!" As your dog gets more skilled, start tossing the paper where it usually lands. Make sure that your dog sees you throw it.

2 Once your dog has the hang of chasing and retrieving the paper, start putting it on the ground when he's not around. Then bring him out, show him the paper, and say, "Get the paper!" At this point, he'll be ready to take the final step—looking for and retrieving the newspaper no matter where it lands.

PUSH THE ELEVATOR BUTTON

Many hotels welcome dogs, but other guests may not, especially when you're all crammed into an elevator and riding to the 53rd floor. A fun way to break the ice is to ask your dog to push the "close door" button. Assuming that your dog is tall enough to reach the button, it's an easy lesson to teach.

1 Begin by teaching your dog to put his front feet on the wall. Stick a small cardboard circle on the wall at about the same height as an elevator button. Pat the spot and say, "Feet up!" With a little practice, your dog will learn to hit the spot every time. When he hits it, say, "Button!" Also give him a lot of praise.

2 Once your dog makes the connection between the "button" on the wall and the real buttons in the elevator, he'll be sure to have an appreciative audience as he rides from floor to floor.

Say Thank You

Most dogs know a few social niceties, but only a few understand the importance of saying thank you. By giving a polite bow when people do nice things, your dog will always get a first-class reception.

1 While your dog is standing, kneel or sit on the floor next to him. Put one hand under his tummy to support his rear end. With the other hand, show him a treat and hold it under his nose.

While keeping his rear up with one hand, slowly move the hand with the treat down toward the floor. Where the treat goes, his nose will follow. As he moves his nose down, say, "Thank you." Then give him the treat and a lot of praise.

2 When his front end is all the way down, tell him, "Stay," so he holds the position for a few seconds.

PART FIVE

MEETING THE NEIGHBORS

These days, most dogs live in cities and suburbs. This means they have to get familiar with situations that their ancestors never thought about, like meeting cats without chasing them, and doing their business in parks and not on the sidewalk.

CHAPTER TWENTY-ONE

LIFE ON A LEASH

In an ideal world, dogs would run free. But dogs today have to deal with traffic and busy sidewalks, not to mention local laws. They need to know how to act on leashes. When they do it well, their people are happy, and they get to go out more often.

No dog has ever captured the essence of social fitness as well as Lassie. No matter what adventures the scriptwriters come up with, this wonderful collie behaves impeccably. She never jumps on people, barks when she isn't supposed to, sniffs people in embarrassing places, or tugs when Jeff or Timmy walk her on a leash—not that she is on a leash very often.

If Lassie lived in the real world instead of on television, she'd spend a lot more time attached to one end of a human-to-canine tether. The wide-open lands of yesteryear have been covered over with shopping malls, housing developments, and four-lane highways. Modern environments are simply too crowded and dangerous for dogs to navigate safely on their own.

In any event, most dogs don't have anywhere near the self-control that Lassie has. Leashes

Good leash training has made these Italian greyhounds well-mannered walkers rather than a handful of trouble.

make it possible for people to keep tabs on their dogs when the dogs would prefer to be doing something else. Moreover, many local governments now have laws requiring dogs to be on leashes when they're out in public. Like it or not, leashes are a fact of life for most dogs today.

Ties That Bind

Leashes may be necessary, but they aren't without hassles for dogs or their owners. From a dog's point of view, wearing a leash and collar is an unwelcome restraint and sometimes a literal pain in the neck. For you, a leash is more likely to be a pain in the shoulder as you pull one way and your dog pulls another. Even when there isn't outright resistance, a walk around the block gets complicated when:

• The leash gets tangled around your legs—or, more often, around your dog's legs—like a Chinese jump rope.

• Your dog pulls so hard on the leash that you feel as though you're training for the chariot race in *Ben-Hur*.

• Your dog suddenly decides to sniff and anoint a tree. When you're walking slowly, this isn't a problem. If you happen to be running, the abrupt braking action can cause you to fall on your face.

• Your dog sees something that puzzles or worries her and stops in her tracks to investigate. She won't move, and neither can you.

• In a valiant attempt to obey leash and pooper-scooper laws at the same time, you engage in a public version of Twister as you struggle to manage the leash and a plastic bag at the same time.

Leash walks will never be as easy as wandering freely in the country or throwing balls in a leashes-optional park. But it doesn't have to be a maddening experience, either. Leashes rarely come with instructions because the principles are pretty simple. But the execution takes a little practice.

What Works for You

Trainers sometimes give the impression that using a leash is a precision art and that everyone should be able to walk down the street in lock-step with their dogs. True, the classic heeling position, in which dogs are practically attached to their owners' left legs, looks nice in dog shows. But this is rarely necessary in real life. There's nothing wrong with having your dog amble somewhere alongside you on a loose leash, says Robin Kovary, director of the American Dog Trainers Network in New York City.

Depending on how much you want to work with your dog, you can achieve as much (or as little) precision as you wish. People who live

This Australian shepherd is totally focused on his owner, whether he's on or off the leash.

in cities and walk on crowded sidewalks usually want their dogs right by their sides. Those who do their walking in suburbia are generally more flexible.

There's no real reason for your dog to always walk on your left side, adds Sarah Wilson, a trainer in Gardiner, New York, and co-author of *Childproofing Your Dog*. This practice originated with hunters. Since they carried their guns over their right forearms, they wanted their dogs on the left for safety. Trainers continue this custom mainly because it's more convenient when all of their students are positioned in the same way.

BREED SPECIFIC

Walking on a leash isn't exactly rocket science, but for some dogs, it may as well be. Siberian huskies have a hard time learning not to pull, because they've been bred to be power plants for sleds. Herding dogs such as shelties (left) tend to run ahead—a genetic throwback to their urges to herd lost sheep—and retrievers want to indulge their tracking instincts by keeping their noses close to the ground.

"There's no magic to this," Wilson says. "It really doesn't matter whether your dog is walking on your right or left side."

There is one aspect of leash training in which there's very little leeway: You need to be consistent. "The rules for walking your dog need to be very clear," says Kimberly Barry, Ph.D., a certified applied animal behaviorist in Austin, Texas. "Consistent training in a positive manner is the key."

Buying a Leash

A leash is nothing more than a tether that links you and your dog together. It can be as simple as a length of rope attached to a bandanna or as beautifully intricate as a braided leather lead attached to a jeweled collar. Style and appearance are certainly one way to choose a leash. More important is function. Different leashes and collars do different jobs. Having the right equipment makes walking your dog a lot more fun. The wrong equipment makes things tough. You won't have much fun if the leash is hurting your hands, and your dog won't have much fun if the collar is hurting her neck.

Regardless of the style, you probably want a leash that's 6 feet long. This is long enough to give dogs freedom to sniff, and short enough to keep them under control. Longer leashes—up to 50 feet in some cases—are good when you're teaching puppies to come, but they're too unwieldy for regular walks.

Nylon or cotton leashes. These have many advantages. They're lightweight, fold easily into a pocket, and are inexpensive. But they're not very comfortable for the people holding them. "Nylon tends to be very slippery, and cotton webbing can give a nasty rope burn," says Deborah Manheim, a professional dog walker in Brooklyn, New York.

Leather leashes. Many people have love-hate relationships with leather leashes. They're heavy; they absorb odors; and they're slow to dry once they get wet. They're also three or four times the price of nylon leashes. Still, many trainers only use leather leashes—in part because they last almost forever, and also because they're comfortable to hold, Manheim says.

Retractable leashes. The main reason that people dislike leashes is that they restrict their dogs' ability to run and explore. Retractable leashes have solved this problem. Ranging in length from about 16 to 32 feet, retractable leashes allow you to play out extra line when the coast is clear, then zip it back in when you want your dog closer. People who own retractable leashes usually love them, but the convenience of freedom comes with a price. The leashes have thick plastic handles that are hard to get a grip on and can be uncomfortable to hold. "I prefer not to use them because if a dog is a puller, the retractable leash encourages this behavior," Manheim adds.

Another problem with retractable leashes has nothing to do with you or your dog, but with other people in the area. The lines are very thin and hard to see. More than a few people have walked between people and their dogs—and tripped because they never saw the leashes.

Specialty leashes. Manufacturers have created an astonishing variety of gear for pets (and people) with special needs. People with arthritis who have trouble holding a leash, for example, may use a product called PuppyPull, which

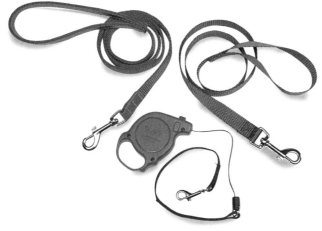

Choosing a leash has more to do with your personal style than with the type of dog you have. Top left and right: nylon leashes; bottom: retractable leash.

POOCH PUZZLER

Why do dogs grab their leashes in their mouths?

Sometimes, dogs get a little confused about who's supposed to hold the leash. Whether it's because they're excited or because they're trying to pull their people along, they may grab hold of the loose end of the leash and refuse to let go.

"Some dogs grab their leashes because they like having things in their mouths, and the leashes are right there," says Kimberly Barry, Ph.D., a certified applied animal behaviorist in Austin, Texas. "Others do it because grabbing the leashes reduces the tension of the collars on their necks."

This impromptu tug-of-war isn't always a problem, but it may cause hitches at both ends of the leash. For dogs, time spent grappling isn't time spent walking. And for people, few things are less appealing than holding the soggy end of a leash.

wraps around the waist and leaves the hands free. For dogs with arthritis or hip problems, there's a leash called Bottom's Up. It slightly raises the dog's rear end as she walks, which helps support her weight.

Couplers. If you're walking two or three small dogs and you don't feel like wrestling with multiple leashes, you'll probably want a coupler. Couplers have two ends: One end attaches to the leash, and the other end has multiple clips that allow you to hook on to several collars. Couplers are convenient and less expensive than buying several leashes. But the collar ends usually aren't

From left: slip or choke collar; nylon collar with plastic clasps; cotton webbing and leather collars in two different sizes.

long enough, so the dogs are always banging into each other. And they don't provide a lot of control, Manheim says.

Buckle collars. Usually made from leather or nylon, these are flat collars that you can adjust in the same way you would a belt. "They are ideal for small, delicate, and sensitive dogs, including puppies, and for adult dogs who walk nicely on a leash," says Kovary.

Head halters. Buckle collars don't give much control when you're working with assertive or unruly dogs. An alternative is the head halter. Made from soft nylon webbing, head halters have two parts: a loop that encircles a dog's muzzle, and a strap that goes behind her neck. They're designed in such a way that when a dog lunges forward, the nose loop pulls her head down and makes her lose her balance. After crashing into herself a few times, even the most headstrong dog learns not to pull against the leash.

"They're similar to horse bridles, which operate on the same principle: Where the head goes, the body must follow," Kovary explains. "They're very good for dogs who bark a lot when they're walking, who lunge at other dogs or people, or who walk along the sidewalk with their heads down in search of goodies."

The webbing on head halters is soft, but it still presses and rubs. Most dogs need a few weeks to get used to it.

Slip collars. Also called choke collars, these have traditionally been recommended by almost all trainers. They're designed in such a way that pulling the leash causes the collar to briefly tighten. This puts uncomfortable pressure on a dog's neck and also makes a jingling sound that dogs dislike. It's an effective way to correct them when they make mistakes.

Attitudes about slip collars have changed in recent years. Trainers still recommend them for dogs who are very independent or headstrong and don't readily respond to commands. "A slip collar may be the only thing that gets her attention," Kovary says. But for most dogs, the collars aren't necessary because there

A body harness is a comfortable alternative to a collar and leash, especially for puppies, small or delicate dogs, or dogs with back problems.

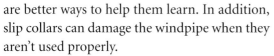

are better ways to help them learn. In addition, slip collars can damage the windpipe when they aren't used properly.

"Slip collars can be very hard on a dog," Kovary says. "A large percentage of dogs don't need them, and a large percentage of owners don't know how to use them."

Body harnesses. Puppies and small dogs have delicate throats and windpipes that can be injured by conventional collars. They often do better with body harnesses. Usually made of nylon webbing, harnesses embrace the torso rather than the neck. Even if you give the leash a stout pull, the pressure will be distributed over a wide area. This makes harnesses more comfortable and safer than conventional collars. And because the harnesses provide back support, they're often recommended for dogs with spinal problems.

Nighttime collars. A lot of people don't get home until dark, which makes the usual walk-the-dog ritual somewhat hazardous. Pet supply stores sell battery-powered collars with flashing lights. The flashes are quite bright and make dogs visible to cars from blocks away.

Taming the Leash

Until someone designs a leash that automatically walks dogs around the block and cleans up after them, people will continue to be attached to one end while their dogs have a great time at the other. There are thousands of trainers and obedience schools in the United States, and most communities have basic-skills classes going on nearly every night. Obedience classes are great places to learn the basics of leash

The mere sight of a leash is enough to launch most dogs into happy orbits. This fox terrier has learned that if she doesn't stand quietly, she doesn't get the walk.

control, but there are a few things that aren't always taught. For example:

Launch quietly. It's impossible for children to be calm when they see Christmas presents under the tree, and it's just as hard for dogs to relax when the leash comes out of the closet. They get so excited, in fact, that it's a challenge just to attach the leash, much less have a tranquil walk. "Proper leash deportment begins before you even put on the leash," Kovary says.

She recommends getting your dog in the right frame of mind by having her sit or lie down. Listening to you and obeying simple commands will focus her attention, Kovary explains. When you aren't in the mood for a struggle, you can simply hang out until she settles down on her own. Either way, don't attach the leash until the manic energy has cooled somewhat.

The most efficient way to hold a leash is to put your thumb through the loop and lay the strap across your palm.

Put your thumb through the loop. Rather than holding the end of the leash as they walk, many people slip their wrists through the loop at the end or wrap the whole thing a few times around their wrists. This keeps your hands free and reduces finger fatigue, but it can also get you hurt, especially if you have a large dog. "If you lose your balance and the leash is wrapped around your wrist, you can't let go of the leash easily," Wilson explains.

The best way to hold a leash is to put your thumb through the loop and drape the end of the strap across your palm. Use your other hand to hold and support the middle of the leash. This position gives you enough leverage to control your dog and is still comfortable enough for long walks, Wilson explains.

Practice control. Once your dog is calm, the leash is attached, and the door is open, it's

Proper leash etiquette requires that dogs walk next to or slightly ahead of people.

time to start working on your basic moves. Dogs need time to get used to leash walks, Kovary says. Until they've had a few lessons, they won't have the foggiest idea what they're supposed to do. To help your dog make the connection between the leash and walking properly, here's a three-part plan that Kovary recommends.

1. As you walk, keep looking at your dog and encourage her along. This isn't to be social, but to focus her attention on you. "Everything outside is going to be a big magnet for her attention. You want to do everything you can to make yourself the biggest magnet out there."

2. Using both hands to manipulate the leash, encourage your dog to walk next to or slightly ahead of you. The idea isn't to pull her around a lot, but to help her understand where her personal space is and what her boundaries are.

A DOG WALKER'S LIFE

While thousands of her fellow New Yorkers are getting their workouts in health clubs, Deborah Manheim is getting hers in the street, thanks to the dozens of straining, pulling, exuberant dogs she takes for walks each day. A professional dog walker in Brooklyn, Manheim exercises as many as five dogs at a time.

That can add up to 350 pounds of pulling canine weight. After a half-hour, she swaps one group of dogs for another, and then another—and she does it for 4 to 8 hours a day.

It can be a challenge to walk even one dog on Brooklyn's crowded streets.

Walking five of them requires dexterity, a strong arm, and an intimate understanding of dogs.

"You need to know who's dominant and who's submissive," she says. "If I have two rambunctious dogs, I have to think about the group and maybe not walk those two together."

Manheim has learned that it doesn't require huge amounts of strength to control her charges. But it does require savvy. "It's totally cool to be controlling a pack of dogs while walking past a 6-foot-3 guy with one unruly Lhasa apso," she says.

"When your dog walks alongside you, she'll be less likely to wrap the leash around you."

3. When you slow down or stop, your dog should match your pace. She won't understand this at first. You can help her make the connection by putting your palm in front of her face as you stop. She'll automatically slow down, and that's when you'll want to give instructions, such as "sit" or "heel."

Give each dog her own leash. Walking two dogs can either double your pleasure or double your trouble. Some professional walkers use leash couplers to link two or more dogs. Manheim recommends using separate leashes,

one or more in each hand. And be sure to take up most of the slack, she adds. Giving two dogs too much freedom almost guarantees that there are going to be tangled feet—theirs or yours.

FAST FIX Dogs who are well-trained (or elderly) can enjoy a slow, stately walk. Dogs who are exuberant and seething with energy, however, need to move quickly—not only because it helps them dispel energy but also because it makes it harder for them to get distracted. Walking fast is the best way to keep dogs focused on you rather than on what's happening around them, says Manheim.

Tied in Knots

There might be a dog who has never gotten tangled in her leash or tripped her owner during an evening walk. But probably not. The length and flexibility that make leashes versatile also make them difficult to control.

Any dog can learn basic leash lessons such as sit or heel in a few weeks. The real challenge comes when you're confronted with real-life problems that aren't always taught in obedience class. Like picking up dog poop when you have a plastic bag in one hand and a squiggling, pulling leash in the other. Or controlling a dog who keeps pulling no matter how much you pull back. Or budging a dog who, for reasons known only to her, simply refuses to move.

None of these situations is difficult to handle—once you know a few tricks.

Cleaning Up Poop

Even Houdini might have found that cleaning up a squishy pile while controlling an eager dog was a serious challenge to his dexterity. People who walk their dogs in public have to deal with this every day. Pet supply stores have some pretty fancy pickup gear, but you don't really need it. The easiest, most efficient way to clean up after your dog also happens to be the cheapest.

Before heading out for your walk, put one or two plastic bags—discarded bread and newspaper wrappers work nicely—in your pocket. When your dog makes a stop, temporarily loop the leash several times around your wrist and put your leash hand inside a plastic bag. Pick up the pile with your bagged hand and use your other hand to turn the bag inside out.

With practice, you can do this in one swift move—it takes about 3 seconds. Twist or knot the top closed and carry it with you until you come to a trash can. People who walk their dogs in city neighborhoods soon have mental maps of the location of every trash can along their usual routes.

Pulling

If dogs went to school, they'd flunk Euclidean geometry. They don't realize—and wouldn't care if they did—that walking in a straight line is the quickest way to get from A to B. Their usual trajectory is a zigzag, usually at a high rate of speed. They know they're on a leash, but they also know that the leash moves when they do—if they pull hard enough.

There are many ways to stop the pulling. Here are a couple that you may want to try.

Don't resist or pull back on the leash when your dog surges forward. Instead, turn your body slightly, plant your feet—and stop. Dogs instinctively pull when something is pulling them, but they tend to give up when they get the feeling that whatever they're attached to isn't going to budge. Plus, stopping abruptly will cause their collars to give a quick snap, a sensation they'd just as soon avoid.

Dogs only strain against their leashes when they're more focused on the world around them than on their owners. To bring your dog's attention back to you, wait until she forges ahead the length of the leash. Then abruptly turn and walk the other way. This move always takes dogs by surprise, and dogs don't like surprises. They soon learn that they're more comfortable when they match their steps with yours.

One way to deal with a pulling dog is to turn your body slightly, plant your feet, and wait. Resume your walk when your dog releases the tension on the leash.

Abruptly turning and walking the other way when your dog starts pulling will give her an unpleasant surprise. She'll give up and learn that it pays to watch you rather than surging ahead.

Balking

It usually happens when dogs see something that scares them. It could be another dog or a

CALL FOR HELP

No one will ever know what they're thinking, but some dogs (usually puppies) get frightened by the oddest things: stairs, lampposts, doorways, even an empty potato chip bag.

Most dogs outgrow their fears, but sometimes they don't—and what began as a little bit of anxiety can turn into a full-fledged phobia. They won't get over it on their own, says Robin Kovary, director of the American Dog Trainers Network in New York City. At soon as you notice signs of unreasonable fears, talk to your veterinarian, who may refer you to a behaviorist. Phobias can be cured, but it's a time-consuming process. In addition, some dogs may need medications such as Prozac (fluoxetine) to help them cope a little more easily.

person approaching, or it could be a street sign halfway up the block. Whatever it is, they usually respond by freezing solid or by trying to pull another way. Balky behavior isn't difficult to stop, but you have to work at it. Merely pulling at the leash won't help because dogs who are scared aren't about to cooperate.

When you're approaching whatever it is your dog is afraid of, put yourself in the middle to create a little distance. Happily encourage your dog to hurry past. You'll probably have to lay on the enthusiasm pretty thick, but as long as she has a buffer zone and a lot of praise, she'll probably hurry past. Then praise her some more and give her a treat.

STRANGE behavior

NAME FRITZ

BREED GREYHOUND

AGE 3

The Behavior Fritz retired from racing soon after his second birthday, but he didn't retire his love for speed. He launches into round-the-house relays a couple of times a day. He leaps on furniture and takes furious laps around the coffee table. But as his owners soon discovered, there are really two Fritzes: Inside Fritz and Outside Fritz.

Inside Fritz is pure energy, exuberant and full of fun. Outside Fritz doesn't care about speed at all. In fact, he gets so frightened when he's out of the house that he barely lifts a paw. He only trembles, ducks his head, tucks his tail, and tries to hide behind his owners' legs. They understand that the racing life can be a hard one, and it breaks their hearts to see how frightened Fritz becomes.

The Solution Sadly, most racing dogs are isolated from the world beyond their kennels and the track. They don't meet many people and they don't go for many walks. At an age when other puppies are exploring the world, most of these dogs are cooped up in crates. "Fritz probably received no socialization in the world outside of the track," says Liz Palika, a trainer in Oceanside, California, and author of *All Dogs Need Some Training*. As with many working greyhounds, he may have developed a fear of open places because he was never exposed to them before.

"His owners will have to concentrate on getting him used to the outside world," Palika explains. Because he's so frightened, they'll have to start small—running in the yard and driveway, for example. Once Fritz feels more comfortable when he's outside his own home, they can start thinking about taking him for walks around the block or to a nearby park. It takes time and patience, but most dogs can learn to overcome this type of fear, she says.

In some cases, in fact, they recover a little too well. Greyhounds are bred to run; the urge for speed is part of their very fiber. "Once Fritz does overcome his fear, he should only be allowed to run in secure locations, because running can be so intoxicating for this breed that they sometimes forget where they are and run right away," says Palika.

CHAPTER TWENTY-TWO

MEETING OTHER DOGS

Some dogs go over the top when greeting other dogs. Some are shy and wary.
And others bristle at the very sight of other dogs. Dogs can have greeting rituals that are
very different from people's—but they can all learn to be a little more gracious.

Stan Chappell of Vienna, Virginia, is a pretty tolerant guy. And he likes most dogs. But when it comes to one dog—his brother-in-law's dachshund, Jackson—his tolerance goes out the window.

"I can't stand it when Jackson arrives at our house," Chappell says. "As soon as he comes in, he goes after my dog, Cory. He starts sniffing Cory's rear end and won't stop. That animal is nothing but a sex maniac."

From a human point of view, Chappell's exasperation is understandable. If any of our human friends greeted us by sniffing between our legs, we'd be appalled, to say the least. We have more discreet ways of saying hello. But dogs routinely sniff each other's private areas—and ours, for that matter. From their perspective, it's the right thing to do.

This is just one of many doggy social gestures that are entirely different from those employed by people; and the differences in perception can lead to clashing agendas. Dogs have a right to be themselves and enjoy the company of other dogs. On the other hand, no one wants to shrink with embarrassment every time their dog encounters another dog. Dogs will never stand up on their hind legs and shake hands, but they can learn to be a little more civil.

Who Are You?

Dogs' greeting rituals are just as complex and multifaceted as our own. They use one greeting when they encounter dogs that they know and another when meeting strangers. Appearances notwithstanding, they're remarkably circumspect and polite in the ways they say hi.

Once dogs make eye contact, they begin walking toward each other. Along the way, they probably stop to sniff some grass or clover. This

This beagle and golden retriever are introducing themselves by sniffing each other's faces. Next, they'll move their attention rearward.

is a way of signaling that they're not aggressive. More important, it demonstrates that they're not about to commit the sin of staring, which is a sign of hostility, says John C. Wright, Ph.D., certified applied animal behaviorist, professor of psychology at Mercer University in Macon, Georgia, and author of *The Dog Who Would Be King*. When they're finally close enough, they start to sniff, usually beginning with the head and ears and then moving south.

This Samoyed's relaxed body language shows that he doesn't feel threatened by the stranger's inspection.

There's a good reason that they sniff the nether regions, Dr. Wright explains. The anal and genital areas—and to a lesser extent, the insides of the ears, along the lips, and the top of the head—are packed with glands that release intriguing, informative scents. A quick sniff tells dogs such things as sex, age, and sexual receptiveness.

Jackson the dachshund probably isn't thinking about sex at all when he sniffs Cory's rear end. In all likelihood, he's simply trying to remember who Cory is.

Social Gestures

Dogs' basic greeting rituals are easy to recognize, but the messages they convey are complex. If there are a lot of dogs in your neighborhood, you'll witnesses all of these signals at one time or another. Knowing what dogs are saying is the only way to know whether the encounter you're witnessing is scary or safe. And it's helpful to remember that all of this sniffing, peeing, and leaning has very little to do with you. It's a dog thing, and human notions of manners are really beside the point.

"Don't mess with me." Dogs are intensely conscious of status and power. Even in today's modern, protected world, where status doesn't play a role in survival, they continue to assert their supremacy by barking furiously, staring and swishing their tails, or growling. A dog who displays these and other aggressive signals is telling other dogs to keep their distance. In addition, he may be warning them to stay away from you. "Sometimes, dogs are trying to take responsibility for protecting their owners," Dr. Wright explains.

"Hi, who are you?" In a world of short leashes, it's difficult for dogs to meet other dogs. The only way they can do it is to strain and pull at their leashes. They're not trying to be disrespectful of you, Dr. Wright explains. They're just trying to fulfill their canine obligations.

"Who's the boss?" Since dogs are always concerned about social status, their first order of business is to determine which, if either, dog deserves special respect. There's no avoiding

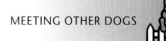

this. All dogs think about leadership. This was a critical concern in the days before dogs decided to cast their lots with people, and the issue is bound to surface whenever two or more dogs meet.

What usually happens is that one dog stands stone-still while the other, more forward dog stands next to and over him. The dog who is dominant may follow this towering move by darting his nose up and down his fellow's spine, as though he were a bird pecking seeds. Assuming that the "lower" dog isn't interested in proclaiming his own high status, it's usually at this point that he rolls over on his back—and possibly urinates all over the sidewalk.

"Yup, I'm the boss." It's a very aggressive move, but dogs do it all the time. Right after they meet and dispense with the sniffing preliminaries, one dog may urinate very near the other one. It's his way of proclaiming that he's the boss of the pair, says Sarah Wilson, a trainer in Gardiner, New York, and co-author of *Childproofing Your Dog*. There's a good chance that the second dog will acquiesce. Or he'll express his disagreement by urinating on top of the first dog's puddle. At this point, there's no predicting what will happen next—it's up to dog number one to decide if he wants to challenge the statement laid down by dog number two. Chances are good, however, that the dogs will dispense with all of this social posturing and simply start to have a good time.

"I want to play." Dogs have an unmistakable way of signaling that they're in the mood for fun. It's called a play bow, and the name describes precisely what they do—lower their front legs close to the ground while sticking their bottoms way up in the air. This posture is usually accompanied by a swiftly wagging tail and a nearly human-looking grin. It means that a dog is in high spirits and is inviting the other dog—or person—to hurry up and play.

"I'm going to win if we fight." Dogs have powerful bodies and equally powerful jaws, but they still prefer posturing to fighting. Conflicts in the wild are costly, and dogs have wisely learned that a good bluff can work just as well as a direct attack and is a heck of a lot safer. But sometimes, they do take that final step. What you're likely to see is one or both dogs rising up on his rear legs and cuffing and grappling with his front paws. It's very similar to the position dogs use when play-fighting, and it's not always easy to tell the difference—except that true aggression is invariably accompanied by snarling and growling. "You'll know in about 5 seconds whether it's going to be a fight or playtime," says Dr. Wright.

The play-bow—a gesture in which dogs stick their rears in the air and wag their tails—is how they invite people and other dogs to join in a game.

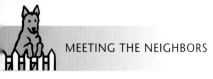

This Border collie is blowing off energy before he goes near other dogs. It's probably the best way to keep him calm.

Peaceful Promenades

You don't have to be fluent in dog to know when basic good manners are being breached. In a way, this has very little to do with canine etiquette and a lot to do with human expectations. It may be natural for dogs to snarl and lunge to establish dominance, for example, but you're not going to win many friends when it's your dog doing the lunging. Dogs will never give up their natural, if somewhat gamey, rituals. But they can adjust their styles to suit the people in their lives. The people, in turn, have to get used to the idea that dogs are going to do some pretty unpleasant things—if not sniffing, then urinating, and if not urinating, then humping. They've been doing them for thousands of years, and they don't need a lot of help from us.

Take the edge off their energy. Most dogs spend a lot of time lying around and not doing much. But there's a volcano of energy under the surface. Like children let out of school on a summer day, they nearly come unhinged with excitement when they get a chance to play and interact. The more their energy is seething, the more likely they are to go overboard with greetings—which means you'll see a lot of bottom-sniffing, humping, leaning, and licking.

Giving dogs lots of exercise can take the edge off their over-the-top excitement, according to Carol Lea Benjamin, a trainer and author of *Dog Problems.* In fact, people who regularly take their dogs out in public often make sure that the first half of the walk is in a relatively dog-free environment. This allows their dogs to blow off steam before they meet other dogs along the way.

Step in and take charge. It would be presumptuous to instruct an Italian on the proper pronunciation of "ciao." Similarly, dogs know their own social rules better than we ever will, which is why it's usually best to step back and let them do what they do. This advice changes, however, when there's aggression in the air.

It's easy to stop problems when both dogs are on leashes. All their people have to do is pull them in different directions. When your dog is on a leash and the other dog isn't, however, you'll have to assert your moral authority indirectly. "Look at the other dog and say, 'Stop' or 'Go away' in a very firm, loud voice," says Kathy McCoubrey, a trainer in Broad Run, Virginia. "This can break the concentration of the other dog so that he'll stop in his tracks. I've tried this myself and found it very effective, even though I'm not a physically imposing person."

Let them choose their friends. All dogs may look more or less alike to us, but they have their own criteria for friendship that have to be respected, says Sandy Myers, owner of Narnia Pet Behavior and Training in Naperville, Illinois. "We can't pick our children's friends, even though we try; and we can't pick our dogs' friends, either," she says. She recommends watching the body language of both dogs when they meet. As long as you see play signals—a loosely wagging tail, a happy grin, and eager sprinting back and forth—you'll know they're getting along.

Tense body language doesn't mean dogs are going to fight, she adds. Many dogs are nervous about meeting other dogs, and they'll naturally be a little stiff. But you still don't want to bring dogs together if the signs aren't right, especially when they're on leashes. Dogs who are running free can approach or run away if they want to. When they're both on leashes, they may feel trapped—and that will make them even more tense and anxious. "I generally cross to the other side of the street when I see that we're approaching an unfamiliar person or dog, and most other dog owners in my subdivision do the same," says Dr. Wright. "Later, if we keep seeing each other, my dog becomes more receptive, and introductions generally go fine."

Walk quickly—in the other direction. Some dogs always have something to prove. If your dog has a chip on his shoulder—or there's another dog in the neighborhood who does—even casual sniff-and-greets can quickly get ugly. Even if the dogs don't get close enough to squabble, you may find yourself struggling to pull the leash one way while your dog is struggling to go the other.

When peace isn't possible, retreat is the only sensible option. Immediately turn and walk the other way when you think there may be an unpleasant confrontation, Dr. Wright recommends. Even dogs who dislike each other on sight can't do much when they're on opposite sides of the street.

Keep your voice down. When dogs do fight, it's natural for their people to shout and yell. It doesn't help, says Dr. Wright. If anything, it increases the level of tension. A better approach is to keep your voice low and employ diversionary tactics, such as moving quickly in the opposite direction.

POOCH PUZZLER

Do dogs have stinky feet?

Despite their reputations for having doggy breath and wet-dog odors, most dogs actually smell pretty good—assuming, of course, that they haven't been rolling in dung or raiding the cat box lately.

But there is one area where dogs smell just as musty as people, and that's on the bottoms of their feet, says John C. Wright, Ph.D., certified applied animal behaviorist, professor of psychology at Mercer University in Macon, Georgia, and author of *The Dog Who Would Be King*. "There are pores in a dog's foot pads through which odor-bearing moisture comes out," says Dr. Wright. "This means a dog can sniff where another dog has walked and know that the first dog has been there."

The odors can be quite strong—but only to dogs. People aren't really aware of the odors, says Dr. Wright. Even if dogs did have a sour-sock smell, they wouldn't want it washed away, because they need the odors to communicate with other dogs.

STOPPING A DOGFIGHT

Most dogfights are nasty, brutish, and short. They rarely last more than a few seconds, but that's more than enough for the dogs to inflict serious injuries. It's up to the humans to break up fights—without getting hurt themselves.

"When your dog is fighting, he probably is not going to be able to recognize you as his loving owner," says Steve Aiken, an animal behaviorist in Wichita, Kansas. "He may be a very sweet licking machine at home, but in the middle of a dogfight, he's acting on tens of thousands of years of instinct. If you get in the middle, expect to get bitten."

There are several ways to stop or at least interrupt a fight. Here are a few strategies that trainers recommend.

Soak them with water. Dogs hate getting splashed, and sometimes spraying the combatants with water from a hose will break them up. It doesn't always work, but for dogs who are too big to separate physically, it may be your only choice.

Put down a barrier. When small dogs are fighting, throw a blanket or even your coat over both dogs. This will protect you from bites and scratches as you physically separate them.

CHAPTER TWENTY-THREE

MEETING CATS

Cats often prefer privacy, but dogs see everything that
moves as a potential plaything. Because of these conflicting agendas,
dogs and cats need a little help working things out.

Cats are small, they zigzag, and they have interesting smells. They're about the best fuzzy play toys a dog could ask for. Cats, of course, have a different perspective, which is why worlds collide when cats and dogs come face-to-face.

Cats get pretty tired of being harassed by man's best friend, and people get pretty tired of rescuing cats who have been scared up trees, or being dragged across the street every time their dogs take off in pursuit.

Teaching dogs to be more considerate of cats is a challenge because every fiber in their bodies wants to give chase. Dogs as well as cats are nat-ural predators whose instincts tell them to chase whatever moves—especially things that are smaller than they are, says Debra Forthman, Ph.D., director of field conservation at Zoo Atlanta in Georgia. The more cats run, the more dogs want to chase them, she explains.

Meeting the Neighbors

Dogs and cats aren't natural enemies, but they are very different. Dogs tend to be social, extroverted, and physical, while cats are more solitary and diffident. "A dog looks at a cat and says, 'Wow! Here's something to play with!'" says Lewis Cooper, D.V.M., a veterinarian in Rockville, Maryland. "The cat just says, 'Get away from me.'"

Cats will never learn to be more like dogs, but dogs can learn to be more catlike—or at least more polite—in their greetings. It's easiest to teach young dogs to respect cats, but even dogs who are set in their ways can learn additional social graces.

Introduce them slowly.
Dogs rarely chase cats whom they live with, because they understand that these little creatures are their friends and deserve a

BREED SPECIFIC

Most dogs chase cats for a quick thrill, but for some breeds it's more like business. Dogs bred for guarding, such as pit bulls and Rottweilers, and those bred for hunting small game, such as beagles and Jack Russell terriers (right), may have a hard time resisting the chase.

147

little respect. You can help them form the same feelings for cats in the neighborhood by making the proper introductions.

"You have to allow them to develop affection for each other, and that means introducing them several times for short periods each time," says Dr. Cooper. When you're out on walks and your dog is on a leash, let him approach cats, but hold him back so he approaches slowly, Dr. Cooper advises. Many cats will welcome this type of controlled interaction and will come up and give a sniff. As often as you can, make additional overtures—to the same cat and to any others you happen to meet—letting your dog get a little closer each time. He'll start to under-

stand that every cat is an individual to be respected, rather than potential prey to be chased.

Show by example. Dogs look to their humans for guidance in how to act in different situations. Dr. Cooper recommends crouching down between your dog and the cat he's meeting. Hold your dog with one hand and pet the cat with the other. "Your dog will begin to see the relationship between you and the cat," he says. After that, he'll want to follow your lead, Dr. Cooper explains.

Watch for signs of tension. Most dogs get along fine with cats, but others will bristle at the very idea. So keep an eye on your dog and back off if he shows signs of aggression, says Mary Beth Dearing, D.V.M., a veterinarian in Alexandria, Virginia.

All under One Roof

It doesn't take a lot of diplomacy for dogs to get along with—or at least ignore—cats on the other side of the street. When they meet cats on their own turf, however, things get a little more complicated. Even though they'll probably learn to get along with a feline who is just joining the family, the first few weeks may be tense. Here's what experts recommend that you do to keep your dog on his best behavior and ensure that the fur doesn't start flying.

Keep them apart—but together. Dogs are very territorial and don't always take kindly to newcomers, whether they're cats or other dogs. Unless you give them time to adjust, they may react in less than positive ways. Dr. Forthman recommends putting up a baby gate with

When people make it clear that cats are welcome members of the family, it doesn't take dogs long to accept the newcomers.

Dogs and cats aren't natural enemies. In fact, they'll often become the best of friends, especially when their owners encourage them to get along.

your dog on one side and the cat on the other. This allows them to see and smell each other for a few days. When your cat is approaching the gate without fear and your dog seems more curious than excited, you can take down the gate and let them mingle, she says.

Let them work it out. People always want to get involved when their pets are bickering, but this usually makes things worse, says Vivian Jamieson, D.V.M., a veterinary ophthalmologist in Mount Pleasant, South Carolina. Dogs and cats need to establish a natural hierarchy in which one pet has lower status relative to the other, she explains. People who step in and scold the one who is more dominant are merely prolonging the struggle. "If you constantly support the submissive one, you're going to encourage more fighting," she says.

Provide for quick escapes. Even in the happiest households, a dog's sense of fun may include such things as nipping, wrestling, or even shaking a cat in his mouth—behavior that's sure to elicit a hiss-and-swat reaction or at least a few moments of panic. Cats always need

a way to escape, says Dr. Forthman. Some people install a cat door that's too small to admit a dog. Others put up a cat tree that allows cats to get high and out of reach in a hurry. Cats who know they can escape whenever they want are much more likely to accept a dog's idea of fun without launching a full-fledged attack.

 **FAST FIX** No matter how much dogs enjoy chasing cats, they usually enjoy food even more. Some veterinarians recommend keeping treats in your pocket for a few days after bringing a new pet into the family. When your dog starts his boisterous behavior, flip him a treat. Dogs can't eat and chase at the same time, and given the choice, they usually opt to eat.

P O O C H ❓❓ P U Z Z L E R

Why do dogs love cat food?

Given a choice between eating dog kibble or cat food, dogs will invariably turn their backs on their own food and clean out the cat's bowl instead. Dogs are naturally competitive when it comes to food, and undoubtedly they enjoy the feeling of "winning" the extra serving. But the main reason that they crave cat chow is that it tastes very good. Cats need more fat in their diets than dogs, so their food is filled with fat flavors. In addition, cats won't eat food unless it has a strong taste and even stronger aroma, says Lewis Cooper, D.V.M., a veterinarian in Rockville, Maryland. The same smells and tastes that cats find so attractive act like magnets for dogs, he explains.

149

CHAPTER TWENTY-FOUR

MEETING STRANGERS

If we spent as much time alone as dogs do, we'd get pretty excited—or nervous, shy, or ecstatic—about meeting people, too. But every dog, whether she gets out every day or once a week, can learn to greet people politely and with polish.

Human greetings must seem strange and standoffish to dogs. We greet strangers with nods of the head and polite handshakes. Dogs are much less reserved. Their tendency is to meet people with all the subtlety of laser-guided missiles: barking with pleasure when people approach, running in excited circles, jumping up for paw-to-chest encounters. Their natural instinct is to be very physical when meeting someone.

In addition, the human world, from their point of view, is a confusing swirl of moving legs and arms, and a babble of words that they don't understand. It's as though every day were a day in Disneyland: Their senses can get overly stimulated, and meeting new people ratchets up the excitement even more. Things that we take for granted—the jangle of keys, the rustle of a parka, the scent of perfume—make them think that wonderful

Dogs who have met a lot of people from a young age learn to take the experience for granted.

things are happening, and they can barely contain themselves.

Some dogs are better social emissaries than others, of course. Those who regularly meet strangers get fairly blasé about the whole thing, while those who rarely meet people tend to go over the top, says Quenten London, a training consultant with the National Institute of Dog Training in Los Angeles, who recommends introducing dogs to as many people as possible while they're still young and impressionable.

Restoring Civility

Americans who travel overseas are often mystified by the social expectations in the different cultures that they visit. Bowing, touching forearms, and kissing are just a few of the socially correct ways that strangers greet each other. The confusion is even greater for dogs here at home. Their every instinct tells them to greet people dog-style. They want to use their mouths, paws, and sometimes their entire bodies to communicate greetings. If they aren't taught not to do these things—and given other, more polite alternatives—their social standing among the neighbors isn't likely to thrive.

Dogs do have one great advantage over people: They're very eager to do the right thing. Even without formal obedience lessons, most dogs can learn the rudiments of human greetings fairly quickly. Here's what experts advise.

Give them time to adjust. It's not an accident that you and your dog will usually spend a few minutes alone before the veterinarian comes into the examining room. Giving dogs a few minutes to explore their surroundings helps them get over the excitement of being someplace new and meeting new people, says Lewis Cooper, D.V.M., a veterinarian in Rockville, Maryland. This makes it easier for veterinarians to look them over and do their jobs, he explains.

You can use a similar technique when you and your dog are out in public. Suppose you're going around the block, where you'll certainly encounter people you haven't seen before. Before setting out, give your dog a chance to get used to being outside. Let her sniff around the

Giving dogs a chance to nose around a bit before going for walks allows them to calm down before meeting others.

front yard for a few minutes. Encourage her to dawdle by the telephone pole on the corner and the fire hydrant around the block. Dogs who have time to absorb the newness of their environments are able to dispel surplus energy and get used to the sights and sounds. This helps them be a little calmer when the environment also includes new people.

Give a silent lesson. Dogs crave our attention and approval, which is why punishment often isn't necessary—just letting them know you don't approve of something is often enough to make them stop. Suppose your dog greets people by jumping up. Pointedly ignoring the

BREED SPECIFIC

Dogs' love for people knows no breed boundaries, but sporting dogs, such as retrievers, setters, pointers, and spaniels, are among the most even-tempered and friendly because they've been bred to work very closely with people.

151

Why do dogs mount people's legs?

Even dogs who are slow to warm up to people sometimes greet them in the most intimate and inappropriate way of all—by firmly wrapping themselves around the nearest leg and eagerly humping away.

Veterinarians call this mounting behavior, and it's extremely common, especially in dogs who haven't been neutered. It's mainly a guy thing, but some females do it, too. It looks sexual, but that's not what it's about, says Jeanne Saddler, a trainer and the owner of Myriad Dog Training in Manhattan, Kansas. It's really about getting ahead in the world.

As with other forms of physical contact, such as jumping up and putting their paws on other dogs' shoulders, dogs mount each other when they want to signal that they're dominant and have greater social status. In the wild, dogs who were dominant ate better than other dogs and had more offspring. It was a good message to send.

Dogs can certainly tell the difference between a person's leg and another dog, but the message is more or less the same: "I'm the one in charge around here, and I'm doing this to make sure you know it, too."

behavior—and, more important, encouraging others to ignore it—takes away the satisfaction. Some dogs will simply give it up, says Nicholas Dodman, professor of behavioral pharmacology and director of the Animal Behavior Clinic at Tufts University School of Veterinary Medicine in North Grafton, Massachusetts, and author of *Dogs Behaving Badly*.

Stand on the leash. It's asking a lot to expect people you don't know to stand still while getting bowled over by 85 pounds of canine excitement. You may need to take more of an active approach. Trainers recommend using the leash to curtail inappropriate greetings. Actually, you don't have to do much of anything. When your dog approaches a stranger with her usual lack of decorum, quickly step on the slack portion of the leash. Whether your dog is going in for a sniff or a full-fledged jump, taking up the slack will bring her to an abrupt halt, says Jeanne Saddler, a trainer and the owner of Myriad Dog Training in Manhattan, Kansas. "This way, no one is the bad guy," she explains. "The only jerking is what the dog did to herself."

Wrap it around your waist. Every dog can learn to greet strangers politely, but it won't happen right away. In the meantime, trainers sometimes recommend wrapping the leash loosely around your waist when

Wrapping the leash around your waist makes it easier to control a dog who is intent on giving an overly exuberant greeting.

people are approaching. This helps in two ways: First, it shortens the leash, giving the dog less room to sniff and lunge. Second, it also allows you to pull your dog back just by swiveling your hips. Putting the brakes on her forward momentum works better than giving a prolonged pull, if only because dogs tend to respond to pulls with pulls of their own. A quick jerk is a message they can't ignore. They don't forget it, either, and they learn that moving quickly toward strangers invariably gets them pulled back.

FAST FIX Dogs learn quickest when their lessons are linked to food. Suppose your dog always lunges forward when people approach. After stopping her forward momentum—by putting your foot on the leash, for example—and waiting a moment for her to calm down, give her a biscuit or some other treat. She'll associate the food with the emotion of the moment, which will be calmness and not excitement, Saddler says. "Before long, your dog will teach herself the lesson she needed to learn," she explains.

It's a Scary World

The vast majority of dogs love people and are excited—maybe too excited—to meet them. But some dogs are simply afraid. They're afraid of people they don't know. They're afraid of people with loud voices or tall people or young people who run around a lot. Sometimes, they're afraid because of something unpleasant that happened

CALL FOR HELP

It's natural for dogs to bark, bristle, or growl when strangers approach their territory. At home, this protective urge helps people feel safe, and it's not entirely a bad thing. When it occurs in public, however, it makes other people nervous—and for good reason. Even small dogs can give very strong bites, which is why aggressive behavior is so scary.

Dogs who act aggressively toward the people around them have forgotten the first and most important part of their covenant: "In exchange for food, love, and a warm place to sleep, we will always remember that you, not we, are the ones in charge."

Aggressive behavior isn't that hard to stop, although you'll probably need help from an expert. It's worth doing right away because dogs who act aggressively invariably get worse unless they're stopped immediately, says Nicholas Dodman, professor of behavioral pharmacology and director of the Animal Behavior Clinic at Tufts University School of Veterinary Medicine in North Grafton, Massachusetts, and author of *Dogs Behaving Badly*.

While your dog is learning new rules, try to avoid making too much eye contact, Dodman adds. Dogs instinctively view direct eye contact as a challenge. Even though most dogs learn to accept eye contact as a perfectly normal human thing, those who tend to be aggressive may not tolerate it at all. So make eye contact only briefly, or, better yet, avoid it entirely until your dog is doing the things she's supposed to do.

before. And sometimes that's just how they are. Dogs who are shy or naturally nervous or who have never been around people very much tend to shy away—or, conversely, to growl or get aggressive—when people come too close. And for these dogs, across the street may feel a little too close.

Except for dogs whose fears run deep, it's usually easy to help them relax around people. As with so many other lessons, it's easiest to teach dogs to be calm and friendly when you pamper their tummies. That's why Saddler developed a special training exercise that she calls the cookie technique. The idea is pretty simple. By teaching dogs to associate a word with their favorite foods, it's possible to actually change their moods just by saying the word. Here's how it works.

1. Give your dog a treat several times a day while saying "cookie." It's not easy for dogs to learn human words, but they have no trouble at all remembering words that indicate that food is about to arrive. Keep doing this for several weeks until your dog gets in a tail-wagging mood whenever she hears the word "cookie."

2. Whenever you take your dog where people are—or when people come to the house—fill your pockets with cookies. "The instant your dog sees a stranger, before she has decided whether

At Your Service

Delta is a little dog who does a big job with amazing grace. The 9-year-old papillon throws every ounce of his 6 pounds (he's a little less than a foot tall) into helping his owner, Lauren Wilson, maintain her mobility and independence. Wilson, who is disabled, has come to count on Delta, an exceptional example of the discipline and abilities of service dogs—pups who are trained to help people with disabilities.

Working together, Wilson and Delta are a strong team. "He's my helper and he's family," says Wilson, of Silver Spring, Maryland. "I use multiple commands to get him to jump on kitchen counters and slide cans and other objects to me, push the proper buttons on the microwave, or even climb into the clothes dryer to retrieve clothes from the back that are beyond my reach." On grocery day, other shoppers watch in amazement as Wilson points out foods from her motorized chair and Delta leaps onto the shelves to deliver the goods.

Few dogs beat Delta when it comes to dedication, intelligence, and a sense of humor. Once, Delta had to spend some time at the veterinarian's. "I asked the vet's assistant not to crate him," Wilson says, "because he would do anything to get back to me." The assistant decided to tuck Delta into a crate anyway. A few moments later, to everyone's surprise, Delta emerged on his own from the vet's back office, followed by a few new friends. "He had not only opened his own door to get back to me," Wilson says, "he had let all the other animals out, as well."

or not she's going to be scared, say 'Do you think he has a cookie?'" When she looks happy at the mention of her favorite word, give her a treat. If you do this all the time, she'll discover that meeting new people always seems to coincide with her favorite activity of all. And it's very hard for dogs to be frightened at the same time that they're thinking about food.

STRANGE behavior

Name CLARA

Breed STANDARD POODLE

Age 2

The Behavior

Clara drinks out of the toilet. That's not too surprising, because most dogs find that the toilet bowl is a convenient place to get a drink. But Clara doesn't stop with a little liquid refreshment. When she's done drinking, she raises her paw and jiggles the handle until the toilet flushes. She stands and watches as the water goes down. Then she walks out of the bathroom. Her owners don't mind that Clara is wasting water. But they're getting a little unnerved—not only because they hear the toilet flushing when they're the only people home but also because it seems crazy that Clara is able to do it at all.

The Solution

Making the mental connection between the toilet handle and the resulting flush is quite an accomplishment. Among dogs, it's nearly the equivalent of discovering quantum physics. It makes sense that a poodle made the great discovery because these dogs are exceptionally bright, says Judith Halliburton, a trainer and behaviorist in Albuquerque, New Mexico, and author of *Raising Rover*.

Halliburton suspects that Clara observed her people pressing the lever and figured that she could do it, too. Even for a poodle, this must have taken some figuring out. She probably fumbled around for a while before she actually made the toilet flush. When she did it, she must have liked what she heard and saw, because she kept doing it. In fact, she has even started to watch as the bowl refills, which means she likes watching water rise as much as watching it fall.

There's another explanation, as well. Most dogs drink their water out of large bowls. The water may get changed every day, but it still gets warm and stale-tasting. It's possible that Clara flushes the toilet to get a drink of fresh, flowing water. Watching the action is just part of the fun.

If Clara's owners truly dislike her newfound bathroom habit, they could stop it just by closing the bathroom door, Halliburton says. Even closing the lid may work because that would take away the visual thrill. Of course, it's always possible that Clara would discover how to raise the lid, in which case they would have to try something else.

CHAPTER TWENTY-FIVE

PLANNING PIT STOPS

Nature's call doesn't always come at convenient times. It sounds in the middle of
the night or on busy sidewalks or on the neighbor's lawn. You can't ignore the call,
but you can work with dogs to ensure that it comes at better times.

Dogs aren't known for their delicate manners or their sense of discretion, as Jennifer Hannum, a university student in Philadelphia, can attest. Every day, she walks her 10-year-old Labrador mix to a pleasant park two blocks from her home; and every day, she has to wait, an embarrassed look on her face, while her dog takes a bathroom break in the middle of the street or in front of the one house where the occupants happen to be outside.

"It doesn't matter if she's been inside for 30 minutes or 8 hours," Hannum says. "She always stops on the spur of the moment, and it's never where I want to stop."

Social Rules, Physical Limits

People with large enclosed yards don't have to worry about their dogs' bathroom habits because their entire lawns make great commodes. Those who live in apartments or big cities, however, often take their dogs for three or four walks a day. Even short walks become an adventure when:

• Dogs insist on watering every vertical object or speck of dirt on the sidewalk.

• They take their bathroom breaks at lousy times, like when you're crossing the street or standing in front of an outdoor cafe.

• They refuse to go at all. This usually happens during rainstorms or at 3:00 A.M., while their owners impatiently wait for them to get with the program.

"Dogs aren't under the same social rules that we are," says Brian Kilcommons, a trainer and behavioral expert in Gardiner, New York, and co-author of *Good Owners, Great Dogs.* "You have to understand that dogs relieve themselves at inappropriate moments, and that dogs have limitations."

One of those limitations, of course, is access. Except for dogs with doggy doors, they only go outside when people take them out. That often means going 10 to 12 hours without a break, and that's stretching the limits of their holding capacity, says Mike Richards, D.V.M., a veterinarian in Cobbs Creek, Virginia.

There's also the social aspect of bathroom breaks. People go for relief, but dogs have more in mind because they use urine as a way of communicating with other dogs, says Kimberly Barry, Ph.D., a certified applied animal behaviorist in Austin, Texas. They prefer to stop in places where other dogs have stopped—at light poles, in neighbors' front yards, or in the middle of the street. And of course, dogs don't have the same social inhibitions that people do. Leaving

a pile on a busy sidewalk is no more embarrassing for them than stopping to sniff a chrysanthemum. Why wait to get to the park when this nice patch of sidewalk is right here?

Planned Convenience

Any dog, even one who hasn't had a lot of formal education, can learn to make his pit stops at times and places that are a little more convenient for you, Kilcommons says.

Keep to a schedule. Dogs have a hazy sense of time, but their internal clocks are as accurate as a Swiss watch. If you take them out at the same times every day—especially after they eat, when everything in their bodies is churning—they will learn to anticipate these breaks and will be less desperate when you walk out the door.

Teach a potty prompt. Just as dogs can easily learn to sit or lie down, they can also learn to do their business when you ask them to. The trick is to practice the commands when they're ready to do what comes naturally. When your dog is squatting or lifting a leg, give a command such as "go now." When he goes—as he surely will—praise the heck out of him, Kilcommons says. If you do this several times a day for a few weeks, your dog will begin to link the words with the action. And once he understands what you're saying, he'll look forward to doing it— and getting the nice praise that follows.

Watch their body language. Even dogs who know what they're supposed to do aren't always able to do it—either because they waited too long before going outside or because their owners weren't paying attention. To help your dog understand that he should always wait for

This Australian shepherd is glad to take his breaks on command, although having a nice tree nearby is always a treat.

the "go" command, you have to watch his body language to see when he's getting restless or uncomfortable. When you see that, quickly take him where you want him to go and give the command. The more you practice together and the fewer accidents there are, the easier it will be for him to time his breaks in ways that are most convenient for you.

FAST FIX Dogs aren't always able to go in a hurry just because their owners want them to. "Take a deep breath and run around the block with him," Kilcommons suggests. Exercise speeds the body's metabolism, and most dogs will be ready to take a break within a few minutes.

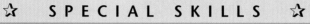

SHAKE HANDS

Shaking hands is always a neighborly thing to do. People do it all the time, and most dogs can learn it, too. For big dogs, especially, an offer to shake hands lets people know that they're friendly as well as socially adept.

1 Ask your dog to sit in front of you. Hold a treat where he can see it, then close your hand so it's out of sight.

2 Put your hand, still closed, just underneath his chin and wait a bit. Eventually, he'll start pawing your hand to get at the treat. As soon as he lifts his paw, praise him and give him the treat. Keep practicing until he starts pawing at your hand as soon as you move it toward his chin. When that happens, start telling him, "Shake hands" when you move your hand forward. Pretty soon, he'll recognize that a proffered hand is always an offer to shake.

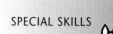

SAY HELLO

Any dog can run up to strangers and poke his nose in private places, but only well-behaved dogs can make visitors feel welcome by actually saying hello—or at least giving a well-mannered bark of greeting.

1 Do whatever it takes to make your dog bark. For some dogs, this will mean having someone call at a certain time, or ringing the doorbell. For others, jumping up and down and acting excited will set them off. As soon as your dog barks, tell him, "Say hello."

2 After the first or second bark, give him the treat. Dogs can't eat and bark at the same time, so he'll quiet down right away. When he does, tell him, "Enough." Keep practicing until your dog barks and stops barking with each command. Then take him around to meet the neighbors.

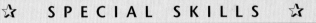

☆ SPECIAL SKILLS ☆

GO TO YOUR PLACE

Friendly dogs are nice to be around, but sometimes they get a little too friendly—following you around, nudging you to play, and generally getting underfoot. That's why every dog should have a place of his own, such as a blanket in a corner, where he'll retire when you tell him to.

1 Hold a treat in front of your dog and use it to lure him to "his" place. Encourage him to lie down. When he starts going down, point to the place and say, "Down. Place." Once he's down, give him the treat.

2 Keep practicing until he has the idea. (As he gets more adept, you can quit saying, "Down," and just say, "Place.") Then, start giving the command from farther away. At first, you'll probably be just 1 to 2 feet away. After awhile, you'll be able to point to the place from across the room and he'll quickly go and lie down.

GET YOUR TOY

Experienced hosts put guests at ease by suggesting something enjoyable that they can do together. Dogs can be good hosts, too, by bringing a toy for guests to play with. It's best to practice this trick inside to ensure that your dog doesn't grab his toy and run off behind the rhododendrons.

1 Toss your dog's favorite toy so it lands a few feet away from him. Tell him, "Get your toy," and encourage him to pick it up. When he picks up the toy, have him bring it to you. Praise him lavishly when he does, then give him a treat. After that, encourage him to play with the toy for a moment.

2 Keep practicing until he keeps bringing you the toy, no matter how far away you're standing. After awhile, he'll be more than willing to retrieve the toy from his basket, as well. To entertain guests, you can sit next to them while giving the command. Or ask them to tell your dog, "Get your toy."

Credits and Acknowledgments

(t=top, b=bottom, l=left, r=right, c=center, F=front, C=cover, B=back)
All photographs are copyright to the sources listed below.

PHOTOGRAPH CREDITS

Ad-Libitum: Stuart Bowey, ic, vib, 2b, 4b, 6t, 7b, 8b, 10t, 11b, 12b, 13t, 14t, 15b, 16b, 17t, 20b, 21t, 23t, 23b, 27t, 28b, 29t, 31t, 32b, 34b, 35b, 36b, 37t, 38b, 39b, 40t, 42b, 44t, 45b, 48b, 49t, 50t, 51b, 52t, 53b, 54b, 55b, 56b, 57b, 58t, 59b, 60b, 63b, 65t, 68t, 69c, 70b, 72b, 73t, 74b, 75b, 76t, 77b, 78t, 79b, 80t, 81t, 88, 91t, 93t, 93b, 94t, 95b, 97b, 99b, 100t, 103t, 104b, 105t, 107t, 109b, 117b, 118b, 119t, 121b, 130b, 131t, 132t, 133b, 134t, 134b, 135t, 136b, 139t, 139b, 135t, 136t, 139b, 140t, 141b, 142t, 143b, 144t, 147b, 149t, 150b, 151t, 152b, 155t, 157t, BCtr, BCbr, BCbl.

Auscape International: Jean-Michel Labat, 98t; Yves Lanceau, 123t; Klein/Hubert-Bios, 136b

Australian Picture Library: John Carnemolla, 25b

Bill Bachman: viiib, 22t, 80b

Norvia Behling: 5b, 46, 66c, BClc

Bruce Coleman Limited: Jane Burton, x, 90b, BCtl

Kent and Donna Dannen: 26b, 120b

Ron Levy: 115t

Ron Kimball: FC

André Martin: 113b

The Photo Library: David Madison, 18

Dale C. Spartas: iic, 25t, 128

Judith E. Strom: 108c, 111t

ILLUSTRATIONS
All illustrations by Chris Wilson/Merilake; icons by Matt Graif

The publisher would like to thank the following people for their assistance in the preparation of this book:
Trudie Craig; Karen Francis at Pawprint; Annabel Fraser; Tracey Jackson.
Special thanks to the following people who kindly brought their dogs to photo shoots:
Kerry Achurch and "Jak"; Lindy Archer and Sue Deehan and "Champagne" and "George"; Tim and Andrea Barnard and "Sam" and "Tessa"; Helen Bateman and "Bonnie"; Esther Blank and "Max"; Corinne and Don Braye and "Minne"; Jenny Bruce and "Stella"; Penny Cass and "Wilma"; Jo Cocks and "Gypsy"; Lindy Coote and "Boo"; Frances Farac and "Madison"; Judith Fox and "Rawson"; Gwynneth Grant and "Max"; Lindy Haynes and "Hudson," "Nelson," and "Panda"; Dinah Holden and "Molly"; Anne Holmes and "Marli"; Ann Howard and "Bella"; Lubasha Macdonald and "Tigra"; Paul McGreevy and "Wally"; Andrew McIntyre and "Abby" and "Daisy"; Rosemary Marin-Guzman and "Biggles"; John Maroulis and "Harry" and "Monty"; John and Hilary Mulquin and "Cleo"; Judith Neilson and "Pepa"; Dan Penny and "Molly"; Jackie Richards and Nick Wiles and "Skipper"; Matthew Robinson and "Jesse"; Denise Rowntree and "Bootsie"; Craig and Melissa Turner and "Carne" and "Flash"; Jan Watson and "Flash" and "Jessie"; Russ Weakley and "Max," "Bob," and "Harry"; Kathryn Weidemier and "Jessika".

Index

Underscored page references indicate sidebars. **Boldface** references indicate illustrations.